Evaluating the Realization of B   ure
Management: Construction an   el

D1539410

DISSERTATION

zur Erlangung des akademischen Grades
doctor rerum politicarum
(Doktor der Wirtschaftswissenschaft)

eingereicht an der

Wirtschaftswissenschaftlichen Fakultät
der Humboldt-Universität zu Berlin

von

Matthias Lange (MScIS, BScIS),
geb. 23.08.1983

Präsident der Humboldt-Universität zu Berlin:
Prof. Dr. Jan-Hendrik Olbertz
Dekan der Wirtschaftswissenschaftlichen Fakultät:
Prof. Dr. Ulrich Kamecke

Gutachter: 1. Prof. Dr. Jan Mendling
                      2. Prof. Dr. Jan Recker

Tag des Kolloquiums: 4. Juni 2012

Cover: © istockphoto.com/samxmeg

Book Copyright © 2012 Matthias Lange

ISBN-13: 978-1479230457 (paperback) 978-3843905589 (hardcover)

ISBN-10: 1479230456 (paperback) 3843905584 (hardcover)

Information in this book have been prepared with due care. Misstakes and errors cannot be completely suspended. Publisher and author do not accept legal responsibility or accountability for misstatements and resulting consequences.

1. Edition 2012

Evaluating the Realization of Benefits from Enterprise Architecture Management:

Construction and Validation of a Theoretical Model

Matthias Lange
MScIS, BScIS
Institute of Information Systems
Humboldt-Universität zu Berlin
Germany
matthias.lange@wiwi.hu-berlin.de

A doctoral thesis submitted to the
School of Business and Economics,
Humboldt-Universität zu Berlin.

Berlin, April 19, 2012.

SUPERVISORY PANEL

Principal Supervisor   **Professor Dr. Jan Mendling**

Vienna University of Economics and Business

Department of Information Systems & Operations

Institute for Information Business

Associate Supervisor   **Professor Dr. Jan Recker**

Queensland University of Technology

Faculty of Science and Technology

Information Systems Discipline

ABSTRACT (ENGLISH)

Enterprise Architecture Management (EAM) is an intensively discussed approach in industry and academia, which aims to facilitate the management of business transformations. The core of EAM is thereby to holistically understand, engineer, and manage an organization's business transformations according to its business strategy. Despite the popularity and potential of EAM, both researchers and practitioners lament a lack of knowledge about the realization of benefits from EAM. To determine these benefits available through EAM, we explore various success dimensions of the EAM benefit realization in this doctoral thesis. To this end, we develop and test a model that explains the role of the success dimensions in the realization of benefits from EAM.

The proposed EAM Benefit Realization Model is based on the DeLone & McLean IS success model, the findings of an extensive literature review, and eleven exploratory interviews. To further test this model, we operationalize it as a measurement instrument based on a Web-based survey. We demonstrate the strong reliability and validity of this measurement instrument in pre-tests and a pilot, and use it subsequently to collect data in a global survey. Based on the collected data from 133 EAM stakeholders, we conduct a confirmatory factor analysis that confirms the existence of an impact of five distinct dimensions on the benefits derived from EAM: 'EAM product quality', 'EAM infrastructure quality', 'EAM service delivery quality', 'EAM cultural aspects', and 'EAM use'.

The findings presented in this thesis demonstrate that direct EAM benefits are realized from the two success factors of 'EAM product quality' and 'EAM use'. Furthermore, the 'EAM cultural aspects' are a central enabler in realizing EAM benefits from the dimensions of 'EAM infrastructure quality' and 'EAM service delivery quality'.

Key Words

Enterprise Architecture, EA, benefits realization, benefit assessment, benefits, structural equation modeling, formative constructs, confirmatory factor analysis.

ABSTRACT (GERMAN)

Enterprise Architecture Management (EAM) ist sowohl in der Forschung als auch in der Praxis ein viel diskutierter Ansatz zur Steuerung von Unternehmenstransformationen. Dabei ist der Kern von EAM das ganzheitliche Verstehen, Planen und Steuern von Unternehmenstransformationen, die der verfolgten Geschäftsstrategie entsprechen und diese umsetzen. Trotz der Popularität und des immensen Potenzials von EAM, herrscht sowohl unter Forschern als auch Praktikern Uneinigkeit über den konkreten Nutzen dieses Ansatzes. Aus diesem Grund untersuchen wir im Rahmen dieser Doktorarbeit, wie aus verschiedenen EAM-Erfolgsdimensionen Nutzen entsteht. Dazu entwickeln und testen wir ein Modell, das die Rolle der herausgestellten Erfolgsdimensionen bei der Nutzenrealisierung erklärt.

Das entwickelte EAM-Nutzenmodell basiert auf dem DeLone & McLean-Nutzenmodell für Informationssysteme, sowie Erkenntnissen aus einer umfassenden Literaturrecherche und elf explorativen Interviews. Um das Modell zu testen, entwickeln wir ein Messinstrument für eine internet-basierte Umfrage. Wir demonstrieren dafür zunächst in Vorabtests und einem Piloten die Zuverlässigkeit und Validität dieses Messinstruments. Dann nutzen wir das Messinstrument, um in einer globalen Umfrage Daten zum weiteren Testen des Modells zu sammeln. Mit Hilfe der 133 gesammelten, validen Antworten von EAM Stakeholdern führen wir eine konfirmative Faktorenanalyse durch, die die Existenz eines Einflusses von fünf verschiedenen Dimensionen auf den Nutzen von EAM bestätigt. Diese Dimensionen sind die EAM Produktqualität, die EAM Infrastrukturqualität, die EAM Dienstleistungsqualität, die EAM Kultur und die EAM Nutzung.

Die Ergebnisse, die in dieser Doktorarbeit vorgestellt werden, zeigen, dass der direkte Nutzen von EAM primär aus den beiden Erfolgsfaktoren der EAM Produktqualität und der EAM Nutzung entstehen. Darüber hinaus sind die kulturellen Aspekte des EAM die zentrale treibende Kraft bei der Entstehung von Nutzen aus den beiden Dimensionen EAM Infrastrukturqualität und Dienstleistungsqualität.

Stichwörter

Unternehmensarchitektur, Unternehmensarchitekturmanagement, Enterprise Architecture, Enterprise Architecture Management, EA, EAM, Nutzen, Nutzenbewertung, Wertorientierung

ACKNOWLEDGEMENTS

Composing these lines is probably the most enjoyable part of this thesis because it provides me with the opportunity to thank wonderful people who are important to me and without whom I would not have been able to complete this project.

First of all, I would like to express my sincere gratitude to my two, supervisors Jan Mendling and Jan Recker. I am very thankful that I was given the opportunity to work with and learn from these two truly inspiring and great academics. Thank you, Jan (Mendling), for giving me all the support, guidance, feedback, and motivation that I needed to write this thesis while providing me with an environment in which to explore, learn, and develop my ideas. And thank you for giving me a second chance after I postponed my PhD some years ago. ;-) Thank you, Jan (Recker), for giving me direction, feedback, and input that was eminently helpful in the development of my concepts. The two of you truly shaped my learning experience, professional development, and research.

Additionally, I would like to thank especially my colleagues who helped me tremendously with their problem solving, support, and feedback as I wrote this thesis. I would also like to thank all the practitioners and researchers who were involved in this research and who provided me with feedback and input.

A very big thank you to my friends in Pittsburgh. Thank you all for the great times and the support that you gave me during my research stay. You made it an unforgettable experience that I will never forget. In particular, I would like to thank David Garlan and Eduardo Miranda for providing me the opportunity to visit Carnegie Mellon University, Len Bass for giving me guidance in and inspiration for my research, and finally Matt Bass for being a good friend. I will certainly be back.

Lastly, but most importantly, I would like to thank those closest to me. I thank my mother and my father, who always believed in me and offered the support and encouragement I needed to develop into the person I am today. Thank you! I also thank my closest friends, my brothers, and my grandfather for their support and company on my journey. Last but not least, I would like to thank Lisa for her understanding, affection, and warmth, all of which I needed to write this thesis.

Matthias Lange
April 2012

PUBLICATIONS FROM THIS THESIS

The research presented in this thesis has yielded a total of four refereed scholarly articles (not counting papers in development or under review) till April 2012 that have been published in conference proceedings and journals. The following table provided an overview of these publications:

Table 0-1 Overview of Published Scholarly Articles Resulting from this Research

Publication	Type	Reference
Lange, M., Mendling, J. (2011): An Experts Perspective on Enterprise Architecture Goals, Framework Adoption and Benefit Assessment. In: Proceedings of the 6th Trends in Enterprise Architecture Research Workshop, 29 August 2011, Helsinki, Finland, 304-313.	Conference Paper	Chapter 2
Lange, M., Mendling, J., Recker, J. (2012): A Comprehensive EA Benefits Realization Model – An Exploratory Study. In: Proceedings of the 45th Hawaii International Conference on Systems Sciences. January 4-7, 2012, Maui, Hawaii, 4230-4239.	Conference Paper	Chapters 3 & 4
Lange, M., Mendling, J., Recker, J. (2012): Realizing Benefits From Enterprise Architecture: A Measurement Model. In: Proceedings of the 20th European Conference on Information Systems. June 10-13, 2012, Barcelona, Spain.	Conference Paper	Chapters 3, 4 & 6
Lange, M., Mendling, J., Recker, J. (2012): Measuring the Realization of Benefits from Enterprise Architecture Management. 8(2).	Journal of EA	Chapters 3 & 4

Furthermore, the following two scholarly articles are in the process of being reviewed for a publication in a journal:

Table 0-2 Overview of Scholarly Articles in Review Resulting from this Research

Publication	Submitted to	Reference
Lange, M., Mendling, J. (2012): Enterprise Architecture Benefit Assessment – A literature review and research directions. In review.	Communications of the AIS	Chapter 2

TABLE OF CONTENTS

LIST OF FIGURES

LIST OF TABLES

LIST OF ABBREVIATIONS

AARS	Adjusted Average R-squared
AHP	Analytic Hierarchy Process
AIS	Association of Information Systems
ANOVA	Analysis of Variance
APC	Average Path Coefficient
ARS	Average R-squared
ATM	Automatic Teller Machine
AVIF	Average Variance Inflation Factor
CBSEM	Covariance-based Structural Equation Modeling
CFA	Confirmatory Factor Analysis
CTB	Change the Business
CIO	Chief Information Officer
DIO	Domain Information Officer
DMSM	DeLone and McLean IS Success Model
DoDAF	United States Department of Defense Architecture Framework
EA	Enterprise Architecture
EAM	Enterprise Architecture Management
EFA	Exploratory Factor Analysis
ERP	Enterprise Resource Planning
GFI	Goodness of Fit Index
GOF	Goodness of Fit
HR	Human Resources
IS	Information Systems
IT	Information Technology
LISREL	Linear structural relations
LV	Latent Variable
MIS	Management Information System
MoDAF	British Ministry of Defence Architecture Framework

NAOMI	Normalized Architecture Organization Maturity Index
PLS	Partial Least Square
POS	Point of Sale
PRM	Probabilistic Relations Models
RoI	Return on Investment
RTB	Run the Business
SAM	Strategic Alignment Model
TAM	Technology Acceptance Model
UML	Unified Modeling Language
UPDM	Unified Profile for DoDAF and MoDAF
TOGAF	The Open Group Architecture Framework
VIF	Variance Inflation Factor

1. Introduction

Going to bed at night
saying we've done something wonderful,
that's what matters to me.
Steve Jobs (1955-2011)

In this doctoral thesis, we explore how benefits are realized from Enterprise Architecture Management (EAM). The objective of this chapter is to introduce the underlying motivation and outline the scope and design of this research. In Section 1.1, we discuss the general motivation behind this research. We then present the problem statement and the purpose of this doctoral thesis in Section 1.2. In Section 1.3, we present the underlying epistemological positioning. After an introduction of the concept of benefits in information systems research in Section 1.4, we discuss the scope of this research in Section 1.5 and the research design in Section 1.6. Finally, we provide an overview of the structure of this doctoral thesis in Section 1.7.

1.1. Motivation

Organizations need to be able to operate in a volatile world in which not only incremental operational changes are necessary to survive in the market; also larger step changes that transform the complete business model of an organization or even an entire industry are part of the common order of business.[1] Many organizations struggle to align the resulting required transformation activities with their business strategies. For example, a recent study on project portfolio management conducted by the Technische Universität Berlin shows that 34% of the interviewed organizations fail to align their transformation projects with their business strategies.[2]

In this context, Enterprise Architecture Management (EAM) is an intensively discussed approach, both in industry and academia, which aims to facilitate the management of an organization's business transformations.[3] The core of EAM is thereby to holistically understand, engineer, and manage an organization's business transformations according

---

[1] E.g., McKinsey (2009)

[2] Meskendahl et al. (2011)

[3] Lankhorst et al. (2009); Tamm et al. (2011)

to its business strategy.[4] EAM translates the broader goals and principles of an organization's business strategy into concrete processes and Information Technology (IT), thereby enabling an organization to realize its goals. These processes and IT systems are subsequently implemented in transformation projects. In this way, Enterprise Architecture Management (EAM) aims to fill the gap between business strategy formulation and the actual implementation of such strategies within the organization's processes and IT systems. To this end, EAM can play a pivotal role in governing an organization's continuous improvement process by first constituting the interface between business strategy and implementation and second supporting the development of the solution architecture in implementation projects.[5]

Over the last decade, EAM has become accepted as a frequently used management instrument in business and IT.[6] More and more organizations employ EAM to manage their vital business transformations, and these organizations make substantial investments in EAM programs.[7] A 2009 study on EAM conducted by Booz & Company confirmed that over 60% of the interviewed executives see their investment in EAM as a top-five priority item that is necessary to successfully implement their strategies.[8] However, many organizations still view EAM as an abstract concept that requires significant investment and whose benefits have not yet been proven.[9] Several organizations consider their EAM programs to have failed because they are not able to justify their investments in EAM by substantiating the benefits of this investment.[10] For examples, a 2007 study of EAM conducted by Infosys reports that about 57% of the surveyed organizations are unable to justify their investments in EAM.[11] Consequently, more and more board members, senior managers, and EAM managers are being asked to demonstrate the benefits of EAM.

Given this need to evaluate the benefits of EAM, many organizations attempt to assess their own EAM programs.[12] However, there is no established, commonly accepted approach for this type of evaluation. Both academia and practice laments a lack of

---

[4] Boh et al. (2007); Ross et al. (2009)

[5] Op 't Land et al. (2009); Proper, Greefhorst (2011); Tamm et al. (2011)

[6] Aier et al. (2008); Bucher et al. (2007); Salmans, Kappelman (2010)

[7] Kaisler et al. (2005); Morganwalp, Sage (2004)

[8] Burns et al. (2009)

[9] Rodrigues, Amaral (2010)

[10] Morganwalp, Sage (2004); Zink (2009)

[11] Aziz, Obitz (2007)

[12] Rodrigues, Amaral (2010)

knowledge about how EAM benefits are realized.[13] To date, a few published studies discuss these EAM benefits explicitly, although they do not provided an answer to the question of how benefits are realized from EAM.[14] In contrast, most published EAM research mentions or discusses EAM benefits only in passing.[15] However, in addition to the interest in this topic in practice discussed above, an increasing interest in the corresponding questions of the benefits of EAM is developing in academia.[16]

In this doctoral thesis, we set out to contribute to the body of knowledge in this area by studying the factors that determine the benefits of EAM.

1.2. Problem Statement and Purpose of this Doctoral Thesis

Scholars in EAM research have no doubt that manifold benefits are associated with EAM.[17] However, there is no knowledge of how these various benefits are interconnected or which factors determine the realization of benefits from EAM. Therefore, the main purpose of this doctoral thesis is to develop a comprehensive EAM benefit model that encompasses and explains the realization of business- and IT-centric EAM benefits. The desired measurement model contributes to the body of knowledge of information systems (IS) research in at least two ways. First, establishing the required theoretical foundations of EAM benefits provides insight into the contribution of EAM to organizations' goals and allows these benefits to be explained and predicted.[18] Second, an understanding of the mechanisms of EAM and of its success factors tangibly justifies investments in EAM, especially in comparison with adjacent management instruments, such as project portfolio management and business process management.[19]

Understanding how EAM generates benefits for an organization is an academically and practically stimulating challenge that must be subdivided to be properly addressed. Therefore, we separate the purpose described above into the following two research questions.

---

[13] Espinosa et al. (2011); Lange, Mendling (2011); Morganwalp, Sage (2004); Zink (2009)

[14] Espinosa et al. (2011); Morganwalp, Sage (2004); Tamm et al. (2011). We discuss the few existing studies in detail in Section 2.3.

[15] For a detailed literature review on existing approaches to evaluate EAM, see Chapter 2.

[16] Espinosa et al. (2011); Tamm et al. (2011)

[17] Boucharas et al. (2010); Ross, Weill (2005)

[18] Morganwalp, Sage (2004); Rodrigues, Amaral (2010)

[19] Johnson et al. (2004); Kappelman et al. (2010)

Research question 1:   What are the success factors and conditions that influence the benefits realized from Enterprise Architecture Management?

As a first step toward the development of the desired EAM benefit realization model, we must identify the factors and conditions that influence the success, and ultimately, the benefits of EAM. Because these factors and conditions span organizational, social, and process-related elements, they are a multidimensional and complex matter that requires a deeper understanding before the realization of benefits from EAM can be addressed. When organizations are conscious of these success factors and conditions, they can define or influence these determinants in a goal-oriented fashion when designing or improving their implementation of EAM. Consequently, making these success factors and conditions explicit already generates value in practice by defining the benefit drivers of EAM. The answer to this research question aims to contribute to the body of knowledge of IS research through an analysis and description of the success factors and conditions of EAM.

Having identified these success factors and conditions, we answer the following second research question:

Research question 2:   How can an organization's realization of the benefits from Enterprise Architecture Management be explained and predicted?

This second research question builds on the identified success factors and conditions of EAM and seeks a model that explains and predicts the realization of EAM benefits. This desired model should connect the EAM success factors and conditions with related benefits. The model should also provide predictions, testable propositions, and causal explanations of how each success factor impacts the realization of EAM benefits. In this way, the desired model aims to contribute to the empirical body of knowledge of information systems (IS) research, first by proposing an explanation for the realization of EAM benefits and second by proposing a testable measurement model and measurement instrument to predict organizations' realization of EAM benefits.

For practice, the outcomes of this research will provide a tool to assess an organization's implementation of EAM. The measurement instrument will allow organizations to identify how their EAM practices currently perform and to map their practice against the desired target state. Furthermore, the measurement instrument can serve as a benchmarking tool. Organizations can use the instrument to benchmark themselves in relation to their industry using the collected empirical data, thereby identifying potential improvements for their implementation of EAM.

1.3. Epistemological Positioning

Having discussed the research problem and research questions in the previous sections, we will now explore the epistemological positioning of this doctoral thesis.

Epistemology is concerned with the questions of how knowledge is obtained and what its related underlying assumptions are.[20] An explicit discussion of the epistemological positioning is fundamental to any research endeavor because this evaluation raises awareness of the limitations of the findings.[21] In particular, an awareness of the type of theory and the philosophical positioning adopted by a study assists in the process of interpreting the findings of the study and ensures the identification of an appropriate answer to the research question.[22] Therefore, in the following sub-sections, we discuss the qualifications of the discipline and its body of knowledge to which this doctoral thesis aims to contribute, consciously explore, and define the type of theory adequate to address our two research questions, and make explicit the philosophical positioning that underlies this research.

Research Discipline

This thesis contributes to the discipline of information systems (IS) research. IS research is an organizational and technical research discipline that studies phenomena related to information systems and is concerned with the intersections between organizations, people, and technology.[23] In particular, an information system is *"any combination of information technology and people's activities using that technology to support operations, management, and decision-making"*.[24] Accordingly, IS research can be defined as a multidisciplinary subject that *"[...] addresses the range of strategic, managerial and operational activities involved in the gathering, processing, storing, distributing and use of information, and its associated technologies, in society and organizations."*[25]

IS research is *multidisciplinary* because it has overlaps and interferes with disciplines such as computer science, systems engineering, management, sociology, and psychology.[26] Thereby, as Lee (2001) argues, IS research *"examines more than just the*

---

[20] Hirschheim (1992)

[21] Becker, Niehaves (2007); Gregor (2006)

[22] Boudreau et al. (2001); Straub (1989)

[23] Hevner et al. (2004); Silver et al. (1995)

[24] Ellison, Moore (2003)

[25] Avison et al. (2005)

[26] Galliers et al. (2006); Orlikowski (2001)

technological system, or just the social system, or even the two side by side; in addition it investigates the phenomena that emerge when the two interact."[27]

In IS research, two different scientific paradigms can be distinguished:[28] (a) *behavioral science*, in which theories explaining or predicting human or organizational behavior are developed and verified; and (b) *design science*, in which new and innovative artifacts are developed to extend the boundaries of human and organizational capabilities. Therefore, design science is understood as a problem-solving process that designs, builds, and evaluates artifacts to meet an identified business need, while behavioral science develops and justifies theories explaining or predicting phenomena related to an identified business need. Consequently, the ultimate goal of design science is utility and of behavioral science is truth.[29]

We argue that the research of EAM in this doctoral thesis is a matter of IS research because EAM is also a *multidisciplinary* approach that *addresses the range of strategic, managerial, and operational activities* used to understand, engineer, and manage an organization's need for transformation. Furthermore, the understanding, engineering, and management of business transformations is concerned with and addresses *information technology and people's activities using that technology to support, manage, and guide decision-making.*

In terms of the employed scientific paradigm of IS research, we focus on the behavioral science paradigm in this doctoral thesis because we develop a model to explain and predict the realization of benefits from EAM.

Theory Type

The type of theory developed through research depends on the underlying research problem at hand, and the researcher should select the desired type of theory accordingly. Gregor (2006) distinguishes between four different primary research goals that can be combined into different types of theory:[30]

- The first goal, *analysis and description,* is concerned with an analysis and description of the researched phenomena, their relationships, and the boundaries within which the phenomena and relationships are relevant.

- The second goal, *explanation,* explains the what, why, how, and when of the researched phenomena using different views and methods for argumentation. The

---

[27] Lee (2001)

[28] Hevner et al. (2004)

[29] Hevner et al. (2004); Holmström et al. (2009); Kuechler, Vaishnavi (2008); Winter (2008)

[30] Gregor (2006)

resulting research outcome usually helps others to generate deeper insight or understanding of the researched phenomenon.

- The third goal, *prediction,* prescribes what will happen with the researched phenomena given that certain conditions hold. Therefore, the predictions are of an approximate or probabilistic nature within the IS discipline.

- The final goal, *prescription,* is a special case of prediction in which the resulting theory is a method or structure that results in an artifact.

Combining the four research goals outlined above, Gregor (2006) distinguishes between the following five types of theory, as presented in Table 1-1:[31]

Table 1-1 Taxonomy of Theory Types

Theory type	Distinguishing attributes
I. Analysis	Says 'what is'. The theory does not extend beyond analysis and description. No causal relationships among phenomena are specified and no predictions are made.
II. Explanation	Says 'what is', 'how', 'why', 'when', 'where'. The theory provides explanations but does not aim to predict with any precision. There are no testable propositions.
III. Prediction	Says 'what is' and 'what will be'. The theory provides predictions and has testable propositions but does not have well-developed justificatory causal explanations.
IV. Explanation and prediction (EP)	Says 'what is', 'how', 'why', 'when', 'where' and 'what will be'. Provides predictions and has both testable propositions and causal explanations.
V. Design and action	Says 'how to do something'. The theory gives explicit prescriptions (e.g., methods, techniques, principles of form and function) for constructing an artifact.

SOURCE: Adapted from Gregor (2006)

Based on this taxonomy, we adopt the research goal of 'explanation and prediction' in this doctoral thesis. First, answering Research Question 1 aims to *explain* the factors that influence EAM benefits, and second, the answer to Research Question 2 seeks to *explain and predict* the relationships between these factors and the EAM benefits. The targeted measurement models will be able to *predict* the future results of EAM benefits in similar settings. The contribution to the body of knowledge in the 'explanation and prediction' classification is manifested in either theory building or testing. In this doctoral thesis, we first develop a theory on the realization of EAM benefits and then test this theory empirically by means of survey research.

---

[31] Gregor (2006)

Philosophical Positioning

Every research project is based on underlying philosophical assumptions about what constitutes 'valid' research. Therefore, it is important to know what these assumptions are when conducting or evaluating research. With respect to the philosophical position of IS research, various divisions are suggested in the literature; Orlikowski et al.'s (1991) threefold division is the most commonly applied one in IS research.[32] Based on Chua (1986)'s work, Orlikowski et al. (1991) describe three different philosophical positions: The positivism, the interpretivism, and the critical position.[33]

Positivism is the predominant perspective in IS research.[34] Positivism underlies the assumption that the studied phenomenon is unique, concrete, and fragmentable and that there exists an ideal, value-free description of the phenomenon in which cause-effect relationships exist that can be identified and tested with deductive logic and analysis using hypothesis.[35] Chen et al. (2004) shows in their research that positivist research accounts for 81% of the published empirical research in IS.[36]

In contrast, *interpretivism* emphasizes the importance of subjective meaning and peoples' approaches to constructing reality. This position aims to explore the meaning and subjects' intentional descriptions of the phenomenon at hand within a social context, both because it explains subjects' states of mind and their related behaviors and because it is constitutive of these behaviors.[37]

The third position, the *critical* position, is based on the belief that social reality is constituted historically. Hence, it is assumed that human beings, organizations, and societies are not limited to one state: on the contrary, they can change states by recognizing their possibilities and acting accordingly.[38]

In this doctoral thesis, we adopt the positivistic position. According to Orlikowski et al. (1991), IS research is classified as positivist if the researcher makes use of formal propositions, hypothesis testing, and quantifiable measures of variables. Furthermore, the researcher must make inferences about phenomena by investigating a sample of a

---

[32] Alaranta (2006)

[33] Chua (1986); Orlikowski, Baroudi (1991)

[34] Boudreau et al. (2001)

[35] Dubé, Paré (2003); Lincoln, Guba (1985); Orlikowski, Baroudi (1991)

[36] Chen, Hirschheim (2004)

[37] Chua (1986); Klein, Myers (1999); Orlikowski, Baroudi (1991); Walsham (2006)

[38] Chua (1986); Orlikowski, Baroudi (1991)

stated population.[39] In this thesis, all of these criteria are met. Based on a literature review, we first identify the *formal propositions* about how EAM success factors yield EAM benefits. Then, we transform these propositions into *testable hypotheses* by operationalizing our research model in means of a measurement instrument. This instrument contains the *quantifiable measures of variables* that are used to empirically test our hypothesis. Based on these results, we draw *conclusions based on our sample* for the general realization of EAM benefits in organizations.[40]

It is important to be aware of the limitations of the positivist position adopted in this thesis, especially when interpreting its findings.[41] While many researchers proposed different limitations for positivism,[42] we focus on the most important limitations in the context of this thesis. Positivist research encourages the development of deterministic explanations for phenomena, relying on research methods that ensure validity, rigor, and replicability. While positivist methods ensure high-quality research and support building on cumulative knowledge across various disciplines, the underlying assumption of the validity of universal, deterministic theories is only fully valid if one suspects that the relationships underlying the phenomena of interest have determinate and unidimensional characteristics.[43] Markus et al. (1988) conclude from their research that these characteristics are not generally given in the case of information systems research that investigates organizational and human aspects.[44] Consequently, interpreting the results of this research on the use of EAM in organizations, we must consider the social contexts that may be influenced by, for example, time or politics. Therefore, we recognize that the realization of EAM benefits is susceptible to organizational and political problems that should be considered when interpreting our findings.

1.4. Benefits in Information Systems Research

Before we elaborate on the scope of this doctoral thesis in the next section, we consider the concept of benefits in information systems.

As already discussed in the first section of this chapter, the research question of how benefits are realized from EAM is still unsolved. Furthermore, in the EAM literature,

---

[39] Orlikowski, Baroudi (1991)

[40] The detailed description of the research design can be found in Section 1.6.

[41] Becker, Niehaves (2007); Gregor (2006)

[42] Weber (2004)

[43] Orlikowski, Baroudi (1990)

[44] Markus, Robey (1988)

benefits are mainly discussed as axiomatic or self-evident.[45] However, because the concept of benefits is multifaceted and ambiguous, as we will show later in this section, it must be clearly defined to avoid misconceptions. These misconceptions are particularly common regarding the questions of both how to measure these benefits and how to draw conclusion about them.[46] However, what exactly are the facets and characteristics of benefits?

In the IS discipline, benefit research has its historical roots in the literature on the effectiveness of IS[47] that measures the impact of IS outputs.[48] Later research – for instance, studies by DeLone et al. (1992), Seddon (1997), and DeLone et al. (2003)[49] – extends this research to models for IS success.[50] These models suggest that IS benefits comprise five dimensions along which benefits can be evaluated:

- `individual impacts' measure the effects on and the results for the user of the IS;[51]

- `organizational impacts' measure the effects on the overall organizational performance;[52]

- `inter-organizational or industry impacts' measure the effects on the performance of the overall industry or the interaction of the organizations;[53]

- `societal impacts' measure the macroeconomic effects on the society;[54] and finally,

- `user satisfaction' measures the user's response to the outcome of the IS.[55]

The last dimension, user satisfaction, is particularly controversial. For example, Seddon (1997) argues that it is merely a proxy for other consequences that should be measured instead directly and that user satisfaction, therefore, should not be mixed up with the

---

[45] Lange, Mendling (2011); Morganwalp, Sage (2004); Zink (2009)

[46] Ravald, Grönroos (1996)

[47] Cronk M. C., Fritzgerald (1997)

[48] Mason (1978); Shannon, Weaver (1949)

[49] DeLone, McLean (1992), (2003); Seddon (1997)

[50] For a detailed description of the IS models, see Section 3.1.

[51] DeLone, McLean (1992)

[52] DeLone, McLean (1992)

[53] Clemons et al. (1993); Clemons, Row (1993)

[54] Seddon (1997)

[55] DeLone, McLean (1992)

other dimensions of IS benefits.[56] Furthermore, these five dimensions define a continuum that must be considered in an integrated manner. This continuum can also comprise negative impacts, i.e., costs, as not all IS outcomes have a positive impact on all stakeholders. This integrated continuum is often referred to as the 'net benefits.'[57] Seddon (1997) defines 'net benefits' more formally as *"the sum of all past and expected future benefits, less all past and expected future costs."*[58]

When measuring these 'net benefits', five different factors determine the size of the effect in addition to the five dimensions described above. First, the measured IS benefits depend on the viewpoint of the stakeholder. Based on their research on organizational effectiveness, Seddon et al. (1999) suggest to distinguish between five different types of stakeholders with differing objectives: the autonomous observer who engages in an objective role and is not involved as a stakeholder, the individual who has his own interests at heart, the group who has its collective interests at heart, the executives or business owners who want the organization to profit, and the country that wants society as a whole to profit.[59] Second, the IS benefits depend on the type of system at hand. Here, Seddon et al. (1999) distinguish between six different types of systems with properties that influence the size and characteristics of the benefits. These include an aspect of an IS such as a single functionality of an application, a single application, a type of IS, all IS used by an organization, an IS development methodology, or an organization's IT function.[60] Third, the measured IS benefits depend on the level of analysis, be it individual, group, organizational, or societal.[61] Finally, the type of data collected for the purpose of analyzing IS benefits will determine the results. The type can be either perceptual, such as an individual's opinion about the benefits, or objective, such as concrete financial measures like the return on investment (ROI).[62]

Based on this discussion of the different factors that determine the measured 'net benefits', Chau et al. (2007) suggest a taxonomy of IS benefits with two axes.[63] The first axis describes the 'net benefits' of IS, composed of the four dimensions of user

---

[56] Seddon (1997)

[57] DeLone, McLean (1992), (2003); Seddon (1997)

[58] Seddon (1997)

[59] Seddon et al. (1999) draw their conclusions primarily from Cameron, Whetten (1983); Grover et al. (1996)

[60] Seddon et al. (1999)

[61] Cameron, Whetten (1983)

[62] E.g., Cameron, Whetten (1983); Chan (2000); Lewis et al. (2005)

[63] Chau et al. (2007)

satisfaction, individual impact, organizational impact, and societal impact. The other axis describes the perspective taken when measuring the IS benefits. This axis is composed of the five elements discussed above: the stakeholder, the type of system, the unit of analysis, the type of data, and the research method. A depiction of this taxonomy can be found in Figure 1-1.

Figure 1-1 Taxonomy of IS Benefits

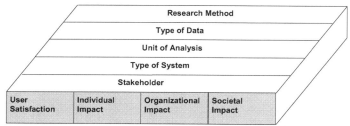

SOURCE: *Adapted from Chau et al. (2007)*

While the taxonomy of IS benefits proposed by Chau et al. (2007) demonstrates the multifaceted dimensions and angles that may be considered when evaluating and measuring IS benefits, a certain ambiguity remains regarding the questions how to instantiate and operationalize these dimensions to measure the concrete IS benefits. Therefore, it is crucial to adjust the taxonomy to the distinct context of the application. Furthermore, IS benefits are typically realized over time and in the long-run, not immediately. The resulting time lags can impede the demonstration of the cause-and-effect relationships between implementation activities and the occurrence of benefits because they are not always proximate in time. For example, a new information system in an organization could require end-user training when it is first introduced, but it is only when the end users become familiar with the new system that they can efficiently use it, leading to positive net benefits. These aspects have consequences for the measurement of benefits and must be considered in addition to the aspects discussed above.[64]

Within the context of EAM, the four dimensions of 'net benefits' – user satisfaction, individual impact, organizational impact, and societal impact – remain valid because they describe the areas in which EAM can create benefits on an abstract, high level. Similarly, the more technical aspects of the measurement of net benefits – the research method, type of data, and unit of analysis – consider more general factors that are also valid in the domain of EAM. For example, the different types of data collected to analyze the EAM are generally the same, whether an information system or EAM is being analyzed. This

---

[64] Rodrigues, Amaral (2010)

similarity occurs because in both cases, the type can be either perceptual or objective. In contrast, two dimensions of this taxonomy, the dimensions stakeholders and type of system, must be adapted to reflect the particularities of this domain and allow a further EAM-specific discussion.

First, the stakeholder dimension must consider the EAM-specific stakeholders and their particular perceptions of the benefits realized from EAM.[65] In this context, an EAM stakeholder is defined as *"[...] an individual, team, or organization (or classes thereof) with interest in, or concerns relative to, an EA."*[66] van der Raadt et al. (2008) identify 27 different EAM stakeholders on four different levels: the enterprise, the domain, the project, and the operational levels.[67] These stakeholders range from board members to the organization's senior management to various analyst roles on the project level representing different people in diverse roles with diverging goals and perspectives. The perspective on EAM benefits held by each of these EAM stakeholders reflects each of their individual needs and expectations.

Second, the dimension type of the system needs to be adjusted to the context of EAM. As previously discussed, for a traditional IS, this dimension differentiates between the different levels of abstraction for an IS, ranging from an aspect of IS, such as one single functionality of an application, to a type of IS, an IS development methodology, and finally an organization's IT function. When these levels of abstraction are translated to the domain of EAM, EAM can be evaluated on three different levels: the EAM products being the outputs created for EAM, the overall Enterprise Architecture (EA) being the actual systems and processes, or the overall EAM of an organization can be evaluated.[68]

In the context of this outlined understanding of IS benefits and the adoption of the taxonomy of IS benefits, we can move on to a detailed discussion of the perspective this thesis takes in researching the realization of EAM benefits. Therefore, we continue in the next section with a discussion of the scope of this research according to the dimensions described above.

1.5. Research Scope

The previous section described the benefits of EAM as a multifaceted and comprehensive topic that we can be discussed in terms of various scopes and on various levels. With respect to the dimensions of benefits discussed above, six design decisions must be

---

[65] Rodrigues, Amaral (2010)

[66] IEEE (2000)

[67] van der Raadt, van Vliet (2008). See Appendix Table A-1 for a list of these stakeholders.

[68] For a detailed description of these levels and their underlying concepts, see Section 2.3.

made to further develop the scope of this doctoral thesis. Figure 1-2 summarizes these design choices and highlights the scope of this research based on the dimensions described above. We present a justification for this scope in the following section.

Figure 1-2 Scope of this Doctoral Thesis

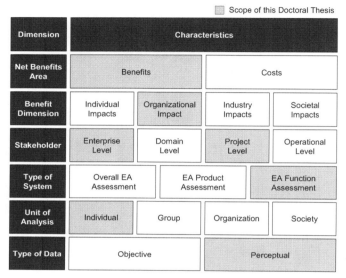

Which Area of Net Benefits Are Explored?

The 'net benefits' comprise both positive impacts, i.e., the benefits, and negative benefits, i.e., costs. Both must be examined to allow what is gained to be compared to what is expended.[69] Only a full consideration of both sides permits a judgment of the net benefits of EAM. However, because the direct costs associated with conducting EAM are much more tangible, we focus in this research on only the benefits. For example, personal costs and material costs, such as software licenses, are tangible costs that can be directly accounted for. We believe that it is more important to focus on the benefits side of the equation because an exploration of the cost side, i.e., what is invested in EAM, would also be unnecessary if the benefits are not trusted.

What Dimensions of Benefits Are Considered?

The benefits of EAM can be studied on individual, organizational, industry, or societal levels.[70] Although these levels influence each other, the different levels cannot be

---

[69] Zeithaml (1988)

[70] Clemons et al. (1993); Clemons, Row (1993); DeLone, McLean (1992)

merged and must be considered independently.[71] Organizational benefits are not a simple summation of the individual benefits and, similarly, the societal benefits are not a simple summation of the organizational benefits. In other words, for example, a decision on the organizational level might not result in an immediate and consistent adoption on the individual level due to resistance.[72] Therefore, we focus our investigation in this doctoral thesis on only one impact of EAM, namely, at the organizational level.

What Stakeholders Are Included in the Scope?

The definition of a clear stakeholder perspective has been a challenge in researching IS success.[73] EAM has many and heterogeneous stakeholders that can be clustered at the enterprise, domain, project, and operational levels.[74] Due to this broad set of stakeholders, viewpoints on the topic can vary significantly. However, the goal of this doctoral thesis is to focus on the enterprise and the project levels while making no distinction between the business and IT sides. We believe that it is important to investigate the viewpoints of these two different stakeholder groups to be able, first, to compare these two groups, and second, to get a holistic view on the topic.

What Type of System Is Investigated?

EAM can be evaluated on three levels:[75] the EAM products being the outcomes created for EAM, the overall EA being the systems and processes in place, or the EAM activities of an organization's implementation of EAM can be evaluated. In this work, we focus on an evaluation of implementations of EAM and how these generate benefits for organizations. A concrete evaluation of the EA design choices or the EA in place is, therefore, beyond the scope of this doctoral thesis. The goal of this doctoral thesis is to examine whether benefits are realized by conducting EAM in general rather than evaluating concrete solutions or outcomes of EAM.

What Unit of Analysis Is Investigated?

The benefits of EAM can be measured on four different levels of analysis: individual, group, organizational, or societal.[76] In this doctoral thesis, we focus on the measurement of benefits as perceived by individuals. This scope is chosen because this area has not

---

[71] Hardgrave, Johnson (2003); Khalifa, Verner (2000)

[72] Hardgrave, Johnson (2003)

[73] Cameron, Whetten (1983); Leidner, Elam (1994); Quinn, Rohrbaugh (1983); Sedera et al. (2006); Tallon et al. (2000); Thong, Yap (1995); Yoon, Guimaraes (1995)

[74] van der Raadt, van Vliet (2008)

[75] For a detailed description of these levels, see also Section 2.3.

[76] Cameron, Whetten (1983)

been investigated and this perspective is the most rudimentary. All other dimensions are superior and comprise aspects of this level.

What Type of Data Are Investigated?

The type of data investigated can be either objective or perceptual.[77] While objective measures provide factual measures, the legitimacy of perceptual measures as a proxy for objective measures is a still open debate in IS. This debate continues for two reasons: First, perceptual measures carry the possibility that interviewees exaggerate their views to their advantage or for self-promotion. Second, the complexity of perceiving organizational performance complicates an accurate assessment of the perceived benefits.[78] However, research has demonstrated a strong correlation between the perceptual measures of organizational performance and the traditional objective measures.[79] This correlation is also consistent with findings from organizational research.[80] Given the time and resource constraints of this doctoral thesis, we use perceptual measures as a proxy to analyze the benefits of EAM because they are easy to obtain while still providing the required insight.

1.6. Research Design

Having discussed the scope of this research, in the following section, we discuss the research design that we employ in this doctoral thesis to achieve our research goal. The research design outlines the research process, including the theories used, the employed research methods, and the desired outcomes.[81] In this way, the research design incorporates the required compromises and trade-offs that are made to accommodate the time, resource, and quality constraints of this doctoral thesis.[82]

When defining research design, researchers note that there is no universal process for the development of scientific knowledge. Instead, theory development is a dynamic process that is not always sequential.[83] Based on Bergmann's (1957) scholarly work, which has also been iterated by others, three common themes have been identified within the scientific process. These themes, on whose foundation research is built, are

---

[77] E.g., Cameron, Whetten (1983); Chan (2000)

[78] Tallon et al. (2000)

[79] Venkatraman, Ramanujam (1987)

[80] Tallon et al. (2000)

[81] Whetten (1989)

[82] Phillips (1976)

[83] Handfield, Melnyk (1998)

observation, induction, and deduction.[84] While the observation uncovers the areas of research and theory development describing the research territory, induction develops broader generalizable theories based on specific observations. These theories are then tested via deduction to predict the future outcomes.[85] Each of these three phases is driven by different research methods. The methods that are appropriate in one phase might be inappropriate in another. Therefore, the researcher must consciously choose the appropriate methods for each phase of the research to fulfill the respective objectives of the three phases.[86] The combination of qualitative and quantitative research methods can help to develop richer insights into the research phenomena than the use of only a quantitative or a qualitative method.[87]

In this research, we employ the three themes of observation, induction, and deduction in a two-phase research design, as suggested by MacKenzie et al. (1978).[88] The first phase, the explorative phase, comprises the themes of observation and induction and develops a model for the realization of benefits from EAM. The second phase, the confirmatory phase, is dedicated to deduction because it tests the model.

To follow a rigorous theory development and validation process in each of these two phases, we utilize a research design employing versatile research methods that are appropriate to the three themes discussed above. Figure 1-3 depicts the steps of this research design, including the employed research methods, the theories used, and the desired research outcome.

Figure 1-3 Overview of the Research Design of this Doctoral Thesis

Phase	Model Building & Refinement: Explorative Phase			Model Operationalization & Testing: Confirmatory Phase		
Theory	EAM Success Factors & Benefits	DLML IS Success Model				
Research method	Literature Review	Conceptualization	Semi-structured Interviews	Model Development & Specification	Survey Operationalization	Structural Equation Modeling
Research outcome	Theoretical Success Factors & Benefits	Theoretical A Priori Model	Revised A Priori Model	Operationalized A-Priori Model	Survey Instrument	Validated Model

[84] Bergmann (1957); Blalock (1969); Bohm (1957); Greer (1969); Kaplan (1964); Popper (1961); Stinchcombe (1968)

[85] Lee, Baskerville (2003); MacKenzie, House (1978); Weick (1989)

[86] Handfield, Melnyk (1998); van de Ven (1989)

[87] Venkatesh et al. (Forthcoming)

[88] MacKenzie, House (1978)

In the first phase of this research, a literature review is used to identify the existing knowledge in the domain of EAM benefits. The theoretical success factors and benefits that are identified in the literature review are then conceptualized in an a priori model. We supplement this model with a practical perspective through semi-structured interviews with EAM experts. In the second phase of this research, the hypotheses of the a priori model are tested with survey research to perform deductive reasoning, theory testing, and extension.[89]

The combination of using a literature review, semi-structured interviews, and survey research employed in this doctoral thesis follows Gable's (1994) suggestion to leverage multiple research methods to improve overall research outcomes in IS.[90] In the social sciences, the use of multiple methods, also called 'triangulation',[91] has a distinct tradition that complements the qualitative and quantitative research methods.[92] Both approaches have their strengths and weaknesses, and each complements the other's incompleteness.[93] Table 1-2 summarizes a comparison of the case study research method, as an example of a qualitative method, and the survey research method, as an example of a quantitative method, according to the characteristics of controllability, deductibility, repeatability, generalizability, discoverability, and representability. The table illustrates how the different methods complement each other. To this end, Kerlinger (1986) and Lee (1989) conclude that the four major weaknesses of case study research are (a) limited controllability because independent variables cannot be manipulated; (b) limited deductibility due to the risk of improper interpretation of the research data; and (c) limited repeatability and (d) generalizability due to limited capabilities to randomize the case study sample.[94] Survey research is stronger than case study research in these areas.[95] Survey research can accurately capture and control the conditions of the survey, allowing repeatability and controllability; provide a foundation for an objective interpretation, allowing good deductibility; and finally, enable random sampling, allowing sound generalizability.[96] With respect to discoverability and representability, Benbasat et al. (1987) forwards three arguments for case study research. First, case study research

---

[89] A detailed description of the research methods employed in this study can be found in the respective chapters.

[90] Crowstone, Myers (2004); Gable (1994), (1996); Sawyer et al. (2005)

[91] Webb et al. (1966)

[92] Jick (1983)

[93] Attewell, Rule (1991)

[94] Kerlinger (1986); Lee (1989)

[95] Attewell, Rule (1991)

[96] Gable (1994)

allows the phenomena of interest to be researched in their natural settings. Second, case study research allows the nature and complexity of the circumstances in which the phenomena take place to be researched, and third, case study research allows valuable insight into emerging topics in changing environments.[97] In survey research, study of these aspects is limited. Survey research is inflexible in discovering and exploring new aspects of the researched phenomena, and it requires an abstraction of the context.[98] As Kaplan et al. (1988) state: *"Stripping of the context buys objectivity and testability at the cost of deeper understanding of what actually is occurring."*[99] Therefore, as depicted in Table 1-2, it can be concluded that in dimensions in which case study research has a low performance, the performance of survey research exhibits better characteristics, and vice versa.

Table 1-2 The Relative Strengths of the Case Study and Survey Research Methods

Dimension	Case Study	Survey
Controllability	Low	Medium
Deductibility	Low	Medium
Repeatability	Low	Medium
Generalizability	Low	High
Discoverability (explorability)	High	Medium
Representability (potential model complexity)	High	Medium

SOURCE: Adapted from Gable (1994)

1.7. The Structure of this Doctoral Thesis

In this chapter, we have introduced the research project of this doctoral thesis by discussing its motivation, problem statement and purpose, epistemological positioning, benefits in IS research, and research scope and design. The remainder of this doctoral thesis describes the research in seven additional chapters, as follows (see Figure 1-4).

Chapter two introduces the backgrounds of EAM. The objective of this chapter is to establish a point of origin for this research. We introduce the foundations of EAM by discussing the EAM background in Section 2.1 and outlining its central concepts and tools in Section 2.2. Furthermore, we discuss the existing approaches to EAM assessment in Section 2.3. We close this chapter with a conclusion in Section 2.4.

In *Chapter three*, we present the results of a literature review on the EAM success factors and EAM benefits. The objective of this chapter is to develop a theoretical a priori model for the realization of EAM benefits. After we presented the existing research in Section

---

[97] Benbasat et al. (1987)

[98] Gable (1994)

[99] Kaplan, Duchon (1988)

3.1, we describe the research method used in the literature review (Section 3.2) and discuss its findings (Section 3.3). The chapter closes with a synthesis (Section 3.4).

In *Chapter four*, we report on the semi-structured expert interviews to conduct an initial validation and exploration of our developed theoretical a priori model. The objective of this chapter is to create a revised version of our model that incorporates feedback from the semi-structured interviews. Therefore, we describe our research approach to the semi-structured interviews in Section 4.1 and outline the findings from these expert interviews (Section 4.2). The revised model for the realization of benefits from EAM is then presented based on the findings (Section 4.3). The chapter closes with a conclusion and the implications for this doctoral thesis (Section 4.4).

In *Chapter five*, we aim to operationalize our revised model by means of a survey instrument. The objective of this chapter is to develop a reliable and valid measurement instrument for the validation of our model. After a discussion of the employed research method (Section 5.1), we outline the formalization of the model to make it operational in Section 5.2, and we describe the development of the measurement instrument as a Web-based survey (Section 5.3). We then report on the pre-testing and pilot of the measurement instrument in Section 5.4. In Section 5.5, we report on the survey administration, and we close the chapter with a synthesis in Section 5.6.

In *Chapter six*, we present an analysis of the data gathered in the survey. The objective of this chapter is to test our revised a priori model. Section 6.1 introduces the data analysis strategy. Next, Section 6.2 provides an overview of the descriptive statistics of the data gathered in the survey. After we have analyzed the implemented measurement items of our measurement instrument using statistical methods in Section 6.3, we explore the validity of alternative model variants for the measurement model in Section 6.4. Finally, we statistically evaluate the measurement model for the realization of benefits from EAM in Section 6.5. The chapter closes with a synthesis in Section 6.6.

Chapter seven discusses the findings of the model testing. The objective of this chapter is to interpret and develop a deeper understanding of the findings. Section 7.1 discusses the overall model. Section 7.2 continues with a discussion of the distinct dimensions of the model, and Section 7.3 elaborates on the removed constructs and measurement items. A discussion of the implications for research and practice follows in Section 7.4. Finally, we close the chapter with a synopsis in Section 7.5.

Chapter eight concludes this research. The objective of this chapter is to provide a summary of its findings and contributions. We summarize the findings of this research in Section 8.1, present the contributions of this research in Section 8.2, and outline the limitations of this doctoral thesis in Section 8.3. Finally, Section 8.4 provides recommendations for future research.

Figure 1-4 A Graphical Representation of the Thesis Outline

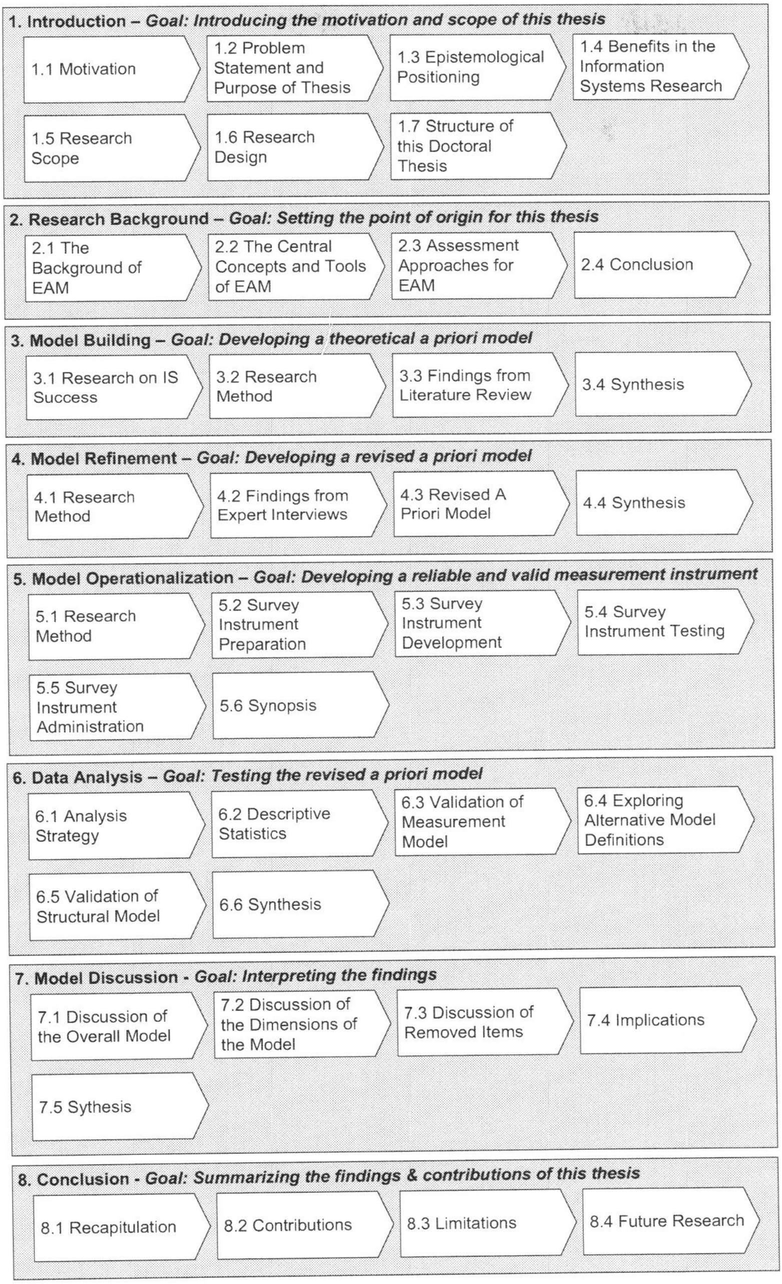

1. Introduction – *Goal: Introducing the motivation and scope of this thesis*

| 1.1 Motivation | 1.2 Problem Statement and Purpose of Thesis | 1.3 Epistemological Positioning | 1.4 Benefits in the Information Systems Research |

| 1.5 Research Scope | 1.6 Research Design | 1.7 Structure of this Doctoral Thesis |

2. Research Background – *Goal: Setting the point of origin for this thesis*

| 2.1 The Background of EAM | 2.2 The Central Concepts and Tools of EAM | 2.3 Assessment Approaches for EAM | 2.4 Conclusion |

3. Model Building – *Goal: Developing a theoretical a priori model*

| 3.1 Research on IS Success | 3.2 Research Method | 3.3 Findings from Literature Review | 3.4 Synthesis |

4. Model Refinement – *Goal: Developing a revised a priori model*

| 4.1 Research Method | 4.2 Findings from Expert Interviews | 4.3 Revised A Priori Model | 4.4 Synthesis |

5. Model Operationalization – *Goal: Developing a reliable and valid measurement instrument*

| 5.1 Research Method | 5.2 Survey Instrument Preparation | 5.3 Survey Instrument Development | 5.4 Survey Instrument Testing |

| 5.5 Survey Instrument Administration | 5.6 Synopsis |

6. Data Analysis – *Goal: Testing the revised a priori model*

| 6.1 Analysis Strategy | 6.2 Descriptive Statistics | 6.3 Validation of Measurement Model | 6.4 Exploring Alternative Model Definitions |

| 6.5 Validation of Structural Model | 6.6 Synthesis |

7. Model Discussion - *Goal: Interpreting the findings*

| 7.1 Discussion of the Overall Model | 7.2 Discussion of the Dimensions of the Model | 7.3 Discussion of Removed Items | 7.4 Implications |

| 7.5 Sythesis |

8. Conclusion - *Goal: Summarizing the findings & contributions of this thesis*

| 8.1 Recapitulation | 8.2 Contributions | 8.3 Limitations | 8.4 Future Research |

2. Research Background

*The act of discovery consists not in finding
new land but in seeing with new eyes.*
Marcel Proust (1871-1922)

Enterprise Architecture Management (EAM) is a management instrument that helps organizations to manage their business transformations.[100] In this chapter, we elaborate on the background of EAM. The objective of this chapter is therefore to establish a point of origin for this research. First, we provide the background of EAM (Section 2.1). We then introduce its central concepts and tools in Section 2.2. In the subsequent Section 2.3, we provide an overview of the existing assessment approaches to evaluating EAM. Finally, we close the chapter with a conclusion in Section 2.4.

2.1. The Background of Enterprise Architecture Management

The Motivation behind EAM

Every enterprise must adjust itself to a changing environment that is shaped by events such as mergers and acquisitions, reinforced regulations and laws, the breakup of monopolies, or technological innovations.[101] In this context, IT fuels the need for change by enabling new business models that further influence the environmental conditions and market dynamics.[102] The resulting changes have significant impacts. For example, in the automotive industry, the development time for a new model shifted from six years to a few months. Similarly, in the banking industry, the time to market changed from nine to twelve months to a few weeks.[103] The incremental operational adjustments of an organization are often insufficient to cope with these changes allowing a business to

---

[100] See Chapter 1.1

[101] Carroll, Hatakenaka (2001); Op 't Land et al. (2009); Wainwrighta, Waring (2004)

[102] Horan (2000); Mulholland et al. (2006); Tapscott (1996)

[103] Op 't Land et al. (2000)

persist in the market. Instead, enterprises need to adopt larger step changes that transform the entire business model of the organization.[104]

However, large, complex organizations struggle to cope with these desired changes because they face challenges such as the following:

- They lack transparency about their current products, processes, or IT.

- They are affected by organizational structures that bear unclear responsibilities, organizational silos, and self-contained business units operating independently.

- They are limited by confining regulations.

- They misalign business needs with IT supply.

- They must manage complex legacy landscapes of IT applications and infrastructure and business processes that provide duplicate functionalities and create unmanageable data silos.[105]

To address these challenges, research shows that each organization needs to gradually develop an understanding of its current operating platform[106] and develop it into a digitized platform, using IT as an enabler. This allows the business to become better, faster, and more profitable than those organizations, which are not doing so.[107] This is accomplished by digitizing business processes and embedding those processes into a foundation for execution that makes the individual process less flexible but the enterprise more agile in a changing world. Because the digitalization of business processes requires clear decisions about individual processes, management attention can be freed up from low-value activities to focus on activities that improve profits and growth.[108]

However, the implementation of these strategic business transformations is a comprehensive endeavor that is associated with a high degree of uncertainty. Therefore, many organizations struggle to align their transformation activities with their business strategies.[109] One management instrument that aims to improve the implementation of business transformations is Enterprise Architecture Management (EAM).

---

[104] Kotter (1995)

[105] Op 't Land et al. (2009)

[106] An operating platform is the collection of implemented business processes and the IT infrastructure of an organization that is uses to execute its business. Ross et al. (2009), p. 26

[107] Ross et al. (2009), p. 2

[108] Ross et al. (2009), p. 5

[109] Henderson, Venkatraman (1993); Meskendahl et al. (2011)

A Definition of Enterprise Architecture Management

To understand and discuss Enterprise Architecture Management (EAM), it is important to understand what architecture is and why it is necessary.

Architecture, in general, is the foundation of any building or construction domain, such as building houses, planning cities, or developing products (e.g., cars).[110] According to the IEEE Computer Society, architecture is defined as "*...the fundamental organization of a system embodied in its components, their relationships to each other, and to the environment, and the principle guiding its design and evolution.*"[111]

The underlying idea of architecture is based on the principle that everything is created twice: first as a vision or plan in our minds and then in reality through action.[112] Therefore, architecture helps to first formally construct the object at hand (e.g., a house, a car, or in our case, an enterprise) and then to communicate the plan. For example, when designing a house, the house owner discusses the rooms, doors, windows, staircases, etc., that he or she has in mind with an architect. Based on this discussion, the architect creates the architecture of the house by means of a master plan. Engineers and builders can then use this master plan as a foundation for more detailed specifications. The formal creation of the architecture, following the initial discussions, ensures that the house, when actually built, complies with what is in the mind of the builder in the first place.[113] In an analogy to the architecture of a house, an organization and any changes within it in the form of adaption or redesign can be designed purposefully and in a systematic and controlled manner with an Enterprise Architecture (EA).[114]

In this doctoral thesis, we define the Enterprise Architecture (EA) as the inherent structures of the "*...main components of [an] organization, its information systems, the ways in which these components work together [...] to achieve defined business objectives, and the way in which the information systems support the business processes of the organization.*"[115]

The management instrument that is concerned with the understanding, engineering, and management of the Enterprise Architecture (EA) is called Enterprise Architecture Management (EAM). The core of EAM is the operationalization of an organization's

---

[110] Lankhorst et al. (2009)

[111] IEEE (2000), p. 9

[112] Covey (2004)

[113] Lankhorst et al. (2009)

[114] Proper, Greefhorst (2011)

[115] Kaisler et al. (2005)

strategy through the transformation of an organization's operating platform.[116] More formally, we define *Enterprise Architecture Management (EAM) as the management activities conducted in an organization to provide direction and practical support in the design, management, and transformation of an Enterprise Architecture (EA) to achieve its strategy. To this end, it establishes, maintains, and uses a coherent set of architecture principles, models, services, and governance structures.*[117]

According to this definition, the term EAM refers to an organization's activities carried out to manage the Enterprise Architecture (EA). In general, organizations have two forms through which they can conduct these *management activities.* The choice of which depends on their maturity. First, more mature organizations have established a dedicated department to conduct EAM. In this case, this department is referred to as the '*EAM function.*'[118] Second, a less mature organization that just started to practice EAM can conduct EAM as a project without a dedicated department. This practice is commonly referred to as an '*EAM initiative.*'[119] However, in this doctoral thesis, we do not explicitly differentiate between these two forms of practice. Therefore, we refer to an organization's implementation of the management activities related to EAM, i.e., the organization-specific instantiation of EAM, as simply as *EAM.*

The Interfaces of EAM

EAM is positioned between the formulation of an organization's business and IT strategies and the organization's program management.[120] The formulation of an organization's business and IT strategies determines the organization's long-range objectives, an evaluation of alternative strategies, and the monitoring of the results.[121] In oppose to this, the implementation of a strategy is executed through a set of projects. Together, these independent projects deliver on some defined objective(s) of the organization and the projects are managed against these objectives within the program management.[122] However, the translation from a strategy into a meaningful program consisting of multiple projects is a challenge for many organizations.[123] Furthermore, traditional program management considers only typical project parameters such as project risks,

---

[116] Tamm et al. (2011)

[117] Adapted from Ahlemann et al. (2012), p. 3

[118] van der Raadt, van Vliet (2008)

[119] Ahlemann et al. (2012)

[120] Op 't Land et al. (2009), p. 21

[121] Armstrong (1982)

[122] The Standard for Program Management, (2008)

[123] Meskendahl et al. (2011)

budgets, and deadlines.[124] Considering only these project parameters carries the risk of optimizing locally at the level of a specific project rather than at the global level, which is the goal of the overall business transformation.[125]

Figure 2-1 Relationship between Strategy, Program Management and EAM

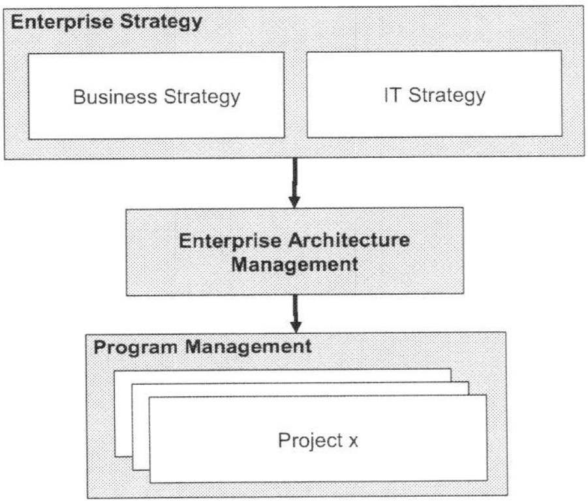

In this context, EAM comes into play, enacting an organization's strategy by translating the strategy's broader principles, capabilities, and goals into concrete implementation projects. These projects implement the respective business processes and supporting IT to enable the organization to realize its goals (see Figure 2-1). Although the role of EAM appears to be similar to strategic management, EAM describes the vision and goals of an organization in greater detail and, hence, provides the glue between strategy formulation and the transformation projects managed within the program management of an organization.[126] Therefore, good EAM practice provides insights to balance an organization's principles, capabilities, and goals based on its strategy and facilitates their translation to daily operations.[127]

Consequently, EAM is an integral part of an organization's processes of change and transformation and its governance.[128] EAM designs and develops the essentials of business and IT and their required evolution.[129] Although EAM historically developed from an IT approach, it is not an IT issue. EAM is rather an indispensable, integrated

---

[124] Bentley (2010); Project Management Institute (2008)

[125] Greefhorst, Proper (2011)

[126] Tamm et al. (2011)

[127] Ross et al. (2009)

[128] Op 't Land et al. (2009)

[129] Lankhorst et al. (2009)

management instrument that aligns business requirements and IT supply to fulfill an organization's goals.[130]

2.2. The Central Concepts and Tools of EAM

To enact an organization's strategy for execution, EAM needs to enable an effective (do the right thing) and efficient (do the thing right) business transformation. Therefore, EAM must cover the steering, coordination, and communication of a business transformation.[131] To this end, EAM builds on a comprehensive set of concepts and tools for the holistic management of an organization's business transformation.[132] These central concepts and tools for EAM, which have been proposed and discussed by both academics and practitioners, are introduced in detail in this section.

From a high-level perspective EAM is typically structured in three different areas: EAM products, EAM processes, and EAM governance.[133] The *EAM processes* are the collection of activities that are conducted in the context of EAM. These EAM processes create the *EAM products* as outcomes. Furthermore, to properly embed the EAM processes in the overall organization, the *EAM governance* defines the EAM responsibilities and the corresponding EAM roles and bodies. These three areas of EAM are designed and implemented according to each organization's specific goals to realize its desired benefits. Figure 2-2 illustrates the relationship between these three areas, the set goals, and the resulting benefits. In the following sub-sections, we elaborate on each of these three areas of EAM by further detailing and defining the central concepts and tools for each of these areas.

Figure 2-2 Taxonomy of EAM Benefit Assessments

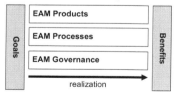

---

[130] Chan, Reich (2007); Ross et al. (2009)

[131] Op 't Land et al. (2009)

[132] Ross et al. (2009)

[133] van der Raadt, van Vliet (2008)

EAM Products

EAM products, which are the outputs of the *EAM processes*, can be classified into two different types: (a) *EA models* and (b) *EAM principles*.[134]

First, *EA models* are, in general, a purposeful abstraction of a relevant part of the reality.[135] They are used in the context of EAM as (a) a means to document the as-is architecture that describes the currently implemented operational environment, (b) as a blueprint for a to-be architecture that describes the desired future target state, (c) as a communication language for changes or to gain alignment, or (d) as a decision-making basis for comparing competing architectural solutions.[136] Thereby, *EA models* are created using modeling languages such as ArchiMate.[137] Each EA model describes various components (e.g., business capabilities, business processes, applications, software components, or data objects) representing the real-world objects of the organization at hand and their relationships. It is important to clearly distinguish between an Enterprise Architecture (EA), and its architectural representation, referred to as an *EA model*. This clear distinction is required as in general linguistic use architecture can have two different meanings: the inherent structure of a system or its representation.[138] The inherent structures of the main components and their relationships are the so-called Enterprise Architecture (EA), which we have defined in the previous section.[139] Implementing this Enterprise Architecture (EA) based on the *EA models* imposes the actual systems. Consequently, the *EA models* describe the implemented system – or the planned system, depending on the timeframe. Similarly, the Enterprise Architecture (EA) refers to the implemented or planned structures of components and relationships of the system. Here, the term system refers to either the business processes or the IT, depending on the object of interest. Figure 2-3 visualizes this architectural triangle of *EA models*, the *Enterprise Architecture (EA),* and the actual *systems*.[140]

---

[134] Ross et al. (1996)

[135] Falkenberg (1998)

[136] Smolander et al. (2008)

[137] OpenGroup

[138] Bass et al. (2002) elaborate on the two meanings of architecture by pointing out that although every system has an architecture, not yet every architecture is explicitly represented.

[139] See Section 2.1.

[140] Stelzer (2009) which is developed based on the so-called semiotic triangle by Lyons (1977) and Ogden, Richards (1923).

Figure 2-3 Architectural Triangle for Enterprise Architecture

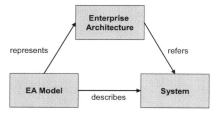

SOURCE: Adapted from Stelzer (2009)

Following the discussion above, three different EA models can be distinguished that differ with respect to their time-reference: (1) the 'as-is architecture', which describes the currently implemented operational environment, (2) the 'to-be architecture', which describes the desired future target state, and (3) the roadmap, which describes the transformation path from the as-is to the to-be architecture. Note the linguistic haziness in this case because the architecture in the 'as-is architecture' or the 'to-be architecture' refers to a type of EA model, not to the Enterprise Architecture (EA) discussed above.

As an example of an EA model, a so-called 'domain map', Figure 2-4 illustrates the Enterprise Architecture (EA) of a bank at the domain level. The domain map depicts the different areas of the bank, referred to as domains in the context of EAM that are necessary to operate its business. Each of these areas – for example, human resources (HR) – must be specified by concrete processes and IT on a more detailed level, such as a payroll application. Further EA models are typically used to detail these domains.

Figure 2-4 EA Model Illustrating the Architecture of a Bank at the Domain Level

Channels							External
Branch FE	Web	Call center	ATM	POS	Email, fax	Mobile	Clearing house

Business management	Product servicing		Transaction engine		Support
Sales	Security	Under-writing	Customer	Processing	Exchanges
Pricing	Accounts	Leasing	Products	Settlement	Cards circuit
Risk	Payments	Collections	Contracts		
Perfor-mance	Cards	Trading	Books		HR
Reporting					Purchasing

Accounting: General ledger, Fixed assets

Support: Real estate

Source: Adapted from Akella et al. (2012)

The second type of EAM products, the EAM principles, is the key means of directing the development and implementation of an Enterprise Architecture (EA).[141] In this doctoral thesis, we define the *EAM principles* as *"an organization's basic philosophies that guide the development of the architecture. [...] Principles provide guidelines and rationales for the constant examination and re-evaluation [of an Enterprise Architecture]."*[142] Hence, the EAM principles aim to guide the organization in the development of its EA.[143] The EAM principles are derived from the relevant goals of the organization and the organizational decisions that have been made in relation to EAM.[144] Accordingly, their guiding nature restricts the design freedom for the development of an EA.[145] Each EAM principle is associated with a rationale that explains the intend of the principle and its concrete implications for implementation.[146] Table 2-1 provides an example of an EAM principle including the related rationale and implications.

Table 2-1 Example of an EAM Principle

Principle	Customers have a single point of contact
Type of principle	Business
Quality attributes	Usability, efficiency
Rationale	▪ It is much more customer friendly when the customer can direct all of his communication to a single point, is serviced directly, and does not have to contact multiple people. ▪ A single point of contact also ensures that consistent information is provided to the customer. ▪ It is more efficient to dedicate resources to handle customer contacts, and prevent interruptions in operational activities.
Implications	▪ There is one access point for customers, which may be a customer contact center or a dedicated person for important customers. ▪ The access point attempts to shield the customer from the internal organization, and handle the request completely. ▪ The access point is provided with sufficient information in order to handle customer requests. ▪ Customers are only directed to others in exceptional situations, and in those cases the access point ensures that the proper information about the customer is forwarded.

Source: Adapted from Greefhorst et al. (2011)

---

[141] Proper, Greefhorst (2011)

[142] Richardson et al. (1990)

[143] Stelzer (2009)

[144] Greefhorst, Proper (2011)

[145] Aier et al. (2011a); Dietz (2008)

[146] Armour et al. (1999); Hoogervorst (2004), (2009); Richardson et al. (1990); Wilkinson (2006)

To support the creation and maintenance of EAM products, *EAM frameworks* provide guidance on how to develop and structure EAM products. While various EAM frameworks are proposed in academia and in practice, the four most frequently cited are the Zachman framework,[147] the TOGAF framework,[148] the DoDAF framework,[149] and the ARIS framework.[150] Although each of these is referred to as an EAM framework, the term is highly ambiguous, and consequently, the actual EAM frameworks differ significantly in what they suggest and what they comprise. For example, the four EAM frameworks here are primarily a combination of an EAM process methodology[151] and an enterprise ontology. Additionally, for historical reasons, the scope of most of these EAM frameworks comprises the design and building of enterprise-wide information systems rather than the management and optimization of the enterprises as a whole. Therefore, these EAM frameworks are often combined or adjusted to specific needs in practice.[152]

Nevertheless, the four EAM frameworks also have some elements in common. Their focus is to provide techniques for a model-based description of the EA, although they do not specify a specific modeling language.[153] To manage the huge number of entities used in the models, the EAM frameworks leverage architectural layers and architectural views as a means of further reducing the complexity of the EA models.[154]

The breakdown of the EA models into different *EAM layers* varies depending on the employed EAM framework. According to Winter et al. (2007), EAM frameworks can be structured along five different layers, each of which represents a different view of the organization:[155]

- The *business architecture* layer depicts the organization's fundamental principles describing, among other entities the strategy, organizational goals, value networks, and offered services/products. Among other things, this layer can be used to analyze and optimize the organization's business model.

---

[147] Zachman (1987), (2003)

[148] The Open Group (2005)

[149] Department Of Defence Architecture Framework Group

[150] IDS Scheer (2005); Scheer (1999)

[151] Note that in comparison to the EAM processes discussed below, the EAM frameworks focus in their process descriptions primarily on the creation of the EAM products. The other areas introduced later are not covered in most EAM frameworks.

[152] Lange, Mendling (2011); Sessions

[153] Lankhorst et al. (2009)

[154] Schekkerman (2006)

[155] Winter, Fischer (2007)

- The *process architecture* layer focuses on the business capabilities and their orchestration to develop, create, and deliver services/products: for example, it describes the required business processes, the related organizational structures, the responsibilities, and the performance indicators. This layer can be used, for example, to analyze and optimize the organization's process landscape.

- The *integration architecture* models the interaction and interconnection of the information system components, describing, e.g., application classes, integration systems, and data flows. Among other things, this layer can be used to analyze and optimize the organization's integration technologies such as an Enterprise Service Bus.

- The *software architecture* comprises software artifacts describing, e.g., services and data structures. This layer can be used, for example, to analyze and optimize the organization's application landscape.

- The *infrastructure architecture* focuses on the technological aspects of computing and communication, describing, for example, the infrastructure services and the infrastructure organization. Among other things, this layer can be used to analyze and optimize the organization's IT infrastructure components.

In addition to the architectural layers, the *architectural views* help adjust the EA models to the particular needs of the different stakeholders. The views disregard unnecessary information and filter the EA model with only the stakeholders' concerns in mind. In the architectural views, the elements of an EA model that are visible to a specific stakeholder depend completely on that stakeholder's needs.[156]

Once available, the EA models are a means of analyzing and optimizing the EA. Bucher et al. (2007) describe eight analytical approaches that help to assess what should be done to efficiently implement an organization's strategy:[157]

- *Benefits analysis* identifies how certain aspects of an organization contribute to its organizational goals and create benefits for the organization. For example, a benefits analysis of the value chain reveals which parts of the value chain contribute to the overall profit of the organization and how much each contributes, allowing problematic areas to be identified.

- *Cost analysis* assigns costs to certain aspects of the EA and allows for the calculation of the financial impacts of changing the architecture. For example, a cost analysis of

---

[156] Lankhorst et al. (2009), pp. 57–58

[157] Bucher et al. (2007)

the support processes can reveal inefficient areas that cause high costs compared to the competitors.

- *Coverage analysis* identifies redundancies and gaps by matching two or more layers. For example, business processes can be mapped to the application landscape to identify which applications are actually not used in an organization's operation.

- *Dependency analysis* investigates the relationships between different EA entities, both on the same layer and between layers. For example, business processes can be mapped to an application to identify which processes will be affected if the application is changed.

- *Heterogeneity analysis* identifies similar entities that are implemented in variants or in different areas that should be reconsidered for standardization. For example, this analysis can reveal how many different technologies are employed as infrastructure components in an organization, causing unnecessary complexity.

- *Interface analysis* typically focuses on the evaluation of the relationship and interfaces within one class of entities (e.g., technical interfaces between software applications). For example, it can determine how many applications in the application landscape communicate over point-to-point interfaces rather than over a central Enterprise Service Bus.

- *Complexity analysis* is strongly related to dependency, heterogeneity, and interface analysis; in addition, it considers aspects such as modularity. For example, it can analyze how many variants of a business process exist that require different IT implementations.

- *Compliance analysis* leverages the transparency created with EA to identify gaps within certain policies and regulatory laws (e.g., Solvency II or Basel II). For example, business processes can be mapped to the regulatory requirements to identify processes that do not comply with the current regulations.

EAM Processes

EAM processes define the activities and the sequences required to conduct EAM. These processes also determine which activities generate which EAM products. Various process models have been proposed in the context of the EAM frameworks.[158] The EAM processes can be categorized into three areas: EAM decision-making, EAM conformance,

---

[158] Pulkkinen (2006)

and EAM delivery.[159] The EAM decision-making processes (a) approve new EAM products or formally approve changes to existing EAM products, and (b) handle escalations regarding EAM conformance, i.e., if a transformation project does not comply with the set EAM principles or guidelines, these processes handle the escalation and reach a decision in this regard. One or more governance bodies (e.g., an EAM board) typically perform these activities. The EAM conformance processes (a) validate the EAM principle conformance, i.e., check the formal compliance of the transformation projects and prepare the related decision-making, (b) provide feedback on the EAM products to the creators, and (c) escalate the EAM exceptions to the respective decision makers. The EAM delivery processes (a) create and maintain EAM products, (b) validate change results to determine whether they conform to the defined EAM principles, and (c) provide support in applying EAM products in transformation projects. The EAM delivery processes also (d) provide advice to guide EAM decision-making. Figure 2-5 depicts these processes.

Figure 2-5 Overview of EAM Processes

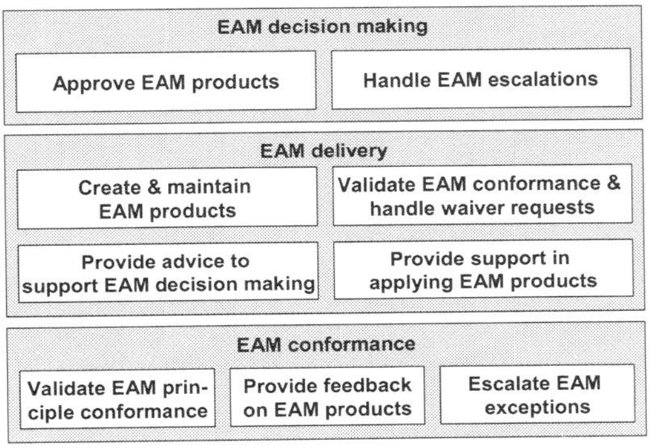

Source: Adapted from van der Raadt et al. (2008)

EAM Governance

EAM governance defines the bodies, roles and responsibilities and their integration into the organization as a whole. EAM governance bodies and roles can range between an informal advisory capacity and a formal decision-making authority.[160] EAM governance bodies provide a formal status to the decision-making about EAM products and the escalations of nonconformity. Effective EAM governance bodies are characterized by various roles that represent potentially conflicting interests, include transparent decision-

---

[159] van der Raadt, van Vliet (2008)

[160] Peterson (2004)

making based on objective principles and criteria, and the proper mandates to enforce decisions.[161] The setup of the EAM governance must be tailored to the organization at hand. Depending on the organizational characteristics, EAM decision-making is implemented with a centralized, decentralized, or federal model for the optimal integration.[162]

Figure 2-6 provides an example of an EAM governance structure. In this example, two EAM governance bodies are in place: the Architecture Review Board, which is responsible for reviewing and approving the EAM products, and the Enterprise Architecture Council, which serves as the decision-making authority for all EAM-related decisions. Both governance bodies are integrated with the business units on the business side, the IT side, and the various transformation projects.[163]

Figure 2-6 Example of an EAM Governance Structure

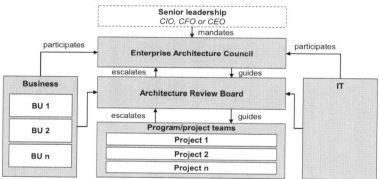

Source: Adapted from Ahlemann et al. (2012)

2.3. Assessment Approaches for EAM

Having introduced in the central concepts and tools of EAM in the previous section, in this section, we shift our focus back to the benefits of EAM. Therefore, this section discusses approaches for EAM the assessment of EAM. Some parts of the results of the following section have also been submitted for publication in Lange et al. (In Review) by the author of this doctoral thesis.[164]

---

[161] van der Raadt, van Vliet (2008)

[162] Peterson (2004)

[163] Gallagher (1974)

[164] Lange, Mendling (In Review), see also Section 'PUBLICATIONS FROM THIS THESIS'

Overview

In the following section, we briefly introduce and discuss along the taxonomy of EAM outlined above existing research on EAM assessment approaches. The scope of an EAM assessment can vary, depending on the perspective taken and units of analysis. An assessment of the overall benefits realized by EAM, an EA model, or an Enterprise Architecture (EA) can all be performed.

To identify the existing research on EAM assessment approaches, we conducted a structured three-step literature review to identify publications, as suggested by Webster and Watson (2002).[165] They recommend beginning with a journal database search and an examination of the related conference proceedings. As a next step, they recommend searching first backward and then forward in the identified literature to identify sources that quote the identified papers or that the identified papers have quoted.[166] We first searched for scientific publications with Google Scholar and CiteSeerX. The findings from this step were supplemented by screening the tables of contents of the top IS journals. Finally, we reviewed the citations of the identified publications to identify further relevant literature. To focus this research, we only identified the benefit assessment literature that directly addressed the area of EAM research and that has, therefore, proven applicable in this context. We disregarded literature from boundary disciplines such as business-IT alignment or software architecture. Consequently, we restricted the key words used in the first step when querying Google Scholar and CiteSeerX to 'enterprise architecture analysis', 'enterprise architecture assessment', 'enterprise architecture benefit', 'enterprise architecture effectiveness', 'enterprise architecture evaluation', and 'enterprise architecture value.' This search yielded 83 publications after excluding redundant hits. To further identify the relevant publications from the top IS publications that may have been missed in the first step, we screened the tables of contents and abstracts of 22 major outlets between January 2000 and December 2010. These publications included the eight AIS senior scholars' basket journals[167] and additional reputable journals from the MIS journal ranking list[168]. This search yielded an additional

---

[165] Webster, Watson (2002). Literature reviews are also introduced in more detail in Section 3.2.

[166] Webster, Watson (2002)

[167] These are the European Journal of Information Systems, Information Systems Journal, Information Systems Research, Journal of AIS, Journal of Information Technology, Journal of MIS, Journal of Strategic Information Systems and MIS Quarterly. AIS (2011)

[168] These are the Academy of Management, ACM Transactions, Communication of the ACM, Communication of the AIS, Data Base, Decision Science, Decision Support Systems, Harvard Business Review, IEEE Computer, IEEE Transactions, Information Management, Management Science, Organizational Science, and Sloan Management Review.

71 identified publications. In the last step, we identified further 18 additional publications by inspecting the citations of the previously identified publications.

Having identified a total of 172 publications, we excluded 121 publications because they either did not fit into the scope outlined above or were not a peer-reviewed publication, as recommended by Baker (2000).[169] The remaining 51 publications remained in the scope of this literature review.

Figure 2-7 Breakdown of the Literature Identified that Addresses EAM Assessment Approaches

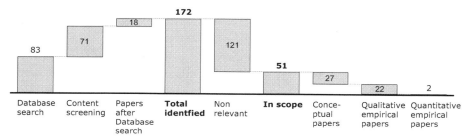

The identified publications are mainly based on conceptual or qualitative empirical findings and are short on quantitative empirical findings, as the following statistic shows. Over half of the 51 identified papers (52%, 27 papers) used a conceptual approach in their research; 44% (22 papers) used a qualitative empirical approach based on case studies, Delphi studies or focus groups; and only the remaining 4% (2 papers) present quantitative empirical findings.

While 13 papers (25%) discuss the assessment of the overall EAM benefits, addressing all elements of our taxonomy, the remaining 38 papers (75%) are concerned with an assessment of singular aspects of EAM, such as the evaluation of EA design alternatives, EAM frameworks or EAM compliance, i.e., a subset of the components of our taxonomy.

In the following paragraphs, we first provide an overview of the identified research that focuses on EAM assessment of the various singular components of our taxonomy, i.e., the components of either EAM products or EAM processes. The research that focuses on the assessment of EAM products primarily suggests approaches to evaluate the as-is or to-be enterprise architectures and is presented in the first sub-section. The papers about the assessment approaches for EAM processes discuss, in particular, how to evaluate the EAM compliance processes and the selection of an appropriate EAM framework and are

---

[169] Baker (2000)

presented in the second sub-section. In the third sub-section, we present existing research about the identified literature for an overall EAM benefit assessment.

Assessment Approaches for EAM Products

The first group, 'EAM product assessment', is concerned with the evaluation of different design decisions or design alternatives of an EA – so-called 'EA scenarios' – for their fit with an organization's goals and their respective requirements. To evaluate the EA scenarios, these approaches either leverage the analysis of EA models or gather information about the EA in a structured manner.[170] Four research streams belong to this category. The streams mainly differ in the methods that they employ to evaluate the EAM products. The first stream is about automated EA model analysis, the second leverages Extended Influence Diagrams for decision-making, the third provides a multicriteria decision-making method, and finally, the fourth uses EA modeling languages to facilitate the assessment.

First, de Boer et al. (2005) propose a concept for an automated evaluation of EA models regarding their static and dynamic behavior.[171] This approach consists of a formal language based on XML to specify the EA models that can be analyzed according to their structural and behavioral properties. While an analysis of the structural properties can, for example, be an analysis of component redundancies, an analysis of the behavioral properties can be, for example, the context-specific interpretation of a component. To define this analytical language, the authors use signatures, i.e., a formal structural representation of the components of an EA. Therefore, the signature consists of a partially ordered set of primitive sorts, i.e., a data type identifier, and a partially ordered set of relationships. In addition, the authors use semantic models for the dynamic analysis, building on these signatures. These semantic models use the concrete sorts and their relationships and model their change over time due to the dynamic behavior. Furthermore, the dynamic behavior is analyzed with scenes and transitions. Scenes are sequences of semantic models, and transitions are the connection between these scenes. As an illustration, the language can describe how a business process of 'register order placement' is formally described and how a second component, an 'employee', can dynamically take different roles in this process. In this illustration, example analyses are also proposed, including checking whether name attributes are defined as XML element names, type checking, and checking whether is-a relationships are anti-symmetric. Furthermore, a process to conduct these analyses is discussed. The authors suggest conducting five steps in this process: create the symbolic model, collect the semantic

---

170 Davoudi et al. (2011)

171 de Boer et al. (2005)

models and the transitions between them, create the rules based on these semantic models and transitions, generalize these rules, and analyze the model based on the identified rules. This presented research focuses on the structural and dynamic representation of the EA components, preparing an automated analysis of the respective EA model. To this end, the suggested approach can be considered as a formal modeling language that provides some capabilities for an automated analysis rather than as an analysis approach for EAM.

Second, *Extended Influence Diagrams* are a model-based approach proposed by Johnson et al. (2006) for the evaluation and comparison of different architectural design alternatives. Johnson et al. (2006) evaluate different existing languages with respect to their decision-making capabilities in the context of EAM. These authors conclude that existing languages are insufficient in the context of EAM in terms of their capability to support firstly uncertainty and secondly multiple levels of abstraction. Hence, they propose to extend the language of influence diagrams accordingly. Johnson et al. (2006) argue that these two extensions are desirable in the context of EAM because the information represented in the EA models is typically associated with a degree of uncertainty and because the existing knowledge is not always available on one level of abstraction.[172] The Extended Influence Diagrams are researched and applied in various contexts as depicted in Table 2-2. Additionally, the authors propose a software tool to conduct the analyses in the context of EAM. In general, these analyses are an evaluation of EA models against context-specific criteria to make EAM-related decisions.[173] An example of this type of a decision-making is the evaluation of an application landscape whether the provided availability of each application is sufficient for the supported business processes. Further researched quality criteria are summarized in Table 2-2. The research of Extended Influence Diagrams focuses on the evaluation of software quality criteria, mainly in a technical sense as described in ISO-9126.[174] Johnson et al. (2006) interpret the term Enterprise Architecture as the application architecture rather than taking a holistic view of the enterprise and including layers such as business processes or infrastructure. Consequently, this research lacks the holistic perspective required to evaluate the overall Enterprise Architecture including all its layers.

---

[172] Johnson et al. (2006); Lagerström et al. (2007)

[173] Buschle et al. (2010); Johnson et al. (2007a); Ullberg et al. (2010)

[174] ISO/IEC (2001)

Table 2-2 The Researched Areas of Application of the Extended Influence Diagrams

Researched area of application	Identified literature
Availability	Holschke et al. (2010); Raderius et al. (2009)
Cyber security	Ekstedt et al. (2009b)
Data accuracy	Närman et al. (2009a)
Interoperability	Ullberg et al. (2008a), (2008b)
Maintainability	Ekstedt et al. (2009a); Gammelgård et al. (2007)
Maintenance management process	Höök et al. (2009)
Organizational performance	Gustafsson et al. (2009)
Process and system dependency analysis	Franke et al. (2009b); Franke et al. (2009a)
Software change project costs	Lagerström et al. (2009b)
System modifiability	Lagerström (2010); Lagerström et al. (2009a), Lagerström et al. (2010)
System quality	Närman et al. (2007); Närman et al. (2009b)

Third, Davoudi et al. (2011) argue that the approaches presented above lack, first, the ability to assign different weights to the evaluated criteria according to an enterprise's needs, and second, the ability to accommodate different views. These authors address the former lack by using the multicriteria decision-making method Analytic Hierarchy Process (AHP), which allows different weights to be assigned to the quality criteria that are used in decision-making.[175] Additionally, the latter lack is addressed by proposing a process that considers the different EAM views for the identification and structuring of the EAM-related decision-making.[176] These views are defined and evaluated according to seven components: (1) a stimulus that requires the architecture to change, (2) a defined source of this stimulus is defined that generates the stimulus, (3) a context in which the stimulus occurs, (4) the architectural view that is determined by the EAM view from which the quality attribute is considered, (5) the related EAM products belonging to the involved EAM view, (6) the potential responses of the enterprise to the stimulus, and finally, (7) the measures for the evaluation of the response of the architecture. Consequently, all the various EAM views are supported in this approach, in contrast to Johnson et al.'s (2006) approach, which only considers the software quality criteria on the application layer. Because some decision makers have problems assigning exact weights to quality criteria, Davoudi et al. (2011) extend their approach using fuzzy logic in further research. This approach eases the assignment of quality criteria to the EA design alternatives for decision makers as no exact weights are required.[177] Nevertheless, Davoudi et al. (2011) limit their research to very specific quality

---

[175] Davoudi, Aliee (2009a), (2009b); Davoudi et al. (2009d); Davoudi et al. (2011)

[176] Davoudi, Aliee (2009c)

[177] Aliee et al. (2010); Davoudi et al. (2009e)

dimensions and do not propose a holistic, integrated set of quality dimensions or criteria to be used in their approach. Consequently, their approach is confined to a limited set of dimensions and requires the identification of appropriate measures for the context of EAM.

Fourth, in contrast to the approaches that focus on the quantitative analysis for decision-making regarding EA scenarios, various researchers propose extensions of the existing modeling languages to incorporate the capabilities of quantitative analysis. Iacob et al. (2005) propose the extension of the ArchiMate modeling language for performance evaluations.[178] They recommend enriching models with data to calculate the top-down workload and the bottom-up performance. Therefore, each model has to be normalized to the ArchiMate metamodel structure to allow the respective calculations. Morkevicius et al. (2010) argue that the latter approach lacks a model-driven evaluation process and suggest an extension of the approach based on the Unified Profile for DoDAF and MODAF (UPDM) standard in the context of performance analysis.[179] This UPDM standard defines a set of UML stereotypes and allows for model-driven evaluations. These evaluations are accomplished using the information contained in the UML stereotypes and aggregating this information to calculate the performance indicators. The authors demonstrate this based on a workload calculation that is aggregated for all the components of the architecture. Buckl et al. (2009b) build on Johnson et al.'s (2006) approach, proposing a method that integrates the required information in the EA models.[180] They suggest augmenting the EA models with quality attributes and causal dependencies and then analyzing these data with the formal Probabilistic Relations Model (PRM) analysis framework proposed by Franke et al. (2009b).[181] This framework calculates the performance indicators considering probabilistic characteristics of architectural components. Yu et al. (2006) go one step further, arguing that models are the appropriate means for a foundation of systematic analysis and rational decision-making while also proposing to leverage intentional modeling to incorporate the transparency of past decisions and the traceability of decisions against their underlying goals.[182] These authors demonstrate how the intentional modeling framework i* can be used in the context of EAM. A third quantitative modeling approach is proposed by Javanbakht et al. (2009). These authors argue that missions, goals, and opportunities must be incorporated into the decision-making process of the improvement or redesign of

---

[178] Iacob, Jonkers (2005)

[179] Morkevicius et al. (2010)

[180] Buckl et al. (2009a); Buckl et al. (2009b)

[181] Franke et al. (2009b)

[182] Yu et al. (2006)

business processes in the context of EAM to allow for informed decisions to be made. Therefore, they suggest a model-based method in their research and propose a supporting software tool that enables the modeling of missions, goals, and opportunities in EA models.[183] However, all these approaches focus on the modeling of information for the purpose of analysis; therefore, they support a quantitative usage of the modeled information. Each of these approaches stops short of suggesting how to use the modeled information for decision-making and what attributes or information exactly need to be modeled.

These four streams of research in the area of EAM product assessment exemplify the manifold research in the area of the analysis of EAM design alternatives. Existing research focuses on the integration of quantitative information in existing modeling approaches and on the research of decision-making procedures and approaches to support rational decision-making. In addition, various different decision-making contexts, e.g., system availability and system performance analysis, have been researched in detail. However, these contexts focus on single quality characteristics in the domain of software applications. Although these software applications are considered enterprise-wide applications, to date, a holistic Enterprise Architecture perspective that considers business, application, and infrastructure aspects has only been suggested by Davoudi et al. (2009c).[184] To the best of our knowledge, a truly holistic perspective on the topic that guides the evaluation of EA scenarios has not yet been researched. Nevertheless, the specific set of parameters that determines the benefits of an EA design alternative would be of interest to both practitioners and academics. Therefore, it is necessary to elaborate on the approaches that guide the assessment of EA design alternatives from a holistic perspective, considering all the various EAM layers, and to answer the research questions such as the following: What dimensions and characteristics of the EA design alternative must be considered to evaluate an EA design alternative holistically? What factors influence the benefits of EA scenarios? How can EA scenarios be evaluated over time?

Assessment Approaches for EAM Processes

The second group, 'EAM process assessment', is concerned with evaluating the conduct of EAM processes. The processes should be evaluated according to whether they are complete, efficient, and purposeful in terms of the organization's goals. In our literature review, we identified four references that focus on this topic, namely an overall EAM process model, an EAM compliance model, an EAM framework selection model, and an EAM pattern collection.

---

[183] Javanbakht et al. (2009)
[184] Davoudi, Aliee (2009c)

Hirvonen et al. (2003) propose an overall EAM process that is similar to the V-Model of software development for EAM. Their definition of the model remains on a rather high level, comprising seven high-level process steps, as follows: (1) 'Project starting', in which the EAM is planned and quality targets are set; (2) 'Preplanning activities', in which the current state is analyzed and requirements are identified; (3) 'EAM construction', in which the a target state is planned for selected areas; (4) 'Planning results', in which the target states are validated and reviewed; (5) 'Implementation and transition plans', in which roadmaps are planned, reviewed and implemented; (6) 'Project ending', in which the project is ended and feedback is gathered; and finally, (7) 'EAM maturity', in which a continuous analysis for improvement opportunities is conducted. More detailed processes or activities within these process steps are not discussed.[185]

Another approach, focusing on EAM compliance, is proposed by Ylimäki et al. (2007) These authors do not explicitly define a process for EAM compliance, instead suggesting perspectives from which EAM compliance should be evaluated, namely the evaluation of EAM goals, of EAM targets, and the concrete evaluations.[186] Both of these presented approaches, namely Hirvonen et al. (2003) and Ylimäki et al. (2007), provide a partial view of the processes required for EAM. A complete reference model for EAM processes as the basis for an assessment of the implemented processes has not yet been proposed. The presented research focuses either on a high-level description of such or on detailing a small area of the EAM processes.

In addition to this research, the selection and evaluation of the right EAM framework for an organization can also be subordinated to this area. Here, Lim et al. (2009) propose a framework to evaluate EAM frameworks and select the appropriate one for the situation at hand.[187] The evaluation is conducted according to the dimensions of view, perspective, scope, and time; for each of these dimensions, the quality attributes are also defined. These core quality attributes are interoperability, flexibility, reusability, scalability, portability, standardization, communication, reduce complexity and alignment and for each dimension, dimension-specific additional attributes are defined as well. This approach focuses on a general evaluation of the frameworks and lacks the ability to evaluate EAM frameworks for the specific organization under consideration. For example, existing knowledge or experiences within an organization with respect to one framework are not considered.

[185] Hirvonen et al. (2003)

[186] Ylimäki et al. (2007)

[187] Lim et al. (2009)

In contrast to this approach, Buckl et al. (2008) propose using EAM patterns to customize and enrich EAM frameworks with best practices according to each organization's needs. The suggested patterns are clustered in methodological patterns (M-Patterns) that describe the steps to be taken to address an EAM concern, viewpoint patterns (V-Patterns) that provide an EAM language to be used by M-Patterns and information patterns (I-Patterns) that supply a model to visualize the data needed for V-Patterns.[188] For example, for an EA model depicting an application landscape, the V-Patterns specify which application should appear in which color depending on factors like how critical the application is to business success. Buckl et al.'s (2008) research focuses on the definition of these patterns in a catalogue and the researchers suggest appropriate selection criteria for the patterns as future research.

Based on the four publications that we identified in this area, we conclude that the research in this area is in its initial stages, and approaches to evaluating the overall EAM process landscape are not yet available. Consequently, we see a need for research on the detailed reference models for EAM processes. These would provide the capability to evaluate an organization's EAM against these reference processes. The related research could answer questions such as the following: What processes and activities must be operated to conduct EAM? How can these reference processes be evaluated against the current organization's practice? As discussed, the suggested approaches to the assessment of the EAM frameworks focus on the general selection and evaluation of the EAM frameworks. How to evaluate EAM frameworks against each specific organization's goals is not discussed. Because the frameworks employed in organizations must always be customized to organizational needs,[189] further research should also define more specific evaluation and selection criteria for the EAM frameworks to allow individual approaches for organizations to be compiled based on an EAM toolbox.

Overall EAM Benefit Assessment

The last group of EAM literature that we identified discusses approaches to the overall assessment of EAM benefits. We identified three different streams of research in this area.

In an exploratory study of 100 organizations, Ross et al. (2005) identify a list of benefits emanating from EAM. They group these benefits into technology-related EAM benefits composed of IT cost, IT responsiveness, and risk management and business-related EAM benefits including shared business platforms, managerial satisfaction, and strategic business impacts. These authors suggest the establishment of a baseline for each of

---

[188] Buckl et al. (2008)
[189] Lange, Mendling (2011)

these dimensions and the monitoring of each of these dimensions to evaluate EAM.[190] Boucharas et al. (2010) also identify the potential benefits of EAM in a literature review. They identify the potential EAM benefits in the existing literature and organize these in a so-called EAM benefit map. These benefits are discussed according to Kaplan and Norton's Strategy Maps:[191] they identify the categories 'financial outcomes benefits', 'customer outcomes benefits', 'innovation processes benefits', 'operations management processes benefits', 'customer management', 'organization capital', 'information capital benefits', and 'human capital'. Furthermore, the authors recommend that their results should be used to establish a business case for EAM based on these identified benefits[192] and propose to research an approach that analyzes the contribution of EAM to the achievement of business goals in future research.[193] In another study, Foorthuis et al. (2010) empirically analyze how EAM conformance leads to EAM benefits.[194] These authors conclude with an empirical model that demonstrates that the EAM compliance assessments of projects, the management propagation of EAM, and the EAM assistants for projects are the main levers that yield conformance of projects to the EA. This conformance, in turn, yields the EAM benefits of business IT alignment, integration, standardization, reduced redundancy, increased project quality, better management of complexity, and accomplished enterprise-wide goals. However, Foorthuis et al. (2010) consider their empirically validated model in this area to be a first version due to the limitations of their study, and they suggest that the model be further tested and validated. Furthermore, they suggest that a monitoring process to track the identified benefits over time is developed.

In another research stream, based on two international case studies, Kluge et al. (2006) adopt the DeLone and McLean IS success model[195] for the domain of EAM. They argue that in the context of EAM the perceived benefits of EAM differs significantly between business and IT representatives and that this type of model can help to explain the process of benefit creation from EAM. Therefore, they cluster the benefit creation process into three stages: potential benefits, being the system quality and information quality in the original model; the perceived benefits, being the intention to use and the user satisfaction in the original model; and the realized benefits, being the net benefits in the original model. Furthermore, they argue that the components of service quality and the

---

[190] Ross, Weill (2005)

[191] Kaplan, Norton (2004)

[192] Boucharas et al. (2010)

[193] van Steenbergen, Brinkkemper (2008)

[194] Foorthuis et al. (2010)

[195] DeLone, McLean (2003)

use of the original model are decisive moderators concerning in organizations' EAM benefit realization. Consequently, they find in the two case studies that these moderators are the EAM presentation strategy (service quality) and the EAM governance strategy (use).[196] Niemi et al. (2009) criticize Kluge et al. (2006) for adopting a narrow "*consideration of the original success model: only the effects of presentation and governance strategies are discussed while other constructs have been left intact.*"[197] Hence, they use the DeLone and McLean IS success model to explain the EAM benefit realization process, but they extend it with four different EAM viewpoints: process, product, outcome and impact and define what the IS success model means in the context of the EAM for each of these viewpoints. These authors employ a previously published case study to exemplify their approach, demonstrating that their model can be applied. Although these approaches provide a good starting point for the adoption of the widely accepted DeLone and McLean IS success model to the context of EAM, a thorough empirical validation has not yet been conducted.[198]

In the third stream of research, in the area of the overall EAM benefit assessment approaches, van der Raadt et al. (2010) propose an assessment model to evaluate an organization's implementation of EAM. The so-called Normalized Architecture Organization Maturity Index (NAOMI) assesses both the efficiency of EAM and how well EAM is incorporated into the overall organizational bodies, roles, structures, and processes. van der Raadt et al. (2010) base their model on two elements: first, an EAM reference model, which is a high-level norm description for EAM, and second, a measurement approach that does not link the efficiency topic to the maturity phases. The authors argue that the latter enables a flexible use of the model in various situations. The model assesses EAM according to the dimensions of management and organization, products, communication and PR, human resources and tools, and work processes by comparing the processes implemented in an organization with best-practice processes. The model is validated and refined in 3 subsequent case studies.[199] Lux et al. (2010) propose a further method for evaluating the benefits of EAM based on the resource-based theory. Their suggested model includes a cause and effect relationship between EAM and organizational performance. They hypothesize that the EAM-related IS resources have an impact on EAM capabilities. In turn, these capabilities have an impact on business processes, which have an impact on business process performance, which has an impact

---

[196] Kluge et al. (2006)

[197] Niemi, Pekkola (2009)

[198] For a more detailed discussion of this research, see Section 3.1.

[199] van der Raadt et al. (2010); van der Raadt et al. (2005); van der Raadt et al. (2007); van der Raadt et al. (2009)

on organizational performance.[200] This model is theoretically developed and verified by one case study. A further empirical validation has not yet been published.

The research in the area of EAM benefit assessment is mainly split into three areas: the research on EAM benefit drivers, IS success models in the context of EAM, and a concept for the overall assessment of EAM against an EAM reference model. A first step to drive the development in this area further may be to link these different areas, allowing the establishment of an overall business case for EAM and an overall assessment method that includes all levels of EAM. Furthermore, measures used to assess the different dimensions of EAM benefits are lacking. These measures would help to conduct the respective assessments in practice. A validation of the conceptually developed approaches is also necessary to confirm the previously developed hypothesis.

2.4. Conclusion

This chapter introduced the foundations of EAM. Based on a literature review, it further detailed the necessity of researching the benefits of EAM. We have discussed how the assessment of EAM is a challenging area of research because evaluating the fulfillment of EAM goals is a complex and long-term endeavor that underlies permanent change. The presented literature review has demonstrated that there is a lack of empirically validated approaches in the area of EAM assessments and that this field of research must develop these empirically validated approaches.[201] Currently, the most wide-spread research areas are EAM product assessments, EAM process assessments and overall EAM benefit assessments. However, there appears to be no common theory within and across these research areas.

Our results show that the in the area of EAM product assessment has focused on decision-making procedures for EAM, but it currently lacks concrete measures to holistically evaluate EAM. The approaches in this area should provide a holistic framework that specifies which dimensions should be considered when conducting a holistic assessment. The current approaches this type of holistic view that considers all EAM layers, such as business, application, and infrastructure; instead, they focus on the application layer alone. Furthermore, to date, concrete measures for these dimensions have not yet been researched. Such measures would allow the assessment of the effectiveness of EAM.

---

[200] Lux et al. (2010)

[201] An overview of the identified literature and the respective research methods used can be found in Appendix B.1.

Similarly, in the second area of EAM benefit approaches discussed here, the assessment of EAM processes, reference models for EAM processes are just beginning to emerge in research and their validation is still pending. Nevertheless, these models are necessary to enable the evaluation of organizations' EAM processes. Research should develop further theory in this area to identify the core processes that EAM should conduct and the extent to which these processes lead to the expected EAM benefits.

In addition to this, in the area of overall EAM benefit assessment, the overall business case of EAM has not yet been researched thoroughly. To close this gap, research should develop additional theories about the benefit drivers of EAM and thoroughly identify validated approaches to evaluate these benefit drivers and how they yield EAM benefits in practice.

3. Model Building

The truth is rarely pure and never simple.
Oscar Wilde (1854-1900)

In this chapter, we develop a theoretical a priori model for the realization of benefits from EAM. In building our model, we draw upon the DeLone and McLean IS success model (DMSM) and discuss our extension of the model in the domain of EAM.[202] After describing the research background of this DMSM (Section 3.1), we describe the research method applied in this chapter in Section 3.2. We then discuss the constructs and propositions of the model that have been identified in an extensive literature review in Section 3.3. In the last section of this chapter (Section 3.4), we close with a synopsis of the main findings. The results of the following chapter have also been published in parts in Lange et al. (2012) by the author of this doctoral thesis.[203]

3.1. Research on IS Success

IS research has a rich tradition of IS success, which includes aspects such as user information satisfaction,[204] task–technology fit,[205] system use,[206] and participation.[207] IS success has been a research topic in the IS literature for at least three decades. Since Keen (1980) posed the question, "What is the dependent variable?" at the first International Conference on Information Systems,[208] scholars have suggested a number of different models to explain IS success and the related success factors from various perspectives.[209] For example, Davis's (1989) Technology Acceptance Model (TAM) uses

---

[202] DeLone, McLean (1992), (2003)

[203] Lange et al. (2012), see also Section "PUBLICATIONS FROM THIS THESIS"

[204] E.g., Shaw et al. (2002)

[205] E.g., Goodhue, Thompson (1995)

[206] E.g., Davis (1989); Venkatesh et al. (2009)

[207] Garrity et al. (2005)

[208] Keen (1980)

[209] Petter, McLean (2009); Urbach et al. (2008)

the Theory of Reasoned Action and Theory of Planned Behavior to explain why one IS is more willingly accepted by users than another.[210]

The main challenge for researchers investigating IS success is the ambiguity of the concept and the multiplicity of IS success constructs suggested in the literature.[211] For example, DeLone et al. (1992) report that 180 studies have utilized over 100 identified measures.[212] Although IS success research covers many different aspects, such as user information satisfaction, task–technology fit, user involvement, and participation,[213] in this doctoral thesis, the aspects of IS benefits are of particular interest. In this context of IS benefits, the dominant model for IS success is the DMSM.[214] In the following, this model is introduced and existing adoptions of the model to the domain of EAM are discussed.

Figure 3-1 The Updated DeLone & McLean IS Success Model

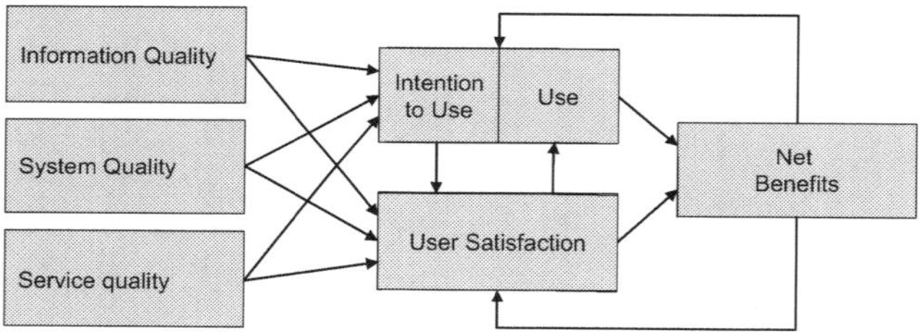

SOURCE: Adapted from DeLone et al. (2003)

The DeLone and McLean IS Success Model

Based on an extensive literature review of IS success measures, DeLone et al. (1992) introduced the DeLone and McLean IS success model (DMSM) as a taxonomy to measure the 'ultimate' dependent variable in IS research: the success of information systems.[215] This model was updated by DeLone et al. (2003) incorporating the findings from empirical and theoretical research on IS success measures that followed their initial work.[216] The updated model of IS success consists of six dimensions (depicted in Figure 3-1) that determine the success of an information system:

---

[210] Davis (1989); Fishbein, Ajzen (1975)

[211] Rai et al. (2002)

[212] DeLone, McLean (1992)

[213] Garrity et al. (2005)

[214] Hu (2003)

[215] DeLone, McLean (1992)

[216] DeLone, McLean (2003)

- *Information quality* refers to the output that is created by an information system. Typical characteristics of this dimension include, for example, accuracy, completeness, consistency, relevance, and timeliness.

- *System quality* refers to the desirable characteristics of the information processing system. Typical characteristics include, for example, like data quality, ease-of-use, flexibility, functionality, importance, integration, portability, and reliability.

- *Service quality* refers to the support of the IS function for the end user of the system. Typical characteristics of this dimension include, for example, technical competence, responsiveness, reliability, and empathy.

- *Use and intention to use* measures the actual usage of the IS and is typically analyzed, for example, based on the characteristics dependency, frequency of use, number of accesses, time of use, and usage pattern.

- *User satisfaction* measures how satisfied the user is with using the information, the system, and the related services. This dimension is typically measured based on the user's delightness, satisfaction, and contentness with respect to the system of interest.

- *Net benefits* measure the outcomes in terms of contribution to the success of individuals, groups, organizations, or society. This dimension is typically characterized by factors such as job performance, decision-making performance, improved productivity, increased sales, and quality of work environment.[217]

The application of the model is highly dependent on the context of analysis. Therefore, when applying the model, the researcher must understand the information system and organization of interest to determine the types of measures used for each dimension. For example, an information system managed by a vendor would have service quality measures for the vendor rather than for the IS department.[218] This context sensitivity poses challenges not only to the application of the model but also to the comparison of different studies.

[217] DeLone, McLean (1992), (2003)
[218] Petter, McLean (2009)

Table 3-1 Overview of the Applications of the DMSM

Object of Analysis		Publication
Single IT application (i.e., the concrete assessment of the success of an application in a concrete organization)	Finance and accounting system	Iivari (2005)
	Data warehouse	Shin (2003)
	E-portal	Cheung et al. (2005)
	Knowledge management system	Clay et al. (2005)
	Picture archiving and communication system	Paré et al. (2005)
	Work time registration system	Bartis et al. (2008)
Type of IT or IT application (i.e., the assessment of a type of application across organizations)	Data warehouse	Nelson et al. (2005); Wixom et al. (2005)
	Delivery information systems	Wilkin et al. (2003)
	E-mail systems	Mao et al. (2004)
	Enterprise systems	Gable et al. (2003); Sedera (2006); Sedera et al. (2004b); Sedera et al. (2004c); Sedera et al. (2004a); Sedera et al. (2004d)
	Knowledge management system	Kulkarni et al. (2006); Wu et al. (2006)
	Knowledge repository systems	Qian et al. (2005)
	Web-based system	Garrity et al. (2005)
	Websites	Schaupp et al. (2006)
All IT applications used by an organization or sub-organization		Almutairi et al. (2005); Bradley et al. (2006); Byrd et al. (2006)
IT function of an organization		Cha-Jan Chang et al. (2005)

SOURCE: Adapted from Urbach et al. (2008)

The DMSM has been applied to various objects of analysis, as depicted in Table 3-1, and in domains other than information systems, such as business process modeling.[219] This fact suggests that the model is widely accepted.[220] Furthermore, Urbach et al. (2008) and Petter et al. (2008) reveal in their literature reviews that the DMSM has been widely validated from an empirical standpoint.[221] However, the DMSM is also criticized in the literature. The criticisms address three main points. First, the DMSM is criticized for being a mixture of a process and a variance model.[222] Combining process and causal explanations in one model is impossible because a variance model describes what dependent factors the independent factors influence and to what degree it does so (if all

---

[219] Sedera et al. (2004d)

[220] Petter et al. (2008)

[221] Petter et al. (2008); Urbach et al. (2008)

[222] Seddon (1997)

other conditions are equal), whereas a process model describes which series of events causes a certain outcome. This series of events cannot be analyzed in a variance model.[223] Furthermore, Seddon (1997) criticizes the ambiguous meaning of the use construct. According to Seddon's (1997) discussion, it can have three different meanings: use can be a proxy for the benefits of IS, the dependent variable for future IS use, or an event in a process that leads to an impact. However, he concludes that the first meaning can be the only correct one in the context of a variance model.[224] Finally, the third main criticism is the underrepresentation of cultural and people aspects in the model. For instance, the role of external players and other cultural aspects that affect IS success is not considered.[225]

Approaches to Applying the DMSM to EAM

According to our characterization of EAM in Chapter 2, EAM is the capability to manage business transformations. EAM builds on EAM methods, tools, and frameworks [226] as well as the people conducting the related EAM processes, which is quite similar to an information system. An information system is defined as *"any combination of information technology and people's activities using that technology to support operations, management, and decision-making"*.[227] Consequently, we argue that an application of the DMSM to the domain of EAM is reasonable because EAM has strong parallels to an information system. EAM can be interpreted as a system that creates outputs such as an information system (i.e., EAM products). Additionally, similar to how an IT system serves as the infrastructure for an information system, EAM is based on infrastructure components, such as organizational structures and tool support. Finally, similar to the IT department that provides services for an information system, EAM provides services to an organization.

In addition, the application of the DMSM to areas such as process modeling or knowledge management has proven the broader applicability of the model to other domains, as discussed above, although DeLone and McLean originally developed the DMSM for information systems only. It can be argued that this model is broadly applicable mainly because the model is based on the generic communication and information influence

---

[223] Markus, Robey (1988)

[224] Seddon (1997)

[225] Ballantine et al. (1996)

[226] Lankhorst et al. (2009)

[227] Ellison, Moore (2003)

theories, which indicates that the model can be used to evaluate the success of any process.[228]

In fact, to the best of our knowledge, two available publications build on this parallel and suggest adapting the DMSM to the domain of EAM, albeit while considering different aspects of EAM, as briefly discussed in Section 2.3.

Kluge et al. (2006) argue that both business and IT stakeholders must be involved in EAM to encourage a comprehensive usage of EAM and to derive its full benefits. Based on two international case studies, the researchers show that EAM typically lacks the involvement of relevant stakeholders, which is an impediment to realizing the full benefits of EAM. This finding brings them to conclude that the DMSM should be adjusted to an 'EAM Value Realization Model' aimed at a greater overall EAM acceptance. The authors reason that the DMSM is suitable because it was originally designed to capture the process of value realization in the IS domain and has been extended in further research to other domains. Consequently, based on their findings from two case studies and the DMSM, the researchers derive the adjusted 'EAM Value Realization Model', which contains service quality and uses as two mediators to facilitate the overall success of EAM. However, this model focuses on the effects of EAM presentation and different governance strategies on the overall success of EAM. Other constructs that may influence the overall success of EAM are not considered in this research. Furthermore, while the study reports on the preliminary findings of two case studies, further validation has yet to be published.[229]

Niemi et al. (2009) pick up the main shortcomings of Kluge et al.'s 'EAM Value Realization Model' and suggest a model that considers additional constructs relevant to the success of EAM.[230] They propose to consider four different viewpoints when evaluating the seven dimensions of the DMSM. The *process viewpoint* considers the EAM planning, development, and management processes. The *products viewpoint* comprises the results of the EAM processes, i.e., the models and principles. The *outcome viewpoint* assesses the results of the implementation of EAM products, i.e., the systems developed. Finally, the *impacts viewpoint* considers the benefits from EAM that arise directly or indirectly from EAM processes or products. The authors illustrate the suggested theoretical application of the DMSM by using a case study that has been earlier published in Andersin et al. (2007), but they do not further validate their suggested approach in

---

[228] Niemi, Pekkola (2009)

[229] Kluge et al. (2006)

[230] Niemi, Pekkola (2009)

later publications.[231] However, in our view, the main limitation of this research is the definitions of the different viewpoints. First, the definitions contain redundancies and white spots. For example, the impact viewpoint has no direct equivalent for five out of its seven dimensions. Second, the viewpoints are not integrated into an overall perspective, and thus, it is not clear how the different viewpoints relate to each other as part of a consistent and integrated theory of the benefits of EAM.[232]

In conclusion, the existing research has suggested applying the DMSM to explain selected characteristics of EAM, but no comprehensive model regarding the realization of EAM benefits has yet been researched and validated.

Adapting the DMSM to an EAM Benefit Realization Model

Using the DMSM as a variance model[233] in this research, we suggest applying the dimensions of the DMSM to the domain of EAM by interpreting the DMSM dimension in the EAM Benefit Realization Model as follows:

EAM product quality is adapted from the information quality dimension in the original model. Originally, this dimension described the output of the information system. Similarly, in the context of EAM, this dimension is concerned with the output of EAM, i.e., the EAM products. The EAM products are the outcomes that store the information required for EAM and the related decision making. The second dimension of the EAM benefit realization model, i.e., the system quality in the original model, is adjusted to form the *EAM infrastructure* provides the required foundation for EAM and therefore determines the formal conditions under which EAM is executed. And finally, the *EAM service delivery quality* replaces the original dimension of service quality. This dimension is concerned with the quality of the EAM services provided to the EAM stakeholder to enact the EA. The original dimensions of the remaining three dimensions, i.e., use, satisfaction, and net benefits, remain intact.

In addition to these adjustments of the DMSM, we introduce another dimension, *EAM cultural aspects,* to address the criticism that cultural and people aspects are underrepresented in the DMSM.[234] This dimension reflects the importance of these aspects, as identified through our literature review. In contrast to the EAM infrastructure quality, which is concerned with the formal conditions, this dimension is concerned with

---

[231] Andersin, Hämäläinen (2007)

[232] Niemi, Pekkola (2009)

[233] Newman, Robey (1992)

[234] Ballantine et al. (1996); Seddon (1997)

the informal (i.e., the 'softer') conditions in which EAM operates. Bean (2010)[235] and Magalhaes et al. (2007)[236] argue that these cultural and social aspects are a fundamental but oft-neglected element of EAM. Therefore, we see a need to represent these aspects in the additional dimension, *EAM cultural aspects,* which will be described in detail later.

Figure 3-2 summarizes our extended model, which we detail in Section 3.3 together with the identified EAM success factor and the benefit constructs.

Figure 3-2 The EAM Benefit Realization Model

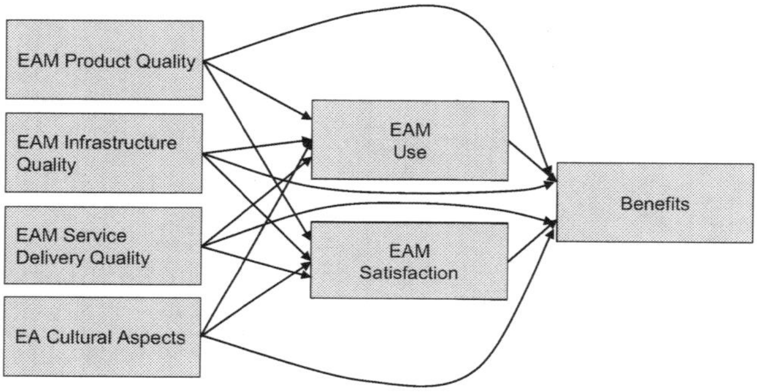

3.2. Research Method

Having no theory for the realization of benefits from EAM, we need to develop an a priori model that can subsequently be validated. An a priori model enables the initial design of the theory-building research,[237] allows for the generation of propositions, and provides a framework to synthesize and integrate the empirical findings.[238]

Steinfield et al. (1990) suggest four approaches to develop a priori models. The first approach *inductively derives the a priori model* from observed patterns of events or behaviors and is often called 'grounded theory building', as the model is 'grounded' in empirical observations.[239] The second approach *develops an a priori model based on a bottom-up analysis* of the conceptual factors that are potentially relevant to the target phenomenon by using a predefined framework. Such a predefined framework could be,

---

[235] Bean (2010)

[236] Magalhaes et al. (2007)

[237] Eisenhardt (1989)

[238] Steinfield, Fulk (1990)

[239] E.g., Glaser, Strauss (2008)

for example, the input-process-output framework through which the researcher identifies the input factors and describes the process that yields the phenomenon of interest as an output. The third approach *extends or modifies existing models to explain a new context*. This approach could, for example, extend theories on individual learning to the context of organizational learning. The fourth approach *applies existing theories in entirely new contexts*. This approach reasons by analogy and could use, for example, theories from physics to explain the IS phenomenon.[240]

In this doctoral thesis, we employ the third approach to develop our a priori model. The DMSM is used as an established theory in the IS discipline and extended to the domain of EAM.[241] However, to adapt the constructs of this model to the domain of EAM, we need to first identify the success factors for EAM and the benefit dimensions. Therefore, we derive a set of EAM success factors and benefits based on a literature review. These factors are then integrated with the DMSM to develop an a priori model for this research.

Thus, the propositions are generated based on a theoretical analysis of the phenomenon at hand, i.e., the realization of benefits from EAM, and are derived by logically deducting predictions about the world based on the theoretical analysis.[242] The propositions postulate associations among the constructs, i.e., an abstraction of a concept of the real world on a theoretical level, and may be conjectural, but they have to be testable. To test them, they are operationalized by an empirical formulation as a hypothesis. A hypothesis is stated as the relationships among empirically observable variables. These relationships between theoretical and empirical concepts are depicted in Figure 3-3.[243]

In the following, we describe our approach to the literature review before detailing how we used the insights from the literature review to derive our EAM benefit realization model and propositions. The operationalization of the model defining the hypotheses and variables on an empirical level is than later presented in Chapter 5.

---

[240] Steinfield, Fulk (1990)

[241] As we focus in this section on the description of the research method, our reasoning why the DMSM is applicable to the domain of EAM can be found in Section 3.1.

[242] Shanks (2002)

[243] Bhattacherjee (2012)

Figure 3-3 Distinction between Theoretical and Empirical Concepts

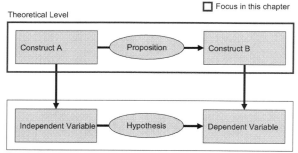

SOURCE: Adapted from Bhattacherjee (2012)

Literature Review

A literature review is essential to gather existing research as a foundation for a research study, assists in positioning and scoping the research, and helps the researcher to integrate the research with existing body of knowledge[244].[245] Therefore, the first step in any research endeavor is to identify the existing research as a foundation and use the quality literature when proposing a new study or new theory.[246] To build a theoretical foundation for the application of the DMSM to the domain of EAM, we conducted a comprehensive review of previous studies in the domain of EAM that identified EAM success factors and EAM benefits.

For this literature review, we applied the structured approach, as suggested by Webster and Watson (2002), to create a complete and sound foundation for this research.[247] In this literature review, we first identified relevant scientific publications by searching scientific databases (ACM Digital Library, AIS Electronic Library, EBSCOhost Business Source Premier, IEEE Xplore, ScienceDirect, and SpringerLink) and by searching the domain-specific outlets Journal of EA and the Trends in EA Research workshop series. Because EAM is a comprehensive discipline and related to various IS topics,[248] we narrowed the focus of our review by excluding studies from boundary disciplines, such as business-IT alignment and software architecture development.

---

[244] The body of knowledge refers to the cumulative research knowledge achieved by "building on each other's [research] results". Iivari et al. (2004).

[245] Hart (1999); Leedy, Ormrod (2009); Shaw (1995b), p. 326

[246] Barnes (2005)

[247] Webster and Watson (2002). See for a detailed description Section 2.3.

[248] Buckl, Matthes (2010)

We used the key word 'enterprise architecture' to query the databases. This search yielded 868 publications. To identify additional publications from IS top publications that may have been missed in the first step, we screened the table of contents and abstracts of the eight AIS senior scholars' basket journals.[249] This search yielded an additional four publications. Having identified 872 publications, we excluded 190 redundant publications. Following the suggestions of Baker (2000), we excluded an additional 82 studies that were not peer-reviewed publications.[250] The remaining 600 publications were further screened by evaluating the titles and abstracts with respect to their fit to our research scope. This step led to the exclusion of 453 publications that addressed topics different from the scope of this thesis, e.g., definitions of a metamodel for EA or discussions on the definition of EA. The remaining 147 publications were analyzed in detail to extract EAM success factors and EAM benefits. These factors could be found in 48 publications, which are used as a foundation for this research. Finally, we analyzed the references of these 48 publications to identify additional, not-yet-covered articles. However, this step did not yield any further publications. This breakdown of the identified literature is also depicted in Figure 3-4.

Figure 3-4 Breakdown of Literature Identified in Literature Review

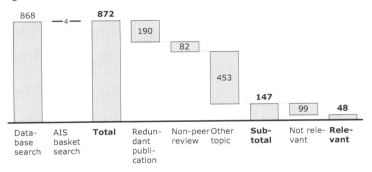

Synthesizing the Identified Literature

The identification of applicable peer-reviewed literature is a necessary condition but not a sufficient condition for a literature review.[251] To be effective and conclusive, a literature review must synthesize the literature based on a concept-centric approach rather than a chronological or author-centric approach.[252] Therefore, the data identified in the

---

[249] Newsted et al. (1998)

[250] Baker (2000)

[251] Shaw (1995a)

[252] Webster, Watson (2002)

literature review must be processed to serve as a foundation that can be used to obtain deeper insights and support theory building.[253]

Therefore, studying the identified 48 publications, we extracted all of the concepts mentioned explicitly or implicitly as EAM success factors. For this extraction, we used the coding procedures suggested in the context of grounded theory.[254] For grounded theory, three different coding processes are suggested. First, open coding refers to the generation of initial concepts from data by identifying elements in the data that are relevant to the research. Second, axial coding uses the concepts identified during the open coding phase and develops and links these concepts into conceptual families. Third, selective coding formalizes the relationships among the conceptual families into theoretical frameworks.[255]

In this thesis, we leveraged the first two coding processes of the coding procedure in grounded theory to identify EAM success factors from the literature. We did not apply the third coding process in this doctoral thesis because the DMSM served as a theoretical foundation. Thus, the development of a theoretical framework was not required.

For the coding, we first read all of the articles completely and marked all of the mentioned factors that supposedly contribute to EAM success in accordance with open coding. Using this approach, we identified 211 potential EAM success factors,[256] such as 'completeness of the as-is architecture documentation improves EAM efficiency'. In the second step, for the axial coding, we used the qualitative data analysis tool NVivo 9 to code and cluster the success factors into conceptual families. That is, we modeled the DMSM in the tool by creating a folder for each of the six dimensions as a basic structure. Next, we assigned NVivo tags ('nodes' in NVivo terms) as units of meaning to each identified potential EAM success factor. To analyze the 211 potential EAM success factors, we coded them as follows:

- When a new success factor emerged, a new node was created and assigned to the appropriate dimension of the DMSM.

- Additional success factors generally supporting an earlier identified factor were assigned to these nodes.

---

[253] Bem (1995)

[254] Not to be mixed up with "Gounded Theory" as a research method, which is not applied in this research.

[255] Corbin, Strauss (2008)

[256] One item being a success factor named in one publication; this includes the redundant count of similar factors that are named by more than one publication.

The results of this proceeding are described in the following section.

3.3. Findings from Literature Review

Building on the insights from the literature review, we present the resulting constructs and propositions of the a priori EAM Benefits Realization Model in the following section.

That is, we detail each dimension of the EAM Benefit Realization Model and the related propositions. We denote in italics each construct with a capital letter for the associated dimension (e.g., *P*), a number for the success factor or benefit (e.g., *P1*), and a lower letter for the sub-dimension or sub-benefit (e.g., *P1a*). This procedure will enable tractability later in this doctoral thesis. As all of the propositions denote an association between an EAM success factor construct and the resulting EAM benefit construct, the propositions focus on a normative description of the EAM success factors. The addition 'to impact EAM net benefits positively' is omitted for each proposition to increase readability, but it should be kept in mind by the reader.

The EAM Product Quality Dimension (P)

EAM products are the artifacts created by EAM and typically comprise at least the as-is architecture, the to-be architecture, and the roadmap. Hence, this dimension is concerned with the information provided by these EAM products, the characteristics of these products, and the quality of this information:

Construct P1:	As-is architecture quality
Proposition P1:	EAM should provide desirable information about the as-is architecture that satisfies the needs of the EAM stakeholders in an effective and efficient way.

This first core product of EAM is the documentation of the current implementation of business processes, IT systems, and infrastructure.[257] It should provide a current (*P1a*)[258] and complete (*P1b*)[259] view of the as-is architecture and provide the right degree of detail (*P1c*)[260].

---

[257] Kaisler et al. (2005); Lankhorst et al. (2009); Schmidt, Buxmann (2011); van der Raadt, van Vliet (2008)

[258] Aier et al. (2011b); Foorthuis et al. (2010); Riege, Aier (2009); Schmidt, Buxmann (2011)

[259] Aier, Schelp (2009); Bricknall et al. (2006); Winter, Fischer (2007)

[260] Pulkkinen (2006); Schmidt, Buxmann (2011); Winter, Fischer (2007)

Construct P2:	To-be architecture quality
Proposition P2:	EAM should provide desirable information about the to-be architecture that satisfies the needs of the EAM stakeholders in an effective and efficient way.

Similar to the as-is architecture, this documentation describes business processes, IT systems and infrastructure but focuses on the desired state in the future. Moreover, the documentation should also provide a complete (*P2a*)[261] view of the desired architecture that provides the correct degree of detail (*P2b*).[262] In addition to these two key characteristics, the to-be architecture should also be adapted regularly to changing conditions because the organization or the environment may change over time (*P2c*).[263]

Construct: P3:	Roadmap quality
Proposition P3:	EAM should provide desirable information about the EAM roadmap that satisfies the needs of the EAM stakeholders in an effective and efficient way.

The EAM roadmap schedules the transformation steps, i.e., the implemented projects, that cause the as-is architecture to evolve step-by-step into the to-be architecture. It brings the transformation steps into a desired sequence that accommodates contextual factors, such as business priorities, budgets, and urgency.[264] The roadmap needs to be feasible given the resource and other organizational constraints (*P3a*),[265] complete in terms of considering all of the relevant steps needed to transform from the as-is architecture to the to-be architecture (*P3b*),[266] and integrated by considering and solving dependencies among different transformation steps (*P3c*).[267]

---

[261] Aier, Schelp (2009); Bricknall et al. (2006); Hjort-Madsen, Pries-Heje (2009); Schmidt, Buxmann (2011)

[262] Pulkkinen (2006); Schmidt, Buxmann (2011); Winter, Fischer (2007)

[263] Schmidt, Buxmann (2011)

[264] Lankhorst et al. (2009)

[265] Seppänen et al. (2009); Zink (2009)

[266] Aier, Schelp (2009); Bricknall et al. (2006)

[267] Halley et al. (2005)

The EAM Infrastructure Quality Dimension (I)

The dimension 'EAM infrastructure quality' is concerned with the condition in which EAM operates. This dimension is concerned with the questions of which EAM infrastructure should be provided to operate EAM most effectively and efficiently.

Construct I1:	EAM mandate definition
Proposition I1:	A clear EAM mandate should define the appointed organizational and business/IT scope of EAM.

The parts of the organization that are in the scope of EAM, i.e., the entities and subsidiaries that are under consideration, should be clearly defined (*I1a*).[268] This scope should be tailored to the intended purposes and management expectations[269] and should consider the desired strategic long-term focus.[270] Next, effectively positioning EAM between the business and IT department appears to create certain advantages (*I1b*).[271] Thereby, being an organizational rather than an IT practice is seen to be beneficial[272] because the former allow organizations to leverage interdisciplinary teams[273] that can continually exchange information between business and IT[274] and that are aligned with business objectives.[275] Furthermore, EAM should be integrated and aligned with boundary functions,[276] such as project portfolio management, business and IT strategy definition, and project management.[277] EAM should be positioned such that it does not compete with these boundary instruments (*I1c*).[278]

Construct I2:	Decision-making centrality
Proposition I2:	Central and local accountabilities should be defined for EAM decision-making.

---

[268] van der Raadt et al. (2007); Zink (2009)

[269] Inji Wijegunaratne et al. (2011); Struck et al. (2010)

[270] Bricknall et al. (2006)

[271] Aier et al. (2011b); Halley et al. (2005); Radeke (2010)

[272] Espinosa et al. (2011)

[273] Aier et al. (2011b)

[274] Aier et al. (2011b); Radeke (2010)

[275] Aier et al. (2011b); Bricknall et al. (2006)

[276] Bricknall et al. (2006); Buckl et al. (2010); Kaisler et al. (2005)

[277] Aier et al. (2011b)

[278] Zink (2009)

Because EAM aims at a holistic optimization of the EAM in alignment with global and long-term objectives, central governance plays a crucial role.[279] The absence of such super-ordinate coordination mechanisms will lead to local and often short-term optimization such that global and long-term objectives will be omitted .[280] Consequently, without the right degree of centralization for budgets (*I2a*), operational process optimization and implementation (*I2b*), application development project prioritization and approval (*F2c*), IT development and implementation (*I2d*) and infrastructure planning and management (*I2e*)[281], EAM compliance and ultimately the pursued EAM goals become unenforceable.

Construct I3:	EAM governance formalization
Proposition I3:	Governance mechanisms should be defined for EAM decision-making.

The EAM governance formalization specifies the formal decision rights to encourage the desired behavior.[282] To do so, the EAM literature suggests using formally defined policies (*I3a*),[283] formalized communication of all stakeholders over boards (*I3b*),[284] formal review gates (*I3c*)[285], and incentives (*I3d*)[286] as formal governance mechanisms.

Construct I4:	EAM framework & tool availability
Proposition I4:	EAM frameworks & tools should serve as the infrastructure that supports the EAM service delivery.

Having an EAM framework in place (*I4a*)[287] guides the EAM service delivery and improves efficiency and effectiveness.[288] Such a framework should be accepted by all relevant stakeholders as a reference for EAM products.[289] To increase the efficiency and

---

[279] Schmidt, Buxmann (2011)

[280] Boh et al. (2007); Schmidt, Buxmann (2011)

[281] Aagesen et al. (2011); Boh et al. (2007); Kamogawa, Okada (2005); Radeke (2011); Radeke (2010)

[282] Aier, Schelp (2009); Weill, Ross (2009)

[283] Schmidt, Buxmann (2011); van der Raadt et al. (2007)

[284] Espinosa et al. (2011); van der Raadt, van Vliet (2008)

[285] Espinosa et al. (2011)

[286] Boh et al. (2007)

[287] Aier et al. (2008); Riege, Aier (2009); van der Raadt et al. (2007)

[288] Bricknall et al. (2006); Kamogawa, Okada (2005); Matthee et al. (2007)

[289] Schmidt, Buxmann (2011)

effectiveness of such a framework, the organization should align the framework with its needs,[290] particularly to set its goals[291] and its stakeholders' needs.[292] Moreover, using EAM tools support (*I4b*)[293] establishes a central repository of EAM products,[294] which enables advanced EAM analyses and a corporate-wide access.[295] In addition to employing an EAM framework and a central EAM tool, reference architectures are discussed in the literature to further increase the efficiency and effectiveness of EAM (*I4c*).[296]

Construct I5:	EAM principle establishment
Proposition I5:	EAM principles guiding the design of the to-be architecture should be in place.

EAM principles are *"fundamental propositions that guide the description, construction, and evaluation of Enterprise Architectures."*[297] They can differ in terms of scope, i.e., they may address business application issues or technical infrastructure issues, and the level of detail.[298] Consequently, they should be directive (*I5a*),[299] specific (*I5b*),[300] and implementable (*I5c*).[301]

Construct I6:	EAM skills availability
Proposition I6:	EAM staff should be well trained and integrated in the organization.

Clearly defining and setting up EAM roles (*I6a*)[302] ensures that all activities are properly assigned and being performed with the right skills. Furthermore, EAM staff should be

---

[290] Buckl et al. (2010); Darling (2008)

[291] Lindström et al. (2006)

[292] Bricknall et al. (2006); Lindström et al. (2006)

[293] Aier, Schelp (2009); Kaisler et al. (2005); Radeke (2010)

[294] Aier et al. (2011b); Schmidt, Buxmann (2011)

[295] Espinosa et al. (2011); Kim, Everest (1994); Kluge et al. (2006); Ross (2003)

[296] Schmidt, Buxmann (2011); Wilson et al. (2011)

[297] Stelzer (2009)

[298] Boh et al. (2007)

[299] Boh et al. (2007); Schmidt, Buxmann (2011)

[300] Schmidt, Buxmann (2011); Sidorova, Kappelman (2011)

[301] Proper, Greefhorst (2011)

[302] Boh et al. (2007)

continually trained (*I6b*).[303] In addition to the right expert knowledge, it is important that EAM staff be well equipped with soft skills, such as facilitation and communication skills (*I6c*)[304] to moderate among all stakeholders.[305] In addition, EAM roles should be well integrated with other organizational roles, and EAM architects should be well linked in the organization to an extensive network (*I6d*).[306] Furthermore, the boundaries among the differing roles in the organization should be clear (*I6e*).[307]

The EAM Service Delivery Dimension (D)

The EAM service delivery is concerned with the EAM services provided to all relevant stakeholders. Therefore, the communication with EAM stakeholders, the compliance validation and decision making, and the support for projects play a crucial role.[308] This dimension is concerned with the EAM services provided to the organization and the characteristics of these services. That is, this dimension does not focus on the particular EAM processes, i.e., it does not focus on processes such as the internal EAM processes used to update EAM products, but on the actual services provided to the stakeholders external to the EAM staff.

Construct D1:	EAM communication
Proposition D1:	EAM should educate EAM stakeholders about the activities of EAM.

The EAM communication should communicate stakeholder-specifically (*D1a*)[309] such that the information is understandable[310] and accessible to all stakeholders.[311] When communicating with EAM stakeholders about acceptance inhibitors, it is also argued that it is important to convince EAM stakeholder of the benefits of EAM, e.g., through success stories (*D1b*).[312] Furthermore, EAM stakeholders should be actively involved to increase

---

[303] Aier, Schelp (2009); Asfaw et al. (2009)

[304] Asfaw et al. (2009); Sidorova, Kappelman (2011)

[305] Ross (2003); Seppänen et al. (2009); Weill, Ross (2009)

[306] Aier et al. (2011b)

[307] Aier, Schelp (2009)

[308] Schmidt, Buxmann (2011); van der Raadt et al. (2007); van der Raadt, van Vliet (2008); van der Raadt et al. (2009)

[309] Hjort-Madsen, Pries-Heje (2009); Isomäki, Liimatainen (2008); Kaisler et al. (2005); van der Raadt et al. (2010)

[310] Inji Wijegunaratne et al. (2011); Kaisler et al. (2005)

[311] Schmidt, Buxmann (2011)

[312] Inji Wijegunaratne et al. (2011); van der Raadt et al. (2010); Zink (2009)

the visibility of EAM outside of the department responsible for EAM (*D1c*).[313] This visibility is said to improve top management cognition of EAM, which, in turn, helps to improve the effects and benefits of EAM.[314]

Construct D2:	EAM management support
Proposition D2:	EAM should support management in deciding on architecture-related topics and assuring project conformance.

Regular project or architecture reviews should be conducted to evaluate whether the set EAM principles are fulfilled (*D2a*).[315] Accordingly, the defined approach for reviews and decision making should be transparent and consistent such they are understandable to all stakeholders (*D2b*).[316] Additionally, violations should be tracked and sanctioned (*D2c*).[317] In addition, top management should be briefed regarding the results of reviews and advised for decision-making proactively (*D2d*).[318]

Construct D3:	EAM project support
Proposition D3:	EAM should be integrated with the actual implementation in transformation projects.

Active involvement in ongoing projects (*D3a*)[319] for architectural considerations and methodical questions is considered to be crucial to compliance and project success.[320] This involvement should also not simply be process-related to achieve compliance; rather EAM experts should spend a significant share of their time on projects by taking an active project role (*D3b*)[321] to ensure the transfer of tacit knowledge.[322]

---

[313] Aier et al. (2011b); Aier, Schelp (2009); Asfaw et al. (2009); Boh et al. (2007); van der Raadt et al. (2007)

[314] Kamogawa, Okada (2005); Struck et al. (2010)

[315] Boh et al. (2007); Bricknall et al. (2006); Schmidt, Buxmann (2011); Ylimäki et al. (2007)

[316] Tanigawa (2004); van der Raadt, van Vliet (2008)

[317] Schmidt, Buxmann (2011)

[318] Ross (2003)

[319] Aagesen et al. (2011); Aier, Schelp (2009); Foorthuis et al. (2010); Radeke (2011)

[320] Aier, Schelp (2009), Bricknall et al. (2006)

[321] Schmidt, Buxmann (2011); Seppänen et al. (2009)

[322] Struck et al. (2010)

The EAM Cultural Aspects Dimension (C)

This fourth dimension, 'EAM cultural aspects', is introduced to accommodate the social aspects of EAM. These social aspects are considered to be a fundamental but oft-neglected part of EAM.[323] Similar to Hill et al. (2008),[324] we define EAM culture as *"the specific collection of [EAM] values and norms that are shared by people and groups in an organization and that control the way they interact with each other and with stakeholders outside the organization."* Therefore, this dimension is concerned with the implicit EAM values and norms that are lived to implement EAM successfully.

Construct C1:	EAM top-management commitment
Preposition C1:	EAM leadership commitment ensures priority and resources.

Various researchers argue that top management support is a crucial component of EAM success. Without a culture of managerial support, EAM fails to resonate within the organization, and resources are rarely assigned to it.[325] Therefore, the degree of top management commitment is a crucial element that helps shape EAM and ensures sufficient resources *(C1a)*.[326] Therefore, top management should emphasize the importance of EAM *(C1b)* and should consequently allocate sufficient time to this topic *(C1c)*. Furthermore, the leadership should be clear and should communicate passion and excitement for EAM *(C1d)*.[327]

Construct C2:	EAM awareness
Proposition C2:	All EAM stakeholders should have a high awareness of EAM.

To be accepted in the organization, EAM should be known by all relevant stakeholders (C2a) and be perceived by all stakeholders as important (C2b)[328]. Furthermore, EAM stakeholders should be educated continually to ensure their awareness and understanding of EAM *(C2c)*.[329]

---

[323] Bean (2010); Magalhaes et al. (2007)

[324] Hill, Jones (2008)

[325] Asfaw et al. (2009); Bricknall et al. (2006); Foorthuis et al. (2010); Isomäki, Liimatainen (2008); Radeke (2011); Radeke (2010)

[326] Matthee et al. (2007); Seppänen et al. (2009); Zink (2009)

[327] Asfaw et al. (2009); Zink (2009)

[328] Espinosa et al. (2011); Isomäki, Liimatainen (2008)

[329] Aier, Schelp (2009)

Construct C3:	EAM understanding
Proposition C3:	A common understanding of EAM should be established for both business and IT employees.

To create an understanding of EAM, an organization must create a common vision for the long term (*C3a*) and a common understanding of EAM for the short term among both its business and IT employees (C3b).[330] Therefore, the understanding should have a clear business purpose and should be integrated into the overall business strategy (*C3c*).[331]

The EAM Use and EAM Satisfaction Dimension (U / S)

The dimensions 'EAM use' and 'EAM satisfaction' remain intact as defined by DeLone and McLean.

Construct U:	EAM use
Proposition U:	EAM should actively use the EAM products, the provided infrastructure, the service delivery, and the established EAM culture for conducting business transformation activities in an organization.

If EAM is not used in the actual transformation activities of an organization, created to-be designs will not be implemented.[332] Therefore, the actual use of EAM is crucial for realizing the benefits from EAM.

Construct S:	EAM satisfaction
Proposition S:	EAM stakeholders should be satisfied with the EAM products, infrastructure, service delivery, and cultural aspects.

Similar to the use construct, the satisfaction of EAM stakeholders is believed to influence EAM benefits. The satisfaction of EAM stakeholders influences the degree to which EAM is used in the future and the belief in the developed concepts, which determines the actual implementation of these concepts.[333] Therefore, satisfaction is viewed as a factor that influences EAM benefits.

---

[330] Asfaw et al. (2009); Espinosa et al. (2011); Isomäki, Liimatainen (2008); Radeke (2010)

[331] Inji Wijegunaratne et al. (2011)

[332] Aier, Schelp (2009); Hjort-Madsen, Pries-Heje (2009)

[333] Aier, Schelp (2009); Bricknall et al. (2006)

The EAM Net Benefits Dimension (B)

Finally, the EAM net benefits dimension describes the ultimate benefits obtained from EAM. Despite a lack of an overview of EAM success factors in the literature, the first literature reviews[334] and practitioner surveys[335] that identify and categorize EAM benefits have recently emerged. Based on their literature review, Tamm et al. (2011) distinguish between the direct and indirect benefits of EAM.[336] They categorize the direct benefits as organizational alignment, information availability, resource portfolio optimization, and resource complementary, but they do not further elaborate on the indirect benefits. The researchers claim that the latter category is impacted by EAM but can also be influenced by additional factors, such as the actual operation of the platform. Using a different approach, Espinosa et al. (2011) categorize EAM benefits by using three different benefit layers: IT, business, and organizational benefits.[337] In contrast to the aforementioned categorizations Foorthuis et al. (2010) categorize the benefits into organization-related and project-related benefits.[338]

Dissecting the literature regarding EAM benefits outlined above, we find that there is significant agreement among the authors in three areas. First, EAM is said to improve efficiency, especially by reducing cost, reducing complexity, increasing integration, and improving utilization. Second, EAM promotes business-IT alignment by creating transparency and establishing a common language. Finally, EAM fosters the ability to change. Nevertheless, the evidence and explanation for these EAM benefits are mostly anecdotal or identified in exploratory studies. In this research, we use these three areas to structure the benefits identified in the literature reviews. Therefore, we do not elaborate further on the interdependencies among and the structures of the different benefit constructs.

Construct B1:	Efficiency benefits
Proposition B1:	EAM enables the reduction of cost.

A well-operating EAM allows for better integration (*B1a*), standardization (*B1b*) and consolidation (*B1c*) processes as well as applications that have often emerged as 'silos' during past years of organic growth. With the transparency created by EAM and clear EAM principles on how to develop and expand, these 'silos' can be broken. Consequently,

---

[334] Boucharas et al. (2010); Tamm et al. (2011)

[335] Espinosa et al. (2011); Lange, Mendling (2011); Salmans, Kappelman (2010)

[336] Tamm et al. (2011)

[337] Espinosa et al. (2011)

[338] Foorthuis et al. (2010); Morganwalp, Sage (2004); Niemi, Soliman (2006); Radeke (2011)

the standardization, consolidation, and integration leads to lower complexity (*B1d*) and better controlled and improved utilization (*B1e*), which, in turn, increases efficiency and reduces costs (B1f).[339] Similarly, using EAM, implementation projects are expected to save resources (*B1g*) and time (*B1h*) and to mitigate risks (*B1i*) because EAM products can be used as a starting point, relevant knowledge can be brought into the projects by actively involving experienced architects, and an overall, integrated approach to planning the EA can help to identify and mitigate project risks early. Furthermore, the use of EAM allows the management of project complexity analogous to the reduction of complexity on the organizational level (*B1j*).[340]

Construct B2:	Effectiveness benefits
Proposition B2:	EAM ensures business-IT alignment.

By improving communication between business and IT, EAM supports the alignment of business and IT and thereby facilitates the achievement of set business goals. First, EAM is said to enable the global optimization of the organization when working under set goals (*B2a*). In doing so, EAM prevents the local optimization of the organization's individual parts. Furthermore, EAM allows business processes to be aligned with the supporting IT applications (*B2b*).[341] This horizontal and vertical business-IT alignment is important for realizing organizational value.[342] Furthermore, EAM provides a common language and a holistic overview of the organization's fundamental aspects, which enable effective communication among the different stakeholders in an organization (*B2c*).[343] Finally, EAM promotes compliance with various regulatory requirements (such as SoX or Basel II compliance) (B2d).[344]

Construct B3:	Flexibility benefits
Proposition B3:	EAM fosters the ability to change.

By rendering the different aspects of the organization transparent, EAM enables the management of the underlying complexity and thus facilitates the identification of

---

[339] Espinosa et al. (2011); Ross et al. (2009); Tamm et al. (2011)

[340] Foorthuis et al. (2010)

[341] Bucher et al. (2007); Hjort-Madsen, Pries-Heje (2009); Ross et al. (2009)

[342] Henderson, Venkatraman (1993)

[343] Foorthuis et al. (2010); Kappelman et al. (2010); Tamm et al. (2011); van der Raadt et al. (2004)

[344] Lankhorst et al. (2009); Schönherr (2009)

required changes (*B3a*).[345] This capability, in turn, allows the organization to deal with its environment effectively, to adjust quickly (*B3b*) and to drive appropriate innovation (*B3c*). Furthermore, this transparency and awareness of organizational structures facilitates cooperation with other organizations by helping the organization to integrate easily with these other organizations (*B3d*).[346]

Table 3-2 summarizes the constructs and the respective sources identified in the literature review.

Table 3-2 Overview of EAM Success Factors Identified from the Literature Review

NVivo Node 1: Identified constructs	NVivo Node 2: Property	Publications
EAM Product Quality Dimension		
(P1) As-is architecture quality	(P1a) Timeliness	Aier et al. (2011b); Foorthuis et al. (2010); Riege et al. (2009); Schmidt et al. (2011)
	(P1b) Completeness	Aier et al. (2009); Bricknall et al. (2006); Winter et al. (2007)
	(P1c) Level of detail	Pulkkinen (2006); Schmidt et al. (2011); Winter et al. (2007)
(P2) To-be architecture quality	(P2a) Timeliness	Aier et al. (2009); Bricknall et al. (2006); Hjort-Madsen et al. (2009); Schmidt et al. (2011)
	(P2b) Completeness	Pulkkinen (2006); Schmidt et al. (2011); Winter et al. (2007)
	(P2c) Level of detail	Schmidt et al. (2011)
(P3) Roadmap quality	(P3a) Feasibility	Seppänen et al. (2009); Zink (2009)
	(P3b) Completeness	Aier et al. (2009); Bricknall et al. (2006)
	(P3c) Consideration of dependencies	Halley et al. (2005)
EAM Infrastructure Quality Dimension		
(I1) Mandate definition	(I1a) Organizational scope	Bricknall et al. (2006); Inji Wijegunaratne et al. (2011); Struck et al. (2010); van der Raadt et al. (2007); Zink (2009)
	(I1b) Business-IT positioning	Aier et al. (2011b); Bricknall et al. (2006); Espinosa et al. (2011); Halley et al. (2005); Radeke (2010)
	(I1c) Alignment with other functions	Aier et al. (2011b); Bricknall et al. (2006); Buckl et al. (2010); Kaisler et al. (2005); Zink (2009)
(I2) Decision-making centrality	(I2a) Capital budgets	Aagesen et al. (2011); Boh et al. (2007); Kamogawa et al. (2005); Radeke (2011); Radeke (2010); Schmidt et al. (2011)
	(I2b) Operational process optimization and implementation	Aagesen et al. (2011); Boh et al. (2007); Kamogawa et al. (2005); Radeke (2011); Radeke (2010); Schmidt et al. (2011)

---

[345] Foorthuis et al. (2010); Schmidt, Buxmann (2011); Tamm et al. (2011)

[346] Hjort-Madsen, Pries-Heje (2009); Jonkers et al. (2006); Morganwalp, Sage (2004)

NVivo Node 1: Identified constructs	NVivo Node 2: Property	Publications
	(I2c) Application development projects prioritization and approval	Aagesen et al. (2011); Boh et al. (2007); Kamogawa et al. (2005); Radeke (2011); Radeke (2010); Schmidt et al. (2011)
	(I2d) IT development and implementation	Aagesen et al. (2011); Boh et al. (2007); Kamogawa et al. (2005); Radeke (2011); Radeke (2010); Schmidt et al. (2011)
	(I2e) Infrastructure planning and management	Aagesen et al. (2011); Boh et al. (2007); Kamogawa et al. (2005); Radeke (2011); Radeke (2010); Schmidt et al. (2011)
(I3) EAM governance formalization	(I3a) Formally defined policies	Schmidt et al. (2011); van der Raadt et al. (2007)
	(I3b) Formal review gates	Espinosa et al. (2011); van der Raadt et al. (2008)
	(I3c) Formal communication	Espinosa et al. (2011)
	(I3d) Incentives	Boh et al. (2007)
(I4) EAM framework & tools availability	(F4a) Framework in place	Aier et al. (2008); Bricknall et al. (2006); Buckl et al. (2010); Darling (2008); Kamogawa et al. (2005); Lindström et al. (2006), (2006); Matthee et al. (2007); Riege et al. (2009); Schmidt et al. (2011); van der Raadt et al. (2007)
	(I4b) EAM tool support established	Aier et al. (2011b); Aier et al. (2009); Espinosa et al. (2011); Kaisler et al. (2005); Kim et al. (1994); Kluge et al. (2006); Radeke (2010); Ross (2003); Schmidt et al. (2011)
	(I4c) Reference architecture established	Schmidt et al. (2011); Wilson et al. (2011)
(I5) EAM principles establishment	(I5a) Directive	Boh et al. (2007); Schmidt et al. (2011)
	(I5b) Specific	Schmidt et al. (2011); Sidorova et al. (2011)
	(I5c) Implementable	Proper et al. (2011)
(I6) EAM skills availability	(I6a) Defined EAM roles	Boh et al. (2007)
	(I6b) Continuous training	Aier et al. (2009); Asfaw et al. (2009)
	(I6c) Soft skills	Asfaw et al. (2009); Ross (2003); Seppänen et al. (2009); Sidorova et al. (2011); Weill et al. (2009)
	(I6d) Extensive networking	Aier et al. (2011b)
	(I6e) Role differentiation from other functions	Aier et al. (2009)
EAM Service Delivery Quality Dimension		
(D1) EAM Communication	(D1a) Stakeholder-specific communications	Hjort-Madsen et al. (2009); Inji Wijegunaratne et al. (2011); Isomäki et al. (2008); Kaisler et al. (2005); Schmidt et al. (2011); van der Raadt et al. (2010)
	(D1b) Communication of the benefits of EAM	Inji Wijegunaratne et al. (2011); van der Raadt et al. (2010); Zink (2009)
	(D1c) Proactive communication	Aier et al. (2011b); Aier et al. (2009); Asfaw et al. (2009); Boh et al. (2007); Kamogawa et al. (2005); Struck et al.

NVivo Node 1: Identified constructs	NVivo Node 2: Property	Publications
		(2010); van der Raadt et al. (2007)
(D2) EAM management support	(D2a) Architecture reviews	Boh et al. (2007); Bricknall et al. (2006); Schmidt et al. (2011); Ylimäki et al. (2007)
	(D2b) Consistent reviews	Tanigawa (2004); van der Raadt et al. (2008)
	(D2c) Tracking and Sanctioning of violations	Schmidt et al. (2011)
	(D2d) Management briefing	Ross (2003)
(D3) EAM project support	(D3a) Active involvement	Aagesen et al. (2011); Aier et al. (2009), (2009); Foorthuis et al. (2010); Radeke (2011), Bricknall et al. (2006)
	(D3b) Active project role	Schmidt et al. (2011); Seppänen et al. (2009); Struck et al. (2010)
EAM Cultural Aspects Dimension		
(C1) EAM top-management Commitment	(C1a) Resource commitment	Asfaw et al. (2009); Bricknall et al. (2006); Foorthuis et al. (2010); Isomäki et al. (2008); Radeke (2011); Radeke (2010)Seppänen 2009 #468}Matthee et al. (2007); Zink (2009)
	(C1b) Assigned importance	Asfaw et al. (2009), (2009); Bricknall et al. (2006); Foorthuis et al. (2010); Isomäki et al. (2008); Radeke (2011); Radeke (2010); Zink (2009)
	(C1c) Time commitment	Asfaw et al. (2009), (2009); Bricknall et al. (2006); Foorthuis et al. (2010); Isomäki et al. (2008); Radeke (2011); Radeke (2010); Zink (2009)
	(C1d) Communication of importance	Asfaw et al. (2009), (2009); Bricknall et al. (2006); Foorthuis et al. (2010); Isomäki et al. (2008); Radeke (2011); Radeke (2010); Zink (2009)
(C2) EAM awareness	(C2a) Stakeholders' awareness	Espinosa et al. (2011); Isomäki et al. (2008)
	(C2b) Stakeholders' understanding of importance	Espinosa et al. (2011); Isomäki et al. (2008)
	(C2c) Stakeholder education	Aier et al. (2009)
(C3) EAM understanding	(C3a) Shared vision	Asfaw et al. (2009); Espinosa et al. (2011); Isomäki et al. (2008); Radeke (2010)
	(C3b) Shared understanding	Asfaw et al. (2009); Espinosa et al. (2011); Isomäki et al. (2008); Radeke (2010)
	(C3c) Alignment of common goals	Inji Wijegunaratne et al. (2011)
EAM Benefits Dimension		
(B1) Efficiency benefits	(B1a) Integrate application/processes	Espinosa et al. (2011); Ross et al. (2009); Tamm et al. (2011)
	(B1b) Standardize applications/processes	Espinosa et al. (2011); Ross et al. (2009); Tamm et al. (2011)

NVivo Node 1: Identified constructs	NVivo Node 2: Property	Publications
	(B1c) Consolidate application/processes	Espinosa et al. (2011); Ross et al. (2009); Tamm et al. (2011)
	(B1d) Control complexity	Espinosa et al. (2011); Ross et al. (2009); Tamm et al. (2011)
	(B1e) Increase utilization	Espinosa et al. (2011); Ross et al. (2009); Tamm et al. (2011)
	(B1f) Reduce cost	Espinosa et al. (2011); Ross et al. (2009); Tamm et al. (2011)
	(B1g) Manage project budget	Foorthuis et al. (2010)
	(B1h) Meet project deadlines	Foorthuis et al. (2010)
	(B1i) Mitigate project risks	Foorthuis et al. (2010)
	(B1j) Manage project complexity	Foorthuis et al. (2010)
(B2) Effectiveness benefits	(B2a) Achieve global optimization	Bucher et al. (2007); Hjort-Madsen et al. (2009); Ross et al. (2009)
	(B2b) Achive business-IT alignment	Bucher et al. (2007); Hjort-Madsen et al. (2009); Ross et al. (2009)
	(B2c) Communicate efficiently	Foorthuis et al. (2010); Kappelman et al. (2010); Tamm et al. (2011); van der Raadt et al. (2004)
	(B2d) Achieve regulatory compliance	Lankhorst et al. (2009); Schönherr (2009)
(B3) Flexibility benefits	(B3a) Identify change	Foorthuis et al. (2010); Schmidt et al. (2011); Tamm et al. (2011)
	(B3b) Respond to market changes	Hjort-Madsen et al. (2009); Jonkers et al. (2006); Morganwalp et al. (2004)
	(B3c) Enable innovation	Hjort-Madsen et al. (2009); Jonkers et al. (2006); Morganwalp et al. (2004)
	(B3d) Cooperate with others	Hjort-Madsen et al. (2009); Jonkers et al. (2006); Morganwalp et al. (2004)

3.4. Synthesis

Based on an extensive literature review, we discussed EAM success factors and EAM benefits as part of our a priori EAM benefit realization model. The described model builds upon the DMSM and considers existing research in the area of EAM as well as related IS and management theories (e.g., prior research on the dimension of cultural aspects). The model is based on existing knowledge about EAM success factors and EAM benefits compiled from a literature review and combines this knowledge into a new comprehensive theoretical model that provides direction and guidance for further theoretical and empirical validation. Figure 3-5 provides an overview of the developed constructs of the a priori EAM Benefit Realization Model.

Figure 3-5 Overview of the Constructs of the Theoretical A Priori Model

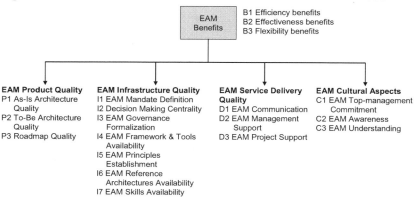

At this stage, the model is a first step to obtaining insights into and beginning a discussion of a theory of the EAM benefit realization. As a result, we posed potential propositions of EAM success factors and EAM benefits based on theoretical findings. However, these potential propositions require further testing and validation. In the next several chapters, we will use this model as a foundation to refine the model based on discussions with experts and to develop and validate a measurement instrument for testing the model.

4. Model Refinement

As a first step towards an initial validation of the model for the realization of benefits from EAM, especially in terms of completeness, we conducted semi-structured interviews with EAM experts. The objective of this chapter is to create a revised version of our model that incorporates the feedback from the semi-structured interviews. Consequently, in this chapter, we describe this initial qualitative evaluation of our model developed in the previous chapter. In particular, the goal is to obtain insights into the adequacy of the theoretically developed model, including its propositions, and to identify additional EAM success factors that are not covered by the existing literature but that are important in practice. Therefore, we first describe in this chapter the use of semi-structured interviews as a qualitative research method in IS research (Section 4.1). We then report on the findings of the semi-structured interviews in Section 4.2 and present the resulting revised model for the realization of benefits from EAM in Section 4.3. We close this chapter with a conclusion and a summary of its main findings in Section 4.4.

4.1. Research Method

As an important data collection techniques in qualitative research,[347] interviewing is the research technique of choice in IS research for almost all types of qualitative research, such as positivist, interpretive, or critical research.[348] Interviews are a means of gathering rich data from people in various roles and situations and help to focus on the subject's world.[349] Rubin et al. (2005) state that qualitative interviews are *"[...] like night-vision goggles, permitting us to see that which is not ordinarily on view and examine that which is looked at but seldom seen."*[350]

---

[347] Myers, Newman (2007); Polkinghorne (2005)

[348] Hesse-Biber, Leavy (2005); Klein, Myers (1999); Myers (1997), (1999); Northcutt, McCoy (2004)

[349] Myers (2009)

[350] Rubin, Rubin (2005)

In IS research, interviews are recognized as appropriate in areas in which research and theory are in their early formative stages because they are a means for the researcher to study IS in its natural setting, to learn about the state-of-the-art in practice, and to build theories based on phenomena observed in practice. Therefore, interviews are a proper basis for research in areas in which only a few previous studies exist.[351]

This situation applies to the present research questions in this doctoral thesis. According to our discussion in the first few chapters of this doctoral thesis, there is a paucity of published theories on the realization of benefits from EAM. Therefore, this research area can be classified as being in a formative stage. Furthermore, EAM is a practical field that must be studied with respect to its natural settings because it is vividly shaped by emerging concepts and new developments in practice. Hence, approaching practitioners is a promising starting point for investigating practitioners' experiences to supplement the theoretical model developed in the previous chapter with a practical perspective and to conduct an initial validation. The insights obtained therein can be leveraged to complement the model developed in the previous chapter with additional or revised constructs and propositions. Consequently, interviews are an appropriate way of conducting research on the realization of EAM benefits in this early phase.

In general, interviews can be classified into three types: structured, unstructured, and semi-structured.[352] *Structured interviews* are characterized by pre-formulated questions, which are typically planned beforehand and asked in a pre-determined order according to a specified time limit. Structured interviews minimize the role of the interviewer such that the interviewer has to ask only pre-determined questions and record the answers without improvising during the interview. The goal is to adopt the same consistent behavior across all interviews. In contrast, *unstructured interviews* have few, if any, pre-formulated questions, and there is usually no time limit. During these unstructured interviews, the role of the interviewer is to elicit as much relevant information from the interviewee as possible, and the interviewer must improvise if the conversation halts. Consequently, there is no attempt to maintain consistency across the interviews. *Semi-structured* interviews are positioned between structured and unstructured interviews. Although semi-structured interviews involve the use of pre-formulated questions, there is no need to adhere to them strictly. If new questions emerge during the interview, the interviewer is encouraged to improvise and follow the flow of these questions. However, because some pre-formulated questions are used, the goal is to achieve some consistency across the interviews. While enabling this consistency, the interviewer has enough freedom to follow interesting aspects of the conversation. This freedom

---

[351] Benbasat et al. (1987)

[352] Myers (2009)

constitutes one of the major advantages of semi-structured interviews, as this approach tries to take the best of structured and unstructured interview while reducing the disadvantages of these two types, such as the inconsistencies across interviews and the lack of opportunity to explore emerging topics.[353] To this end, semi-structured interviews provide some further advantages. First, they enable researchers to confirm what is already known while learning something new. Second, semi-structured interviews allow researchers to discuss a topic with the interviewee in a conversational rather than a structured manner. In such an environment, interviewees are more open to discussing sensitive topics. Third, the interviewer can flexibly react to the interviewee if interesting topics emerge or questions arise.[354]

In this doctoral thesis, we employ semi-structured interviews to perform an initial validation of our model for the realization of EAM benefits. Given that the objectives in this research phase are to conduct an initial validation of the developed model for EAM benefits and to identify EAM success factors that are not yet covered by the model, the interviews must address both explanatory and exploratory elements. The explanatory elements are needed to obtain preliminary insights that can help evaluate the constructs and the propositions of our model, and the exploratory elements aim at bringing a practical perspective to the theoretical model by adding constructs and propositions that are potentially missing in the literature.[355] Semi-structured interviews best fit the objectives of this research phase for several reasons. First, semi-structured interviews allow us to conduct a structured discussion of our model with the interviewees. This discussion is required to conduct an initial evaluation of our model in an explanatory manner. Second, semi-structured interviews allow for flexibility when discussing additional potential EAM success factors in an exploratory manner. This flexibility is needed to identify EAM success factors that are not covered by the model developed thus far and that are consequently not covered in the existing literature, though they are important in practice.

4.1.1.   Preparing the Interviews

Before conducting the semi-structured interviews, we must prepare thoroughly for them. Accordingly, we must define the concrete objectives of the semi-structured interviews, define the target audience, select appropriate interviewing techniques, define an interview guide, and mitigate potential problems.

---

[353] Myers (2009); Yin (2011), pp. 133–135

[354] Myers (2009)

[355] Yin (2003)

Objectives of Semi-structured Interviews

The objectives of the semi-structured interviews are two-fold. First, the semi-structured interviews shall serve as an initial evaluation that allows us to obtain insights into the adequacy of the theoretically developed model, including its propositions and constructs (i.e., an investigation into whether the model reflects the experiences of the interviewees). Second, the semi-structured interviews aim to identify additional EAM success factors that are not covered by the existing literature but that are important in practice. Therefore, this research phase will focus on proving the plausibility and completeness of the model rather than on performing a broad empirical validation.[356] Consequently, the data collected in the semi-structured interviews must support the plausibility and completeness of the model rather than provide statistical evidence of the validity of the model.

Defining the Target Audience

Regarding the selection of the target audience, Eisenhardt (1989) suggests that researchers define specific characteristics for the target audience to control for extraneous variation. Accordingly, researchers should strive for a theoretic sampling approach that identifies potential interview partners who can contribute to the replication and extension of the emergent theory. Given the resource constraints of any study, the selection of interview partners should further maximize what can be learned in the available period of time.[357]

Therefore, the characteristics of the interview participants should be consistent with the objectives of these semi-structured interviews (i.e., to evaluate the model for completeness and plausibility). Because different stakeholders may have different perspectives on the topic,[358] a broad and multifaceted range of different views must be considered when selecting the participants for the interviews. Given the scope of the present thesis on the organizational level,[359] this thesis must cover these multiple perspectives to be representative of an overall organizational perspective.

In general, to discuss EAM success factors, the interviewees must have some expertise and experience in the domain of EAM. Therefore, we focus on EAM experts, including EAM experts who operate at the senior management level of enterprises (mostly 'Head of

---

[356] Which is done in the later phases of this doctoral thesis when we empirically validate the mdoel by means of a Web-based survey. See Chapter 5 – 7.

[357] Eisenhardt (1989)

[358] Cameron, Whetten (1983); Leidner, Elam (1994); Quinn, Rohrbaugh (1983); Sedera et al. (2006); Tallon et al. (2000); Thong, Yap (1995); Yoon, Guimaraes (1995)

[359] See Section 1.6.

Enterprise Architecture' or an equivalent title) and experienced consultants who can complement the experiences of the enterprise experts. Having significant experience in the domain of EAM indicates that the interviewee understands EAM benefits and what works vs. what does not work. This background is needed because EAM is a long-term activity that generates value over time and does not necessarily yield direct benefits.[360] Further, it is important to consider both the business and IT perspectives on the topic because they may have differing views. Therefore, the interviewee sample shall comprise both people with business backgrounds and people with IT backgrounds.

Technique Selection

The application of proven interviewing techniques helps to generate systematically richer data that can be used, in turn, to generate deeper insights.[361] However, Myers et al. (2007) and Schultze et al. (2011) identify in their research a lack of methodological sophistication with respect to interview-based IS research. They argue that overcoming this lack of sophistication and employing proven techniques will improve qualitative research in IS.[362] Consequently, we base our semi-structured interviews on proven interviewing techniques. Three such interviewing techniques frequently used in IS research are appreciative, laddering, and photo-diary interviewing.[363] *Appreciative interviewing* is a guided inquiry from social science that looks for the best in people and the relevant world around them. The purpose is to turn attention away from dysfunctions, anomalies, and deviant behaviors and to focus on strengths, possibilities, goodwill, and the grace of the phenomenon at hand.[364] *Laddering interviews[365]* are used to inquire about the content and structure of an interviewee's perception of the phenomenon at hand.[366] To elicit the interviewee's perception, the researcher conducts the laddering interview in two phases. First, the general differences among elements are discussed. Second, the relationships among the elements are investigated by laddering the key distinctions.[367] Thus, the researcher encourages the interviewee to elaborate on

---

[360] Rodrigues, Amaral (2010)

[361] Schultze, Avital (2011)

[362] Myers, Newman (2007); Schultze, Avital (2011)

[363] Schultze, Avital (2011)

[364] Avital, Te'eni D. (2009); Avital et al. (2009); Michael (2005)

[365] Also frequently considered in IS to be part of the Repertory Grid (or RipGrid) method which is an interviewing technique using factor analysis to determine personality measures. Tan F. B., Hunter (2002)

[366] Davis, Hufnagel (2007); Kelly (1955); Napier et al. (2009)

[367] Reynolds, Gutman J. (1988)

the relationships among the elements by asking how and why questions.[368] Finally, photo-diary interviews enrich the interviews with diaries and visual representations to render the interview more concrete in terms of precision, context, and evidence. During the interview, diaries and visual representations are used to discuss the phenomenon in detail and illustrate background information.[369] Table 4-1 summarizes the main differences between these three introduced techniques.

Table 4-1 Summary of Interviewing Techniques

Interview approach	Appreciative interview	Laddering interview	Photo-diary interview
Study objective	Core capabilities, design requirements, success factors, and aspirations	Personal constructs systems, its structures and hierarchical relationships	Meaningful incidents and explanation of events, behaviors, and emotions in that context
Interview questions disposition	Positively deviant and action oriented	Structure and pattern seeking	Re-constructive, critical, and self-reflexive
Data generation logic & discussion aids	Reframe lived experience with a positive lens to construct pathways to aspired futures	Compare and contrast through triads and means-ends analysis	Reflect through annotated visual snapshot to capture event and informant's situated emotions and thoughts
Interviewer role	Help with positive reframing	Give examples and probe	Facilitate the interpretation of photo-diary entries

SOURCE: Adapted from Schultze et al. (2011)

In this doctoral thesis, we apply the technique of laddering interviews for the explanatory part of the semi-structured interviews, i.e., the first objective is to gain insight into the validity of our theoretically developed constructs and propositions. This technique is a promising one for investigating whether the theoretically derived propositions appear among the respective constructs in practice. With this technique, the constructs can be differentiated in detail in the interviews, and the propositions can be investigated. Furthermore, the technique promotes deeper insight into the interviewees' reasoning for these propositions. Developed for market research, laddering is an in-depth, one-on-one interviewing technique that originally aimed to understand how product attributes provide value to customers. Using this technique, the interviewer investigates how product attributes lead to consequences that generate value for the customer.[370] This

---

[368] Hunter (1997)

[369] Bagnoli (2009); Latham (2003); Rubin, Rubin (2005)

[370] Reynolds, Gutman J. (1988)

laddering process is explored by repeatedly asking how and why questions until the resulting value is reached.[371] For this research, we relate the identified EAM success factors one after the other to the potential benefits by asking, for examples, for the EAM success factor '(P1) As-is product quality' the question 'How does the as-is product quality lead to EAM benefits?' After the interviewees provide their explanations, the underlying reasons for the interviewees' answers are further 'laddered' by asking appropriate how and why questions. In general, two approaches are common in laddering: soft laddering and hard laddering.[372] Whereas hard laddering limits the interview to pre-determined elements and constructs, in soft laddering, interviewees generate their own elements and constructs.[373] As we have a given model that we want to evaluate with the semi-structured interviews, we use the hard laddering approach in our interviews. Therefore, the constructs of the model are first introduced, and then their relationships are 'laddered' by the interviewees.

Defining an Interview Guide

In semi-structured interviews, the questions are typically formulated before the interview.[374] Considering the discussion above, we design an interview guide to direct the researcher as the interviews are conducted. An interview guide should include introductory comments, a list of topic headings or possible key questions, a set of associated prompts, and closing comments.[375]

When designing the interview guide, we divided the semi-structured interview into two phases. The first phase focuses on open questions designed to identify EAM success factors and benefits. The second phase introduces and discusses the theoretically developed model. Dividing the semi-structured interviews into these two phases allows us to avoid biasing the interviewee when the model is introduced. Consequently, the interviewees should identify missing success factors and benefit constructs without having any prior knowledge of the model.

The interview guide begins with a comprehensive introduction to the interview. This part includes a statement of appreciation, an introduction to the interviewer, the background of the research study, and a discussion of the interviewee's right to confidentiality. The interview itself has four sections. The first section gathers some demographic statistics. The second and third sections aim to identify missing EAM success factors and benefit

---

[371] Hunter (1997)

[372] Veludo-de-Oliveira et al. (2006)

[373] Schultze, Avital (2011)

[374] Myers (2009); Yin (2011), pp. 133–135

[375] Robson (2011)

constructs. The fourth section discusses the constructs and propositions of the theoretically developed model for an initial validation. Table 4-2 provides an overview of the questions in the interview guide. The complete interview guide can be found in Appendix C.

Table 4-2 Guiding Questions for Semi-structured Interviews by Sections

Section 1.	**Demographics** 1. What are your enterprise's demographics? 2. What is your personal experience with EAM?
Section 2.	**EAM benefits** 1. What benefits do you realize with EAM? 2. How do these benefits differ on the organizational and project-level?
Section 3.	**EAM success factors** 1. According to your experiences, what are the success factors for EAM? 2. How are these success factors linked to the benefits of EAM?
Section 4.	**Discussion of the theoretically developed EAM benefits realization model** 1. How did you experience [insert different model constructs] as a success factor for EAM? 2. How does [insert different model constructs] lead to EAM benefits?

Mitigating Potential Pitfalls

While conducting interviews, researchers may encounter some difficulties that compromise the quality of the research results.[376] Therefore, the interviewer must be aware of the potential pitfalls and discuss potential mitigation approaches. Based on Myers et al. (2007), Table 4-3 summarizes the potential difficulties, problems, and pitfalls of interviews:

Table 4-3 Potential Difficulties, Problems, and Pitfalls of Interviews

Potential pitfalls	Description
Artificiality of the interview	The qualitative interview interrogates someone who is a complete stranger; it asks subjects to give or to create opinions under time pressure.
Lack of trust	As the interviewer is a complete stranger, the interviewee is likely to be concerned with the degree to which the interviewer can be trusted. Thus, the interviewee may choose not to divulge information that he or she considers to be "sensitive". If this information is important to the research, the data-gathering process remains incomplete.
Lack of time	Lack of time for the interview may mean that the data gathered are incomplete. However, it can also lead to the opposite problem: subjects may create opinions under time pressure that they do not strongly believe in. In this case, more data are gathered, but the gathered data are not entirely reliable.
Level of entry	The level at which the researcher enters the organization is crucial (Buchanan et al. (1988)). For example, if a researcher enters at a lower level, it may prove difficult, if not impossible,

---

[376] E.g. Fontana, Frey (2000); Myers (2009)

Potential pitfalls	Description
	to interview senior managers at a later date. In some organizations, talking to union members can bar access to the management and vice versa. Additionally, gatekeepers may inhibit the researcher's ability to access a broader range of subjects.
Elite bias	A researcher may interview only certain people of high status (key informants) and, as a result, fail to obtain an understanding of the broader situation. Miles et al. (1994) discuss the bias introduced in qualitative research by interviewing the "stars" in an organization. Studies affected by elite bias overweight data from articulate, well-informed, usually high-status informants and under-represent data from intractable, less articulate, lower-status employees (Heiskanen et al. (1997)).
Hawthorne effects	Qualitative interviews are intrusive and can change the situation. The interviewer is not an invisible, neutral entity; rather, the interviewer is part of the interactions that they seek to study, and this relationship influences those interactions (Fontana et al. (2000)). The researcher may intrude upon the social setting and interfere with people's behavior.
Constructing knowledge	Naive interviewers may think that they are like sponges, simply soaking up data that are already there. They may not realize that in addition to gathering data, they are also actively constructing knowledge (Fontana et al. (2000)). In response to an interviewer, interviewees construct their stories; they are reflecting on issues that they may have never explicitly considered before. Interviewees usually want to appear knowledgeable and rational. Hence, they strive to construct a story that is logical and consistent.
Ambiguity of language	The meaning of our words is often ambiguous, and it is not always clear that subjects fully understand the questions. Fontana et al. (2000) states, "Asking questions and getting answers is a much harder task than it may seem at first. The spoken or written word has always a residue of ambiguity, no matter how carefully we word the questions or how carefully we report or code the answers" (Fontana et al. (2000, p. 645)).
Interviews can go wrong	Interviews are fraught with fears, problems and pitfalls. It is possible for an interviewer to offend or insult an interviewee unintentionally; in these cases, the interview might be abandoned altogether (Hermanns (2004)).

SOURCE: Adapted from Myers et al. (2007)

To improve the quality of this research, we discussed mitigation strategies for these common pitfalls upfront. With these mitigation strategies in place, the goal was to control for a good outcome as much as possible before the interviews and during the interviews. However, we have to keep in mind that generating a good outcome is not always possible, and the effectiveness of these mitigation strategies must be assessed during the analysis of the outcomes of the interviews.

Because the interviews for this doctoral thesis were mainly conducted with people who were complete strangers to the interviewer, the artificiality of the interview was mitigated by ensuring that an initial base of trust between the interviewee and the interviewer was established through an extensive introduction phase. Additionally, we did not impose a time limit on the interviews such that the interviewees had enough time to answer the questions and were not under time pressure.

Building a base of trust at the beginning of the interview also aimed to mitigate the *lack of trust*. Furthermore, the interviewer assured full confidentiality at the beginning of the interview and offered the interviewee an opportunity to review the notes.

To prevent the *lack of time* from compromising the quality of the data gathered, we did not impose a time limit on the interviews. Furthermore, the interviews were scheduled, to a degree as great as possible, with enough buffer time upfront such that the interviewee would not run short of time because of another appointment.

The *level of entry* pitfall was mitigated by approaching senior managers. As discussed earlier, the target participants of the semi-structured interviews were mostly 'Heads of Enterprise Architecture' or their equivalents, which assured a certain level of seniority.

To avoid an *elite bias*, we selected different organizations and different types of experts for the interviews.[377] The different perspectives of such heterogeneous participants should provide broad and manifold insights.

To control for the *Hawthorne effects,* the interviewer must be aware of this effect and adjust his or her behavior during the interviews. Robson (2011) provides some general advice for interviewers. First, the interviewer should listen more than speak. The interviewer should not use the interview to demonstrate his or her personal experiences and opinions but should seek to elicit those of the interviewee. Second, the questions should be presented in a straightforward, neutral, and non-threatening way such that the interviewee is not biased by the questions, confused by them, or compelled to adopt a defensive stance. Third, the interviewer should avoid cues that lead the interviewee to answer in a certain way. The interviewer must avoid both verbal and non-verbal cues. Last, the interviewer should enjoy the interview and positively encourage the interviewee to talk more about his or her experiences and opinions.[378]

Because interviewees can *construct knowledge* during the interview, the best mitigation strategy for this pitfall is to be aware of it and to probe the interviewee as much as possible. To do so, interviewers should repeatedly ask the respondents to reiterate the how and why of the reasons under discussion.[379]

---

[377] In particular, industry experts, experienced consultants, and academics. See also above in this section and in Section 4.1.2.

[378] Robson (2011)

[379] Fontana, Frey (2000)

To avoid the *ambiguity of language*, we extensively describe the constructs under discussion in the interviews. However, the risk of a certain level of ambiguity, especially in the domain of EAM, remains. Asking questions to clarify the interviewees' understanding and answers helps to identify further potential problems with ambiguity.[380]

Last, the *interview may go wrong*. Unfortunately, there is no active mitigation strategy that can ensure that the interview does not go wrong, but fortunately, during the course of our interviews, nothing happened to classify one of the interviews as having 'gone wrong'.

4.1.2.   Conducting the Interviews

After preparing the interviews, we conducted eleven interviews from June to July 2011. In the following, we describe in detail the selection of the interview participants and the interview process.

Selection of Interview Participants

Aiming for a broad and diverse range of participants for the semi-structured interviews,[381] we identified the interviewees through a judgmental procedure that considers the following factors: years of experience in EAM, position in the organization, organizational focus, and expert type. Table 4-4 lists the factors considered when selecting the interviewees, including a detailed description, the possible values, and the desired characteristics of interview participants.

Table 4-4 Overview of Criteria for Selecting the Interview Participants

Factors	Description	Possible value	Desired characteristic
Years of experience in EAM	Years of experience the interviewee has with EAM	Number of years	> 3 years
Position in the organization	Interviewee's current position	Job title	Senior position
Organizational focus	Interviewee's organizational focus when conducting EAM	Business or IT	50% business and 50% IT
Expert type	Interviewee's type of expertise	Industry expert or EAM consultant	50% industry experts and 50% EAM consultants

Based on the defined factors, we compiled a list of experts by searching the German professional community platform XING and by calling upon personal contacts. This list

---

[380] Robson (2011)

[381] See Section 4.1.1.

comprised 76 EAM experts who were contacted individually. Face-to-face interviews were then set up with eleven experts who were willing to participate. Among these participating experts, we did not identify any systematic omissions or bias in the responses in terms of associated organizational position, expert type, positioning in the organization, or years of experience.

The interviewed EAM experts covered both EAM experts at a senior management level from enterprises (mostly 'Heads of Enterprise Architecture' or their equivalents) and experienced consultants who can complement the experiences of these enterprise experts.

Table 4-5 Overview of the Participants in the Semi-structured Interviews

Expert ID	Expert Type	Organizational Focus	Years of Experience	Position in the Organization
Expert 1	Industry (Logistics)	Business	12	Chief Architect
Expert 2	Industry (Financial)	Business	7	CIO
Expert 3	Industry (Retail)	IT	16	Head of Enterprise Architecture
Expert 4	Industry (Healthcare)	IT	11	Head of Enterprise Architecture
Expert 5	Industry (Telecommunication)	IT	7	Head of Enterprise Architecture
Expert 6	EAM Consultant (Project-level)	Business	16	Senior EAM Consultant
Expert 7	EAM Consultant (Top-management)	Business	13	Senior EAM Consultant
Expert 8	EAM Consultant (Top-management)	Business	7	Senior EAM Consultant
Expert 9	EAM Consultant (Top-management)	Business	23	Senior EAM Consultant
Expert 10	EAM Consultant (Project-level)	IT	16	Senior EAM Consultant
Expert 11	EAM Consultant (Project-level)	IT	8	Senior EAM Consultant

The interviewees who participated in the semi-structured interviews covered a broad and diverse range of participants, as required for the theoretical sampling. With 12.4 years of experience on average, the participants had high levels of seniority and senior job positions. Further, 45.5% are industry experts, and 54.5% are EAM consultants. Additionally, 54.5% have a business background, and 45.5% have an IT background. Hence, the participants fulfilled all of the desired characteristics.

According to Eisenhardt (1989), four to ten explorative observations enable a reasonably good replication logic. However, she admits that there is no general rule regarding the ideal number. To determine the number of observations, researchers should consider resource constraints, opportunities and feasibility issues. Furthermore, if theoretical saturation is reached, researchers should stop gathering additional observations.[382] Theoretical saturation occurs if incremental insights about the researched phenomenon are minimal and if only previously observed phenomena and relationships are witnessed.[383]

Figure 4-1 Theoretical Saturation for EAM Benefit Constructs

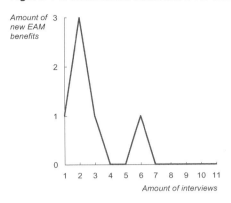

Figure 4-2 Theoretical Saturation for EAM Success Factor Constructs

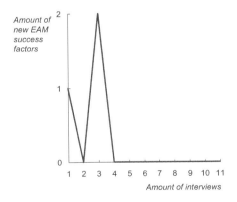

In this doctoral thesis, the insights gained with additional interviews decreased to a minimum after seven interviews. As Figure 4-1 shows, the last additional EAM benefit construct was identified in the sixth interview. Similarly, Figure 4-2 shows that after three interviews, no new EAM success factors were identified. Therefore, we can conclude

---

[382] Eisenhardt (1989); Glaser, Strauss (1969)

[383] Napier et al. (2009); Tan F. B., Hunter (2002)

that the number of interviews conducted for this doctoral thesis was sufficient to achieve theoretical saturation.

Conducting the Interviews

Following our pre-specified interview guide, we conducted eleven interviews from June to July 2011. In the interviews, each of which lasted approximately 90 to 120 minutes, we first asked open questions about the expert's experiences with EAM benefits and EAM success factors and then discussed the expert's experiences with EAM success factors along the dimensions of our model. Because five of the eleven experts were not close to our location, we conducted these interviews by telephone. Long-term studies show that telephone interviews are as effective as face-to-face interviews.[384]

The principal researcher of this doctoral thesis conducted all of the interviews. Robson (2011) states that the researcher should also be the interviewer in small-scale research projects.[385] During the interview, the interviewer took notes on the answers, and each interview was subsequently coded and analyzed, as described in the following section.

4.1.3.   Analyzing the Interviews

Following the interviews, we coded the results in the same way that we coded our findings from the literature review.[386] With this approach, we were able to identify additions and changes to our theoretically developed model and derive a revised model that incorporates the findings from these semi-structured interviews.

To analyze the interviews, we needed a textual data analysis technique that would allow us to identify emerging aspects as meaningful constructs that could supplement our theoretically developed model. Here, we also used the coding and analysis procedures suggested in the context of grounded theory.[387]

The coding for this content analysis was performed using NVivo. First, we went through all of the interviews completely and identified all of the success factors and benefits that the interviewees claimed contributed to EAM success in accordance with open coding. Second, for the axial coding, we clustered the success factors into conceptual families in NVivo. Thus, we modeled the theoretically developed model in NVivo by creating a folder for each of the previously identified dimensions as a basic structure. Next, we modeled the remaining elements (i.e., the success factors and benefits) of the theoretically

---

[384] Rogers (1976)

[385] Robson (2011)

[386] Compare Section 3.2.

[387] Corbin, Strauss (2008)

developed model by using NVivo tags (i.e., 'nodes' in NVivo). To identify additional constructs and potential changes, we coded the findings from the interviews as follows:

- When a new success factor or benefit emerged, a new node was created and assigned to the appropriate dimension of the DMSM.

- Additional success factors or benefits generally supporting a certain earlier identified factor were assigned to these nodes.

Finally, after the revised model was developed with this proceeding, we numbered the changes for tracking purposes. The results of this proceeding are discussed in the following section.

4.2. Findings from Expert Interviews

Our eleven semi-structured interviews generally confirmed the findings from our literature review. All of the experts agreed that when compared with their experiences, the proposed constructs are relevant and influential. They also generally believed that the suggested model, which establishes an instrument that measures the value of EAM, provides valuable insights for practice. In the following, we discuss the additions and changes identified during the semi-structured interviews. First, we discuss the additions and changes to our theoretically developed a priori model on the construct level. We then present the detailed insights about each sub-aspects of the construct that we obtained in the interviews during the discussion of our theoretically developed a priori model. As a result, we focus on describing the qualitative insights rather than on presenting empirical findings because the objective of the interviews was to identify qualitative insights rather than to conduct an empirical validation with statistical significance.[388]

When we detail our findings, we denote in italics for tracking purposes each addition or change to the constructs and each new insight to a construct sub-dimension with a capital letter (i.e., A, C or I, respectively), a sequential number (e.g., A1), and a lower letter for the associated dimension (e.g., A1b).

4.2.1. Identification of Missing Constructs

EAM Benefit Constructs

Asking our experts in the semi-structured interviews about the benefits of EAM, the EAM experts agreed mainly with the theoretically identified benefits, as all of the theoretically identified benefits were mentioned by at least some of the experts. Figure 4-3 shows how

---

[388] See also detailed discussion of this scope in Section 4.1.

often the interviewees mentioned each EAM benefit. In addition, the interviews uncovered five additional benefits, which are described in the following:

Figure 4-3 EAM Benefit Constructs Identified in the Expert Interviews

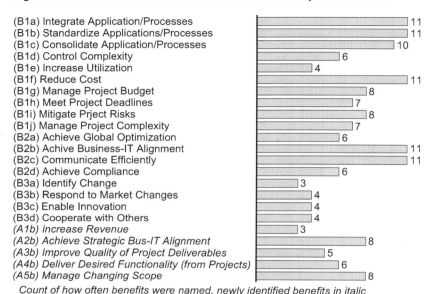

(B1a) Integrate Application/Processes — 11
(B1b) Standardize Applications/Processes — 11
(B1c) Consolidate Application/Processes — 10
(B1d) Control Complexity — 6
(B1e) Increase Utilization — 4
(B1f) Reduce Cost — 11
(B1g) Manage Project Budget — 8
(B1h) Meet Project Deadlines — 7
(B1i) Mitigate Prject Risks — 8
(B1j) Manage Project Complexity — 7
(B2a) Achieve Global Optimization — 6
(B2b) Achive Business-IT Alignment — 11
(B2c) Communicate Efficiently — 11
(B2d) Achieve Compliance — 6
(B3a) Identify Change — 3
(B3b) Respond to Market Changes — 4
(B3c) Enable Innovation — 4
(B3d) Cooperate with Others — 4
(A1b) Increase Revenue — 3
(A2b) Achieve Strategic Bus-IT Alignment — 8
(A3b) Improve Quality of Project Deliverables — 5
(A4b) Deliver Desired Functionality (from Projects) — 6
(A5b) Manage Changing Scope — 8

Count of how often benefits were named, newly identified benefits in italic

Addition *A1b*: **Benefits should be extended by the factor 'increase in revenue'**

The first additional EAM benefit is *'increase in revenue'*. Three experts mentioned that an increase in efficiency can be achieved with EAM by, for example, reducing costs or by enabling an increase in revenue. As Expert 7 mentioned, EAM *"...mostly focuses on cost reductions, but revenues need to be considered as a potential benefit as well. Especially for organizations that use EAM for IT enablement, this source of benefits is important."*[389] This finding is also consistent with our theoretical discussion of net benefits in the introduction of this thesis.[390] Cost and benefits are two sides of the same coin, and both need to be considered when discussing value. Consequently, if EAM benefits consider cost reduction, an increase in revenue must also be considered.

---

[389] Quote Expert 7.

[390] See Section 1.4.

Addition *A2b*:   **Benefits should distinguish between strategic and operational alignment**

The second additional benefit of EAM is that it enables organizations to '*achieve strategic business-IT alignment*'. One of the stated EAM benefits identified during the literature review is business-IT alignment. However, during the interviews, eight experts noted that business-IT strategy alignment must be distinguished from business process-IT alignment because "*…alignment can be achieved generally on two levels: between business and IT strategy as well as between processes and IT. EAM ideally synchronizes and aligns both.*"[391] Henderson et al. (1993) support this view with their Strategic Alignment Model (SAM), which makes a similar distinction.[392] Therefore, we distinguish between these two alignments in the following and split the EAM benefit of strategic alignment into operational and strategic alignments.[393]

Addition *A3b*:   **Benefits should be extended by the factor 'improve quality of project deliverables'**

Seven experts emphasized that in addition to the organizational benefits of EAM, EAM yields project benefits. Traditional program management only considers typical project parameters, such as project risks, budgets, and deadlines, whereas EAM considers other project parameters.[394] First, in addition to the improvements in the traditional financial and time-related project parameters already included in the theoretically developed a priori model, five experts argued that EAM impacts the quality of project deliverables: "*Making the dependencies across the different architectural layers explicit helps to improve quality and allows for an alignment not only between business and IT but also across all layers, which results in better quality.*"[395]

Addition *A4b*:   **Benefits should be extended by the factor 'improve project delivery of functionality'**

Furthermore, six EAM experts stated that EAM helps improve not only the quality of project deliverables but also the delivery of the required functionality. For example, with respect to the improved delivery of the functionality, Expert 1 argues, "*By having an overview of how different projects link to each other, individual projects can better*

---

[391] Quote Expert 10.

[392] Henderson, Venkatraman (1993)

[393] Henderson, Venkatraman (1993) call these two in their SAM strategic integration, i.e., the alignment of business and IT strategy, and functional integration, i.e., the alignment of business and IT infrastructure and processes.

[394] Bentley (2010); Project Management Institute (2008)

[395] Quote Expert 11.

integrate their deliverables in the existing landscape and hence deliver functionality that better fits the requirements of the overall Enterprise Architecture." [396]

Addition *A5b*: **Benefits to be extended by the factor 'manage changing project scope'**

In addition, EAM allows organizations to cope with changing scopes across projects, as 8 experts recalled. Expert 7 argues, *"Enterprise architects have an integrating role across projects and not only help to align the scopes across projects but also help the projects to stick to their scopes."* [397]

Change *C1b*: **Importance of the difference between organizational and project benefits important**

With respect to the sub-dimensions of the benefit constructs, six EAM experts highlighted the importance of differentiating between the project-level and organization-level benefits. This distinction is also discussed in the literature.[398] For example, Expert 9 highlights this difference in the following: *"The benefits realized on a project level might be different from those realized for the overall organization. There is a difference in both the time horizon and the source of value. For example, from a project perspective, the existence of a well-documented as-is architecture can be beneficial, but this documentation might have no immediate relevance to the overall organization."*[399] Similarly, Expert 3 argues, *"The benefits realized from EAM for different stakeholders can differ significantly depending on whether you look at the benefits from a project level or an organizational level."*[400] Therefore, the project-level and organization-level benefits should be differentiated from one another.

EAM Success Factor Constructs

Having presented the additions to the EAM benefit constructs of our theoretically developed model, we now discuss the EAM success factor constructs of this model. Here, we identified two additional constructs on the construct level and one major change in a construct during the semi-structured interviews.

There are few changes on this level mainly because the constructs are on a fairly abstract level that comprises various sub-dimensions. In the following, we discuss 11 changes and additions to these sub-dimensions alongside the existing constructs. To differentiate

---

[396] Quote Expert 1.

[397] Quote Expert 7.

[398] E.g., Tamm et al. (2011)

[399] Quote Expert 9.

[400] Quote Expert 3.

these changes and additions to these sub-dimensions from those discussed with respect to the dimensions, we discuss them as 'key insights' in the sub-dimension. They are similarly numbered for tracking purposes with an 'K' along with a sequential number and a letter for the associated construct (e.g., *K1p*).

Figure 4-4 EAM Success Factor Constructs Identified in the Expert Interviews

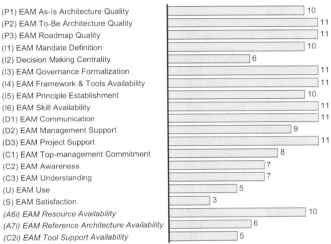

Count of how often success factors were named, newly identified factors in italic

In summary, the EAM experts mainly agreed with the theoretically identified EAM success factor constructs as well. All of the theoretically identified EAM success factor constructs were mentioned as well by at least some experts. Figure 4-4 illustrates how often the interviewees mentioned each EAM success factor construct. However, the interviews unveiled two additions and one major change in the constructs.

Addition A6i: The construct 'EAM resource availability' should be added as an important aspect to the EAM infrastructure quality dimension

Ten of the interviewed experts agreed that EAM resources are an important aspect of the EAM infrastructure quality. Only when sufficient funding, staffing, and time to conduct EAM is available, EAM can be successful. Expert 5 states that *"EAM requires not only the commitment of the leadership to the topic but also a significant investment."* Expert 1 adds, *"Financial resources are not the only resource required to run an EAM function successfully. There must also be sufficient time to conduct the tasks. EAM is not something you can do within one day."[401]*

Addition A7i: **The construct 'EAM reference architecture availability' should be added as an important aspect to the EAM infrastructure quality dimension**

Six experts mentioned the importance of using reference architectures to guide the design of a to-be architecture. Reference architectures refer to industry standards and best-practice architectures, such as eTOM[402] and ITIL,[403] which are used as a guideline for the development of a to-be architecture. Expert 6 states that *"using these reference architectures allows organizations to avoid reinventing the wheel while using best practices that are the de facto industry standard."*[404]

Change C2i: **The 'EAM tool support availability' should be separated from the 'EAM framework & tool availability' construct**

In our theoretically developed a priori model, we have a construct called 'EAM frameworks & tools'. However, in the semi-structured interviews, five experts argued that this construct should be separated into two constructs: 'EAM frameworks' and 'EAM tool support'. The experts argued that these constructs should be split because frameworks and tools have different impacts on EAM benefits. Expert 3 quoted a saying in the IT world, *"a fool with a tool is still a fool"*, which suggests that the best tool might influence the EAM benefits but does not guarantee the success of an organization's implementation of an EAM framework. Further, Expert 8 argued, *"Although most tools are accompanied by a suggested framework, most organizations need to adjust the suggested approach to be successful."*[405] These findings are also further supported by current research, which shows that most organizations adopt a framework or create their own by cherry picking.[406] Consequently, we converted the construct 'EAM frameworks & tools' into two separate ones: 'EAM frameworks' and 'EAM tool support'.

After discussing the additions and changes to the EAM success factor constructs, we now discuss the insights that we obtained from the semi-structured interviews for each sub-dimension. We discuss these insights in terms of the four quality dimensions: EAM

---

[401] Quote Expert 1.

[402] tmforum

[403] OGC (26.02.2012)

[404] Quote Expert 6.

[405] Quote Expert 8.

[406] Lange, Mendling (2011)

product quality, EAM infrastructure quality, EAM service delivery quality, and EAM cultural aspects.

EAM Product Quality

Key Insight *K1p*: Properties of as-is and to-be products should be used as quality indicators for the EAM roadmap as well

In the theoretically developed a priori model, we argued that as-is and to-be products should be characterized by three main quality attributes: timeliness (P1a/P2a), completeness (P1b/P2b), and level of detail (P1c/P2c). In contrast, the third EAM product (i.e., the EAM roadmap) was characterized by two other quality attributes: feasibility (P3a) and consideration of dependencies (P3c). The only similar quality attribute was completeness (P3b). However, the experts argued that timeliness and completeness are also important properties that indicate a high-quality roadmap: *"Having an up-to-date roadmap with the right level of detail is also important in this context. Why would you need a well-integrated and feasible roadmap that is on an excessively high level?"*[407] Therefore, these attributes should also be considered when assessing the quality of the roadmap.

EAM Infrastructure Quality

Key Insight *K2i*: Business-IT positioning should be split into business-IT aspects and organizational focus

For the 'EAM mandate' construct, we argued in the theoretically developed model that effectively positioning EAM between the business and IT departments generated certain advantages (*I1b*).[408] However, we concluded from the interviews that it is important to position the EAM in an organizationally correct manner and to cover both the business and IT aspects (i.e., to include both business processes and the underlying IT systems) when discussing EAM. In the following, Expert 1 argues in line with this idea: *"Regardless of whether EAM is positioned on the business or IT side of the organization, EAM should cover both the business and IT aspects of the enterprise architecture."*[409]

Key Insight *K3i*: The centrality of regulatory compliance and EAM decision-making should be considered for the centrality of decision-making as well

The degree of central decision making covers capital budgets (*I2a*), operational process optimization and implementation (*I2b*), application development project prioritization and

---

[407] Quote Expert 6.

[408] Aier et al. (2011b); Halley et al. (2005); Radeke (2010)

[409] Quote Expert 1.

approval (*I2c*), IT development and implementation (*I2d*), and infrastructure planning and management (*I2e*)[410] in the theoretically developed model. However, Expert 9 reports that the decision-making processes directly related to EAM and to regulatory compliance should also be considered in this context. He argues, *"The decision making related to EAM and regulatory compliance management is not necessarily included in these aspects and can also be organized either centrally or decentrally."*[411]

Key Insight *K4i*: Informal agreements and waivers should be an indicator for the degree of EAM formality

With respect to the formality of EAM (*I3*), Expert 7 argues that a common problem concerns not only the lack of a formal definition for the EAM governance mechanisms but also the questions of whether shortcuts designed to avoid them are common. Specifically, Expert 7 states, *"However, formal governance bodies and EAM processes are defined in many organizations, and we often see people making informal agreements or even giving official waivers of EAM principles that undermine the long-term goals and the resulting benefits that EAM should yield."*[412] Therefore, the 'EAM formal governance' construct should cover these aspects as well. Waivers and informal agreements should be avoided to achieve the long-term goals and full potential of EAM.

Key Insight *K5i*: EAM principle sub-dimensions should be characterized along the different EAM layers

In our theoretically developed model, we argued that the EAM principles need to be directive (*F5a*), specific (*F5b*), and implementable (*F5c*) to yield EAM benefits. However, the experts argue that there are different levels of abstraction for EAM principles and that EAM principles can have a hierarchy of abstraction. Hence, these characteristics do not apply for all EAM principles. Greefhorst et al. (2011) support this argument in their research.[413] More importantly, the experts argue, *"It is important to have EAM principles specified for the different EAM layer. Having EAM principles from the business layer to the infrastructure layer allows organizations to solve a broad range of architectural issues."*[414] Therefore, the experts suggest differentiating the existence of EAM principles

---

[410] Aagesen et al. (2011); Boh et al. (2007); Kamogawa, Okada (2005); Radeke (2011); Radeke (2010)

[411] Quote Expert 9.

[412] Quote Expert 7,

[413] Greefhorst, Proper (2011), pp. 41–43

[414] Quote Expert 6.

in terms of the addressed scope, which ranges from business application issues to technical infrastructure issues.[415]

Key Insight *K6i*: Job rotation should be considered as an important concept to improve the EAM skills

The interviews highlighted the importance of the soft skills of EAM staff and their organizational networks to the success of EAM. Expert 9 stated, "*Communication is a truly important skill for an architect, if not the most important one.*"[416] Expert 4 reports that an important concept for improving the skills of enterprise architects is job rotation: "*Rotating around different roles [...] not only improves the learning experience of the enterprise architect but also allows for a wider acceptance of the enterprise architect in our organization. People in our organizations no longer see enterprise architects as pedants who do nothing but define EAM principles; rather, we see enterprise architects as important contributors to the success of our projects and as people who have deep knowledge and serve as valuable integrators across different projects.*"[417] Therefore, the concept of job rotation is added to the construct.

EAM Service Delivery Quality

Key Insight *K7s*: Simplicity should be considered as an important aspect of EAM communication

In the following, Expert 6 argues that an important aspect of EAM communication is the simplicity of the communication: "*EAM is a topic that is not easily understood by everyone. Hence, communication in a simple und understandable way is important for successfully communicating with stakeholders.*"[418] Therefore, the aspect of simplicity should be considered when discussing successful EAM communication.

Key Insight *K8s*: The active involvement of management in EAM decisions and their implementation should be considered when evaluating the EAM management support

"*It is not enough to have well-defined EAM processes and good EAM decisions. If the leadership is not involved in these processes and decisions, EAM cannot be fully realized.*"[419] This expert quote emphasizes the importance of the involvement of management in EAM. Expert 10 concurs and states, "*Leadership should be involved in not only EAM planning and the related decision making but also in the actual execution of*

---

[415] Boh et al. (2007); Winter, Fischer (2007)

[416] Quote Expert 9.

[417] Quote Expert 4.

[418] Quote Expert 6.

[419] Quote Expert 7.

what is planned and decided."[420] Therefore, when evaluating the support of EAM management, the management's involvement in the actual decision making, the EAM planning, and the EAM execution should be considered.

Key Insight *K9s*: The review of EAM principle should be a regular management activity

In addition to the active involvement of management in EAM, EAM principles should be regularly reviewed by the management. Expert 2 argues, *"To have an effective and efficient enterprise architecture, it is not enough to define EAM principles once. They also have to be reviewed regularly, and it needs to be checked whether they are still in line with the current strategy.*"[421] Therefore, to be efficient and effective, the management activities should include such reviews.

Key Insight *K10s*: The integrating role of enterprise architects across projects is an important factor for the EAM project support

Furthermore, the role of enterprise architects is crucial for aligning and integrating the projects across the organization from an EAM perspective. This integration is also a critical step towards the implementation of the to-be architecture. To this end, Expert 7 argues, *"Enterprise architects have an integrating role across projects and not only help to align the scopes across projects but also help the projects to stick to their scopes."* [422]

EAM Cultural Aspects

Key Insight *K11c*: Cultural aspects are a highly important concern for EAM

With respect to the cultural aspects, our interviewed experts confirmed the need for a thorough consideration of cultural aspects when discussing the realization of EAM benefits. In their experience, this dimension is one of the most important factors when establishing an EAM practice. In particular, the interviewees highlighted three points. First, the experts view top management support for EAM as a key success factor. For example, Expert 7 states, *"Without the involvement of the top management, you can design the best enterprise architecture in the world, but the actual implementation will never happen. Top management needs to understand what we are doing.*"[423] Our interviewed experts further agreed that top management support ensures the availability of required resources and helps to foster acceptance of the architecture within the organization. Second, the experts suggested that building a community around EAM helps to establish EAM and shape a supportive culture. The active establishment of an

---

[420] Quote Expert 10.

[421] Quote Expert 2.

[422] Quote Expert 2.

[423] Quote Expert 7.

EAM community involves not only direct EAM roles but also people from other functions who engage in EAM topics. Expert 8 supports this suggestion by stating, *"Both the enterprise architects and the people implementing the enterprise architecture need to be convinced to support EAM. Therefore, you need to build a community around the topic by involving and engaging the different stakeholders in EAM."*[424] A community ensures that EAM is not only conducted in a department dedicated to EAM but also supported by the main stakeholders. Third, the establishment of an EAM culture is said to mitigate the perception of EAM as an ivory tower that slows down projects with its policies and guidelines. An EAM culture helps to communicate the value of EAM, especially for transformation projects.

4.2.2.   Discussion of Propositions

In addition to discussing the constructs of our model, we discussed the propositions of the theoretical a priori model in the semi-structured interviews. In general, the interviewees agreed that the theoretically identified success factors impact the realization of benefits from EAM. However, some experts remarked that the use and satisfaction construct might not be related to the realized benefits, as proposed in the propositions. These remarks are discussed in detail in the following and tested later along with the empirical validation of the model.

Key Insight *K12prop*:   **Culture can also be seen as dependent on EAM products, EAM infrastructure and EAM service delivery**

Although all of the interviewees agreed that cultural aspects are an important factor in the domain of EAM, the role of these aspects was challenged by two experts. These two experts highlighted the potential role of cultural aspects as a factor dependent on the EAM products, EAM infrastructure, and EAM service delivery dimensions because these three dimensions will impact the EAM culture. For example, Expert 8 states that he *"...would see how an EAM function is designed as being relevant to what culture evolves from this setup. However, I can also see that the overall organizational culture impacts how EAM is perceived."*[425]

Key Insight *K13prop*:   **The intention to use EAM could be influenced by whether it is mandatory to use EAM**

Expert 11 mentioned that the intention to use EAM might also depend on whether it is mandatory to use EAM: *"Especially in government operations, EAM is regulated by law in some countries, such as the USA. Here, we see that the intention to use EAM is not always driven by personal preference; rather, its use is mandatory."* Consequently, the

---

[424] Quote Expert 8.

[425] Quote Expert 8.

use construct might not always have the same influence on the realized benefits. Such concerns with mandatory use have also been discussed in light of the original DMSM. The main criticism here is that use cannot be seen as a measure of success if use is actually mandatory.[426]

Key Insight *K14prop*: **Satisfaction has no direct impact on benefits but is a mediator for use**

Furthermore, three of the interviewees conjectured that satisfaction might have no strong impact on EAM benefits because this construct might describe a mediator for use but not for benefits. Expert 5 commented, *"I would say that a high level of satisfaction can increase the use of EAM. However, how would satisfaction directly impact the benefits of EAM?"[427]* Therefore, the proposition that the benefits of EAM will increase if EAM stakeholders are satisfied with EAM products, EAM infrastructure, EAM service delivery, and EAM cultural aspects may not be valid.

4.3. Revised Model

Having discussed the main findings from the semi-structured interviews in detail in the previous section, we apply these findings to the theoretical a priori model to develop a revised model in this section.

The following Table 4-6 summarizes the findings from the semi-structured interviews and presents the revised a priori model. The revised constructs are presented along with their properties. For traceability, the table refers either to the original part of the theoretically developed model or to the findings from the semi-structured interviews that triggered the change in the reference label.

Table 4-6 Overview of Revised A Priori Constructs

Identified Constructs	Property	Refe-rence
EAM Product Quality Dimension		
(PQ1) As-is architecture auality	(PQ1a) Timeliness	(P1a)
	(PQ1b) Completeness	(P1b)
	(PQ1c) Level of detail	(P1c)
(PQ2) To-be architecture auality	(PQ2a) Timeliness	(P2a)
	(PQ2b) Completeness	(P2b)
	(PQ2c) Level of detail	(P2c)
(PQ3) Roadmap quality	(PQ3a) Timeliness	(K1p)
	(PQ3b) Completeness	(P3b)
	(PQ3c) Level of detail	(K1p)

---

[426] DeLone, McLean (2003); Lassila, Brancheau (1999)

[427] Quote Expert 5.

Identified Constructs	Property	Reference
	(PQ3d) Feasibility	(P3a)
	(PQ3e) Consideration of dependencies	(P3c)

EAM Infrastructure Quality Dimension

Identified Constructs	Property	Reference
(IQ1) EAM mandate definition	(IQ1a) Organizational scope	(I1a)
	(IQ1b) Covered business-IT aspects	(K2i)
	(IQ1c) Organizational business-IT focus	(K2i)
	(IQ1d) Alignment with other functions	(I1c)
(IQ2) Decision-making centralization	(IQ2a) Capital budgets	(I2a)
	(IQ2b) Operational process optimization and implementation	(I2b)
	(IQ2c) Application development projects prioritization and approval	(I2c)
	(IQ2d) IT development and implementation	(I2d)
	(IQ2e) Infrastructure planning and management	(I2e)
	(IQ2f) Compliance management	(K3i)
	(IQ2e) EAM definition and implementation	(K3i)
(IQ3) EAM governance formalization	(IQ3a) Formally defined approval process	(I3a)
	(IQ3b) EAM principle compliance	(I3b)
	(IQ3c) Occurrence of informal agreements	(K4i)
	(IQ3d) Penalties for EAM principle violations	(I3d)
	(IQ3e) Frequent waivers	(K4i)
(IQ4) EAM framework availability	(IQ4a) Standardized FW in place	(C2i)
	(IQ4b) Use industry standards	(C2i)
	(IQ4c) Accepted among stakeholders	(C2i)
(IQ5) EAM tool support availability	(IQ5a) Established tool support	(C2i)
	(IQ5b) Central repository provided	(C2i)
	(IQ5c) Accepted among stakeholders	(C2i)
(IQ6) EAM reference architectures Availability	(IQ6a) Established reference architecture	(A7i)
	(IQ6b) Guide to-be design	(A7i)
	(IQ6c) Used without major adjustments	(A7i)
(IQ7) EAM principles establishment	(IQ7a) Business architecture	(K5i)
	(IQ7b) Application architecture	(K5i)
	(IQ7c) Technology architecture	(K5i)
	(IQ7d) Integration architecture	(K5i)
	(IQ7e) Data architecture	(K5i)
(IQ8) EAM skills availability	(IQ6a) Defined EAM roles	(I6a)
	(IQ6b) Ongoing training	(I6b)
	(IQ6c) Good communication skills	(I6c)
	(IQ6d) Extensive networking in organization	(I6d)
	(IQ6e) High EAM expert knowledge	(I6c)
	(IQ6f) Role differentiation from other functions	(I6e)
	(IQ6g) Job rotation	(K6i)
(IQ9) EAM resources availability	(IQ9a) Financial resources	(A6i)
	(IQ9b) People resources	(A6i)

Identified Constructs	Property	Reference
	(IQ9c) Time resources	(A6i)

EAM Service Delivery Quality Dimension

Identified Constructs	Property	Reference
(SQ1) EAM communication	(SQ1a) Stakeholder-specific communications	(D1a)
	(SQ1b) Communication of the benefits of EA	(D1b)
	(SQ1c) Proactive communication	(D1c)
	(SQ1d) Simple and understandable communication	(I7s)
(SQ2) EAM management support	(SQ2a) Projects checked for conformance	(D2a)
	(SQ2b) Top management involved in decision-making	(D2b)
	(SQ2c) Regular EAM principle review	(I9s)
	(SQ2d) Management briefing	(D2d)
	(SQ2e) Top management is actively involved in EAM planning	(I8s)
	(SQ2f) Top management involved in execution	(I8s)
(SQ3) EAM project support	(SQ3a) Active involvement	(D3a)
	(SQ3b) Active project role	(D3b)
	(SQ3c) Integrating role across projects	(A10s)

EAM Cultural Aspects Dimension

Identified Constructs	Property	Reference
(CA1) EAM top-management commitment	(CA1a) Resource commitment	(C1a)
	(CA1b) Assigned importance	(C1b)
	(CA1c) Time commitment	(C1c)
	(CA1d) Communication of importance	(C1d)
(CA2) EAM awareness	(CA2a) Stakeholders' awareness	(C2a)
	(CA2b) Stakeholders' understanding of importance	(C2b)
	(CA2c) Stakeholder education	(C2c)
(CA3) EAM understanding	(CA3a) Shared vision	(C3a)
	(CA3b) Shared understanding	(C3b)
	(CA3c) Alignment of common goals	(C3c)

EAM Benefits Dimension

Identified Constructs	Property	Reference
(OB1) Organizational efficiency benefits	(OB1a) Integrate application/processes	(B1a)
	(OB1b) Standardize application/processes	(B1b)
	(OB1c) Consolidate application/processes	(B1c)
	(OB1d) Control complexity	(B1d)
	(OB1e) Increase utilization	(B1e)
	(OB1f) Reduce cost	(B1f)
	(OB1g) Increase revenue	(A1b)
(OB2) Organizational effectiveness benefits	(OB2a) Global optimization	(B2a)
	(OB2b) Operational business-IT alignment	(A2b)
	(OB2c) Efficient communication	(B2c)
	(OB2d) Strategic business-IT alignment	(A2b)
(OB3) Organizational flexibility benefits	(OB3a) Identify change	(B3a)
	(OB3b) Respond to market	(B3b)
	(OB3c) Enable innovation	(B3c)

Identified Constructs	Property	Reference
	(OB3d) Cooperate with others	(B3d)
(PB1) Project efficiency benefits	(PB1a) Manage project budget	(B1g)
	(PB1b) Meet project deadlines	(B1h)
	(PB1c) Mitigate project risks	(B1i)
	(PB1d) Manage project complexity	(B1j)
(PB2) Project effectiveness benefits	(PB2a) Improve quality of project deliverables	(A3b)
	(PB2b) Deliver desired functionality (from projects)	(A4b)
(PB3) Project flexibility benefits	(PB3a) Manage changing project scope	(A5b)

In addition to revising the model constructs, we revised the propositions of the model. Table 4-7 summarizes the revised propositions, which include three new and one revised propositions. Further, the table indicates which propositions find support in the semi-structured interviews and which have been challenged. The latter are marked with a checkmark in parentheses. The validity of these challenged propositions will be further investigated, particularly during the empirical validation of the model in the following chapters.[428]

Table 4-7 Overview of Revised Propositions

Dimension	New number	Old number	Proposition	Support
(PQ) EAM product quality	PQ	P	High EAM product quality should be provided by EAM.	✓
	PQ1	P1	EAM should provide desirable information about the as-is architecture that satisfies the needs of the EAM stakeholders in an effective and efficient way.	✓
	PQ2	P2	EAM should provide desirable information about the to-be architecture that satisfies the needs of the EAM stakeholders in an effective and efficient way.	✓
	PQ3	P3	EAM should provide desirable information about the EAM roadmap that satisfies the needs of the EAM stakeholders in an effective and efficient way.	✓
(IQ) EAM infrastructure quality	PQ	I	High EAM Infrastructure Setup Quality should be provided by EAM.	✓
	IQ1	I1	A clear EAM mandate should define the appointed organizational and business/IT scope of EAM.	
	IQ2	I2	Central and local accountabilities should be defined for EAM decision-making.	✓

---

[428] Note again that the addition "to positively impact EAM net benefits" is omitted for each proposition to increase readability.

Dimension	New number	Old number	Proposition	Support
	IQ3	I3	Governance mechanisms should be defined for EAM decision-making.	✓
	IQ4	I4 (rev.)	The EAM frameworks should serve as an infrastructure to support the EAM service delivery.	✓
	IQ5	NEW	The EAM tool support should serve as an infrastructure to support the EAM service delivery.	✓
	IQ6	NEW	The EAM reference architectures should serve as an infrastructure to support the EAM service delivery.	✓
	IQ7	I5	The EAM principles guiding the design of the to-be architecture should be in place.	✓
	IQ8	I6	EAM staff should be well trained and integrated into the organization.	✓
	IQ9	NEW	Sufficient EAM resources should be available.	✓
(SQ) EAM service delivery quality	SQ	D	High EAM Service Delivery Quality should be provided by EAM.	✓
	SQ1	D1	EAM should educate EAM stakeholders about the activities of EAM.	✓
	SQ2	D2	EAM should support the management in deciding on architecture-related topics and assuring project conformance.	✓
	SQ3	D3	EAM should integrate with the actual implementation in transformation projects.	✓
(CA) EAM cultural aspects	CA	C	A good EAM culture should be established for EAM.	✓
	CA1	C1	EAM leadership commitment ensures priority and resources.	✓
	CA2	C2	All EAM stakeholders must have a high awareness of EAM.	✓
	CA3	C3	A common understanding of EAM should be established for both business and IT employees.	✓
(U) Use	U	U	EAM should actively use EAM products, the provided infrastructure, the service delivery, and the established EAM culture for conducting business transformation activities in an organization.	(✓)
(S) Satisfaction	S	S	EAM stakeholders should be satisfied with the EAM products, infrastructure, service delivery, and cultural aspects.	(✓)

4.4. Synthesis

To explore and contextualize our theoretically developed a priori model, we conducted eleven interviews with senior industry experts and experienced EAM consultants. These expert interviews confirmed the findings from our literature review. Based on their experiences, all of the experts agreed that the proposed dimensions are relevant and influential. They also confirmed that the practical relevance and value of the suggested model allows it to measure the benefits realized from EAM.

In particular, the interviewed experts confirmed the need for a thorough consideration of cultural aspects in this context. This consideration was one of the major changes introduced by our model in comparison with the DMSM. However, some experts argued that these cultural aspects may act as a dependent factor on the dimensions of EAM product quality, EAM infrastructure quality, and EAM service delivery quality because these dimensions will impact the EAM culture. Furthermore, two experts hypothesized that satisfaction has no strong impact on EAM benefits because it may describe a moderator for use but not for benefits.

On the basis of the qualitative insights gathered, the revised EAM Benefit Realization Model, which includes cultural aspects as a moderator, is depicted in Figure 4-5. It considers EAM culture as a dependent variable in relation to EAM product quality, EAM infrastructure quality, and EAM service delivery quality (compare this model with the a priori model based on our literature review on the left).

Figure 4-5 Comparison of the Theoretical (left) and Revised A Priori Model (right)

However, the relationships among the constructs, as depicted in Figure 4-5, must be further investigated. To do so, we operationalize the model in the following chapter to conduct an empirical validation via a Web-based survey. Figure 4-6 summarizes the constructs of the revised a priori model that is operationalized in the next chapter independent of their relationships, i.e., the underlying propositions.

Figure 4-6 Overview Constructs of Revised A Priori Model

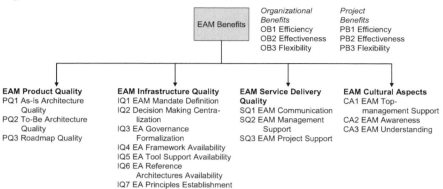

EAM Product Quality
PQ1 As-Is Architecture
    Quality
PQ2 To-Be Architecture
    Quality
PQ3 Roadmap Quality

EAM Infrastructure Quality
IQ1 EAM Mandate Definition
IQ2 Decision Making Centra-
    lization
IQ3 EA Governance
    Formalization
IQ4 EA Framework Availability
IQ5 EA Tool Support Availability
IQ6 EA Reference
    Architectures Availability
IQ7 EA Principles Establishment
IQ8 EA Skills Availability
IQ9 EA Resources Availability

EAM Service Delivery
Quality
SQ1 EAM Communication
SQ2 EAM Management
    Support
SQ3 EAM Project Support

EAM Cultural Aspects
CA1 EAM Top-
    management Support
CA2 EAM Awareness
CA3 EAM Understanding

5.   Model Operationalization

*An idea that is developed and put into action
is more important than an idea that exists only as an idea.*
Buddha

In the previous chapters of this doctoral thesis, we have described a theoretical a priori model for the realization of benefits from Enterprise Architecture Management (EAM). The model was designed according to a literature review and revised based on insights from semi-structured interviews with EAM experts. The remainder of this thesis is concerned with the empirical validation of this model. In this chapter, we describe the operationalization of the model in a Web-based survey as a first step towards this empirical validation. Therefore, the objective of this chapter is to design a Web-based survey that facilitates the measurement of the constructs and relationships of the model discussed in the previous chapters. The chapter is divided into six sections. In Section 5.1, we describe the research methods applied to operationalize the model. Section 5.2 discusses the preparation of the constructs and propositions of the model for its operationalization as a survey. In Section 5.3, the survey is described. In Section 5.4, we test the survey. Section 5.5 describes the survey administration. We conclude with a synopsis of the key findings in Section 5.6.

5.1. Research Method

Having developed the revised model in the previous chapter, we validate the model in this chapter. Previously, we described the constructs and propositions of the model in an exploratory manner. These constructs and propositions are based on a theoretical analysis of the literature and semi-structured interviews. However, the constructs and propositions are an abstraction that describes a phenomenon of theoretical interest.[429] In other words, the constructs are latent and not directly measurable.[430] Therefore, for an empirical validation that tests and measures the constructs in an explanatory manner, we must empirically operationalize the constructs by operationally defining them in terms of variables and hypotheses. A hypothesis is proposed as the relationship between

---

[429] Edwards, Bagozzi (2000)

[430] Bagozzi (1979)

empirically observable variables. The relationships between theoretical and empirical concepts are depicted in Figure 5-1.[431]

Figure 5-1 Distinction Between Theoretical and Empirical Concepts

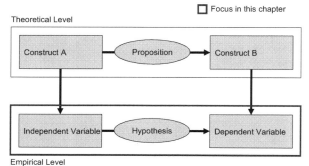

SOURCE: *Adapted from Bhattacherjee (2012)*

The empirical measurement of a variable requires measures, also referred to as indicators or items that are quantifiable and observable scores obtained through surveys, interviews, observations, or other empirical means.[432]

In this doctoral thesis, we use survey research to empirically validate our model. Therefore, we must first define our constructs empirically and then design a measurement instrument, a survey, to gather the quantitative data required by the empirical validation. This definition is presented after the following introduction to survey research.

Empirical Validation by Means of Survey Research

As an important measurement tools in applied social research,[433] survey research refers to a set of quantitative techniques to collect data and create statistics for empirical analysis.[434] Generally, survey research encompasses any measurement procedure that involves asking questions in a structured attempt to gather information about the characteristics, actions, perceptions, attitudes, or opinions of a large group, such as a group of individuals or organizations. The studied group is referred to as the survey

---

[431] Bhattacherjee (2012); Note the focus in Figure 5-1 is on the empirical level that is discussed in the following.

[432] Edwards, Bagozzi (2000)

[433] Trochim

[434] Fowler (2009); Tanur (1982)

population.[435] A survey can take many forms, such as an opinion survey for journalism, a marketing survey for product design, or in our case, a scientific survey for empirical research. In addition, the method employed to survey the participants can vary and may include a face-to-face interview, a written document, such as traditional mail or e-mail, a telephone interview, or an online questionnaire.[436]

Scientific surveys are important in at least three ways. First, a scientific survey is an empirical method that produces standardized information to quantitatively describe certain portions of the study population. The survey analysis is concerned with identifying the relationships between variables or with descriptively projecting findings from a predefined population.[437] Second, a scientific survey collects information by asking people predefined and structured questions, and their answers constitute data that can be analyzed empirically. Third, a scientific survey collects data from only a fraction of the study population. This so-called sample allows generalizations to the entire population. Therefore, the sample must be large enough to allow statistical analysis.[438]

In social and IS research, the survey is an important quantitative research methods.[439] Survey research is popular because of several inherent strengths compared with other research methods.[440] First, survey research is an excellent method to measure phenomena that cannot be observed directly, such as attitudes or preferences. Second, survey research facilitates the collection of data from a population that is too large to be observed directly, such as a large group of people distributed over a country. Third, survey research is preferred by certain respondents because this type of research allows them to answer conveniently without the intrusion of the researcher. Fourth, survey research is economical in cost and time. Fifth, a large sample gathered through survey research allows small effects to be analyzed, even when multiple variables are considered.[441] However, survey research has certain disadvantages.[442]

In addition to these general advantages and disadvantages of survey research, Pinsonneault et al. (1993) suggest four aspects that should be considered when selecting

---

[435] Tanur (1982)

[436] Fowler (2009)

[437] Glock (1967)

[438] Pinsonneault, Kraemer (1993)

[439] Trochim (2001)

[440] Palvia et al. (2004); to put this in perspective, the next frequently used research method is the design of conceptual frameworks and models with 11.6%.

[441] Bhattacherjee (2012)

[442] We discuss the disadvantages later in section 5.3 when we discuss the design of the survey.

survey research as a research method.[443] These four aspects apply all to the present research:

- *Survey research is appropriate when the central question of the research is 'What is happening?' and 'How is something happening?'* In the present thesis, the key reason to conduct survey research is to answer the research question 'How can the benefits of enterprise architecture management for an organization be explained and predicted?' The main goal is to understand and explain the how and why of EAM benefits.

- *Survey research is appropriate when controlling the independent and dependent variables is impossible or undesirable.* Controlling the variables in a laboratory setting is impossible for the research question at hand for two reasons. First, EAM success factors and the resulting benefits are practical phenomena that can only be observed in practice, not in a laboratory. Second, controlling for all potential endogenous effects in this research is neither desirable nor practically manageable.

- *Survey research is appropriate when a study of the phenomenon is desired in its natural setting.* In the present thesis, we study EAM success factors and EAM benefits perceived by individuals for their organization. Therefore, we must conduct this research in the natural organizational setting.

- *Survey research is appropriate when the studied phenomena occurred in the recent past or in the present.* EAM is a relatively young research area guided by recent developments in practice.[444] Therefore, a timely study of EAM in practice is required to achieve results relevant to the objectives of the present work.

Operationalizing the Revised A Priori Model

Having established that survey research is an appropriate research method to empirically validate our revised a priori model, we discuss how we operationalized the model to develop the survey instrument in the following.

Developing a validated measurement instrument, i.e., operationalizing the a priori model, is a critical step in empirically validating our a priori model. Boudreau et al.'s (2001) research findings suggest that "*the field has advanced in many areas, but, overall, it appears that a majority of published studies are still not sufficiently validating their*

---

[443] Pinsonneault, Kraemer (1993)

[444] Lankhorst et al. (2009); Op 't Land et al. (2009)

instruments."[445] To derive valid statistical conclusions about the phenomenon of interest, however, it is important to validate the empirical measurement instrument.[446]

Thus, our main objectives are to develop measurement items that are valid and reliable.[447] Both are required for an adequate measurement of the construct of interest, as represented by the analogy of shooting targets in Figure 5-2.

Figure 5-2 Comparison of Reliability and Validity

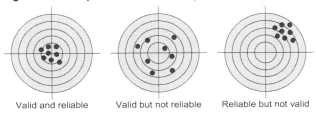

Valid and reliable   Valid but not reliable   Reliable but not valid

Source: Adapted from Bhattacherjee (2012)

Formally, reliability is the extent to which the measurement item of a construct is consistent or dependable. Reliability means that a measurement item provides consistency but not necessarily accuracy. Validity, also known as construct validity, is the extent to which a measurement item adequately reflects the underlying construct. With respect to the validity of the measurement procedures,[448] four types of validity can be differentiated.[449] *Convergent validity* is the degree to which a measurement item resembles the construct that the item measures. *Discriminant validity* is the degree to which a measurement item does not measure other constructs that the item is not intended to measure. *Content validity* is the extent to which a set of measurement items reflects the content domain of the construct that the item measures. *Face validity* is the extent to which a measurement item, 'on its face', seems to be a reasonable measure of the construct underlying the item.[450]

Consequently, it is important to rigorously validate the measurement instrument to operationalize our a priori model according to these four different types of validity. MacKenzie et al. (2011) suggests a ten step approach for developing IS measurement

---

[445] Boudreau et al. (2001)

[446] Straub (1989)

[447] The validity and reliability of a measurement item are also called "psychometric properties".

[448] Note that the validity of hypotheses testing procedures are not discussed here. We will come back to these in Chapter 6.

[449] Bhattacherjee (2012)

[450] Campbell, Fiske (1959)

instruments.[451] In the present thesis, we slightly adjust this approach because the design and implementation of the survey instrument are absent. Therefore, we have added an additional step: survey design. This approach is depicted in Figure 5-3. In the following, we describe these steps and provide a basic introduction. In the remaining sections of this chapter, we describe the implementation of these steps.

Figure 5-3 Overview of Measurement Instrument Development Approach

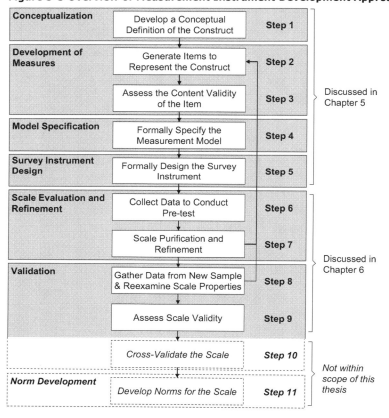

Source: Adapted from MacKenzie et al. (2011)

The first step is to *develop a conceptual definition of the construct*.[452] It is crucial to understand what is to be measured and to define the conceptual domain of the construct,

---

[451] This approach was choosen as it accommodates the development of both reflective and formative constructs. An introduction to the difference is given later in Section 5.2.1.

[452] See Section 5.2.1 for the detailed results of this step.

what the construct is intended to capture, and how the construct differs from other constructs. The construct and its theme must be unambiguously defined and consistent with prior research.[453] For the subsequent assessment of content validity, the construct should be as clear and concise as possible.[454]

The next step is to *generate items that represent the constructs*.[455] Here, the researcher can use a variety of sources, including the literature, deduction from theoretical definitions, previous research on the construct, and expert suggestions.[456] Existing measurement items should be used as much as possible.[457] To generate these construct items we adopt an approch as suggested by Recker (2008), which is detailed in the next section.[458]

Once the construct items have been identified, the next step is to *assess the content validity of the items*.[459] According to Straub et al. (2004), content validity is *"the degree to which items in an instrument reflect the content universe to which the instrument will be generalized."*[460] Thus, in this step, two questions must be answered: First, does the individual item represent an aspect of the content domain of the construct? Second, do the items as a set represent the overall content domain of the construct?

The fourth step is to *formally specify the measurement model* then.[461] The measurement model must describe the expected relationships between the indicators and the related construct or construct sub-dimensions that the indicators are intended to measure. In addition, this step defines the scale of the measurement item. Because the analysis of the model requires this step, we postpone discussing this step until the next chapter, in which we discuss it with the analysis of the data gathered through the survey.[462]

---

[453] MacKenzie (2003)

[454] Churchill (1979); Hinkin (1995)

[455] See Section 5.2.2 for the detailed results of this step.

[456] Churchill (1979); Haynes et al. (1995); Nunnally, Bernstein (1994)

[457] Boudreau et al. (2001); Straub (1989)

[458] Recker (2008)

[459] See Section 5.2.2 for the detailed results of this step.

[460] Straub et al. (2004)

[461] See Section 6.3 for the detailed results of this step.

[462] In this thesis, we have postponed this step and describe it in Chapter 6 as this step is required for the empirical validation of the model based on the survey data rather than for the instrument design and implementation.

After the model with all of the items has been formally specified, the next step is to *formally design the survey*.[463] This step is not included in MacKenzie's (2003) original approach. However, we introduced this step because logic requires it as the next stage before collecting pre-test data. In addition to the lack of rigorous measurement items, IS scholars have criticized the inadequate design and validation of IS survey instruments.[464] Adding this step as an explicit part of the approach improves the survey implementation.

When the survey instrument has been developed, the sixth step is to *collect data to conduct a pre-test*. It is important to determine the appropriate population sample to gather the correct sample data.

After the pre-test data are collected, the seventh step is *scale purification and refinement*.[465] This step includes an examination of the psychometric properties of the scale and an evaluation of the convergent, discriminant, and nomological validity. Consequently, problematic measurement items must be refined or eliminated.

After the scale has been refined, the eighth step is to *gather data from a new sample and reexamine the scale properties*. This step is required because items are often added, changed, or dropped in the previous steps, and new data are required to re-estimate the measurement model. In the present thesis, due to time and resource constraints, we conduct only two iterations of this process.[466]

The same constraints apply to the next step, *assessing the scale validity*.[467] This step reassesses the validity of the measurement instrument and measurement items in a manner similar to that of step seven.

The tenth step is to *cross-validate the scale*. This step validates the psychometric properties using a new sample, which should be a second population to which the measurement item is expected to relate. However, because of time and resource constraints, this step is not performed in the present thesis.[468]

---

[463] See Section 5.3 for the detailed results of this step.

[464] King, He (2005); Straub (1989)

[465] See Section 5.4 for the detailed results of this step.

[466] This second iteration is reported with the model analysis in Chapter 6.

[467] This second iteration is reported with the model analysis in Chapter 6.

[468] MacKenzie et al. (2011) points out that such practical limitations can prevent a complete conduction of his suggested steps. However they should be discussed in the limitations which can be found in Section 8.3.

Finally, the eleventh step is to *develop norms for the scale*. [469] This step aids the interpretation of the scores on the scale. An interpretation of the scores of the measurement items is only possible in relation to a frame of reference. Therefore, it is important to know, for example, something about the distribution of the scores in various populations.[470]

These last two steps are outside the scope of the present thesis. To complete these two steps, the study must be repeated. Due to time and resource constraints, this repetition should be part of future research.

In the following, we report on the execution of the steps outlined above to develop a validated measurement instrument for our EAM Benefit Realization Model.

5.2. Survey Instrument Preparation

Towards the operationalization of our a priori model, we first prepare the development of the survey instrument by conducting the first four steps of MacKenzie et al.'s (2011) approach.[471] First, we revisit the constructs of the a priori model and develop the conceptual construct definitions formally in this section. Then, we develop the measures for each of the constructs and finally we specify the measurement model formally.

5.2.1. Development of Conceptual Construct Definitions

As the first step in the operationalization of our a priori model, in this section, we conceptually define the construct. This step ensures that the target construct is precisely defined.[472] The lack of a proper definition can lead to problems in the validation of the measurement instrument by undermining construct validity, statistical conclusion validity, and internal validity.[473] Therefore, clear, concise, and unambiguous construct definitions are desired.[474] MacKenzie et al. (2011) suggest four factors that should be considered to generate good construct definitions, as presented below.[475]

The first step is to consider how the constructs have been used in prior research or by practitioners. The goal of such a literature review is thereby to identify previous terms and related constructs. The goal of interviewing experts is to identify further aspects or

---

[469] See for details on this step Chapter 7 in which the model is discussed in interpreted.

[470] Spector (1992)

[471] MacKenzie et al. (2011)

[472] Clark, Watson (1995)

[473] MacKenzie (2003)

[474] Churchill (1979); Hinkin (1995)

[475] MacKenzie et al. (2011)

attributes of the construct.[476] In this research, we have conducted this step through a literature review and semi-structured interviews. The results are used to formally define the constructs.[477]

The second step is to formally specify the construct, which includes defining the general property type of the focal construct[478] and the entity to which the construct applies.[479] The general property type to which the focal construct refers can be a thought, a feeling, a perception, an action, an outcome, or an intrinsic characteristic. The entity is the object to which the property type applies, which can be, for example, a person, an organization, or a process.[480] In this research, because we will ask EAM stakeholders about the perceived EAM success factors and benefits, the general property type for all constructs is a perception. Accordingly, the entity for all constructs is EAM stakeholders.[481]

The third step is to specify the theme of the construct, which involves describing the attributes and characteristics of the construct, specifying the stability of the construct, and determining the dimensionality of the construct. The attributes and characteristics should be a set of fundamental attributes and characteristics that are necessary and sufficient for the construct and unique attributes that are specific to the focal construct.[482] The stability must be determined over time, across situations, and across cases.[483] Furthermore, the dimensionality of the construct must be assessed by determining whether the focal construct possesses multiple sub-dimensions. The sub-dimensions of all multidimensional constructs must be defined with the same rigor as the focal construct. The multidimensionality of a construct can be determined by asking the following two questions:

- How distinctive are the essential characteristics?

- Would eliminating any of the characteristics restrict the domain of the construct?

If the elimination of an essential characteristic would not restrict the domain of the construct, then the construct is conceptually onedimensional. If the essential characteristic cannot be eliminated without restricting the conceptual domain, then the

---

[476] MacKenzie et al. (2011); Sartori

[477] See Chapter 3 and 4.

[478] Schwab (1980)

[479] Kozlowski, Klein (2000)

[480] MacKenzie et al. (2011)

[481] See Section 1.5 where we have specified the scope of this doctoral thesis.

[482] MacKenzie et al. (2011)

[483] Chaplin et al. (1988)

construct is multidimensional.[484] For multidimensional constructs, the relationship between the sub-dimensions must be determined[485] which can be achieved by asking the following questions:

- Are the sub-dimensions manifestations of the construct, or are they defining characteristics?

- Does the construct exist separately from the construct sub-dimensions, or is the construct a function of the sub-dimensions?

- Would a change in the construct necessarily result in a change of all sub-dimensions, or could a change result in a change of only one sub-dimension?

If the sub-dimensions are defining characteristics, the construct is a function of the sub-dimensions, and changing one sub-dimension results in a change of the construct, then the construct is a formative construct. In this case, the sub-dimensions of the formative construct are formative indicators. In contrast, if the sub-dimensions are a manifestation of the construct, the construct exists separately of its sub-dimensions, and a change in the construct results necessarily in a change of all sub-dimensions, then the construct is a reflective construct. In this case, the sub-dimensions of the reflective construct are reflective indicators.[486] Generally, the difference between formatively and reflectively defined constructs is the manner in which the sub-dimensions are linked to the construct.[487] For reflectively defined constructs, the sub-dimensions reflect the underlying construct. For formatively defined constructs, the sub-dimensions together form the underlying construct.[488] The literature agrees that the two are not inherently the same.[489] Therefore, the choice between them must be based on a clearly defined

---

[484] MacKenzie et al. (2011)

[485] Bollen, Lennox (1991); Jarvis et al. (2003a); Wong et al. (2008)

[486] MacKenzie et al. (2011)

[487] Edwards, Bagozzi (2000)

[488] Diamantopoulos (2010)

[489] E.g., Baxter (2009); Howell et al. (2007), (2008) A remark on the difference of the two: A reflectively measured construct is not necessarily the same construct when measured with formative indicators: The standard example is the construct "intoxication". It could be measured either reflectively by assessing the symptoms of feeling drunk, or it could be measured formatively by evaluating a person's intake of alcoholic drinks. Although both approaches may be viewed as measuring the same „intoxication", the first set of indicators captures "self-perceived intoxication", whereas the second indicators measures "actual (objective) intoxication." These are actually two different constructs.

focal construct.[490] An assessment of the multidimensionality and thus the formative or reflective definitions, according to the above questions, for the constructs of the revised model can be found in Appendix D.1.[491] An excerpt of the attributes and characteristics determined in this step can be found in the formal construct definitions in Table 5-1. The stability over time is for all constructs, i.e., the EAM success factor constructs and the EAM benefit constructs, the same. The constructs are not stable because a change in their characteristics accompanies a changing EAM maturity. With such a change in the maturity, the characteristics of the EAM success factors and the resulting EAM benefits are expected to change if the survey is conducted repeatedly over time.[492]

Finally, the fourth step is to define the construct in unambiguous terms and to write down the definition. The construct definitions should be clear and concise, should disallow multiple interpretations, should define the construct positively and without jargon and should not be tautological.[493]

The following Table 5-1 provides examples of construct definitions for the revised a priori model according to the steps described above. A complete list of definitions can be found in Appendix D.1. The results of the assessment whether the constructs are formative or reflective can be found in Appendix D.2.

Table 5-1 Sample Construct Definitions of the Revised A Priori Model

(Sub-)Construct Name	Construct Order	Definition	Internal Reference
EAM Product Quality			
(PQ1) As-Is Architecture Quality	1st	An EAM stakeholder's perceived extent to which all desirable information about the as-is architecture is provided to satisfy the organization's needs.	*see below*
(PQ1a) Timeliness	2nd	An EAM stakeholder's perceived extent to which all desirable information about the as-is architecture is provided timely.	(P1a)
(PQ1b) Completeness	2nd	An EAM stakeholder's perceived extent to which all desirable information about the as-is architecture is provided completely.	(P1b)
(PQ1c) Level of Detail	2nd	An EAM stakeholder's perceived extent to which all desirable information about the as-is architecture is provided in the right level of detail.	(P1c)
...	...	...	...

---

[490] Barki (2008); MacKenzie (2003)

[491] See Appendix D.1.

[492] Ross et al. (2009)

[493] MacKenzie et al. (2011)

5.2.2.   Development of Measures

After formally specifying the constructs, the next step is to define a set of measurement items that represents the constructs and its sub-dimensions. This set can then be used in the survey to obtain empirical data. To identify the measurement items, researchers can use a variety of sources, including literature reviews, deduction from theoretical definitions, previous research on the construct, and expert suggestions.[494] The goal of this step is to generate a set of measurement items that comprises all essential aspects of the construct while minimizing the extent to which the measurement item measures aspects outside the focal construct.[495] Therefore, the measurement items must be valid and reliable; a goal that is best achieved with an iterative design of valid and reliable measurement items that are crucial to any empirical research.[496] In the past, poor theory development and a lack of methodological rigor have led to mixed and inconclusive empirical research results.[497] Therefore, IS researchers have called for rigorously developed and validated domain-appropriate measurement instruments.[498]

In addition to ensuring the validity and reliability of measurement items, to conduct research using a sound set of measurement items, it is important to reuse existing measurement items and to determine the correct number of items. It is strongly suggested that existing measurement items should be relied upon as much as possible.[499] Reusing existing measurement items expedites the research,[500] and ensures the high quality of the measurement items because they have been previously validated and proven useful. Furthermore, the results can be compared with those of previous studies.[501] With respect to the number of measurement items, IS research suggests that one set of empirical indicators should be employed for each theoretical constructs because the use of a single measurement item may result in measurement error and may compromise content and construct validity.[502] However, too many measurement items for each construct may create a response-pattern bias.[503] Therefore, the number

---

[494] Churchill (1979); Haynes et al. (1995); Nunnally, Bernstein (1994)

[495] Diamantopoulos, Siguaw (2006)

[496] Flynn et al. (1990), Froehle, Roth (2004)

[497] Moore, Benbasat (1991); Straub (1989)

[498] E.g., Straub (1989)

[499] Bagozzi, Phillips (1982); Boudreau et al. (2001); Straub (1989)

[500] Danziger, Kraemer (1991)

[501] Ives Blake, Olson (1984); Straub (1989)

[502] Barki, Hartwick (1989), Nunnally, Bernstein (1994)

[503] Anastasi, Urbina (1996)

of measurement items per construct should allow adequate measurement of the construct domain while remaining as low as possible.[504]

Following this reuse principle, we conducted a literature review to identify established measurement items in IS research. To identify these items, we screened the tables of contents and abstracts of the eight AIS senior scholars' basket journals for relevant publications and searched scientific databases (ACM Digital Library, AIS Electronic Library, EBSCOhost Business Source Premier, IEEE Xplore, ScienceDirect, and SpringerLink) for quantitative studies that suggested relevant measurement items.[505] In addition, we searched the 'Survey Instruments in IS' database for measurement items that fit our research.[506] We gathered measurement items for nine of our twenty constructs. Based on this pre-existing foundation, the measurement items can be grouped into three categories according to the measurement definitions as suggested by Recker (2008).[507] First, for constructs for which measurement items exist, we must adjust the definitions and wording to the domain of interest in this research. Second, for perceptional constructs for which no measurement items exist, we must develop and validate new measurement items. Third, for simple, non-perceptual constructs, such as years of experience in EA, we must develop simple measurement items. In the following, we discuss the three different categories of measurement items.

Adoption of Measurement Items

The reuse of validated measurement items allows researchers to rely on previously proven measurement items. These measurement items improve research results while reducing the required research resources.[508] Bagozzi et al. (1982) recommend using pre-validated measurement items when an a priori theory exists and when these measurement items have clearly demonstrated validity and reliability in previous studies. Therefore, based on existing theory, we reuse nine such measurement items for the constructs of our revised a priori model. The nine measurement items adopted for this thesis have been previously used in empirical studies and have been proven valid and reliable.[509]

In each of these nine constructs, we slightly reworded the measurement items to adapt the items to the context of the present thesis. For the formative constructs, we selected

---

[504] Cronbach, Meehl (1955)

[505] Newsted et al. (1998)

[506] Newsted et al. (1998)

[507] Recker (2008)

[508] Lewis et al. (2005)

[509] The original definition of these constructs can be found in Appendix D.3.

the items with respect to the characteristics, i.e., the different sub-dimensions, of the definition so that every item reflects one characteristic. For the reflective constructs,[510] we followed the recommendation of Nunnally et al. (1994) and used three items as a measure per construct.[511] Furthermore, the definitions and wording of the measurement items were adapted to suit the present thesis. All items were operationalized using a seven-point Likert scale[512] with endpoints labeled 'strongly agree' and 'strongly disagree'.[513] Table 5-2 summarizes the adopted measurement items for the nine constructs.[514] In the following, we discuss the adoptions for each construct.

---

[510] These are in particular the constructs 'use' and 'satisfaction'

[511] Nunnally, Bernstein (1994)

[512] Lickert (1932)

[513] An exception is hereby the construct 'Extend of Centralization' that is operationalized with the end points 'decentralized along business lines' and 'centralized'.

[514] Note: The listed measurement items are the final items used in the survey that have been changed and reworded iteratively. Further adjustments have been done in the pre-testing phase of the survey. See for these changes Section 5.4.

Table 5-2 Adopted Measurement Items for the Revised A Priori Model

Construct	Adopted construct definition	No	Item	Adopted from
(PQ1) As-is architecture quality	An EAM stakeholder's perceived extent to which all desirable information about the as-is architecture is provided to satisfy the organization's needs.		Information provided by EAM about the as-is architecture is...	
		PQ1a	...always timely	Gable et al. (2008)
		PQ1b	...complete	Gable et al. (2008)
		PQ1c	...detailed	Gable et al. (2008)
		PQ1d	...easy to understand	Gable et al. (2008)
		PQ1e	...unavailable elsewhere	Gable et al. (2008)
(PQ2) To-be architecture quality	An EAM stakeholder's perceived extent to which all desirable information about the to-be architecture is provided to satisfy the organization's needs.		Information provided by EAM about the to-be architecture is...	
		PQ2a	...always timely	Gable et al. (2008)
		PQ2b	...complete	Gable et al. (2008)
		PQ2c	...detailed	Gable et al. (2008)
		PQ2d	...easy to understand	Gable et al. (2008)
		PQ2e	...unavailable elsewhere	Gable et al. (2008)
(PQ3) Roadmap quality	An EAM stakeholder's perceived extent to which all desirable information about the roadmap is provided to satisfy the organization's needs.		Information provided by EAM about the roadmap architecture is...	
		PQ3a	...always timely	Gable et al. (2008)
		PQ3b	...complete	Gable et al. (2008)
		PQ3c	...detailed	Gable et al. (2008)
		PQ3d	...easy to understand	Gable et al. (2008)
		PQ3e	...unavailable elsewhere	Gable et al. (2008)
(IQ2) Decision-making centralization	An EAM stakeholder's perceived extent to which a central decision-making has been defined.		How would you rate the extent of centralization for the respective decision-making in your company?	
		IQ2a	Capital budget	Boh et al. (2007)
		IQ2b	Operational process optimization and implementation	Boh et al. (2007)
		IQ2c	Application development projects prioritization and approval	Boh et al. (2007)
		IQ2d	IT development and implementation	Boh et al. (2007)
		IQ2e	Infrastructure planning and management	Boh et al. (2007)

Con-struct	Adopted construct definition	No	Item	Adopted from
		IQ2f	Enterprise Architecture definition and implementation	Boh et al. (2007)
		IQ2g	Compliance management	Boh et al. (2007)
(IQ7) EAM principles establishment	An EAM stakeholder's perceived extent to which EAM principles have been established.		We have effective EAM principles in place for our...	
		IQ7a	Business architecture	Boh et al. (2007)
		IQ7b	Application architecture	Boh et al. (2007)
		IQ7c	Technology architecture	Boh et al. (2007)
		IQ7d	Integration architecture	Boh et al. (2007)
		IQ7e	Data architecture	Boh et al. (2007)
(Use) EAM use	An EAM stakeholder's perceived extent to which EAM stakeholder intend to continue to engage in Enterprise Architecture Management.	Use1	If we remain with our approach to EAM, the EAM stakeholders' intention would be to continue to engage in EAM.	Bhattacherjee (2001); Recker (2008)
		Use2	In the future, I expect that the EAM stakeholder will continue to engage in EAM.	Bhattacherjee (2001); Recker (2008)
		Use3	EAM stakeholders prefer to continue to use our approach to EAM over other approaches to EAM.	Bhattacherjee (2001); Recker (2008)
		Use4	Regulatory requirements mandate the use of Enterprise Architecture in our organization.	Bhattacherjee (2001); Recker (2008)
(Sat) EAM satisfaction	An EAM stakeholder's perceived extent to which EAM stakeholder feels satisfied about their overall experience with the use of EAM.		EAM stakeholders feel...	
		Sat1	...contented about their overall experience with our approach to EAM.	Recker (2008); Spreng et al. (1996)
		Sat2	...satisfied about their overall experience with our approach to EAM.	Recker (2008); Spreng et al. (1996)
		Sat3	...delighted about their overall experience with our approach to EAM.	Recker (2008); Spreng et al. (1996)
(OB) Organizational benefits	An EAM stakeholder's perceived extent to which EAM yields organizational benefits.		Our EAM turns out to be a good instrument to...	
		OB1a	...integrate applications.	Foorthuis et al. (2010)
		OB1b	...integrate processes.	Foorthuis et al. (2010)
		OB1c	...standardize applications.	Foorthuis et al. (2010)
		OB1d	...standardize processes.	Foorthuis et al. (2010)
		OB1e	...consolidate applications.	Foorthuis et al. (2010)
		OB1f	...consolidate processes.	Foorthuis et al. (2010)

Con-struct	Adopted construct definition	No	Item	Adopted from
		OB1g	...control the complexity of the organization.	Foorthuis et al. (2010)
		OB1h	...increase the utilization of resources.	Foorthuis et al. (2010)
		OB1i	...reduce costs.	Foorthuis et al. (2010)
		OB1j	...increase revenue.	Foorthuis et al. (2010)
		OB2a	...accomplish enterprise-wide goals, instead of (possibly conflicting) local optimizations.	Foorthuis et al. (2010)
		OB2b	...achieve an optimal fit between IT and the business processes it supports.	Foorthuis et al. (2010)
		OB2c	...achieve an optimal fit between IT strategy and business strategy.	Foorthuis et al. (2010)
		OB2d	...effectively communicate among different stakeholders.	Foorthuis et al. (2010)
		OB2e	...achieve compliance to regulatory requirements	Foorthuis et al. (2010)
		OB3a	...identify and trigger required changes in the organization.	Foorthuis et al. (2010)
		OB3b	...enable the organization to respond to changes in the outside world in an agile fashion.	Foorthuis et al. (2010)
		OB3c	...enable innovation.	Foorthuis et al. (2010)
		OB3d	...cooperate with other organizations effectively and efficiently.	Foorthuis et al. (2010)
(PB) Project-related bene-fits	An EAM stakeholder's perceived extent to which EAM yields project-related benefits.		Our projects leveraging EAM turn out to...	
		PB1a	...meet their budget more often than projects that do not leverage EAM.	Foorthuis et al. (2010)
		PB1b	...meet their deadlines more often than projects that do not leverage EAM.	Foorthuis et al. (2010)
		PB1c	...mitigate risks better than projects that do not leverage EAM.	Foorthuis et al. (2010)
		PB1d	...be better equipped to deal with complexity than projects that do not leverage EAM.	Foorthuis et al. (2010)
		PB2a	...deliver the desired quality more often than projects that do not leverage EAM.	Foorthuis et al. (2010)
		PB2b	...deliver the desired functionality more often than projects that do not leverage EAM.	Foorthuis et al. (2010)
		PB3a	...be able to adjust their scope to changing requirements more easily than projects that do not leverage EAM.	Foorthuis et al. (2010)

The '*(PQ1) as-is architecture quality*' construct is measured using five measurement items adopted from the scale of Gable et al. (2008).[515] The original scale measures information quality in the context of the DMSM for ten different characteristics: importance, desirability, availability, usability, readability, accurateness, conciseness, timeliness, and uniqueness. Aligning these characteristics with our construct definition in the domain of EAM, we included five dimensions out of these ten in our measurement instrument: timeliness, completeness, level of detail, understandability, and uniqueness. Although the first three characteristics accord with the literature review and the expert interviews, we included two additional characteristics because we believe they are important in the context of EAM. First, the understandability characteristic accords with the need for simple communication in EAM, which we have included in the revised model in the '(SQ1) EAM communication' construct.[516] Similarly, we argue that the uniqueness characteristic holds true for the EAM context because providing information that is unavailable elsewhere is a key EAM proposition that creates value for the organization.

Similar to the definition of the construct '(PQ1) as-is architecture quality', we use the same measurement items for the construct '*(PQ2) to-be architecture quality*' and '*(PQ3) roadmap quality*'. As shown in the literature review and the expert interviews,[517] the desired characteristics of these constructs are similar for these three constructs. Consequently, we employ the same measurement items and relate them to a different object, namely the to-be architecture and the roadmap.

The construct '*(IQ2) Decision Making Centralization*' is measured using the three measurement items adopted from Boh et al. (2007). In their study, Boh et al. (2007) measure the extent of centralization for infrastructure planning and management, application development project prioritization and approval, and IT development and implementation.[518] Because their study is focused on IT aspects, we must extend the study to include business aspects. Therefore, we supplement the three existing measurement items with three aspects identified in the literature review and expert interviews.[519] We add measurement items in the same manner as for the existing IT aspects. The additional measurement items are capital budget, operational business process optimization and implementation, EAM definition and implementation, and compliance management.

---

[515] Gable et al. (2008)

[516] See the construct '(SQ1d) Simple and understandable communication' in Sections 3.3 and 4.2.

[517] See Sections 3.3 and 4.2.

[518] Boh et al. (2007)

[519] See Sections 3.3 and 4.2.

The construct '(IQ7) EAM principles establishment' is also adopted from Boh et al. (2007). Boh et al. (2007) measure the EAM principles, which they term EAM standards, with measurement items for the infrastructure architecture, the integration architecture, and the data architecture. Again, the business aspects are missing. Moreover, as identified in the literature review, a measurement item for the application architecture is missing. Therefore, we add these two measurement items, whose definition resembles that of the three existing ones. The resulting set of five measurement items accords with our literature review and expert interviews. Furthermore, these five measurement items accord with the EAM layering approach, as described by {Winter 2007 #365), which divides enterprise architecture into these five aspects.[520]

The measurement items for the '(USE) EAM use', or, more formally, the 'intention to use' construct, are adopted from Recker (2008) and Bhattacherjee (2001). We use four measurement items for this construct. Three measurement items measure different aspects of the intent to use: one item measures the current intent in relation to control over this decision, the second item measures future usage intentions, and the third measures intent in relation to alternatives. The fourth measurement item explicitly measures whether the use is mandatory.

For the construct '(SAT) EAM satisfaction', we use three measurement items adopted from Recker (2008) and Spreng et al. (1996). Originally developed for the domain of camcorder user satisfaction, the measurement instrument of Spreng et al. (1996) comprises the three semantic dimensions of satisfaction: contention, satisfaction, and delightedness. The measurement items used here resemble other adoptions in IS research,[521] but they are adapted to the domain of EAM.

The '(OB) organizational benefit' construct is mainly based on the work of Foorthuis et al. (2010).[522] We used their definition of EAM benefit measurement items and adopted the wording according to our definition of seven of the existing measurement items. Five further items that were identified in our literature review and expert interviews were not covered. For these measurement items, we created measurement items similar to existing ones. One item covered several different aspects, and we divided this measurement item into six different items in accordance with Nederhof's (1985) recommendation to avoid double-barreled items. Nederhof recommends that double-barreled items should be split into single-idea statements; if this is impossible, the

---

[520] As discussed in the Section 2.1, Winter, Fischer (2007) differentiates between the five architectural layers business, application, integration, technology, and data layer.

[521] E.g., Gable et al. (2008); Recker (2008)

[522] Foorthuis et al. (2010)

double-barreled items should be eliminated altogether.[523] However, in this case, it was possible to divide the measurement item into separate measurement items. A detailed overview of the adoptions, the introduced measurement items and a justification can be found in Appendix D.4.

Similarly, for the '(PB) project benefits' construct, we adopted six existing measurement items and introduced one new measurement item based on the measurement items of Foorthuis et al. (2010).[524]

Because certain measurement items discussed above are not simple adoptions but cover new characteristics that are unique to the present thesis, a detailed assessment of their validity is required. Therefore, in the next section, we validate these measurement items with the validation of the newly defined measurement items. This assessment accords with Petter et al. (2007), who recommend examining adopted measurement items that have been validated and used in previous research.[525]

Construction of Measurement Items

The measurement items for the nine constructs described in the previous sub-section are based on minor adoptions of existing measurement instruments. However, for the remaining thirteen constructs, no existing measurement item could be found in the literature. Therefore, in this section, we develop and validate measurement items for the remaining thirteen constructs.

Generally, measurement items should be developed in multiple stages that include validation steps during the creation phase rather than the application phase of the measurement items. Early validation is vital for the research results.[526] Furthermore, researchers have criticized as superficial the solely qualitative validation of measurement items prior to an empirical study.[527] Therefore, to develop measurement items for the constructs that are not covered in the literature, a multi-step procedure is required that generates valid and reliable measurement items and validates them quantitatively before the study is conducted. Here, content validity is a central indicator of quality measurement items. As a description of the extent to which a measurement item reflects a particular theoretical construct,[528] content validity is a necessary precondition to

---

[523] Nederhof (1985)

[524] Foorthuis et al. (2010)

[525] Petter et al. (2007)

[526] Flynn et al. (1990); Froehle, Roth (2004); Stratman, Roth (2002)

[527] Hinkin (1995)

[528] Kerlinger (1986)

establishing construct validity. Although a variety of methods have been proposed, most methods focus on defining measurement items for reflectively defined constructs.[529] These methods make assumptions about the direction of the relationship between the items. Therefore, the methods cannot be applied to formative constructs without adaptation.[530] Construct validity is particularly important for formative constructs because a lack of content validity is a particularly serious problem for these constructs.[531]

To address this problem, MacKenzie et al. (2011) recommend using the approach suggested by Hinkin et al. (1999) and illustrated by Yao et al. (2007) for formatively defined constructs.[532] This approach consists of two phases. First, the measurement items for each construct are generated. Second, content validity is checked for the developed measurement items. In contrast to reflective measurement items, further assessments of formative constructs with respect to reliability and other aspects of validity cannot be assessed before a comprehensive amount of data has been collected.[533] Therefore, the validation of the formative measure prior to the data analysis focuses only on content validity.

When generating the measurement items, it is important to develop a set of measurement items that is closely linked to the construct definition. As with formatively defined constructs, the measurement items determine the latent variable rather than vice versa, and the set of measurement items is inextricably linked to the construct definition. Therefore, a *"breadth of definition is extremely important to causal indicators"*[534] because if all facets of the construct are not considered, relevant indicators, and thus an essential part of the construct, will be excluded [535] Additionally, it is important to pay attention to the manner in which the items are written when defining the measurement items. Generally, the wording of the measurement items should be as simple and precise as possible. Ambiguous and unfamiliar terms should be clarified, and overly complicated syntax should be simple, specific and concise. Formulations that contain obvious social

---

[529] Diamantopoulos, Winklhofer (2001); Hinkin, Tracey (1999); Lawshe (1975); Schriesheim et al. (1993)

[530] MacKenzie et al. (2011); Schriesheim et al. (1993)

[531] Petter et al. (2007)

[532] Hinkin, Tracey (1999); MacKenzie et al. (2011); Yao et al. (2007)

[533] Petter et al. (2007).

[534] Nunnally, Bernstein (1994)

[535] Diamantopoulos, Winklhofer (2001)

desirability should be avoided.[536] When formulating the measurement items, double-barreled items should be avoided and split into single-idea statements. If splitting is impossible, the double-barreled items should be eliminated.[537]

Following these principles, we developed measurement items for each of the thirteen constructs. Again, all items are operationalized using a seven-point Likert scale.[538] As above, for these measurement items, the scale end points are labeled 'strongly agree' and 'strongly disagree'. Table 5-3 summarizes the developed measurement items for the thirteen constructs.[539]

[536] DeVellis (1991); Peterson (2000); Podsakoff et al. (2003); Spector (1992)

[537] Nederhof (1985)

[538] Lickert (1932)

[539] Note: The listed measurement items are the final items used in the survey that have been changed and reworded iteratively. Further adjustments have been done in the pre-testing phase of the survey. See for these changes Section 5.4.

Table 5-3 Defined Measurement Items for Revised A Priori Model

Construct	Construct definition	No	Item
(IQ1) EAM mandate definition	An EAM stakeholder's perceived extent to which the appointed scope of EAM has been defined.	IQ1a	Organizational entities and subsidiaries covered by EAM have been clearly specified.
		IQ1b	Our EAM takes care of both business and IT aspects.
		IQ1c	Our EAM has an organizational/ business focus rather than an IT focus.
		IQ1d	Our EAM is well aligned with other boundary functions (such as project portfolio management, strategic planning)
(IQ3) EAM governance formalization	An EAM stakeholder's perceived extent to which the EAM governance mechanisms are formalized.	IQ3a	We have well-defined approval processes to ensure project conformance to EAM principles.
		IQ3b	Internal directives require compliance with EAM principles for all projects.
		IQ3c	EAM principles are ignored and informal agreements are reached to handle certain situations.
		IQ3d	There are penalties for violating EAM principles.
		IQ3e	Waivers of EAM principles are often granted.
(IQ4) EAM framework availability	An EAM stakeholder's perceived extent to which EAM frameworks support EAM activities.	IQ4a	We have a standardized EAM framework in place.
		IQ4b	We employ elements of industry standards (e.g., TOGAF) to complement our own EAM framework.
		IQ4c	Our EAM framework is accepted by all EAM stakeholders.
(IQ5) EAM tool support availability	An EAM stakeholder's perceived extent to which EAM tool support supports EAM activities.	IQ5a	We have established software tool support for our EAM activities.
		IQ5b	We have software tools that provide access to a central repository.
		IQ5c	Our software tools for EAM are accepted among all relevant stakeholders.
(IQ6) EAM reference architectures availability	An EAM stakeholder's perceived extent to which EAM reference architectures support EAM activities	IQ6a	We have established EAM reference architectures.
		IQ6b	EAM reference architectures are used to guide the definition of our to-be architecture.
		IQ6c	We use EAM reference architectures without major adjustments.
(IQ8) EAM skills availability	An EAM stakeholder's perceived extent to which all desirable EAM skills are available to the organization.	IQ8a	We have job descriptions for EAM roles.
		IQ8b	EAM staff receives ongoing training.
		IQ8c	EAM staff has a high level of communication skills.
		IQ8d	EAM staff is well networked in the organization.
		IQ8e	EAM staff has a high level of EAM expert knowledge.
		IQ8f	EAM roles are clearly distinguished from other roles outside the EAM function (such as IT portfolio managers).
		IQ8g	EAM staff participates in a job rotation.

Construct	Description	Code	Item
(IQ9) EAM resources availability	An EAM stakeholder's perceived extent to which all desirable EAM resources are organization.	IQ9a	Our EAM function receives sufficient funding.
		IQ9b	Our EAM function has adequate staffing to support its needs.
		IQ9c	Our EAM function has sufficient time to complete its tasks.
(SQ1) EAM communication	An EAM stakeholder's perceived extent to which the communication of the EAM function fulfills the varying EAM stakeholders' needs.		*The EAM function communicates...*
		SQ1a	... with all stakeholder groups according to their needs.
		SQ1b	... successfully the value of EAM to all EAM stakeholders.
		SQ1c	... proactively with all stakeholder groups.
		SQ1d	... with all stakeholders always as simply and understandably as possible.
(SQ2) EAM top-management support	An EAM stakeholder's perceived extent to which the EAM function provides desired services to the management.	SQ2a	Projects are regularly checked for conformance with EAM principles.
		SQ2b	Top-management is involved in EAM decision-making.
		SQ2c	We regularly review our EAM principles.
		SQ2d	Top-management is briefed regarding review results.
		SQ2e	Top-management is actively involved in EAM planning.
		SQ2d	Top-management is involved in executing EAM decisions.
(SQ3) EAM project support	An EAM stakeholder's perceived extent to which the EAM function provides desired services to the projects.	SQ3a	Enterprise Architects consult implementation projects regarding architectural considerations.
		SQ3b	Enterprise Architects play an active role in implementation projects working actively on project teams.
		SQ3c	Enterprise Architects take an integrating role across projects.
(CA1) top-management commitment	An EAM stakeholder's perceived extent to which top management is engaged in EA.	CA1a	Top-level managers allocate adequate resources for EA.
		CA1b	EAM is of high importance to top-level managers.
		CA1c	Top-level managers allocate sufficient time for EA.
		CA1d	Top-level managers communicate the importance of EAM to the organization.
(CA2) EAM awareness	An EAM stakeholder's perceived extent to which the organization is aware of EAM.	CA2a	EAM stakeholders are aware of the EAM function.
		CA2b	EAM stakeholders understand the importance of EA.
		CA2c	EAM stakeholders who not work in the EAM function but are involved in EAM are frequently trained to better understand EA.
(CA3) EAM understanding	An EAM stakeholder's perceived extent to which a common EAM understanding has been established among all EAM stakeholders.	CA3a	Business and IT employees have a shared vision for EA.
		CA3b	Business and IT employees have a shared understanding of EA.
		CA3c	Our current business objectives are in line with our approach to EAM.

Testing Content Validity of Measurement Items

Next, these measurement items are assessed for content validity. Content validity is the *"degree to which items in an instrument reflect the content universe to which the instrument will be generalized."*[540] To test for content validity, we employ the approach suggested by Hinkin et al. (1999). In this approach, a matrix is constructed in which the different construct definitions are listed on one axis and the measurement items are listed on the other axis (see Table 5-4). By means of this matrix, probands rate the degree to which each item reflects the construct definition using a Likert scale with 1 being 'not at all' and 5 being 'completely'. The results are used to conduct a one-way repeated ANOVA (analysis of variance)[541] to assess whether the rating of one measurement item for one construct differs from the rating for the other constructs. If the F-statistic of this test is significant, the mean rating for the measurement item on the hypothesized construct can be compared with the mean ratings of all other constructs. If the mean rating for the measurement item on the hypothesized construct is higher than the others, then content validity can be assumed.[542]

To conduct this assessment, we asked eight master's students who attended a course in enterprise architecture to conduct the rating toward the end of the semester. In this approach, when selecting raters, scholars argue for the importance of ensuring sufficient intellectual ability or a conceptual understanding of the measurement items and construct definitions. For example, Anderson (1991) recommend selecting raters from the main population of interest. However, Hinkin (1995) and Schriesheim et al. (1993) argue that college students must only understand the task.[543] Due to the resource constraints of this thesis, we chose master's students to conduct the assessment. We argue that the choice of master's students who have a background in EAM ensures the intellectual ability to rate the measurement items and constructs.

When rating the newly developed measurement items, we included the adopted items discussed in the previous section. We included all measurement items from all formatively defined constructs to ensure good content validity throughout the study. However, this approach resulted in a large matrix with a high number of measurement items and construct definitions.[544] Therefore, we split the raters into two groups. The

---

[540] Straub et al. (2004)

[541] Note: It is essential to use a one-way ANOVA as each rater makes multiple ratings for each item making an adjustment to the error term. MacKenzie et al. (2011)

[542] Hinkin, Tracey (1999); Yao et al. (2007)

[543] Anderson, Gerbing (1991); Hinkin (1995); Schriesheim et al. (1993)

[544] Concretely, 113 measurement items and 20 construct definitions.

first group rated the fit of the measurement items to the first ten construct definitions. The second group rated the fit to the remaining ten construct definitions. This procedure avoided overburdening the raters. Based on psychological-judgment research, Schriesheim et al. (1993) argue that raters can distinguish a maximum of eight to ten different aspects at a time.[545]

Table 5-4 Example of Item Rating Matrix

	Construct definitions			
	An EAM stakeholder's perceived extent to which all desirable information about the as-is architecture is provided to satisfy the organization's needs.	An EAM stakeholder's perceived extent to which all desirable information about the to-be architecture is provided to satisfy the organization's needs.	An EAM stakeholder's perceived extent to which all desirable information about the roadmap is provided to satisfy the organization's needs.	...
Information provided by the EAM function about the ASIS architecture is in a form that is readily usable.	3	2	1	...
Information provided by the EAM function about the ASIS architecture is in a form that seems to be exactly what is needed.	5	1	1	...
...	...	...	...	...

The results of this assessment suggest good content validity for the measurement items. All F-statistics are between 7.2 and 38.1, well above the critical f of 1.76 for all measurement items. For all conducted ANOVAs, the p-value is smaller than 0.05, which suggests statistical significance. In addition, the highest mean for all measurement items always correlates with the hypothesized construct that the measurement item is intended to measure. The detailed results of this assessment can be found in Appendix D.5. Due to these positive results, we decided to proceed with all measurement items. However,

---

[545] Schriesheim et al. (1993)

these results should be interpreted only as a first indicator of content validity and should be accepted with caution because of the small sample of eight participants.

Operationalization of All Other Scales

Thus far, we have adopted and developed measurement items to operationalize the constructs of our model. In addition to the theoretical constructs of the model, the survey should gather data on organizational and personal demographics as contextual factors. Because these factors are expected to be moderating or control variables, the factors were developed without a full-scale measurement development approach, as in the previous section. Instead, after the factors were implemented in the survey instrument, these measurement items were evaluated for face validity in the survey pilot phase.[546]

The first measurement item for the organizational demographics is the *organizational perspective* from which the survey is answered. Based on their differing perspectives on the organization, the respondents are differentiated into those who answer based on an overall perspective and those who answer for part of the organization, such as a single business unit or geography.

Next, to capture the organization's demographics, we incorporated nine measurement items. First, a measurement item measures the *organization type*, that is, whether the organization is publicly traded, privately held, non-profit, or a government organization. Second, the industry is determined with a measurement item based on seventeen different categories adopted from the ISIC Rev. 4.[547] Next, in seven text fields, information is requested on the location of the *organization's headquarters*, the *number of countries* in which the organization is present, the *number of employees*, the *number of employees working under EAM*, the *total revenue and IT spending* in 2010, and for the *number of years the organization has used EAM*.

The approach to EAM might be determined by the business strategy that the organization is pursuing. Therefore, we integrate a measurement item that measures the

---

[546] Note: The listed measurement items are the final items used in the survey that have been changed and reworded iteratively. Further adjustments have been done in the pre-testing phase of the survey. See for these changes Section 5.4.

[547] UN ISIC Rev.4 Standard (2008). The detailed categories are: Aerospace & Defence; Automotive & Assembly; Basic Materials; Banking; Chemicals; Consultancy; Consumer Goods; Electronics & Semiconductors; Energy; Healthcaren; Information Technology; Insurance; Private Equity; Public Services; Retail & Wholesale; Telecom & Media; Travel; Transport & Logistics

organization's strategy archetype. The archetypes are categorized according to cost, quality, innovation and niche leadership.[548]

Next, the survey incorporates a measurement item for personal demographics, which is a question about the *participant's primary job*. This question is asked to determine whether the correct target group has been addressed by the survey. An additional measurement item asks the participants for the number of years they have had *experience with EAM*. Another measurement item gathers data about the *time a participant spends on projects*. This item seeks to measure the participant's experience with implementation projects rather than activities in the line function of the organization.

Three additional measurement items gather information about the participant's position in the organization. First, the *level of seniority* is measured with a seven-point Likert scale with the endpoints 'operational' and 'executive' to measure whether the participant is employed on a CxO / top-management level or an operational level. Second, the participant's *organizational positioning* and the participant's *orientation between business and IT* is measured separately with two measurement items that use a seven-point Likert scale with the endpoints 'IT-oriented' and 'business-oriented'.

The respective measurement items can be found in the survey instrument in Appendix D.7.

5.3. Survey Instrument Development

Once the constructs are defined and the related measurement items are developed, the next step is to implement the measurement items in a Web-based survey. In this section, we describe the rationale for selecting a Web-based survey and detail the survey's implementation.

Rational for Choosing a Web-based Survey

With the spread of the Internet and e-mail, new distribution channels for surveys have emerged.[549] Rather than mailed, paper-based surveys, Web-based surveys are increasingly employed for survey research.[550] Web-based surveys obtain the same survey-content results as traditional surveys with faster distribution and response

---

[548] Dess, Davis (1984); Porter (1980)

[549] Fricker, Schonlau (2002)

[550] Lazar, Preece (1999)

cycles.[551] Furthermore, Web-based surveys are efficient in terms of the time, cost, and the effort required to conduct an electronic survey.[552]

Table 5-5 provides an overview of the differences in terms of these properties for mail-, fax-, and Web-based surveys.[553] The convenience discussed above can be observed in this table, in which Web-based surveys show key advantages in speed, return cost, labor, and variable cost compared with paper-based surveys. However, mail-based surveys have advantages in achievable coverage and required expertise. Fax-based surveys score between paper-based and Web-based surveys in all dimensions. However, fax surveys are particularly good at identifying incorrect addresses.

Table 5-5 Comparison of Mail, Fax, and Web-based Surveys

Factor	Mail	Fax	Web-based
Coverage	High	Low	Low
Speed	Low	High	High
Return Cost	Preaddressed/Prestamped	800 return fax number	No cost to the envelope
Incentives	Cash/Non-cash incentives can be incentives	Coupons may be included	Coupons may be included
Wrong address	Low	Low	High
Labor needed	High	Medium	Low
Expertise to conduct	Low	Medium	High
Variable Cost / each survey	About $ 1.00	About $ 0.50	No cost

Source: Adapted from Cobanoglu et al. (2001)

In addition to the advantages of Web-based surveys over mail surveys, certain disadvantages exist, which are discussed below. Table 5-6 compares the advantages of Web-based surveys and traditional mailed surveys.

The most obvious difference between Web-based and mailed surveys is the potential risk of response bias and coverage errors.[554] Because Web-based surveys require participants to have computer literacy and Internet access, coverage errors can occur when parts of the population have no Internet access and therefore are not covered by the survey. Further, a response bias can occur when parts of the population have Internet access but are not familiar with the technology used to complete the survey.[555] However, this response bias occurs only with populations with no Internet access or low Internet literacy, which is not the case for the present thesis. Because we focus in this

---

[551] Taylor (2000); Yun, Trumbo (2000)

[552] Couper, Traugott (2001); Wyatt (2000)

[553] Perkins (2004)

[554] Cole (2005)

[555] Wade, Parent (2001)

thesis on EAM stakeholders in large organizations, the target population of this research can be assumed to have a high educational level and the required technological competence. In contrast, mail surveys are more accessible to groups with limited financial resources, certain racial and ethnic minorities, individuals of lower education, older age groups, or others who may be underrepresented because they lack computer or internet access. It can be assumed that our target population does not include these groups.

Table 5-6 Overview of Web-based and Mailed Surveys

Strengths of Web-based surveys	Strengths of mailed surveys
The sampling instrument is available 24-7 at a location convenient to the respondent	Computer literacy by the participants is not required
Less time required for delivery of the instrument to participants, the administrator's receipt of responses, data entry and analysis and feedback	Fewer concerns about preservation of confidentiality than when a Web-based instrument is used
The Web-based instrument allows inclusion of text, images, and sound	The greater control that can be exercised over the administration of non-electronic instruments in a classroom and the correspondingly higher rate of completed responses
Direct and accurate electronic transmission (coding and analysis) of quantitative and qualitative data;	Some individuals in a sample may not have access to the hardware and software required to complete a Web-based instrument
Potential for customized feedback, including survey results, supplied directly to the respondent, and based on response content	A non-electronic instrument is generally more accessible to groups with limited financial resources, some racial and ethnic minorities, individuals of lower education, older age groups, or others who may be underrepresented because they lack computer or internet access

Source: Based on Perkins (2004)

The greater control that can be exercised over the administration of non-electronic instruments in a classroom may increase the rate of completed responses. However, this control is not feasible for the desired target population because the individuals are too remotely distributed and may not have the time to participate in a classroom experiment. Furthermore, to overcome confidentiality concerns, our Web-based survey allows participants to remain completely anonymous and to skip any question. In addition, our Web-based survey provides confidentiality agreements.

Consequently, Web-based surveys provide significantly more advantages in the context of this thesis than traditional mail surveys. Therefore, we decided to conduct the survey research in this thesis using a Web-based survey. This decision accords with the findings of Kaplowitz et al. (2004) who recommend the use of a Web-based survey for a population in which every member has Internet access because a Web-based survey achieves results comparable to those of a traditional mail survey while providing significant advantages.[556]

Designing the Web-based Survey

Research on self-administered surveys suggests that the instrument's design is highly important if unbiased answers are to be obtained from the respondents.[557] Therefore, in the following section, we describe how we carefully designed the survey's technological implementation, the implementation of missing technical capabilities, and formal and content-related aspects.

The Web-based survey instrument was *technologically implemented* using the survey provider Survey Monkey.[558] We chose this survey provider after careful consideration of different providers[559] and options to implement our survey because Survey Monkey seemed to fulfill all of our requirements while providing good reliability, performance, and quality for an acceptable price. Survey Monkey enabled us to implement the survey with all required features with reasonable effort while providing global accessibility for the target population, good service levels in terms of availability, performance, support, and high usability for the survey participants and administrators, and state-of-the art surveying capabilities. Furthermore, Andrews et al. (2003) recommends a set of additional quality criteria for the implementation of a Web-based survey. The assessment of our survey implementation can be found in Table 5-7.[560] With respect to these quality criteria, we were able to fulfill thirteen out of fifteen criteria by implementing our survey with Survey Monkey. Only the capability to provide links to definitions and to track the sources of participants was lacking but required for the present thesis.[561] To compensate for these deficiencies, we implemented these capabilities in addition to those available through Survey Monkey, as described below.

---

[556] Kaplowitz et al. (2004)

[557] Schwarz (1995); Schwarz et al. (1991)

[558] http://www.surveymonkey.net/home/

[559] Wright (2005) In particular Active Websurvey, Apian Software, Create Survey, EZSurvey, FormSite, HostedSurvey, InfoPoll, InstantSurvey, KeySurvey, Perseus, PollPro, Quask, Ridgecrest, SumQuest, SuperSurvey, SurveyCrafter, SurveyMonkey, SurveySite, WebSurveyor, and Zoomerang

[560] Andrews et al. (2003)

[561] Preece. J. et al. (2002); Yun, Trumbo (2000)

Table 5-7 Survey Implementation Quality Criteria

Quality criteria	Reference	Addressed in this Thesis
Supports multiple platforms and browsers/e-mail clients	Yun et al. (2000)	**Yes.** Survey Monkey is compatible with common operating systems (tested for Windows, Linux, MacOS) and browsers (tested for Firefox, Opera, Internet Explorer, Chrome, Safari)
Controls for browser settings	Yun et al. (2000)	**Yes.** Survey Monkey allows participants with activated cookies and without. All other browser settings have no impact on the survey
Detects multiple submissions automatically	Yun et al. (2000)	**Yes.** Survey Monkey allows each participant to participate only once by setting cookies
Presents questions in a logical or adaptive manner, for example, provides control of when and how questions are displayed	Kehoe et al. (1996); Norman et al. (2001)	**Yes.** Survey Monkey allows adaptive questioning; however, adaptive questioning was not desirable or required for the present thesis
Allows saving responses before completion	Smith (1997)	**Yes.** Survey Monkey saves each response and does not require the submission of intermediate results
Collects open-ended or quantified-option responses	Bachmann et al. (1996); Kiesler et al. (1986); Loke et al. (1995); Schaefer et al. (1998); Yun et al. (2000)	**Yes.** Survey Monkey allows various question types, including open-ended questions. For each section, an open-ended question was included asking the participant for comments on previous answers
Provides automatic feedback with completion	Smith (1997)	**Yes.** After completion of the survey with Survey Monkey, final remarks are presented to the participant
Uses paper questionnaire design principles	Dillman (2000); Oppenheim (1992); Preece. J. et al. (2002); Witmer et al. (1999)	**Yes.** Survey Monkey allows surveys to be designed similar to paper-based surveys. When designing the survey, we considered these principles
Provides automatic transfer of responses to a database	Kehoe et al. (1996); McCoy et al. (2001) Smith (1997)	**Yes.** Survey Monkey stores all responses in a central database that can be downloaded to a local computer in various formats, including Excel and SPSS
Prevents survey alteration	Witmer et al. (1999)	**Yes.** Survey Monkey allows the survey designer to set certain limitations. Participants cannot change the survey
Provides response control and economical displays	Preece. J. et al. (2002); Stanton (1998)	**Yes.** Survey Monkey adjusts the display economically according to the browser. Response control can be activated where required
Provides for links to definitions, menus, button and check box options, animation, sound, graphics options, and so forth	Preece. J. et al. (2002); Yun et al. (2000)	**No.** Survey Monkey allows no incorporation of additional websites with definitions; however, we included at the top of each page an overview of the terms used on the website, including definitions

Quality criteria	Reference	Addressed in this Thesis
Does not require familiarity with survey presentation software	Sheehan et al. (1999)	**Yes.** Survey Monkey can be used with basic Internet experience. No additional knowledge is required
Displays appear quickly to participant	Couper et al. (2001)	**Yes.** Survey Monkey's performance was tested and judged reliable and sufficiently fast
Tracks response source of response failure	Paolo et al. (2000)	**Partly.** Survey Monkey provides only limited tracking of response sources (e.g., only if invitations are sent by Survey Monkey). Because the tracking capability was insufficient for this thesis, we programmed our own tracking

Source: Adapted from Andrews et al. (2003)

Because we were unable to track the sources of the respondents or to provide an overview of the survey's general access statistics, we *compensated for* Survey Monkey's missing technical capabilities with a simple website that provided an access point to the survey. We desired tracking capability for the sources of the respondents because we distributed the survey over different channels and wanted to analyze the response rate per channel. Additionally, we wanted more general, near-real time access statistics to observe how effectively our survey invitations enabled us to respond quickly to participants, e.g., to follow up on incomplete surveys. Therefore, we programmed an entry website to provide the required tracking and analytic capabilities. This website collected the required data and forwarded the participant directly to our survey on Survey Monkey. The access website was a simple PHP script analyzing the referring URL. The script determines the URL for a referral, transferred the source information to Survey Monkey as an identifier, and tracked the referral with Google Analytics for statistical purposes. People accessing the website without a referral received a prompt for a password and contact details to confirm the password. This practice ensured that people who randomly accessed the website, e.g., by finding the site through a search engine, could be identified. However, if a referral was included in the URL, the participant is immediately forwarded to the survey. Screenshots of the website, including and excluding referrals, can be found in Appendix D.6.

With respect to *formal and content-related aspects*, we considered various guidelines and principles. When forwarded to the survey, a prospective participant first encountered a motivational welcome screen that provided the purpose of this research, an estimate of the time required to participate, the expected participation benefits, and the confidentiality agreement.[562] Additionally, the prospective participant received general instructions for participating in the survey, such as how and from what perspective to

---

[562] Dillman et al. (1999)

answer the questions. In addition, the prospective participant could determine the reward for participating in the survey. As an incentive to participate, each participant could choose to receive the full study report and an individual benchmark in which their answers were compared to those of their peers in the industry.

After the survey officially began, it was divided into ten separate webpages. For each dimension of the model, one website displayed the related questions.[563] Then, after all sections were completed, the survey closed by thanking the participant and asking for references to potential new participants. The final survey implementation can be found in a print-friendly version in Appendix D.7. When designing the survey, we considered various design recommendations discussed in the literature. All questions were designed to be fully visible, easily comprehensive, and easily answerable, in a manner similar to how the questions would be presented in a paper-based survey.[564] Specific instructions were provided for each question.[565] All questions were formulated as clearly as possible to avoid leading questions, social desirability, and negative wording.[566] Further, for each domain-specific term, a definition was presented at the beginning of each section to avoid ambiguity. Clarity was ensured by reviewing each question in the first pilot survey line by line with the pilot participants. Clear, seven-point Likert scales were presented with a description of the endpoints.[567] No questions were compulsory, and questions could easily be skipped. Participants were able to move forward and backward in the survey.[568]

5.4. Survey Instrument Testing

By pre-testing and piloting, a researcher can improve a survey significantly before the study is conducted, which leads to improved research results. Therefore, in this section, we test the implemented survey before presenting the survey to the sample population. In addition to the lack of rigorous measurement items, the inadequate testing and

---

[563] There were eight sections / distinct Web-pages for the dimensions of the model being EAM product quality, EAM infrastructure quality, EAM service delivery quality, EAM cultural aspects, use and satisfaction and finally EAM benefits.

[564] Dillman et al. (2010); Dillman et al. (1999)

[565] Dillman et al. (1999)

[566] Hinkin (1995); Roberts et al. (1993)

[567] Garland (1990)

[568] Dillman et al. (1999)

validation of survey instruments in IS research has been criticized.[569] The pre-testing and piloting has three emphases:

1. the usability of the survey layout and user interface,
2. the intelligibility of the questions, and
3. the validity and reliability of the survey instrument.[570]

In the present doctoral thesis, we tested the survey instrument in an iterative, two-step approach. First, we pre-tested the survey instrument in face-to-face interviews. Next, we conducted a small pilot test. The results of each of these iterations were used to improve the survey.

Pre-testing the Survey Instrument

Before conducting a pilot test with a small sample of the target population, we pre-tested the survey in a face-to-face setting to identify any difficulties that may not be apparent by reading the survey.[571] The pre-test objectives were to assess the face validity and further improve the content validity; that is, to discuss whether the individual item represents the desired content domain of the construct and whether the item set collectively represents the entire content domain of the construct.

We pre-tested the survey instrument with fifteen pre-test participants. Of these fifteen participants, five were EAM experts who were familiar with the model from the expert interviews, five were EAM experts who were not familiar with the model and five participants had no specific EAM knowledge but were familiar with information systems. This approach, using different levels of expertise, allowed us to ensure that the developed measurement items were understood by a diverse population of interest.[572]

During the pre-test, the participants were provided with the Web-based survey, and a researcher observed them answering the questions. The researcher took notes for immediate feedback. After answering each question, the participant and the researcher discussed how each question could be improved in terms of wording, item selection, and item completeness to increase content validity. After discussing each question, the researcher asked the participant for additional feedback on the survey's layout and structure. Furthermore, the participant and the researcher discussed the instructions and definitions. This procedure aimed to establish face validity.

---

[569] King, He (2005); Straub (1989)

[570] Jr. Scornavacca et al. (2004)

[571] Boudreau et al. (2001)

[572] Anderson, Gerbing (1991)

Table 5-8 Overview the Pre-test Participants

Pre-Tester ID	Model known?	Years of EAM experience	Position in the organization
Pre-Tester 1	Yes	25	Senior EAM consultant
Pre-Tester 2	Yes	16	Senior EAM consultant
Pre-Tester 3	Yes	7	Senior EAM consultant
Pre-Tester 4	Yes	13	Senior EAM consultant
Pre-Tester 5	Yes	16	Senior EAM consultant
Pre-Tester 6	No	11	Senior EAM consultant
Pre-Tester 7	No	23	Senior EAM consultant
Pre-Tester 8	No	27	Senior EAM consultant
Pre-Tester 9	No	9	Senior EAM consultant
Pre-Tester 10	No	16	Head of EA
Pre-Tester 11	No	N/A	IS Academic
Pre-Tester 12	No	N/A	IS Academic
Pre-Tester 13	No	N/A	IS Academic
Pre-Tester 14	No	N/A	IS Academic
Pre-Tester 15	No	N/A	IS Academic

The pre-test resulted in changes in the wording of the items and definitions, layout improvements to improve readability, and changes in order. After each pre-test, the resulting changes were incorporated into the survey to enable the next pre-tester to provide feedback on the revised survey instrument.

Piloting the Survey Instrument

After the pre-tests, we conducted a pilot test. A pilot test releases the survey to a small sample of the target population that has characteristics close to those of the desired sample.[573] We released the survey over the Internet to a group of twelve pilot testers. These testers were mainly EAM stakeholders who were personally known to the authors. Of the twelve invited pilot testers, 50% participated in the test. The objective of this test was to improve the survey's face and content validity. However, this pilot test was not conducted with the participants under observation. Rather, the researcher provided no support in the survey environment. In this pilot, we collected feedback on the survey's understandability and usability by means of feedback text fields that were incorporated into each survey webpage. The participants were told that they were participating in a pilot survey and were instructed to provide feedback in the additional text boxes placed in the survey masks. The demographics of the participants can be found in Table 5-9.

---

[573] Attewell, Rule (1991)

Table 5-9 Overview of Pilot-test Participants

Pre-Tester ID	Industry	Position in the organization	Partici-pated?
Pilot-Tester 1	Retail	Head of EA	Yes
Pilot-Tester 2	Healthcare	Head of EA	No
Pilot-Tester 3	Public Sector	Head of EA	Yes
Pilot-Tester 4	Telecommunication	Head of EA	No
Pilot-Tester 5	Healthcare	Head of EA	No
Pilot-Tester 6	Telecommunication	Head of EA	No
Pilot-Tester 7	Banking	Head of EA	Yes
Pilot-Tester 8	Banking	CIO	No
Pilot-Tester 9	Banking	Head of EA	Yes
Pilot-Tester 10	Banking	Enterprise Architect	No
Pilot-Tester 11	Healthcare	CIO	Yes
Pilot-Tester 12	Logistics	Enterprise Architect	Yes

We used the results of the pilot phase to further establish face and content validity. Because most measures in the survey are formatively defined, traditional measures, such as Cronbach's alpha, are not appropriate to measure validity due to the limited explanatory power of traditional measures in this context.[574] Based on the pilot-test feedback, we slightly adjusted the survey.[575] The results suggested that the overall performance of the Web-based survey seemed stable, and the survey provider, Survey Monkey, collected and reported all data without difficulties.

5.5. Survey Instrument Administration

Because the pre-test and pilot test can be considered successful, in September 2011, we released the adjusted survey for data collection. To gather conclusive data, the survey must be released to an eligible sample of the target population and a sufficiently representative survey sample, i.e., an adequate response rate, must be ensured.[576]

In this section, we discuss the desired target population, the required sample size, and an appropriate sampling procedure and contact strategy to gather conclusive data.

---

[574] Cenfetelli, Bassellier (2009)

[575] The changes were mainly a rewording the measurement items and changing the layout and structure. For example, the question for the e-mail address was put from the last to the first page to be ableto follow-up on participants who did not complete the survey.

[576] Fan, Yan (2010)

Determining the Target Population and the Required Sample Size

To gather conclusive data, before releasing the survey instrument, the first step is to identify the relevant target population. With respect to the unit of analysis, the target population is those people who are most knowledgeable about the studied phenomenon.[577] In the present thesis, the unit of analysis is EAM stakeholders who are knowledgeable about the benefits of EAM to their organization. Therefore, potential survey participants should have EAM experience and should have observed how benefits proliferate over time.[578]

This target population is the basis for a sample of sufficient size to allow rigorous and conclusive statistical testing. In true random sampling, basic statistics says that the larger the sample, the more accurate the estimates.[579] Therefore, a large sample is desirable. The size of the sample is ideally determined by four factors: (1) an acceptable level of sampling error, (2) the population size, (3) the variation of the population with respect to the characteristics of interest, and (4) the smallest subgroup in the sample that is required to calculate estimates.[580] Based on these factors, various approaches are suggested to determine the appropriate sample size.[581] However, in research practice, insufficient information about the sample population impedes the calculation of the sample size based on these approaches.

Researchers have suggested various arguments and guidelines to determine the required sample size when information about the researched population is insufficient. For example, Guadagnoli et al. (1988) suggest a minimum sample size of 150 to calculate accurate factor-analysis results given a high internal reliability of the measurement items. However, these fixed sample size recommendations do not consider the complexity of the tested model. Therefore, item-to-sample ratios aim to include the complexity of the model. The recommended item-to-sample ratios generally range from 1:5 to 1:10.[582]

However, these ratios are controversial. For instance, some IS scholars argue that in a Partial Least Square (PLS) analysis,[583] smaller sample sizes determined with item-to-

---

[577] Huber, Power (1985)

[578] See Section 1.5.

[579] Goodhue et al. (2006), (2012)

[580] Salant, Dillman (1994)

[581] E.g., Cohen (1992); Krejjcie (1970)

[582] E.g., Barclay et al. (1995); Chin (1998); Chin et al. (2003); Gefen et al. (2000)

[583] PLS is a analysis technique to test empirical models. We introduce this technique in Section 6.1 in detail.

sample ratios are appropriate, in contrast to techniques such as LISREL or regression analysis.[584] Recent research shows that these arguments are wrong. Based on Monte Carlo simulations, Goodhue et al. (2012) find that PLS analysis has no advantage over other techniques for abnormal data or small sample sizes. Therefore, to determine the minimum sample size required to obtain adequate power, they recommend determining the sample size based on the approach of Cohen (1988), which considers the four factors discussed above and does not rely on item-to-sample ratios for PLS analysis.[585] Furthermore, Goodhue et al. (2012) suggest that none of the techniques demonstrate excessive false positives with smaller sample sizes and that PLS analysis has the least number of false positives compared with other techniques. However, non-significant relationships might not be detected using small sample sizes. Consequently, given that small sample sizes and hypothesized paths are not statistically significant, Goodhue et al. (2012) recommend further testing with larger sample sizes.[586]

In this research, we cannot employ Cohen's approach due to a lack of information about the population's characteristics. Therefore, the best estimates for the sample size can be made with a heuristic based on the item-to-sample ratios. For the formative constructs and PLS analysis, which is used to test our research model and discussed in the following chapter, scholars recommend a minimum sample size of 5 to 10 times the number of predictors in the most complex relationship.[587] In the present thesis, the most complex predictors each have 7 predictors, which indicates a minimum sample size of 70.[588] However, given Goodhue et al. (2012), the research results must be interpreted carefully.

Defining the Sampling Procedure and Contact Strategy

The sampling procedure is concerned with drawing individuals from the population to enable a generalization about the phenomena of interest for the total population.[589] Here, the most critical aspect is to reduce the sampling, coverage, and non-response errors. A sampling error occurs when a non-representative sample is drawn from the population. A coverage error occurs when not all individuals of the survey population have an equal or known chance of being selected for participation. Finally, a non-

---

[584] E.g., Barclay et al. (1995); Chin (1998); Chin et al. (2003); Gefen et al. (2000)

[585] Cohen (1988)

[586] Goodhue et al. (2012)

[587] E.g., Barclay et al. (1995); Chin (1998); Chin et al. (2003); Gefen et al. (2000)

[588] These are constructs IQ2 and IQ8. We discuss the details of the model again in Section 6.3.

[589] Pinsonneault, Kraemer (1993)

response error occurs when people who responded to the survey are different from the sampled individuals who did not respond.[590]

First, to reduce the sampling error, random selection procedures ensure the selection of an appropriate sample frame that constitutes a subset of the population that adequately represents the unit of analysis.[591] However, in research practice, these procedures are often impossible for the same reasons that defining the appropriate sample size is impossible: the information about the target population is insufficient. In the present thesis, for instance, an exhaustive list of organizations that use EAM and the EAM stakeholders in those organizations are not known. Therefore, a random sampling procedure cannot be applied, and a judgmental sampling technique must be used to identify as many EAM stakeholders as possible.

Second, to reduce coverage error, the survey should be available over a broad range of channels.[592] As discussed in the previous section, because the target population can be assumed to have Internet access, basing a survey on the Web was not considered a possible cause of coverage error. Therefore, it was important to call the attention of EAM stakeholders to the Web-based survey in various ways. For our research, we sent out 915 invitations (see Figure 5-4) using five channels. Eight hundred personal e-mail invitations were sent to personal and relevant contacts identified by the Internet websites LinkedIn and XING.[593] Further, 53 survey invitations were posted on Internet forums at LinkedIn and XING that were relevant to the topic of EAM (e.g., CIO Forum, IT European Enterprise Architecture, EAM Group), and 42 invitations were sent to other EAM groups that maintained mailing lists for EAM stakeholders (e.g., the Association of EA, Opengroup, the Netherlands Architecture Forum). In addition, we asked the survey participants for further contacts, which produced 19 additional contacts to whom we sent invitations.[594] Finally, we posted an invitation to participate on Twitter. With this approach, we reached a broad variety of EAM stakeholders. Because people can be member of more than one of the included groups or forums, we decided to send out the invitations consecutively to avoid spamming them. Therefore, the invitations were sent consecutively between September and October 2011.

---

[590] Dillman (2000), p. 11

[591] Pinsonneault, Kraemer (1993)

[592] Dillman (2000), p. 11

[593] See www.linkedin.com and www.xing.com; for the invitation e-mails see Appendix D.8

[594] For the referral e-mails see D.8.2.

Figure 5-4 Overview of Contact Channels

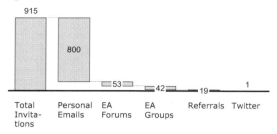

915

800

53   42   19   1

| Total Invita- tions | Personal Emails | EA Forums | EA Groups | Referrals | Twitter |

Third, to reduce the non-response error, Sivio et al. (2006) recommend minimizing the cost of participation, maximizing the benefits of participation, and building trust before and during the survey. In the following, in accordance with these recommendations, we describe how we aimed to increase the response rate and to minimize the non-response error.[595]

To *minimize the cost of participating* in the survey, condescending language, embarrassment, and any inconvenience should be avoided. Further, the questionnaire should be short, easy and interesting for the participant.[596] With an estimated duration of 45 minutes, the survey in the present thesis was not short. However, we designed the survey to be as clear as possible by using, for example, similar structures throughout the survey. Furthermore, we paid attention to the wording of the questions and integrated definitions where required to make each question as easy to understand as possible.

To *maximize the benefits of participating*, the questionnaire should be interesting.[597] In addition to starting and ending the survey with words of appreciation to the participants, we offered the participants more tangible benefits, which have been shown to have a positive effect on the response rate.[598] First, we offered to send the participants a copy of the report resulting from the survey. Second, participants could request a personalized benchmark that showed how their answers compared with the average answers in their industry. Receiving the report and the benchmark allowed the participants to identify

---

[595] Sivio et al. (2006)

[596] Sivio et al. (2006)

[597] Sivio et al. (2006)

[598] Cobanoglu, Cobanoglu (2003)

ways to improve their EAM.[599] Two hundred fifty-eight participants asked to receive the final results, and 205 participants asked for a personalized benchmark.[600]

To *build trust*, Sivio et al. (2006) recommend finding a survey sponsor and working with key managers.[601] We implemented these recommendations in two ways. First, we prominently presented the survey as a collaboration between the Humboldt-Universität zu Berlin and the Vienna University of Economics and Business.[602] Second, in advertising the survey in EAM groups, we asked the group manager to forward our invitation. Further, we aimed to build trust by revealing our full contact details in every contact to avoid appearing anonymous.

In addition to these three principles to improve the response rate, we used a personalized contact strategy in the survey follow-up. Research shows that contacting potential participants in a personal manner, particularly when following-up, increases the response rate significantly.[603] Every person who received a personal invitation but did not access the invitation link to the survey within 5 days received a personal reminder e-mail.[604] To those who participated in the survey but did not answer all of the questions, we sent a reminder within 48 hours of receiving the response requesting completion of the survey.[605]

In conclusion, with the sampling procedure and contact strategy described above, we attempted to distribute the survey as widely as possible and used various strategies to minimize sampling, coverage, and non-response errors. Given the time and resource constraints of this thesis, we believe that every practical means of advertising the survey was used. During the surveying phase, from September 2, 2011 to February 29, 2012, we received 311 responses. Of the received responses, 133 (42.8%) were complete and

---

[599] See Appendix D.8.3.

[600] This amount is fairly high compared to those who participated in total as we asked to provide the e-mail before in the beginning to be able to follow up if participants did not complete the survey. Consequently, this number includes also participants who did not complete the survey.

[601] Sivio et al. (2006)

[602] The author's and the principle supervisor's associated institutions.

[603] E.g., Cook et al. (2000); Deutskens et al. (2004); Fan, Yan (2010); Sánchez-Fernández et al. (2012)

[604] We have sent in total 113 reminder e-mails for participation; see Appendix D.8.4 for an example.

[605] We have sent in total 295 reminder e-mails for completion; see Appendix D.8.5 for an example.

usable for the validation of our model. We well exceeded our minimum required sample of 70.

5.6. Synopsis

In this chapter, we have discussed the operationalization of the revised model. In addition to the adoption and development of measurement items for the constructs of the model, we have described the development, implementation, testing, and administration of the corresponding survey.

Table 5-10 Evaluation of Survey Design and Administration

Survey attributes	This survey
Type of survey research	
Exploratory (XPY) or Explanatory	**XNY.** This survey attempts to test the proposed revised model for the recognition of EAM benefits.
Cross-sectional (CS) or Longitudinal (L)	**CS.** The survey gathers data on various organizations from individuals in various organizations and countries.
General	
1. Is the unit of analysis clearly defined for the study?	**Yes.** The unit of analysis is an EAM stakeholder with a business and IT background. See Section 5.5.
2. Does the instrument consistently reflect that unit of analysis	**Yes.** The instructions for the survey and the measurement items reflect the unit of analysis.
3. Is the respondent(s) chosen appropriate for the research question?	**Yes.** The target population, EAM stakeholders, is chosen and explicitly invited to participate in this doctoral thesis. A statement on the website clarified the target population, and demographic questions ensured that the respondents are part of the target population.
4. Is any form of triangulation used to cross validate results?	**Yes.** The development of the model is based on expert interviews. The adoption and development of the measurement items takes into account the findings from these interviews and findings from a literature review.
Measurement Error	
5. Are multiitem variables used?	**Yes.** Each construct of the research model is measured by multiple measurement items.
6. Is content validity assessed?	**Yes.** Content validity is assessed during the development of the measurement items and during the pre-test of the survey instrument
7. Is field-based pre-testing of measures performed?	**Yes.** Two rounds of pre-testing are conducted.
8. Is reliability assessed?	**No.** Traditional reliability assessments cannot be applied to formative constructs.
9. Is construct validity assessed?	**Yes.** Construct validity is assessed in terms of content validity.
10. Is pilot data used for purification measures or are existing validated measures used?	**No.** Because traditional purification cannot be applied to formative constructs, the measurement items are only purified in terms of content validation.
11. Are confirmatory methods used?	**No.** Traditional reliability assessments cannot be applied to formative constructs.

154

Survey attributes	This survey
Sampling error	
12. Is the sample frame defined and justified?	**Yes.** Section 5.5 describes the sample frame employed to select survey respondents.
13. Is random sampling used from the sample frame?	**No.** Due to limited information about the target population, random sampling is impossible.
14. Is the response rate over 20%	**Unknown.** Due to limited information about the target population, the response rate cannot be calculated.
15. Is non-response bias estimated?	**Yes.** Due to limited information about the target population, standard techniques for estimating the non-response bias are not applicable. However, sampling heuristics to establish the non-response bias in the Web-based survey are discussed and applied in Chapter 6.
Internal Validity Error	
16. Are attempts made to establish internal validity of the findings?	**Yes.** PLS analysis is employed to test for internal validity in Chapter 6.
17. Is there sufficient statistical power to reduce statistical conclusion error?	**Yes.** A minimum sample size of 70 was calculated in accordance with sample estimation heuristics.

Source: Adapted from Mlhotra et al. (1998)

As discussed in Table 5-10, the survey instrument was designed to fulfill all criteria for 'good quality'. Although not all criteria were applicable or could be satisfied, we conclude from the discussion that the survey research in the present thesis is of acceptable quality. In the next chapter, we use the data gathered by the survey to empirically test our model.

6. Data Analysis

In post-capitalism, power comes from transmitting information to make it productive, not from hiding it.
Peter F. Drucker (1909-1995)

In this chapter, we present our analysis of the data from the survey that we have conducted to test our revised a priori model for the realization of benefits from EAM. The objective of this chapter is to test our revised a priori model. This chapter focuses on steps six to nine of MacKenzie et al.'s (2011) measurement instrument development approach, which we have introduced in the previous chapter.[606] After an introduction in Section 6.1 to the data analysis strategy used in this context, Section 6.2 presents the descriptive statistics for the survey sample along with tests and a preliminary discussions of the suitability of the data for the subsequent statistical analysis. In Section 6.3, we present the results obtained from the statistical analysis of the measurement items. In Section 6.4, after this analysis, we discuss the fitness of the developed model; we also assess the structural properties of our a priori model in Section 6.5. Finally, we close the chapter with a synthesis in Section 6.6.

6.1. Analysis Strategy

In the previous chapter, we described how we collected empirical data on the realization of benefits from EAM using the survey instrument developed; in this chapter, we describe the analysis of these data to validate our a priori model. In this analysis, we employ a Structural Equation Modeling (SEM) approach as our data analysis method.

SEM is considered to be a second-generation data analysis technique[607] and is acknowledged as the state of the art for high-quality statistical data analysis in many disciplines, including IS, marketing, and organizational research.[608] In general terms, SEM is a statistical method that is used in multivariate data analysis. Thus, the goal is to

---

[606] See Section 5.1.

[607] Bagozzi, Phillips (1982). Second generation data analysis techniques (such as PLS) are capable of analysing more than one layer of linkages between independent and dependent variables, which first generation data analysis techniques (such as ANOVA) cannot. Gefen et al. (2000)

[608] Chin et al. (2003); Gefen et al. (2011); Gefen et al. (2000); Sarstedt et al. (2011)

study the relationships between dependent and independent variables. SEM allows the researcher to analyze one or more competing models to determine which ones fit the data and what particular model hypotheses are supported by the data.[609]

Conducting SEM

An SEM analysis should generally be divided into two steps: the validation of the measurement model and the testing of the structural model.[610] To validate the measurement model, one analyzes the relationships of the observed measurement items to their hypothesized latent constructs. In contrast, testing a structural model involves analyzing the relationships of the constructs to one another as hypothesized by a particular theory. Although the two steps can be conducted simultaneously with modern SEM software, a two-step approach is preferred because it can reduce interpretational confounding.[611] Interpretational confounding *"occurs when insufficient attention is given to the relative extent to which different sources of empirical meaning underlie the estimation of weights for epistemic statements linking an unobserved variable to its indicators."*[612] In other words, interpretational confounding occurs when a structural model is incorrectly specified and this misspecification remains undetected.[613] Conducting an SEM analysis in two parts makes it possible to identify and resolve potential misspecifications in the structural model. In this doctoral thesis, therefore, having validated the measurement model, we develop putative alternative models and assess their goodness of fit, i.e., how well they fit the data, before analyzing the favored model in detail.[614]

To conduct data analysis with SEM, two distinct statistical techniques can be employed: (a) covariance analysis, which is conducted using software such as AMOS, EQS, or LISREL, and (2) partial least square (PLS) analysis, which is conducted using software such as SmartPLS, PLS-Graph, or WarpPLS.[615] These two types of SEM vary primarily in terms of the objectives of the analysis, the statistical assumptions made, and the resulting fit statistics.[616] For example, whereas the statistical objective of PLS is to obtain a high R-squared with significant p-values and hence to reject the null hypothesis of no-

---

[609] Bollen (2011)

[610] Bollen (1989)

[611] Anderson, Gerbing D. (1988)

[612] Burt (1976)

[613] Bollen (2007)

[614] See Section 6.4.

[615] Barclay et al. (1995); Chin (1998)

[616] Gefen et al. (2000)

effect,[617] the objective of covariance-based SEM is to demonstrate that the null hypothesis is insignificant and hence that the complete set of paths as specified in the model is plausible. In other words, the statistical objective of covariance-based SEM is to show that the examined model is validated by the data analysis.[618] Furthermore, the choice of technique affects the results and their interpretation. Cenfetelli et al. (2009) note that especially when formative constructs are analyzed, these distinct differences must be considered. Whereas covariance-based SEM includes an error term that can be interpreted, this is not the case for PLS techniques, which can yield to inflated weights.

Table 6-1 Comparison of PLS and CBSEM

Criteria	PLS	CBSEM
Objective	Prediction-oriented	Parameter-oriented
Approach	Variance-based	Covariance-based
Assumption	Predictor specification (nonparametric)	Typically multivariate normal distribution and independent observations (parametric)
Parameter estimates	Consistent as indicators and sample size increase (i.e., consistency at large)	Consistent
Latent variable scores	Explicitly estimated	Indeterminate
Epistemic relationship between an LV and its measures	Can be modeled in either formative or reflective mode	Typically only with reflective indicators. However, the formative mode is also supported.
Implications	Optimal for prediction accuracy	Optimal for parameter accuracy
Model complexity	Large complexity (e.g., 100 constructs and 1,000 indicators)	Small to moderate complexity (e.g., less than 100 indicators)
Type of optimization	Locally iterative	Globally iterative
Significance tests	Only by means of simulations; restricted validity	Available
Availability of global Goodness of Fit (GoF) metrics	Are currently being developed and discussed	Established GoF metrics available

Source: Adapted from Chin et al. (1999)

In selecting one of the two approaches, researchers have made different arguments. Chin et al. (1999) provide an overview of the main differences depicted Table 6-1. Based on this table, it can be concluded that the PLS approach is optimal for prediction accuracy and the CBSEM approach for parameter accuracy because of the respective statistical

---

[617] Barclay et al. (1995)

[618] Bollen (1989); Hair (1995)

foundations of the approaches. Furthermore, PLS is better suited for highly complex models, whereas CBSEM is better suited for less complex models.

In addition, based on a literature review, Urbach et al. (2010) identify the following arguments that researchers make in selecting PLS:[619]

- PLS does not require normal-distributed input data.

- PLS can be used with complex structural equation models with a large number of constructs.

- PLS is usable with both reflective and formative constructs.

- PLS is especially useful for prediction

However, some arguments that are given in literature for chosing PLS should be examined through a critical lens because many of them are controversial or have been confuted. For example, in recent research, Goodhue et al. (2012) confuted the argument that PLS requires smaller sample sizes.[620] Furthermore, formative constructs can also be evaluated using a covariance-based SEM approach, which is often not considered in literature.[621]

Nevertheless, we decided to conduct the SEM analysis in this doctoral thesis using PLS for two primary reasons. First, our revised a priori model has a large number of constructs that can be handled more efficiently using PLS. Second, the model mainly contains formatively defined constructs, and these are more compatible with established PLS software.[622] Therefore, we conclude that a PLS approach is more consistent with the objectives of this research.

The PLS Method

Having chosen PLS as an analysis technique, we briefly present the basic concepts associated with PLS. The PLS algorithm was originally developed by Wold (1966) and was subsequently further developed by various researchers.[623]

PLS uses two iterative procedures to minimize the variance between the dependent variables based on a partial least squares approach.[624] The first procedure, the

---

[619] Urbach, Ahlemann (2010); Note that confuted arguments that Urbach, Ahlemann (2010) identified in their literature review have been omitted in this list.

[620] Goodhue et al. (2006), (2012)

[621] Diamantopoulos (2011)

[622] Urbach, Ahlemann (2010)

[623] Wold (1966)

approximation of the outer model, estimates the weights for all of the latent variables as aggregates of the measurement variables. In the first iteration, the weights are made equal for each block of measurement variables, and scores for the latent variables are calculated. In further iterations, more appropriate scores are calculated via regression. Then, in the second procedure, the approximation of the inner model is calculated based on proxies calculated for each endogenous latent variable based on its association with other latent variables. The results of this regression are used as a starting point for the next round of estimates for the outer and inner models. The algorithm stops when no significant improvement is achieved. Then, based on the results, further statistics are computed, such as factor loadings and path coefficients.[625]

There are several tools available that employ this algorithm. The most established ones are SmartPLS,[626] PLS-Graph,[627] and WarpPLS.[628]

We chose WarpPLS because in the context of this doctoral thesis, it presents some advantages over the other available options. First, it can handle the complexity of the research model at hand. Second, it automatically calculates most of the key statistics required for our analysis. Third, it calculates several model fit indices and variance inflation factor (VIF) coefficients for the latent variable predictors, which other off-the-shelf software does not do. Such information is required for a deeper analysis.[629]

In this chapter, we outlined the foundation of the data analysis; in the next section, we present the descriptive statistical analysis of the data collected.

6.2. Descriptive Statistics

Descriptive statistics communicate the basic features of the data in a study by providing simple summaries for the data sample.[630] These descriptions of the characteristics of the sample are intended to simplify the organization and presentation of the data for further discussion.[631] For instance, one might estimate the non-response error associated with

---

[624] Chin (1998)

[625] Tenenhaus et al. (2005); Urbach, Ahlemann (2010)

[626] Ringle et al. (2005)

[627] Chin (2001)

[628] Kock (2011)

[629] Kock (2011)

[630] Trochim (2001)

[631] Gravetter, Wallnau (2011)

the collected data, identify potential violations of assumptions required for further statistical analysis, or answer individual research questions.[632]

Accordingly, in the following, we describe the demographics of the sample data, analyze the data for potential non-response bias, and assess whether assumptions necessary for the statistical testing conducted in the subsequent sections are met.

Overview of Key Demographics

Responding to our invitation to participate in the survey, 747 people accessed our survey website between September 2, 2011, and February 29, 2012. Of those who accessed the website, 311 (41.6%) started the survey, and 133 (42.8% of those who started the survey) completed the survey. In the following, we detail the descriptive statistics and contrast them with the corresponding statistics for other surveys related to EAM. This allows us to discuss the representativeness of the collected survey data and the generalizability of the data.[633]

6.2.1.   Survey Access Demographics

As outlined in Section 5.5, we used five different channels to advertise our survey. Our invitations in EAM groups attracted the most attention. Through this channel, 313 people (41.9%) accessed our survey. As the second most frequently used invitation channel, EAM forums attracted 182 (24.4%) of the people who accessed the survey. An additional 76 people (10.8%) accessed our survey in response to either a personal invitation (70 people, 9.4%) or a personal recommendation (6 people, 0.8%). A social media post via Twitter attracted 29 people (3.9%). Of the people who accessed our survey, 147 (19.7%) were not referred to the survey by one of these means. These people might have found their way to our survey through search engines or broken links. In addition, of those who accessed the survey, 59.7% were in Europe, 18.5% were in North America, and 15.9% were in Australasia.[634] Thus, the individuals from these three continents account for 94.1% of the sample (see Figure 6-1).

---

[632] Sue, Ritter (2007)

[633] Kaplowitz et al. (2004)

[634] Analysis based on Google (2012).

Figure 6-1 Participant by Invitation Channels and Location

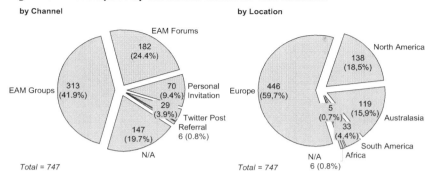

by Channel

by Location

EAM Forums
182 (24.4%)

EAM Groups 313 (41.9%)

70 (9.4%) Personal Invitation

29 (3.9%) Twitter Post

147 (19.7%) N/A

Referral 6 (0.8%)

Total = 747

North America 138 (18,5%)

Europe 446 (59,7%)

5 (0,7%) 119 (15,9%) Australasia

33 (4.4%) South America

Africa

N/A 6 (0.8%)

Total = 747

A comparison of the people who accessed the survey and those who actually participated finds that 311 people (41.6%) started the survey and 151 (20.2%) actually completed it. However, these figures vary by continent and by invitation channel (see Figure 6-2). For instance, the conversion rates in Europe, North America, Australasia, and South America are close to the average conversion rate of 20.2%. Only those people in Africa and those who did not provide a location differ significantly from the rest of the sample. However, because few people in Africa accessed and took the survey, the significantly above-average conversion rate may be due to the small sample. In contrast, the conversion rate analyzed by invitation channel shows that the invitations in EAM forums and EAM groups yielded conversion rates (19.9% and 16.9%, respectively) that are similar to the average conversion rate of 20.2%. In contrast, the conversion rates for personal invitations (34.3%) and personal recommendations (71.4%) are far above this average. This finding is consistent with previous research findings suggesting that personalized invitations yield improved survey response rates.[635] The conversion rate for Twitter, however, at 0%, is the lowest. One potential explanation for this is that Twitter, although it has a large user base, is not popular among the stakeholders targeted for this survey.

---

[635] E.g., Cook et al. (2000); Deutskens et al. (2004); Fan, Yan (2010); Sánchez-Fernández et al. (2012)

Figure 6-2 Comparison of Survey Participants and Drop-outs

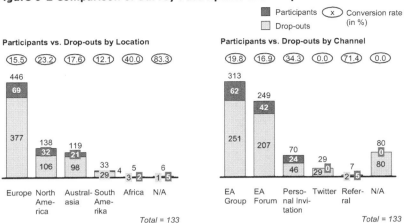

Organizational Demographics

The survey collected data from organizations in 34 countries. The headquarters of approximately 92% of the organizations are located in Europe (51.9%), North America (24.1%), or Australasia (15.8%) (see Figure 6-3). This geographic distribution is similar to that of previous empirical studies in EAM. Boh et al. (2007) report that the largest share of EAM stakeholders are in Europe and North America (88% in the two locations combined).[636] However, other empirical EAM research is often focused on particular geographic locations for reasons of practicality. For example, Foorthuis et al. (2010) focus on the Netherlands, whereas Schmidt et al. (2011) use mainly respondents from Germany and Switzerland (due to the geographic proximity of those countries, they argue).[637] In this research, the top three countries in which the headquarters of the participating organizations are located are the USA (20.3%), Germany (14.3%), and the Netherlands (13.5%) (see Figure 6-3). The large number of participating countries illustrates the global nature of the survey. Figure 6-4 illustrates the geographic distribution of the headquarters of the participating organizations on a heat map.

---

[636] Boh et al. (2007)

[637] Foorthuis et al. (2010); Riege, Aier (2009)

Figure 6-3 Location of Organizations' Headquarters by Continent and Country

by Continent

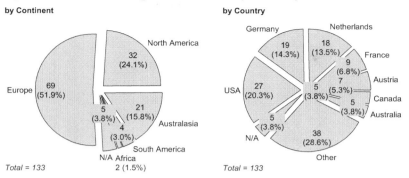

North America
32 (24.1%)

Europe
69 (51.9%)

5 (3.8%)

21 (15.8%)
Australasia

4 (3.0%)

South America

N/A Africa
2 (1.5%)

Total = 133

by Country

Germany
19 (14.3%)

Netherlands
18 (13.5%)

France
9 (6.8%)

Austria
7 (5.3%)

USA
27 (20.3%)

5 (3.8%)

Canada
5 (3.8%)
Australia

5 (3.8%)

N/A
38 (28.6%)

Other

Total = 133

Figure 6-4 Organizations' Location of Headquarters Visualized on Map

<10

10-24

25-50

>50

Three-quarters of the participating organizations are either publicly traded or privately held. Only 17.3% are governmental institutions, and 7.5% are non-profit organizations (see Figure 6-5). The majority of the participants work in the information, communication, entertainment, and recreation industries (25.6%) or in the financial and insurance industry (24.1%) (see Figure 6-5).

Figure 6-5 Participants by Type of Organization and Industry

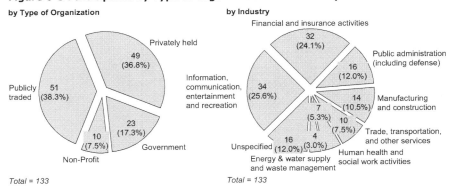

by Type of Organization

by Industry

Total = 133

Total = 133

The prevalence of these two groups of industries is consistent with the findings of previous studies. For example, Bucher et al. (2007) present an EAM study in which 62.5% of the participants are from financial and insurance institutions, 15.0% are from telecommunication and software companies, and 12.5% are from the manufacturing industry.[638] Similarly, Foorthuis et al. (2010) present an EAM study in which 32.8% of the participants are from governmental institutions, 30.4% from the financial and insurance industry, 12.3% from the information and media industry, 6.5% from the manufacturing industry, and 18.0% from other industries.[639] The financial and insurance industry is also dominant (with a figure of 47%) in the EAM study presented by Boh et al. (2007).[640] Although these three studies differ in their coverage of the industries, it can be concluded that in all of the studies, three sectors are prevalent: the financial and insurance industry; the information, communication, entertainment, and recreation industry; and public administration. In this research, the survey data show a focus on these industries as well. Given that the distributions are largely similar, there is no reason to suspect that our distribution of industry sectors is not representative.

[638] Bucher et al. (2007)

[639] Foorthuis et al. (2010)

[640] Boh et al. (2007)

Figure 6-6 Participants by Organizations' Total Employees and EAM Employees

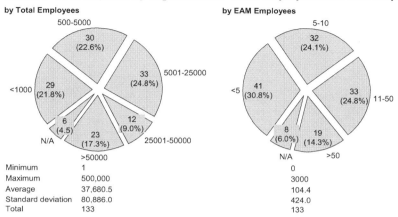

	by Total Employees	by EAM Employees
Minimum	1	0
Maximum	500,000	3000
Average	37,680.5	104.4
Standard deviation	80,886.0	424.0
Total	133	133

The number of employees at the participating organizations is generally more than 37,000, and 65% of the organizations have more than 1,000 employees. These figures are slightly lower than those that Boh et al. (2007) report in their EAM study, in which approximately 90% of the participating organizations have more than 1,000 employees.[641] However, this finding is similar to that of Foorthuis et al. (2010) in their EAM study, in which 72.3% of the organizations have more than 2,000 employees.[642] Given that EAM requires a certain organization size, we assume that our collected sample data are representative. Furthermore, our sample data show an average of 104.4 EAM employees and indicate that more than three-quarters of the organizations employ 50 or more EAM employees (see Figure 6-6). Because we could not identify any prior empirical study that indicated the size of these organizations, we could not cross-validate these demographics with prior research.

6.2.2.   Personal Demographics

In the survey, we asked the participants about their current work, their position within the managerial and organizational structures, the time they spent on projects, their EAM experience, their organizational positioning, and their business-IT orientation. In the following, we discuss these personal demographics and compare them with the corresponding statistics from the existing research.

---

[641] Boh et al. (2007)

[642] Foorthuis et al. (2010)

Figure 6-7 Participants by Managerial Position and Current Job Function

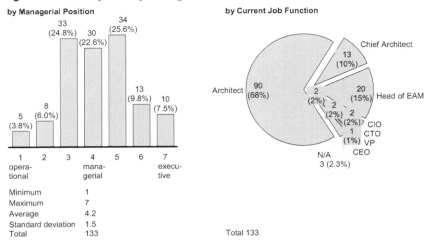

by Managerial Position

by Current Job Function

Minimum 1
Maximum 7
Average 4.2
Standard deviation 1.5
Total 133

Total 133

Approximately three-quarters of our survey participants consider themselves (on a Likert scale from 1 as operational and 4 as managerial to 7 as executive) as primarily managerial (73.0% provided values between 3 and 5; see Figure 6-7). This finding accurately reflects the distribution of the participant's' current positions. Of the participants, 75.5% are either architects or chief architects, and 20.3% are in senior management roles. This finding is consistent with those of the EAM study reported by Struck et al. (2010), which indicate that more than 84% of the participants are architects, although the authors do not provide further details.[643] Likewise, Boh et al. (2007) report in their study that 70% are architects, 17% are CxOs, and 13% are in other roles.[644]

Furthermore, the participants reported spending an average of 52.2% of their time on projects; these figures ranged from 0% to 100% (see Figure 6-8). In the survey, 87.2% of the participants report that they have more than 1 year of experience with EAM; the average figure is 7.1 years of experience with EAM. Therefore, the majority of the participants have experience with EAM, and it can be assumed that they are capable of assessing the benefits of EAM and have witnessed the proliferation of EAM benefits over time. Thus, the sample is consistent with the aforementioned assumption that the survey-takers should be EAM stakeholders with long-term experience with EAM.[645]

---

[643] Struck et al. (2010)

[644] Boh et al. (2007)

[645] See Section 1.5 in which we have discussed the need for experienced participants..

Figure 6-8 Participants by Time Spent on Projects and EAM Experience

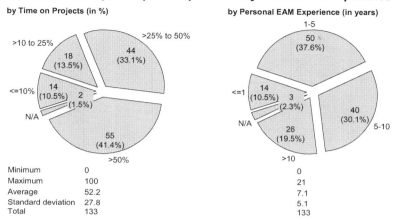

Minimum	0		0
Maximum	100		21
Average	52.2		7.1
Standard deviation	27.8		5.1
Total	133		133

Figure 6-9 Participants by Organizational Position and Business-IT Orientation

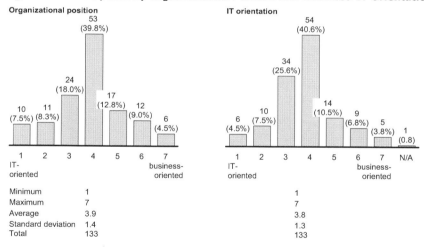

Minimum	1		1
Maximum	7		7
Average	3.9		3.8
Standard deviation	1.4		1.3
Total	133		133

Finally, our data sample includes a sufficient distribution of participants with business and IT backgrounds. On a scale on which 1 indicates that one's position is IT oriented, 33.8% report having a current role in IT (i.e., they provided answers between 1 and 3), 39.8% report having a role in between (i.e., they provided an answer of 4), and 26.3% report having a business role. Similarly, 37.6% report having an IT background, 40.6% report having a background that includes both business and IT, and 21.6% report having a business background (see Figure 6-9). These results indicate that as desired, our survey participants are involved in both IT and business.[646]

6.2.3. Estimation of Non-response Error

Having discussed the demographics of our sample data, we now analyze the potential for non-response error. Even if a survey is well designed, the missing opinions of individuals who did not or could not respond may distort the estimates for the overall population. Non-response bias occurs if the survey data do not reflect a systematic difference between the answers of respondents and non-respondents. The magnitude of this difference times the proportion of non-respondents and respondents is referred to as the expected size of the non-response bias.[647] If the survey respondents differ substantially from the non-respondents, it becomes risky to generalize about the intended population based in the sample.[648] Consequently, non-response error may threaten the external validity of a study and its statistical conclusion validity.[649]

As a means to evaluate non-response error and the resulting validity of the data, Dooley et al. (2003) suggest five methods:[650]

■ Based on the assumption that late respondents have characteristics similar to those of non-respondents, the first method statistically compares early and late respondents to estimate the non-response error. There are different approaches to operationally defining early and late respondents in using this method. One is to operationally define late respondents by identifying successive waves of responses to a questionnaire. For example, late respondents might be those in the last wave of respondents after follow-ups to a questionnaire. Another approach involves identifying the first 20% and the last 20% of the respondents and comparing them or even splitting the sample into two parts according to the response dates. The percentage used for this purpose may also vary between 10% and 50%. The actual comparison between the early and late respondents is based on the primary variables of interest (e.g., the demographics of the participants). If the test indicates that there are no differences between the two groups, it can be assumed that there is no significant non-response error.

---

[646] See Section 1.5 in which we have discussed the need for both business-oriented as well as IT-oriented participants.

[647] Pearl, Fairley (1985)

[648] Sivio et al. (2006)

[649] King, He (2005); Sivio et al. (2006)

[650] Dooley, Lindner (2003)

- Second, a regression analysis using 'days to respond' as a regression variable can indicate non-response error. In this approach, the 'days to respond' variable is coded as a continuous variable and is used as an independent variable in regression equations. The primary variables of interest are regressed on the independent variable. If the analysis does not yield any statistically significant results, it can be assumed that there is no significant non-response error.

- Third, the respondents can be compared with the non-respondents. To compare the respondents and the non-respondents, one must obtain the demographics of a sample of non-respondents. This sample is then used to identify differences between the non-respondents and the survey sample. When using this approach, one should obtain a minimum of twenty responses from a random sample of non-respondents. If no sample of twenty or more non-respondents can be obtained, this method can also be used in combination with one of the two aforementioned methods.

- Fourth, the characteristics of the respondents in a sample can be compared with the known characteristics of the population. If the analysis of the similarities and differences between the respondents and the target population shows no significant differences, it can be assumed that there is no significant non-response error.

- Finally, Dooley et al. (2003) suggest that if the four methods discussed above are not effective, non-response error can be ignored as an indicator of external validity. However, it should be noted that this approach does not help one to assess external validity.

The methods discussed here allow for the ex post assessment of non-response error based on the collected sample. However, efforts to control for non-response error should begin with the design and implementation of the survey instrument.[651] For instance, appropriate sampling is recommended as a way to maximize participation. The a priori measures from the present research are presented in Section 5.5. In the ex post analysis in this research, we make a comparison between early and late respondents. Because information about the overall population is not available, this is the most promising approach to estimating non-response bias in the present thesis.

To compare the groups of early and late respondents, we use a Chi-square test to determine whether they have equal distributions with regard to the key demographics,[652] both organizational and personal. Table 6-2 provides the results of these Chi-square

---

[651] Dillman et al. (1999)

[652] Burkell (2003); Miller, Smith (1983)

tests. Because the p-value is p>0.05 for all of the demographic variables, the results indicate that there are no significant differences in the distribution of early versus late respondents given a 0.05 confidence level.

Table 6-2 Chi-square Test of Early vs. Late Survey Respondents

Demographic variable	p-value
Organizational demographics	
Perspective	0.597
Type of organization	0.143
Industry	0.121
Headquarters	0.245
Employees	0.273
EAM employees	0.415
Revenue	0.336
IT spending	0.265
EAM experience	0.394
Personal demographics	
Job function	0.532
Managerial positioning	0.680
Time on projects	0.280
Organizational positioning	0.772
IT orientation	0.394
EAM experience	0.150

6.2.4. Evaluation of the Data Suitability for Statistical Analysis

Thus far, we have discussed the descriptive statistics of the collected sample and assessed the non-response error of the sample. To prepare for the statistical analysis of the measurement model and the structural model, we must screen the data to determine their suitability for statistical analysis. When one is conducting an SEM analysis, and particularly when one is employing PLS, the data should exhibit multivariate normality.[653] Marcoulides et al. (2006) note that when moderately non-normal data are considered, a significantly larger sample size is required for PLS.[654] Recent PLS research indicates the deleterious impact of using non-normal data.[655]

Normality is one of the most common assumptions used in the development and application of statistical approaches. More than 40 such testing approaches can be identified in the literature. These approaches can be either graphical or numerical.

---

[653] Marcoulides et al. (2009)

[654] Marcoulides, Saunders (2006)

[655] Chin, Dibbern (2009)

Whereas graphical methods plot the distribution of a random variable or the difference between the data and an empirical distribution for visual testing, numerical methods can be used to calculate summary statistics or conduct statistical tests of normality.[656] Surprisingly, some commonly used tests of normality, such as the Kolmogorov-Smirnov test or the chi-square goodness of fit test, are criticized in the literature as having such low power that they should not be used to test normality.[657] Instead, the performance of moment tests and the Wilk-Shapiro test are recommended.[658]

In this doctoral thesis, we test the normality of the collected survey data using a sample moment test of skewness and kurtosis statistics. The analysis of the skewness and kurtosis statistics for each measurement item indicates that the thresholds suggested by Stevens (2009) (skewness < 2 and kurtosis < 7) are not exceeded for any measurement items (see Appendix E.1).[659]

6.2.5.   Summary of Descriptive Data Analysis

Having analyzed the demographics, the non-response error, and the statistical properties of the data, we can conclude that the data can be used for the purposes of this thesis. Based on the descriptive statistics, no significant deviation of our data from those used in other reported EAM research could be identified. Furthermore, neither non-response error nor noticeable problems with the suitability of the data (i.e., non-normality) could be identified. Therefore, we proceed with our analysis of the data.

6.3. Validation of Measurement Items

Before we validate the structural model of our revised a priori model, we further explore the validity and reliability of the measurement items. In Section 5.4, we have discussed the measurement instruments a priori to the data collection. Now, we evaluate the measurement items ex post based on the data collected using the survey.

In this doctoral thesis, we use WarpPLS 2.0 to evaluate the measurement items.[660] We modeled the a priori model in WarpPLS and analyzed the results for the outer PLS model. The outer PLS model in a PLS analysis is dependent only on the relationships of the measurement items to the latent variables (LVs).[661] Therefore, we do not consider the

---

[656] Thode (2002)

[657] D'Agostino et al. (1990)

[658] Thode (2002)

[659] Stevens (2009)

[660] Kock (2011)

[661] Tenenhaus et al. (2005)

relationships between the latent variables themselves, i.e., the inner model, in this section. Instead, we use the results of the inner PLS model to validate the structural model in Section 6.4 and 6.5. Table 6-3, Table 6-4, and Table 6-5 summarize the results of this analysis of the outer model that are discussed in the following.

Table 6-3 Properties of Latent Variables (LV)

Construct	Number of items	Cronbach's alpha	Goldstein-Dillon's ρ	Construct composite reliabilities	AVE	Adequacy coefficient
Reflective constructs						
Use	4	0,794	0,717	0,869	0,630	0,783
Sat	3	0,941	0,729	0,962	0,895	0,946
Benefit	26	0,964	0,931	0,967	0,529	0,725
Formative constructs						
PQ1	5	0,711	0,861	0,817	0,520	0,520
PQ2	5	0,828	0,728	0,884	0,619	0,763
PQ3	5	0,847	0,735	0,897	0,649	0,781
IQ1	4	0,687	0,674	0,810	0,517	0,718
IQ2	7	0,690	0,705	0,791	0,359	0,588
IQ3	5	0,611	0,581	0,731	0,436	0,553
IQ4	3	0,779	0,675	0,872	0,694	0,833
IQ5	3	0,857	0,700	0,913	0,779	0,882
IQ6	3	0,844	0,695	0,906	0,764	0,873
IQ7	5	0,813	0,740	0,873	0,586	0,753
IQ8	7	0,877	0,801	0,905	0,578	0,758
IQ9	3	0,870	0,705	0,921	0,795	0,891
SQ1	4	0,902	0,755	0,931	0,772	0,879
SQ2	6	0,890	0,796	0,917	0,651	0,802
SQ3	3	0,871	0,705	0,921	0,795	0,892
CA1	4	0,928	0,767	0,949	0,822	0,906
CA2	3	0,794	0,681	0,880	0,709	0,842
CA3	3	0,838	0,691	0,904	0,759	0,868

Table 6-4 Item Loadings and their p-values for Reflective Latent Variables (LV)

LV	Item	Loadings	p-value	LV	Item	Loadings	p-value
Use	USE1	0.885	<0.001	Benefits	OB2a	0.743	<0.001
	USE2	0.884	<0.001	(cont.)	OB2b	0.749	<0.001
	USE3	0.789	<0.001		OB2c	0.788	<0.001
	USE4	0.575	0.003		OB2d	0.782	<0.001
Sat	SAT1	0.945	<0.001		OB2e	0.649	<0.001
	SAT2	0.978	<0.001		OB3a	0.724	<0.001
	SAT3	0.914	<0.001		OB3b	0.769	<0.001
Benefit	OB1a	0.766	<0.001		OB3c	0.746	<0.001
	OB1b	0.678	<0.001		OB3d	0.723	<0.001
	OB1c	0.719	<0.001		PB1a	0.613	<0.001
	OB1d	0.653	<0.001		PB1b	0.598	<0.001
	OB1e	0.773	<0.001		PB1c	0.716	<0.001
	OB1f	0.692	<0.001		PB1d	0.775	<0.001
	OB1g	0.778	<0.001		PB2a	0.691	<0.001
	OB1h	0.783	<0.001		PB2b	0.686	<0.001
	OB1i	0.828	<0.001		PB3a	0.708	<0.001
	OB1j	0.721	<0.001				

Table 6-5 Loadings, Weights, and Variance Inflation Factors (VIFs) for Formative Latent Variables (LV)

LV	Item	Loading	Weight	VIF	LV	Item	Loading	Weight	VIF
PQ1	PQ1a	0.766	0.295	1.66	IQ7	IQ7a	0.488	0.167	1.31
	PQ1b	0.764	0.294	1.58		IQ7b	0.874	0.298	2.68
	PQ1c	0.859	0.330	2.37		IQ7c	0.821	0.280	2.48
	PQ1d	0.831	0.319	1.97		IQ7e	0.780	0.780	1.69
	PQ1e	*0.050*	*0.019*	1.17	IQ8	IQ8a	0.746	0.746	2.35
PQ2	PQ2a	0.808	0.261	1.92		IQ8b	0.778	0.778	2.63
	PQ2b	0.867	0.280	2.47		IQ8c	0.801	0.801	2.21
	PQ2c	0.874	0.282	2.75		IQ8d	0.617	0.617	1.53
	PQ2d	0.883	0.286	2.68		IQ8e	0.791	0.791	2.30
	PQ2e	*0.381*	*0.123*	1.13		IQ8f	0.790	0.790	2.38
PQ3	PQ3a	0.856	0.264	2.37		IQ8g	0.783	0.783	2.06
	PQ3b	0.882	0.272	2.79	IQ9	IQ9a	0.918	0.918	3.04
	PQ3c	0.906	0.279	3.33		IQ9b	0.913	0.913	2.95
	PQ3d	0.874	0.269	2.67		IQ9c	0.842	0.842	1.82
	PQ3e	*0.388*	*0.119*	1.09	SQ1	SQ1a	0.877	0.877	2.68
IQ1	IQ1a	0.670	0.324	1.32		SQ1b	0.904	0.904	3.14
	IQ1b	0.728	0.352	1.35		SQ1c	0.883	0.883	2.63
	IQ1c	0.708	0.343	1.39		SQ1d	0.850	0.850	2.23
	IQ1d	0.767	0.371	1.45	SQ2	SQ2a	0.663	0.663	1.60
IQ2	*IQ2a*	*0.391*	*0.156*	1.12		SQ2b	0.717	0.717	1.85
	IQ2b	0.608	0.242	1.37		SQ2c	0.822	0.822	2.51
	IQ2c	*0.478*	*0.190*	1.20		SQ2d	0.882	0.882	4.10
	IQ2d	0.734	0.292	1.52		SQ2e	0.885	0.885	4.38
	IQ2e	0.662	0.264	1.39		SQ2f	0.845	0.845	3.54
	IQ2f	0.694	0.276	1.41	SQ3	SQ3a	0.868	0.868	2.03
	IQ2g	0.549	0.219	1.19		SQ3b	0.907	0.907	2.61
IQ3	IQ3a	0.870	0.399	2.35		SQ3c	0.900	0.900	2.50
	IQ3b	0.901	0.413	2.66		CA1a	0.932		
	IQ3c	0.746	0.342	1.45		CA1b	0.869		
	IQ3d	*0.015*	*0.007*	1.33		CA1c	0.922		
	IQ3e	*0.233*	*0.107*	1.27	CA1	CA1d	0.902		
IQ4	IQ4a	0.872	0.419	1.86		CA2a	0.872		
	IQ4b	0.802	0.385	1.51		CA2b	0.849		
	IQ4c	0.824	0.396	1.62	CA2	CA2c	0.804		
IQ5	IQ5a	0.909	0.389	2.78		CA3a	0.919		
	IQ5b	0.908	0.389	2.76		CA3b	0.92		
	IQ5c	0.828	0.354	1.72	CA3	CA3c	0.765		
IQ6	IQ6a	0.900	0.393	2.56					
	IQ6b	0.903	0.394	2.59					
	IQ6c	0.815	0.356	1.63					

Having calculated the statistics for the outer PLS model, we can use the data gathered above to test the measurement items. In general, the measurement items must be evaluated for unidimensionality; convergent, discriminant, and criterion validity; and reliability.[662] Because different tests are required to analyze and interpret formatively and reflectively defined latent constructs,[663] we discuss both types of latent constructs separately below.

Unidimensionality

When all of the measurement items that are related to one latent construct represent one underlying trait, the latent construct is unidimensional.[664] Because formative constructs are by definition multidimensional, unidimensionality needs to be tested only for reflectively defined constructs.[665] For these constructs, unidimensionality is a prerequisite for analyzing the validity and reliability of the constructs.[666] The most commonly used measure of unidimensionality for reflective constructs is Cronbach's Alpha.[667] The Cronbach's Alpha must be at least 0.6 for a reflective construct to be considered unidimensional.[668] In addition, we assess Dillon–Goldstein's ρ, which is considered to be a better indicator than the traditional Cronbach's Alpha.[669] A construct is considered to be unidimensional if the Dillon–Goldstein's ρ is larger than 0.7.

In this doctoral thesis, all of the reflective constructs have a Cronbach's Alpha of at least 0.79 and a Dillon–Goldstein's ρ of 0.72 (see Table 6-3). This finding suggests that all of the reflective constructs are unidimensional.

Convergent Validity

Indicating the extent to which a measure relates to the construct it is intended to measure,[670] convergent validity is (like unidimensionality) irrelevant for formative constructs because formative constructs do not necessarily imply that the indicators are

---

662 Anderson, Gerbing D. (1988); Bollen (1989); Chin (1998); MacKenzie et al. (2011)

663 MacKenzie et al. (2011)

664 Anderson, Gerbing D. (1988); Segars (1997)

665 Jarvis et al. (2003b)

666 Nunnally, Bernstein (1994)

667 Cronbach, Meehl (1955)

668 E.g., Nunnally, Bernstein (1994). Other scholars recommend at least a value of 0.7, e.g., Moore, Benbasat (1991), or even 0.8, e.g., Straub (1989).

669 Chin (1998)

670 Bhattacherjee (2012)

correlated.[671] For reflective constructs, convergent validity can be assessed by evaluating three statistics:[672] (a) the factor loadings of the reflective measurement items should be significant and at least 0.6, (2) the construct composite reliabilities should exceed 0.8 and (3) the average variance extracted (AVE) should exceed 0.5, i.e., it should exceed the amount of variance due to measurement error.

In this doctoral thesis, all but one of the item loadings of the reflective constructs are between 0.613 and 0.978 and are significant at $p < 0.001$. Only the measurement item 'Use4' has a value of 0.575 and 'PB1b' has a value of 0.598, which are both below the threshold of 0.6 with a p at 0.003 and 0.001 respectively (see Table 6-4). As Table 6-3 shows, the construct composite reliability is between 0.869 and 0.967 for all reflective constructs, and the AVE for all reflective constructs is between 0.529 and 0.895; both are above the recommended threshold of 0.8 and 0.5 respectively.

Therefore, only two measurement items, 'Use2' and 'PB1b', do not meet the criteria for convergent validity. Whether these items should be removed will be discussed later.[673]

Discriminant Validity

Discriminant validity is the extent to which an item reflects its construct as opposed to all of the other items in the measurement model. Thus, discriminant validity is tested by evaluating whether the measurement items that should not be related are indeed unrelated. Discriminant validity must be tested on two levels: at the construct level (i.e., for the first-order latent constructs) and the measurement level (i.e., for the different measurement items).[674] At the construct level, Fornell et al. (1981) suggest measuring discriminant validity by evaluating whether the constructs' correlations exceed the square root of the AVE for the construct in question.[675] This test can be used for reflective and formative constructs.[676] At the measurement item level, the traditional tests for discriminant validity are not valid for formative constructs because formative constructs do not require measurement items to be unrelated. For reflective constructs, their

---

[671] MacKenzie et al. (2011)

[672] Fornell, Larcker (1981)

[673] We discuss the disputable measurement items at the end of this section, when all tests are done.

[674] MacKenzie et al. (2011)

[675] Fornell, Larcker (1981)

[676] MacKenzie et al. (2005)

loadings should be significantly lower than the cross-loadings on all other factors to indicate discriminant validity.[677]

At the construct level, for all except two constructs, the correlations do not exceed the square root of the AVE (see Appendix Table E-4). The problematic indicators 'PQ2' and 'PQ3' are discussed below. At the measurement level, all of the reflectively defined constructs show cross-loadings that are much lower than the respective factor loadings (at least 0.3), which indicates the discriminant validity of our reflective indicators (see Appendix Table E-3).

Reliability

Reliability is the extent to which a measurement item is dependable and consistent: i.e., the internal consistency of a measurement item.[678] In testing reliability, again, one cannot analyze formative constructs using the traditional approach that is employed with reflective constructs. The reliability of a formative measurement item can be tested using a test-retest reliability test or an inter-rater reliability test.[679] In addition, a sound indicator of reliability in such cases is the composite reliability, which should be above the threshold of 0.7.[680] To assess the consistency reliability of a set of reflectively defined measurement items, Cronbach's Alpha is again used.[681] When Cronbach's Alpha is used to assess reliability, a threshold of 0.8 is recommended.[682]

In the present thesis, all but two Cronbach's Alphas are above the recommended threshold of 0.8, as is shown in Table 6-3. Only the reflective construct 'Use' is below the threshold; this finding is discussed later. For the formatively defined constructs, the test-retest reliability and inter-rater reliability tests are not performed. To analyze the test-retest reliability would have required a second round of data collection that could not be conducted in this thesis because of resource and time constraints. The inter-rater reliability test requires knowledge about the different raters, which was not available either. However, it was possible to assess the composite reliabilities of the formative constructs (see Table 6-3). All composite reliabilities are above 0.73 and are thus above the recommended threshold, which indicates consistency reliability.

---

[677] Straub et al. (2004)

[678] Bhattacherjee (2012)

[679] MacKenzie et al. (2011)

[680] Chin (1998); Fornell, Larcker (1981); Wetzels, Odekerken-Schröder (2009)

[681] Bollen, Lennox (1991)

[682] Nunnally, Bernstein (1994)

Criterion Validity

Criterion validity is the extent to which a measurement item is consistent with an independent, external measurement item that is intended to measure the same construct.[683] In the present thesis, this test was not performed because there were no alternative measures for the constructs examined.

Construct Validity for Formative Constructs

As indicated above, the traditional tests used to assess the validity and reliability of formative constructs are limited in their applicability.[684] Convergent and discriminant validity and consistency cannot be assessed for formative constructs as they are for reflective constructs because the indicators do not necessarily need to be correlated in the former case.[685] Formatively defined measurement items may be positively correlated, negatively correlated, or completely uncorrelated with one another. Moreover, if traditional measures are used, indicators may be removed that are essential to the domain of the construct, and this may compromise the definition of the construct.[686]

Edwards (2001) recommends assessing the construct validity of formative constructs by determining the strength of the relationship between a set of formative measurement items and a formative construct using the adequacy coefficient (R^2_a).[687] The adequacy coefficient is calculated by summing the squared correlations between the construct and its indicators and dividing this figure by the number of indicators. R^2_a values greater than 0.5 indicate that the majority of the variance in the indicators is shared with the construct.[688] For the formative constructs in this thesis, the adequacy coefficients (R^2_a) are between 0.520 and 0.944 and therewith above the threshold of 0.5 (see Table 6-3).

In addition to evaluating the convergent validity of formative constructs by analyzing the adequacy coefficient (R^2_a), one must further analyze the validity of the formative constructs by assessing the significance and strength of the path from the measurement item to the composite latent construct.[689] These weights indicate how much of the variance of the construct is explained by the indicator and thus the weights should be

---

[683] Bhattacherjee (2012)

[684] MacKenzie et al. (2005)

[685] MacKenzie et al. (2011)

[686] Diamantopoulos (2011)

[687] Edwards (2001)

[688] MacKenzie et al. (2011)

[689] Cenfetelli, Bassellier (2009); MacKenzie et al. (2011)

significant.[690] Thus, the number of indicators has an impact on the strength of the relationship because a construct cannot have more than 100% of its variance explained.[691] In addition to determining the weights that indicate the relative contribution of each indicator, one should also assess the absolute contribution of each indicator by analyzing the loadings.[692] Furthermore, formative indicators should be assessed for conceptual redundancy.[693] Cenfetelli et al. (2009) recommend using the Variance Inflation Factor (VIF), which should be less than 10.[694]

Here, problematic loadings can be identified for the measurement items 'PQ1e', 'PQ2e', 'PQ3e', 'IQ2a', 'IQ2c', 'IQ3d', and 'IQ3e', as shown in Table 6-5. For these indicators, the weights also appear to be problematic because they are significantly lower than those of the other indicators of the respective constructs. In our thesis, the maximum VIF is 4.36, as shown in Table 6-5. Hence, the VIFs suggest appropriate levels of conceptual redundancy.

Discussion of Problematic Indicators

Based on these test results, we conclude that three constructs and seven measurement items are problematic in terms of their reliability and validity. Table 6-6 summarizes these issues. Below, we discuss how these problems are addressed.

Table 6-6 Overview of Identified Issues with Measurement Items

Con-struct	Mea-sure	Defi-nition	Identified issue
Use	N/A	Reflective	Reliability: Cronbach's Alpha 0.79 (below 0.8 threshold)
	Use4	Reflective	Convergent validity: Loading 0.57 (below 0.6 threshold)
PQ1	PQ1e	Formative	Construct validity: Loadings and weights low
PQ2	N/A	Formative	Discriminant validity: Square root AVE < construct correlations
	PQ2e	Formative	Construct validity: Loadings and weights low
PQ3	N/A	Formative	Discriminant validity: Square root AVE < construct correlations
	PQ3e	Formative	Construct validity: Loadings and weights low
IQ2	IQ2a	Formative	Construct validity: Loadings and weights low
	IQ2c	Formative	Construct validity: Loadings and weights low
IQ3	PQ3d	Formative	Construct validity: Loadings and weights low
	PQ3e	Formative	Construct validity: Loadings and weights low
PB	PB1b	Reflective	Convergent validity: Loading 0.598 (below 0.6 threshold)

[690] Bollen, Lennox (1991)

[691] Cenfetelli, Bassellier (2009)

[692] MacKenzie et al. (2011)

[693] Cenfetelli, Bassellier (2009)

[694] Mathieson, Peacock (2001)

The reflective construct 'Use' does not have the expected reliability at the construct level, and measurement item 'Use4' does not display the necessary convergent validity. Therefore, we decided to remove the item 'Use4' from the construct. The remaining three items are still appropriate for use in measuring the 'Use' construct; removing the measurement item 'Use4' improves the reliability of the construct and its convergent validity.

The formative indicators 'PQ1e' 'PQ2e', and 'PQ3e' represent the as-is, to-be, and roadmap for the attribute 'available elsewhere' for EAM products. We added these measurement items during the construct definition process because this item is commonly measured in the context of the original DMSM. However, this measurement item was not identified in the literature review for our a priori model or during the expert interviews for the revised a priori model. It appears that the redundant availability of EAM information does not influence the realization of EAM benefits. Hence, we argue that these items can be removed without compromising the definition of the formative constructs. Removing these items also resolves the issue with the discriminant validity of the constructs 'PQ2' and 'PQ3'.

Similarly, the other two problematic indicators 'IQ3d' and 'IQ3e', which are concerned with ignoring or waiving EAM principles, do not seem to have an impact. This might be because the EAM principles can also be employed at a later stage; temporarily waiving them may not have an impact on the long-term benefits. Therefore, we believe that removing these items does not compromise the definition of the 'IQ3' construct.

The formative measurement items 'IQ2a', which indicates the centrality of capital budgets, and 'IQ2c', which indicates the centrality of process improvement decisions, have low loadings and weights. However, we believe that these aspects are important to the definition of the construct 'Extent of centralization' and argue that they should be retained but observed closely in the remainder of the study. MacKenzie et al. (2011) argue that measurements should be retained if the construct definition will be compromised otherwise. Only if the VIF is below 10, the loadings and weights are insignificant, and the construct definition will not be compromised should the measurement item be removed.[695] Otherwise, the measurement item should be further explored in the subsequent analysis.[696] In our case, the measurement items 'IQ2a' and 'IQ2c' also have VIFs below 3. Because this is a much lower and more conservative threshold than, for example, the one recommended by Petter et al. (2007),[697] and

---

[695] MacKenzie et al. (2011)

[696] Cenfetelli, Bassellier (2009)

[697] Petter et al. (2007)

because the construct definition would be compromised, we opt to retain these measurement items.

Finally, the analysis of the convergent validity showed that the reflective item 'PB1b' is below the threshold of 0.6. However as the loading is just 0.2pp below the threshold and the p-value at <0.001 showed significant results, we decided to retain this item and observe it closely in the remainder of the study.

6.4. Exploring Alternative Formal Model Definitions

Having tested the reliability and validity of our measurement items and eliminated the problematic items, we now test the validity of the revised a priori model.

To assess the fit of a model, researchers can employ either exploratory factor analysis (EFA) or confirmatory factor analysis (CFA). Whereas EFA is a method of exploring an underlying factor structure without an a priori specification, CFA uses an a priori specification for the factor structure and loadings.[698] Because we have already developed an a priori model and CFA is recommended in scenarios with a strong a priori theory, we use this approach to assess the model fit.

CFA requires one or more putative models proposing different sets of latent variables (factors) that may account for the covariance of a set of observed variables. These plausible model variants need to be derived based on the a priori designation of plausible factor patterns in previous theoretical or empirical work. The variants are then explicitly tested statistically against the sample data.[699] Evermann et al. (2011) state that this type of procedure for testing model variants offers rich and interesting insights into the data and is similar to theory-building approaches in qualitative research.[700] Furthermore, relaxing the assumption that there is one model that fits the data and testing different variants prevents interpretational confounding, as discussed in Section 6.1.

In Chapter 4, we developed one such model variant, the revised a priori model. However, this model follows from various different assumptions and design decisions based on the earlier discussion. Other alternative a priori models could also be developed that might fit the data better. The next section discusses such alternatives.

6.4.1.   Development of Model Variants

Based on our understanding of the literature and the interviews, we developed six different conceptualizations of EAM benefit realization. There should theoretically be a

---

[698] Venkatraman (1989)

[699] Anderson, Gerbing D. (1988); Bagozzi (1980); Bollen (1989); Doll et al. (1994)

[700] Evermann, Tate. Mary (2011)

vast set of conceptual models that may fit the data, which results from combining the constructs of the measurement model discussed in Section 6.3 and relating these to each other by varying propositions. Nevertheless, we selected only those putative models that logically build on the findings from our literature review and expert interviews.

To develop and logically restrict the model variants for this research, we defined the following five assumptions based on our earlier findings in this doctoral thesis. First, each of the 18 first-order constructs, which have been operationalized with the latent variables discussed in the previous section,[701] belongs to one second-order construct, i.e., a success dimension, as theoretically defined. Therewith, we did not hypothesize a change in the association between first-order and second-order constructs as these have been uniquely assigned based on theoretical reasoning.[702] For example, the first order construct '(PQ1) As-is architecture quality' is always a sub-dimension of the second-order construct '(PQ) EAM product quality' and must not be reassigned to any other second-order construct. Second, the second-order constructs 'EAM product quality', 'EAM infrastructure quality', and 'EAM service delivery quality' must be included in the model alternatives because these identified success factors are hypothesized to have a critical role in the realization of EAM benefits. Third, the 'EAM benefit' construct must be included in all model alternatives as the dependent variable because this is the central construct that we aim to explain. Fourth, the 'EAM cultural aspects' must be included in the alternatives due to its hypothesized critical role in the realization of EAM benefits, but can be either hypothesized as an independent variable or as a moderator. We derived this assumption based on the insights from our semi-structured interviews. In the interviews, some experts highlighted the potential role of the cultural aspects as a dependent factor from the dimensions 'EAM product quality', 'EAM infrastructure quality', and 'EAM service delivery quality' rather than an independent factor as these dimensions will have an impact on the cultural aspects.[703] Fifth, based on the DMSM, we consider 'EAM use' and 'EAM satisfaction', as potential moderators. However, based on findings from previous research on the DMSM and also the expert interviews, the role of the 'EAM satisfaction' construct is questioned.[704] Therefore, we also considered the removal of this 'EAM satisfaction' construct, while still having 'EAM use' as a mediator.

Based on these five theoretical assumptions, six model alternatives are possible. We describe and explain these putative models in the following. We also present the different models in Figure 6-10.

---

[701] See Section 6.3, in particular Table 6-5.

[702] See Section 3.1 and Section 4.2.2.

[703] See Section 4.2.2 – Key insight I12prop.

[704] See Section 3.1 and Section 4.2.2 – Key insight I14prop.

- Model 1 conceptualizes EAM benefits as a factor that is directly caused by the four EAM success dimensions 'EAM product quality', 'EAM infrastructure quality', 'EAM service delivery quality', and 'EAM cultural aspects' that have been identified in the literature. Following our five assumptions above, this conceptualization is the simplest model that relates the identified success factors with the realized EAM benefits.

- Model 2 conceptualizes EAM benefits as a factor that is directly caused by three of the four identified success dimensions, whereas the fourth factor – namely, the 'EAM cultural aspects' – is understood as a mediating factor. This interpretation of the cultural aspects as a mediator emerged from our expert interviews.

- Model 3 conceptualizes 'EAM benefits' as in the original theory of the DMSM model. The four identified success dimensions 'EAM product quality', 'EAM infrastructure quality', 'EAM service delivery quality', and 'EAM cultural aspects' are the independent variables that generate the EAM benefits. 'EAM use' and 'EAM satisfaction' are used as mediators. This model is the closest to the original DMSM and to our initial theoretical model.[705]

- Model 4 integrates the theoretical arguments underpinning Model 2 and Model 3. It positions the 'EAM cultural aspects', 'EAM Use', and 'EAM satisfaction' as mediators. The three EAM success dimensions 'EAM product quality', 'EAM infrastructure quality', and 'EAM service delivery quality' are modeled as independent variables. This model is the revised a priori model that was developed in Chapter 4.

- Model 5 draws on the argument identified in the expert interviews that satisfaction has no strong impact on EAM benefits. Only the 'EAM cultural aspects' and 'EAM use' are employed as mediators in this model. The remaining 3 success dimensions still have a direct impact on the EAM benefits but are influenced by these two mediators. This model is a variation on our revised a priori model that incorporates the suggestion to remove the 'EAM satisfaction' culled from our expert interviews.

- Model 6 combines the reasoning underpinning Model 3 with the argument, as identified from the expert interviews, that 'EAM satisfaction' does not have a significant impact on EAM benefits. This model considers the four EAM success dimensions 'EAM product quality', 'EAM infrastructure quality', 'EAM service delivery quality', and 'EAM cultural aspects' as independent variables. The only mediator in this model is 'EAM use'.

---

[705] This is the model developed based on the literature review in Chapter 3.

For each of these models, one would normally specify distinct hypotheses that translate the propositions discussed in Section 4.2.2 for empirical validation. These hypotheses would be in the form "'(PQ1) As-Is quality' has a positive impact on EAM Benefits." However, for the sake of brevity, we do not explicitly formulate all hypotheses associated with the six models discussed above. Instead, we refer to the illustration in Figure 6-10 and the overview in Table 6-7. Each arrow in Figure 6-10 represents one hypothesis with a positive impact in the direction of the arrow. An arrow from PQ to EAM benefits represents the hypothesis, 'PQ positively influences EAM benefits'.

Table 6-7 Overview of Hypotheses, Related Propositions, and Associated Models

Hypo-thesis	Propo-sition	Description	Model					
			1	2	3	4	5	6
H1	PQ	EAM product quality positively affects EAM benefits	✓	✓	✓	✓	✓	✓
H2	IQ	EAM infrastructure quality positively affects EAM benefits	✓	✓	✓	✓	✓	✓
H3	SQ	EAM service delivery quality positively affects EAM benefits	✓	✓	✓	✓	✓	✓
H4	CA	EAM cultural aspects positively affect EAM benefits	✓	✓	✓	✓	✓	✓
H5	Use	EAM use positively affects EAM benefits			✓	✓	✓	✓
H6	Sat	EAM satisfaction positively affects EAM benefits			✓	✓		
H7	Use / PQ	EAM product quality positively affects EAM use			✓	✓	✓	✓
H8	Use / IQ	EAM infrastructure quality positively affects EAM use			✓	✓	✓	✓
H9	Use / SQ	EAM service delivery quality positively affects EAM use			✓	✓	✓	✓
H10	Use / CA	EAM cultural aspects affects EAM use			✓	✓	✓	✓
H11	Sat / Use	EAM cultural aspects positively affects EAM satisfaction			✓	✓		
H12	Sat / PQ	EAM product quality positively affects EAM satisfaction			✓	✓		
H13	Sat / IQ	EAM infrastructure quality positively affects EAM satisfaction			✓	✓		
H14	Sat / SQ	EAM service delivery quality positively affects EAM satisfaction			✓	✓		
H15	Sat / CA	A good EAM culture positively affects EAM satisfaction			✓	✓		
H16	CA / PQ	EAM product quality positively affects EAM cultural aspects		✓		✓	✓	
H17	CA / IQ	EAM infrastructure quality positively affects EAM cultural aspects		✓		✓	✓	
H18	CA / SQ	EAM service delivery quality positively affects EAM cultural aspects		✓		✓	✓	

Figure 6-10 Alternative Models for Confirmatory Factor Analysis

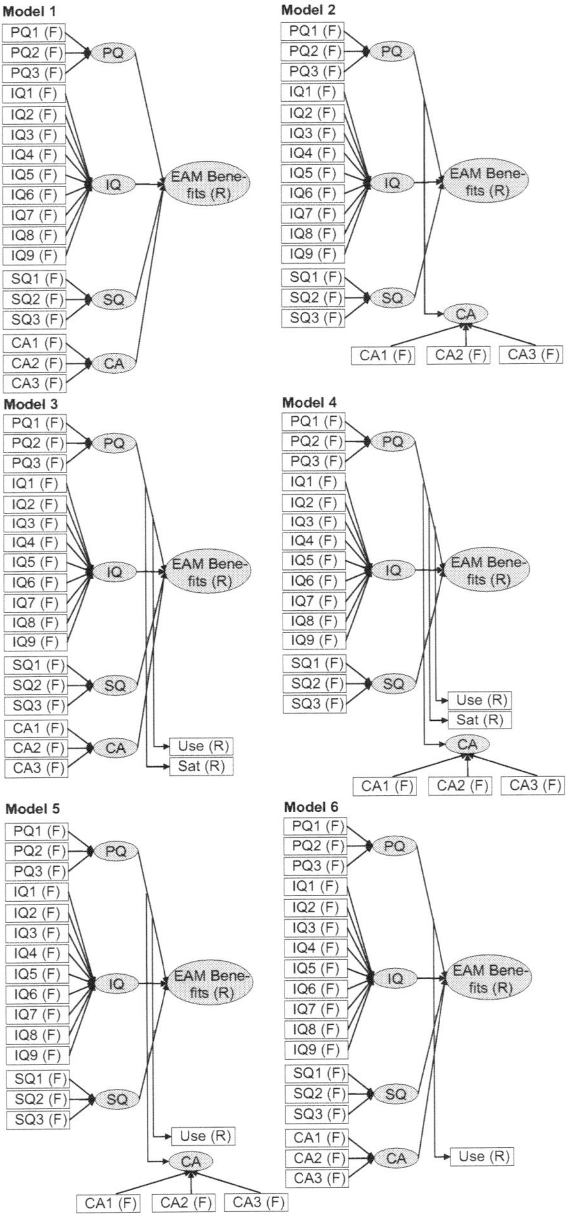

(F) Formatively defined constructs and (R) reflectively defined constructs

6.4.2. Assessing the Model Fit for the Model Variants

Next, we statistically tested each of the models discussed above against the collected empirical data to determine the model fit. We analyzed the data from the survey using a structural equation modeling (SEM) approach and WarpPLS 2.[706]

Here, we test the research models using a two-step approach.[707] First, the quality of the alternative models is assessed by determining the overall fit to identify which model fits the original data better. Then, we evaluate the structural model in detail to determine the best variant.[708]

Because our model contains both formative and reflective constructs, we cannot employ traditional global fit indicators, for example χ^2, because these can only be used with models with reflective models.[709] Kock (2011) recommends that the p-values for the average path coefficient (APC) and the average R-squared (ARS) be lower than 0.05 and that the average variance inflation factor (AVIF) be lower than 5.[710] Furthermore, Tenenhaus et al. (2005) recommend calculating a goodness-of-fit index (GoF) defined as the geometric mean of the average communality of the exogenous constructs and the average R^2 of the endogenous constructs.[711] Wetzels et al. (2009) suggest the following evaluation categories for this GFI: $GoF_{small}=0.1$, $GoF_{medium}=0.25$, and $GoF_{large}=0.36$.[712] Although the R-squared statistic measures the percentage of variability explained by the model, it is criticized as being of limited use in indicating model fit because it is an increasing function of the number of terms in the model. The adjusted R-squared takes this problem into account by adjusting the R-square by the number of terms in the model. Hence, the adjusted R-squared increases only if the predictive power of the model increases.[713] Consequently, we also provide the average adjusted R-squared (AARS) as a

---

[706] Kock (2011)

[707] Anderson, Gerbing D. (1988)

[708] Gefen et al. (2000)

[709] MacKenzie et al. (2011)

[710] Kock (2011). See also Hair et al. (2010); Henseler et al. (2009)

[711] Tenenhaus et al. (2005)

[712] Wetzels, Odekerken-Schröder (2009). Wetzels, Odekerken-Schröder (2009) derives the values from Cohen (1988) who suggests the effect sizes of R^2 to $R^2_{small}=0.02$, $R^2_{medium}=0.13$, and $R^2_{large}=0.26$ and Fornell, Larcker (1981) who suggest for the communarlity that equals in the case of PLS the AVE a cut off value of 0.5.

[713] Hoerl, Snee (2012)

fit index and calculated the Tenenhaus et al. (2005) Goodness-of-Fit index, which is also based on this statistic.[714] The results of these tests are presented in Table Table 6-8.

Table 6-8 Overview of Model Variants and their Fit Indices

	Best Range	Model 1	Model 2	Model 3	Model 4	Model 5	Model 6
Average Path Coefficient (APC)	–	0.210	0.240	0.177	0.194	0.222	0.202
Average R-squared (ARS)	–	0.544	0.559	0.540	0.548	0.555	0.545
Average adj. R-squared (AARS)	–	0.530	0.547	0.523	0.522	0.541	0.532
Average Variance Inflation Factor (AVIF)	<5	2.491	2.493	2.566	2.555	2.496	2.496
Goodness-of-Fit (based on R^2)	–	0.6034	0.6453	0.6426	0.6426	0.6465	0.6410
Goodness-of-Fit (based on adj. R^2)	–	0.6282	0.6383	0.6326	0.6319	0.6384	0.6327
p-Value of Average Path Coefficient	<0.05	<0.001	<0.001	<0.001	<0.001	<0.001	<0.001
p-Value of Average R-squared	<0.05	<0.001	<0.001	<0.001	<0.001	<0.001	<0.001
p-Value of adj. Average R-squared	<0.05	<0.001	<0.001	<0.001	<0.001	<0.001	<0.001

The results of these fit tests indicate that all of the models fulfill the Kock (2011) criteria.[715] The p-values for all of the models are below the recommended threshold of 0.05, and the AVIFs, which are between 2.491 and 2.566, are well below the threshold of 5. For all of the models, Tenenhaus et al.'s (2005) GoF (traditional and adjusted) is above the threshold of 0.36 for large effect sizes. However, comparing the latter GoF indices indicates that Model 5 is superior to the others based on the traditional Goodness-of-Fit index but only slightly (0.01pp) better than Model 2 based on the Goodness-of-Fit index calculated with the adjusted R^2. Because the adjusted R^2 takes into account the complexity of the model, this Goodness-of-Fit index should be favored. This conclusion can also be reached by more closely considering the APCs and ARSs. In general, the addition of a new latent variable to a model should increase the ARS, even if the new variable is weakly associated with the existing ones. However, this addition should generally lead to a decrease in the APC because the path coefficient associated with the new latent variable will be low. Consequently, the APC and ARS only increase together if the newly added latent variable increases the overall predictive and

---

[714] Tenenhaus et al. (2005)

[715] Kock (2011)

explanatory power of the model.[716] As can be seen from the results, the addition of latent variables to Models 2 and 5 (as compared with the simplest model, Model 1) increases the APCs; the ARSs and AARSs also increase. This means that the predictive power of these models improves when additional variables are added. For Models 3, 4, and 6, this is not the case. Here, the addition of latent variables decreases the APCs, and the ARSs and AARSs also decrease[717] or increase only slightly.[718] Consequently, the suggested Models 3, 4, and 6 do not increase the predictive power of the basic model, whereas Models 2 and 5 do increase its predictive power.

However, the GoF as suggested by Tenenhaus et al. (2005) is not a formal procedure for determining global model fit. Instead, the GoF serves as a diagnostic value.[719] Therefore, in the next chapter, we discuss when the structural model is validated and address the distinct differences between the six models introduced above. Based on the GoF assessment, Model 5 should be favored.

6.5. Validation of the Structural Model

Once the measurement model and the model fit have been analyzed, the structural model should be evaluated in detail. To test these hypotheses, we modeled all six models in WarpPLS again using the revised set of measurement items based on the removals discussed in Section 6.3.

The structural models of the six model variants are hierarchical construct models, i.e., models with second-order or higher-order constructs, which are also called multidimensional construct models. Similar to first-order constructs, the hiearchical constructs are often called reflective or formative. However, a formative or reflective conceptualization is problematic, because a hiearchical, second-order construct does not exist separate from its dimensions.[720] Therefore, hierarchical constructs are differentiated between aggregate and superordinate hierarchical constructs. For superordinate constructs, the general concept that the construct represents becomes manifest in its sub-dimensions, i.e., the relationship flows from the construct to its sub-dimensions. For aggregate constructs, the construct combines its sub-dimensions into a general concept, i.e. the relationship flows from the sub-dimensions to the construct.[721]

---

[716] Kock (2011)

[717] This is the case for model 3.

[718] This is the case for model 4 and 6.

[719] Wetzels, Odekerken-Schröder (2009)

[720] Wright et al. (2012)

[721] Edwards (2001); Law et al. (1998); Polites et al. (2011); Wong et al. (2008)

The hierarchical constructs used in our six models are all aggregate constructs, as the sub-dimensions form the respective hierarchical construct. For the assessment of such aggregate hierarchical constructs, similar assessments as for formative constructs are required. We discuss these assessments in the following.

Figure 6-11 Inner and Outer Structural Models for Hierarchical Construct Models Using Example of Model 5

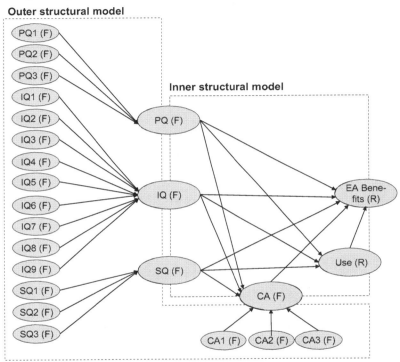

The hierarchical construct models must be assessed in two steps. First, the outer model must be evaluated in a manner similar to that used with the measurement model. Then, the inner model needs to be evaluated.[722] Figure 6-11 illustrates the inner and outer models using the example of Model 5.

To validate the six different hierarchical structural models, we use the approach recommended by MacKenzie et al. (2011).[723] Our six discussed models vary only in terms of the paths between the constructs of the inner structural model; the outer

---

[722] MacKenzie et al. (2011); Wetzels, Odekerken-Schröder (2009); Wright et al. (2012)

[723] MacKenzie et al. (2011)

structural model for all six variants is the same.[724] Hence, in what follows, we discuss the outer model for the six variants and then the different variants of the inner model.

Validation of the Outer Structural Model

As a means of assessing the construct validity of the outer-model constructs, MacKenzie et al. (2011) recommends a validation approach that is fairly similar to that used with the measurement items. He suggests starting by evaluating the AVE for each first-order sub-dimension; this value should be greater than 0.50. Next, the adequacy coefficient (R^2_a) should be examined. These values should be similar to the thresholds for the measurement items, i.e., larger than 0.8.

Table 6-9 Overview of Key Statistics for the Outer Structural Model Constructs

Second-order Construct	Number of items	Cronbach's alpha coefficients	Adequacy coefficient (R^2_a)	Average variance extracted
PQ	3	0,899	0,937	0,833
IQ	9	0,848	0,884	*0,479*
SQ	3	0,821	0,894	0,738
CA	3	0,848	0,908	0,767
Benefits	26	0,964	0,967	0,529

As shown in Table 6-9, the reliability coefficients are well above the threshold of 0.8, and for all except one construct, the AVE is above the threshold of 0.5. Only the 'IQ' construct is slightly below the threshold of 0.5. We discuss this problematic construct at the end of this section.

To assess the construct validity of the hierarchical aggregate constructs, we assess the significance and strength of the path from the first-order composite latent construct to the second-order composite latent construct, i.e., the constructs of the outer model. Significant weights indicate that the first-order constructs explain the outer structural model constructs.[725] In this context, as in evaluating the first-order constructs, one must remember that the number of indicators has an impact on the strength of the relationship because a construct cannot have more than 100% of its variance explained.[726] We also assess the absolute contribution of each first-order construct by evaluating the loadings.[727] Finally, the composite first-order constructs should be

---

[724] Note that the constructs use and satisfsaction although part of the inner model and altered here as well, are discussed as first-order constructs in Section 6.3.

[725] Bollen, Lennox (1991)

[726] Cenfetelli, Bassellier (2009)

[727] MacKenzie et al. (2011)

assessed for conceptual redundancy.[728] A threshold of 10 should be used to assess conceptual redundancy based on the Variance Inflation Factors (VIF).[729]

Table 6-10 Loadings, Weights, Significances, and VIF for Outer Structural Model

LV	Item	Loading	Weight	p-value	VIF
PQ	PQ1	0.874	0.35	<0.001	2.177
	PQ2	0.936	0.374	<0.001	3.826
	PQ3	0.927	0.371	<0.001	3.576
IQ	IQ1	0.663	0.154	<0.001	1.543
	IQ2	*0.157*	*0.036*	*0.203*	*1.065*
	IQ3	0.729	0.169	<0.001	1.883
	IQ4	0.782	0.181	<0.001	2.146
	IQ5	0.626	0.145	<0.001	1.521
	IQ6	0.774	0.18	<0.001	2.091
	IQ7	0.77	0.179	<0.001	2.032
	IQ8	0.827	0.192	<0.001	2.507
	IQ9	0.662	0.153	<0.001	1.738
SQ	SQ1	0.904	0.408	<0.001	2.379
	SQ2	0.862	0.389	<0.001	2.029
	SQ3	0.809	0.365	<0.001	1.608
CA	CA1	0.863	0.375	<0.001	1.978
	CA2	0.862	0.374	<0.001	1.967
	CA3	0.902	0.392	<0.001	2.400

These assessments indicate that only the construct 'IQ2 Extent of centralization' is problematic (see Table 6-10). The loadings of this construct are not significant, nor is its p-value.[730] The other loadings of the outer structural model constructs are between 0.626 and 0.936 with p-values at <0.001; thus, these constructs are significant. The VIFs are between 1.543 and 3.576 and thus are also well below the threshold of 10. Given the number of items per outer structural model construct, the weights are also appropriate.[731]

With respect to the reliability of the outer structural model constructs, a dedicated reliability assessment for formatively defined second-order constructs is not required. As Edwards (2001) argues, *"[R]eliability is not an issue of debate when a multidimensional*

---

[728] Cenfetelli, Bassellier (2009)

[729] Mathieson, Peacock (2001)

[730] A discussion of how to handle this first-order construct follows at the end of this section.

[731] Note that a common threshold for indicator weights has not been recommended but the maximum possible average standardized indicator weight is 0.316 given 10 indicators. Cenfetelli, Bassellier (2009)

construct and its dimensions are treated as latent variables that contain no measurement error."[732]

Based on the analysis of the structural model, we identified issues with the outer structural model construct 'IQ.' First, the average variance extracted (AVE) was below the threshold of 0.5. Second, the loading of the first-order construct, 'IQ2 Extent of centralization', was not significant and showed no significant p-value. Consequently, we decided to drop this first-order construct as it also showed issues with two measurement items, which we have discussed in Section 6.3.[733] Because this construct addresses the degree of centrality of several decision-making areas, it can be argued that the centrality of the decision-making areas have no direct significant impact on the realization of EAM benefits.[734]

Validation of the Inner Structural Model

To examine the inner structural model and validate our hypotheses, we analyzed the path coefficients and the associated path significance using WarpPLS for all six models. The respective values are shown in Table 6-11. Based on these results, three categories of hypotheses can be discussed. The first category is those hypotheses that are not supported by any of the models. The second category is those hypotheses are supported by all of the relevant models, and the third category is those that are supported by some of the relevant models.

None of the models supported hypotheses H2, H6, H7, H8, H9, H12, and H13, as the path coefficients and associated significance values demonstrate. Therefore, we can already conclude without evaluating a dedicated model that these hypotheses find no support in our data. There is no evidence of a direct positive impact of the 'EAM infrastructure quality' on 'EAM benefits' (H2). In addition, the data show no support for a positive impact of 'EAM satisfaction' on 'EAM benefits' (H6). Also, there is no evidence of a positive impact of 'EAM product quality', 'EAM infrastructure quality', or 'EAM service delivery quality' on 'EAM use' (H7-H9). Finally, we could not identify any support for the hypothesis that 'EAM product quality' and 'EAM infrastructure quality' have a positive impact on 'EAM satisfaction' (H12 and H13).

---

[732] Edwards (2001), p. 60

[733] Namely 'IQ2a Capital budgets' and 'IQ2c Application development projects prioritization and approval'

[734] We discuss this in detail in Section 7.3.

Table 6-11 Overview of Path Coefficients of the Six Model Variants

Hypo-thesis	Path	Model 1	Model 2	Model 3	Model 4	Model 5	Model 6
H1	PQ -> Ben	0.12^{ns}	0.12^{ns}	$0.14*$	$0.14*$	$0.141*$	$0.141*$
H2	IQ -> Ben	0.149^{ns}	0.149^{ns}	0.132^{ns}	0.132^{ns}	0.131^{ns}	0.131^{ns}
H3	SQ -> Ben	$0.204*$	$0.204*$	0.169^{ns}	0.169^{ns}	0.172^{ns}	0.172^{ns}
H4	CA -> Ben	$0.367*$	$0.367*$	0.2^{ns}	0.2^{ns}	0.202^{ns}	0.202^{ns}
H5	Use -> Ben	—	—	$0.269**$	$0.269**$	$0.272**$	$0.272**$
H6	Sat -> Ben	—	—	0.008^{ns}	0.008^{ns}	—	—
H7	PQ -> Use	—	—	-0.07^{ns}	-0.07^{ns}	-0.076^{ns}	-0.076^{ns}
H8	IQ -> Use	—	—	0.099^{ns}	0.099^{ns}	0.092^{ns}	0.092^{ns}
H9	SQ -> Use	—	—	0.033^{ns}	0.033^{ns}	0.163^{ns}	0.163^{ns}
H10	CA -> Use	—	—	$0.382***$	$0.382***$	$0.573***$	$0.573***$
H11	Sat -> Use	—	—	$0.413***$	$0.413***$	—	—
H12	PQ -> Sat	—	—	-0.012^{ns}	-0.012^{ns}	—	—
H13	IQ -> Sat	—	—	0.002^{ns}	0.002^{ns}	—	—
H14	SQ -> Sat	—	—	$0.259*$	$0.259*$	—	—
H15	CA -> Sat	—	—	$0.465***$	$0.465***$	—	—
H16	PQ -> CA	—	$0.198*$	—	$0.198*$	$0.198*$	—
H17	IQ -> CA	—	$0.279**$	—	$0.279**$	$0.279**$	—
H18	SQ -> CA	—	$0.365**$	—	$0.365**$	$0.365**$	—

Legend: ^{ns} - not significant, *** - p<0.001, ** - P<0.01, * - p<0.05;
grey shaded – paths with significant weights

The data supported hypotheses *H5, H10, H11, H14,* and *H15-H18 in all model variants.* First, the hypothesis that 'EAM use' has a positive impact on 'EAM benefits' (*H5*) finds support in all of the relevant models and also has fairly stable path coefficients (either 0.269 or 0.271) across the different models. Similarly, the hypothesis that 'EAM cultural aspects' have a positive impact on 'EAM use' (*H10)* is supported by the data.

However, in those models in which hypothesis H11 is included, the path coefficient for hypothesis H10 decreases from 0.573 to 0.382. This may be because 'EAM satisfaction' explains some of the variance in 'EAM use' that (if 'EAM satisfaction' is not modeled) is otherwise already explained by 'EAM cultural aspects' as a proxy for 'EAM use'. As an indicator of such conceptual redundancy, this type of multicollinearity can also be revealed by the VIF and the AVIF.[735] Including the concept of satisfaction in Model 4 increases the AVIF from 2.496 (the corresponding figure for Model 5) to 2.555. More specifically, this increase in the AVIF can also be observed by examining the VIF of hypothesis H10 (see Table 6-12). The VIF increases from 2.231 in Model 5 (in which EAM satisfaction is not included) to 2.633 in Model 4 (in which it is included). However, in all

---

[735] Cenfetelli, Bassellier (2009)

of the models in which EAM satisfaction is included – namely, Models 3 and 4 – there is support for hypothesis H11.

For those models that include satisfaction, the data also support the hypotheses that 'EAM service delivery quality' (H14) and 'EAM cultural aspects' (H15) positively influence 'EAM satisfaction'. Finally, all of the models that include culture as a mediator – namely, Models 2, 4, and 5 – support the hypotheses that 'EAM product quality' (H16), 'EAM infrastructure quality' (H17), and 'EAM service delivery quality' (H18) have a positive impact on 'EAM cultural aspects'.

Table 6-12 Overview of VIFs for the Six Model Variants

Hypo-thesis	Path	Model 1	Model 2	Model 3	Model 4	Model 5	Model 6
H1	PQ->Ben	1.947	1.947	1.960	1.960	1.959	1.959
H2	IQ->Ben	2.817	2.817	2.832	2.832	2.826	2.826
H3	SQ->Ben	2.946	2.946	3.217	3.217	2.973	2.973
H4	CA->Ben	2.254	2.254	3.049	3.049	2.972	2.972
H5	Use->Ben	—	—	2.263	2.263	1.935	1.935
H6	Sat->Ben	—	—	2.281	2.281	—	—
H7	PQ->Use	—	—	1.937	1.937	1.937	1.937
H8	IQ->Use	—	—	2.797	2.797	2.796	2.796
H9	SQ->Use	—	—	3.023	3.023	2.836	2.836
H10	CA->Use	—	—	2.633	2.633	2.231	2.231
H11	Sat->Use	—	—	1.896	1.896	—	—
H12	PQ->Sat	—	—	2.128	2.128	—	—
H13	IQ->Sat	—	—	3.208	3.208	—	—
H14	SQ->Sat	—	—	3.146	3.146	—	—
H15	CA->Sat	—	—	2.126	2.126	—	—
H16	PQ->CA	—	1.866	—	1.866	1.866	—
H17	IQ->CA	—	2.791	—	2.791	2.791	—
H18	SQ->CA	—	2.830	—	2.830	2.830	—
Average VIF		*2.491*	*2.493*	*2.566*	*2.555*	*2.496*	*2.496*

Finally, the third category of hypotheses that have alternating support are the hypotheses that 'EAM product quality' (H1), 'EAM service delivery quality' (H3), and 'EAM cultural aspects' (H4) directly and positively affect 'EAM benefits'. In this category, the significance of these hypotheses depends on the inclusion of the 'EAM use' construct. We can sort the models that are relevant to this discussion into two groups. The first group includes Model 1 and Model 2, whereas the second includes the remaining models: Models 3 through 6. These two groups of models show that if hypotheses H1-H4 and H16-H18 are included in the models, the same path coefficients and path significance are found.[736] In group one, H1 is significant, whereas H3 and H4 are insignificant. In contrast, in group two, in which all of the models include the EAM use construct, H1 is not significant, whereas H3 and H4 are significant (see Table 6-11). Consequently, we can conclude that the inclusion of the use construct has an impact on significance and is the main driver of these changes in significance.

Table 6-13 Overview of R-square for Model Variants

	Model 1	Model 2	Model 3	Model 4	Model 5	Model 6
Ben	0.544	0.544	0.582	0.582	0.582	0.582
CA		0.574		0.574	0.574	
Use			0.599	0.599	0.509	0.509
Sat			0.439	0.439		
Average	*0.544*	*0.559*	*0.540*	*0.548*	*0.555*	*0.545*

Based on the discussion of the two groups, we can conclude that including the 'EAM Use' construct causes the greatest change in the path coefficients and path significance. An analysis of the explanatory power of the models yields the same insights. The R-squares for the EAM benefit constructs increase from $R^2=0.544$ for the first group[737] to $R^2=0.582$ for the second group,[738] when the 'EAM Use' construct is included. Hence, the use construct allows us to explain 3.8pp more of the variance in EAM benefits than is possible when we use Model 1 or 2 (see Table 6-13). In addition, the conceptual redundancy does not increase significantly when we include the 'EAM Use' construct because the AVIFs remain stable. We conclude this by observing the difference between the AVIF values for Model 1 and Model 6 and the difference between those values for Model 2 and Model 5.[739] Including the 'EAM use' construct increases the AVIF by just 0.5pp and 0.3pp, respectively. Only the VIF for the path from 'EAM cultural aspects' to 'EAM benefits' increases by a figure as high as 71.8pp in both cases (from Models 1 and 2 to Models 5 and 6), indicating a conceptual overlap between the two corresponding constructs.[740] The VIFs of all of the other paths remain stable, with changes of less than 2.7pp at most. Therefore, we conclude that given the increased explanatory power and fairly stable AVIFs, the models in the second group that include the 'EAM Use' construct, i.e., Models 3-6, are preferable.

---

[736] Note that the path coefficents in group two change only by 0.3pp depending on the inclusion of the satisfaction construct.

[737] This are Models 1 and 2.

[738] This are Models 3 to 6.

[739] The difference between these is exactly the inclusion of the 'EAM use' construct.

[740] See Table 6-12.

In Models 3-6, the R-squares for the 'EAM Benefit' construct remain stable. Therefore, it can be concluded that including the 'EAM satisfaction' construct (Models 3 and 4) or the 'EAM cultural aspects' construct as a mediator (Models 4 and 5) does not improve the explanatory power of the model with respect to 'EAM benefits.' However, whereas including the 'EAM satisfaction' construct increases the AVIF by only 7pp (from Model 6 to Model 3) and 5.9pp (from Model 5 to Model 4),[741] there is a change of 40.2pp in the VIF for the path from 'EAM cultural aspects' to 'EAM Use', a change of 16.95pp in the VIF for the path from 'EAM Use' to 'EAM benefits', a change of 30.8pp in the VIF for the path from 'EAM service delivery quality' to 'EAM benefits', and a change of 18.7pp in the VIF for the path from 'EAM service delivery quality' to 'EAM Use'. The VIFs for the remaining paths exhibit smaller changes. However, these findings indicated that although the explanatory power does not improve, the conceptual redundancy increases when the 'EAM satisfaction' construct is added. Consequently, Models 5 and 6, which do not include the 'EAM satisfaction' construct, should be favored.

The final difference between the remaining models, Models 5 and 6, is the positioning of the 'EAM cultural aspects' construct as a mediator. Whereas Model 6 includes this construct as a second-order construct, Model 5 includes 'EAM cultural aspects' as a mediator that is influenced by 'EAM product quality', 'EAM infrastructure quality', and 'EAM service delivery quality'. As discussed above, including this construct does not improve the R-squared value. However, the AVIF and all of the VIFs remain the same for these models (see Table 6-12). Therefore, including the 'EAM cultural aspects' construct as a mediator does not increase conceptual redundancy; instead, it helps to explain the role of culture in the realization of EAM benefits. Hence, we argue that Model 5 is preferable to Model 6.

Based on this discussion, we come to the same conclusion recommended based on Tenenhaus et al.'s GoF: Model 5 is the superior model from the analyzed set. The diagnostic characteristics of the GoF as discussed in Section 6.4.2 further support our conclusion.

---

[741] See again Table 6-12.

6.6. Synthesis

This chapter analyzed the data collected using our survey instrument to validate our a priori model. We examined the descriptive statistics for the data, the potential non-response error, and the fit of the data. These analyses suggested that the data are appropriate for use in further analysis. Next, we analyzed the measurement model and identified eleven measures or constructs with problematic characteristics. These findings resulted in the removal of the measurement items 'Use4', 'PQ1e', 'PQ2e', 'PQ3e', 'IQ3d', and 'IQ3e' to improve the overall measurement model.

Table 6-14 Overview of Hypotheses, Related Propositions, and Associated Models

Hypo-thesis	Propo-sition	Description	Model inde-pendent	Model 5
H1	PQ	EAM product quality positively affects EAM benefits	md	✓
H2	IQ	EAM infrastructure quality positively affects EAM benefits	ns	ns
H3	SQ	EAM service delivery quality positively affects EAM benefits	md	ns
H4	CA	EAM cultural aspects positively effect EAM benefits	md	ns
H5	Use	EAM use positively affects EAM benefits	✓	✓
H6	Sat	EAM satisfaction positively affects EAM benefits	ns	ni
H7	Use / PQ	EAM product quality positively affects EAM use	ns	ns
H8	Use / IQ	EAM infrastructure quality positively affects EAM use	ns	ns
H9	Use / SQ	EAM service delivery quality positively affects EAM use	ns	ns
H10	Use / CA	EAM cultural aspects affects EAM use	✓	✓
H11	Sat / Use	EAM cultural aspects positively affects EAM satisfaction	✓	ni
H12	Sat / PQ	EAM product quality positively affects EAM satisfaction	ns	ni
H13	Sat / IQ	EAM infrastructure quality positively affects EAM satisfaction	ns	ni
H14	Sat / SQ	EAM service delivery quality positively affects EAM satisfaction	✓	ni
H15	Sat / CA	A good EAM culture positively affects EAM satisfaction	✓	ni
H16	CA / PQ	EAM product quality positively affects EAM cultural aspects	✓	✓
H17	CA / IQ	EAM infrastructure quality positively affects EAM cultural aspects	✓	✓
H18	CA / SQ	EAM service delivery quality positively affects EAM cultural aspects	✓	✓

Legend: ns – not significant, ni – not included, md – model dependent,
✓ - significant in all models where included

Finally, we discussed several structural model variants to determine to what degree they fit the collected data. Model 5 exhibited the best fit, both in terms of Goodness-of-Fit and based on the detailed discussion. Interestingly, this model is different than our initially developed or revised a priori model. However, it fairly closely resembles our revised a priori model. Nevertheless, unlike the latter, Model 5 does not include the 'EAM Satisfaction' construct. Table 6-14 provides an overview of the hypotheses and indicates whether each is supported by the data. Overall, eight hypotheses are supported by all of the models, seven are not supported by any of the models, and three hypotheses are supported by some models. Model 5 supports six hypotheses. We will discuss these findings in detail in Chapter 7.

7.   Model Discussion

Thus far, we have analyzed our model from a statistical point of view. This chapter will interpret our results and discuss our findings in the context of other research. Therefore, we first discuss the findings from an overall model perspective in Section 7.1. We then focus on the distinct dimensions and their items in the next section (Section 7.2). We continue to discuss the removed measurement items in Section 7.3. Based on this material, we review the implications of this research in Section 7.4. Finally, we conclude this chapter with a synthesis in Section 7.5.

7.1. Discussion of the Overall Model

As indicated at the end of the previous chapter, six hypotheses associated with Model 5 were significant. This finding indicates the general viability of the suggested research model as a means of explaining the realization of EAM benefits. On average, the research model explained 58.2% ($R^2=0.582$)[742] of the variance in the EAM benefits. The amount of variance explained by the model is acceptable given that the empirical studies of EAM typically explain between 10% and 70% of the variance. For example, in their study of the effectiveness of EAM principles, Boh et al. (2007) report a R-square between $R^2=0.303$ and $R^2=0.455$; in their study of EAM techniques and project conformance, Foorthuis et al. (2010) report an R-square between $R^2=0.098$ and $R^2=0.691$; and in their study of IT-centric benefits, Schmidt et al. (2011) report a R-square between $R^2=0.28$ and $R^2=0.40$.

By exploring alternative models, we improved the conceptual redundancy of the model and thus increased its parsimony. Toward this end, we varied the structural model and statistically analyzed the role of the constructs 'EAM Use', 'EAM satisfaction', and 'EAM cultural aspects.' As a result, we removed the 'EAM satisfaction' construct from our

---

[742] For comparability reasons, we report here the traditional R^2 that is reported as well in the quoted research. The more appropriate adjusted average R-square is in the case of this research actually $R^2=0.541$.

revised a priori model because it did not contribute to the explanatory power of the model but inflated the model and undermined its parsimony. All of the other hypothesized constructs proved to be relevant to the realization of EAM benefits.

Figure 7-1 Overview of the Resulting EAM Benefit Realization Model Including the Significant Paths

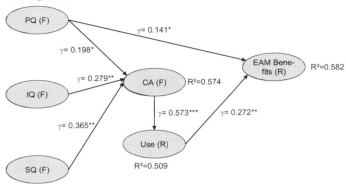

Legend: path coefficients: ns - not significant, *** - p<0.001, ** - P<0.01, * - p<0.05
Note that figure illustrates significant paths only

Showing only the significant paths, Figure 7-1 illustrates the resulting model. In this model, two constructs have a direct, significant impact on the realization of EAM benefits. These constructs are 'EAM use', which has the strongest impact on the realization of EAM benefits ($\gamma=0.271$), and 'EAM product quality', which has approximately half of the impact that 'EAM use' has ($\gamma=0.141$). The remaining three constructs have an exclusively indirect impact on the realization of EAM benefits. 'EAM product quality' ($\gamma=0.198$), 'EAM infrastructure quality' ($\gamma=0.279$), and 'EAM service delivery quality' ($\gamma=0.365$) influence the EAM cultural aspects. These three dimensions explain 57.4% ($R^2=0.574$) of the variance in the 'EAM cultural aspect' construct. The cultural aspects, in turn, influence the use of EAM ($\gamma=0.573$) and explain 50.9% ($R^2=0.509$) of the variance in 'EAM use'. In the next part of this section, we discuss the roles of the included constructs in this overall structural model.

EAM Cultural Aspects

As we expected based on the literature review and our expert interviews, the importance of EAM culture is strongly indicated by our model. The 'EAM cultural aspects' are central. Influenced by the three success factors of 'EAM product quality', 'EAM infrastructure quality', and 'EAM service delivery quality', the cultural aspects appear to strongly influence 'EAM use' ($\gamma=0.573$) and to be a key mediator for the two constructs 'EAM infrastructure quality' and 'EAM service delivery quality' and the dependent variable EAM benefits. Because the two constructs 'EAM infrastructure quality' and 'EAM service delivery quality' do not have a significant impact either directly on the benefits of EAM or indirectly on 'EAM use', the construct 'EAM cultural aspects' is central to the role of the EAM infrastructure and EAM service delivery in realizing EAM benefits. Therefore, the construct 'EAM cultural aspects' can be seen as an important but indirect enabler for EAM benefits.

Because strategic planning is fairly similar to EAM,[743] this finding appears to be similar to those of Cleland et al. (1974). These authors conclude from their research on strategic planning that the success of long-term planning is more sensitive to cultural aspects than to the techniques employed.[744] These findings are consistent with the findings of this research. The employed techniques, in our model the 'EAM infrastructure quality', have no direct impact on the realization of EAM benefits but influence the 'EAM cultural aspects'. Thus, the techniques employed in the domain of EAM are also subordinate to the cultural aspects that influence the realization of EAM benefits.

This finding regarding the central role of culture is also consistent with other earlier research findings. Zink (2009) presents a qualitative EAM study that highlights 'EAM understanding' and 'EAM leadership involvement' as central enablers of EAM success.[745] In addition, organizational research findings show the central role of culture in the realization of benefits. For example, Lee et al. (2004) and Gordon et al. (2007) find evidence in their research that a strong culture is associated with better organizational performance, i.e., the success of the overall organization.[746] This study reconfirms these effects in the domain of EAM.

EAM Use

The role of the construct 'EAM use' is similar to that of the construct 'EAM cultural aspects' in promoting the benefits of EAM. This construct is the only construct other than 'EAM product quality' that directly, significantly influences 'EAM benefits' ($\gamma=0.271$). An organization can understand, plan, and manage an Enterprise Architecture, but EAM only yields benefits if the organization actually implements the planned architecture. Thus, the 'EAM use' construct is a necessary precondition for EAM benefits and, hence, is one of the key drivers in our model.

---

[743] See the relationship between strategic planing, EAM, and traditional program management discussed in Section 2.1.

[744] Cleland, King (1974)

[745] Zink (2009)

[746] Gordon, DiTomaso (2007); Lee, Yu (2004)

These findings are also consistent with earlier EAM research. Schmidt et al. (2011) conclude in their study that EAM stakeholder participation, which one can interpret as a proxy for use, is fundamental to the realization of IT benefits from EAM.[747] In many other domains in which researchers have applied the DMSM, however, the use construct has also either been insignificant or has exhibited conceptual overlap with the success measures employed. For example, Bandara et al. (2006) removed the use construct from their model for project modeling success because the former overlapped significantly with the overall success construct in their model.[748] Based on a review of the literature on the DMSM, Petter et al. (2008) conclude that this dimension receives moderate support overall.[749] For example, although Zuh et al. (2005) present a study in which the use of online IS for e-businesses has a significant positive impact on organizational benefits in both developing and developed countries,[750] Geldermann (2002) reports that the duration, as an indicator for use, using a system is not significantly correlated with organizational benefits.[751] In our case, however, the construct 'EAM use' added explanatory power to the model and did not increase the conceptual redundancy of the model. Hence, we conclude that the 'EAM Use' construct is a central element of EAM benefits.[752]

EAM Product Quality

The 'EAM product quality' construct is the second construct, besides the 'EAM Use' construct (γ=0.271) construct, that has a significant positive impact on the realization of EAM benefits. This impact, however, is approximately half the size of the impact of the construct 'EAM Use' (γ=0.141). As communication vehicles that create transparency by providing information about the current and future architecture and the transformation roadmap, EAM products seem as though they yield such immediate benefits plausibly. Transformation projects can use the EAM products immediately for their project activities and hence provide benefits on the project-level such as an acceleration of project setup times, easier scoping, and efficient communication. This use of EAM products does not even require a deeper understanding of EAM, or in other words a strong EAM culture, to unfold the related EAM benefits. However, using EAM products alone does not

---

[747] Schmidt, Buxmann (2011)

[748] Bandara et al. (2006)

[749] Petter et al. (2008)

[750] Zuh, Kraemer (2005)

[751] Geldermann (2002)

[752] See Section 6.5.

substantially improve an organization. Hence, the associated benefits are relatively low compared to those obtained by organizations using EAM that have a strong EAM culture.

In earlier research, Schmidt et al. (2011) find that EAM product quality has a similar impact on IT-related EAM benefits and a similar impact size.[753] They conclude that the relatively low impact could be due to the fact that EAM products primarily create informational transparency rather than impacting IT evolution in a regulatory manner. The authors further conclude that the impact is relatively low because firms that focus on EAM products alone do not substantially improve with respect to their EAM goals.[754]

EAM Infrastructure Quality and EAM Service Delivery Quality

The next two EAM dimensions, 'EAM infrastructure quality' and 'EAM service delivery quality' have no direct impact on the realization of EAM benefits but have an indirect impact through 'EAM cultural aspects'. Unlike EAM products, these dimensions do not have an immediate role in the realization of EAM benefits. Given the underlying factors, this conclusion appears to be reasonable. Without an understanding and an awareness of EAM, i.e., an appropriate EAM culture, and actual use, neither the EAM infrastructure nor EAM service delivery will yield immediate benefits at the organizational or project level. In contrast, EAM products can be employed on a project level without a deeper understanding of EAM. For example, EAM tool support could improve the efficiency of EAM processes but would not yield immediate organizational benefits on its own, nor could it be used on a project level without a deeper understanding of EAM. Therefore, 'EAM infrastructure quality' and 'EAM service delivery quality' appear to be hygiene factors in a sense. They need to be in place for EAM to operate, and their characteristics shape the EAM culture, but their existence alone is not sufficient to ensure EAM benefits.

To the best of our knowledge, these empirical findings regarding the role of EAM culture in the benefits derived from EAM infrastructure and EAM services are the first ones in this research area. Therefore, they cannot be compared to other findings.

Satisfaction

Finally, 'EAM satisfaction' is not part of the resulting model because it did not contribute to the explanatory power of our model for the realization of EAM benefits. Therefore, we can conclude that the 'EAM Satisfaction' construct, as hypothesized in the revised a priori model, does not seem to be a moderate for the realization of EAM benefits. As briefly

---

[753] 'EA documentation', which is the construct in their study equivalent to our 'EAM product quality' is $\gamma=0.16$ in their research in comparison to $\gamma=0.141$ in this study. Schmidt, Buxmann (2011)

[754] Schmidt, Buxmann (2011)

discussed in the previous chapter, including the 'EAM Satisfaction' construct in the model increased the conceptual redundancy of the model and decreased the strength of the link between the 'EAM cultural aspects' and 'EAM use'.[755] This finding suggests that the 'EAM Satisfaction' and 'EAM Use' constructs have strong conceptual redundancy.

These findings are similar to those from other disciplines in which the DMSM has been used. For example, Gable et al. (2003) remove the satisfaction construct in using the DMSM to analyze ERP system success because it added little explanatory power.[756] The authors argue that pure satisfaction items do not reflect a distinct dimension of success but are rather just additional measures of overall success. This reasoning is also consistent with the findings of Teo et al. (1998).[757] In their study of the impact of IT investment and performance impact measures, these authors conclude that satisfaction is not a distinct dimension. Similarly, Sedera et al. (2004b) eliminated the satisfaction construct from their model of business process modeling success because of its limited explanatory power; they argue that satisfaction is redundant given a comprehensive set of other success measures.[758] In the domain of EAM, van der Raadt et al. (2010) similarly theorize that the stakeholders are satisfied when their individual goals are met. Consequently, the authors argue that benefits and satisfaction are closely related and even congruent.[759]

7.2. Discussion of the Dimensions of the Model

Having discussed the overall model and the relationships between each dimension, we now discuss the details of each of these dimensions. Thereby, we detail the dimensions of the model and discuss how the different sub-dimensions influence their respective superior dimension 'EAM product quality, 'EAM infrastructure quality', and 'EAM service delivery quality' respectively.

EAM Product Quality

The 'EAM product quality' dimension includes the sub-dimensions '(PQ1) EAM as-is architecture quality', '(PQ2) EAM to-be architecture quality', and '(PQ3) EAM roadmap quality'. All of the sub-dimensions impact the overall 'EAM product quality' dimension

---

[755] In those models in which the 'Satisfaction' construct is included, the path coefficient of the path from 'EAM cultural aspects' to 'EAM use' drops from $\gamma=0.573$ to $\gamma=0.382$. See Section 6.5.

[756] Gable et al. (2003)

[757] Teo, Wong (1998)

[758] Sedera, Gable (2004b); Sedera, Tan (2005)

[759] van der Raadt et al. (2010). Note that these are no empirical finding but theoretically postulated hypotheses that are not tested by the authors.

significantly at p<0.001. Figure 7-2 illustrates the model excerpts for the 'EAM product quality' dimension, its sub-dimensions, and the respective measurement items.

Figure 7-2 Model Excerpt from 'EAM Product Quality' Including the Path Weights

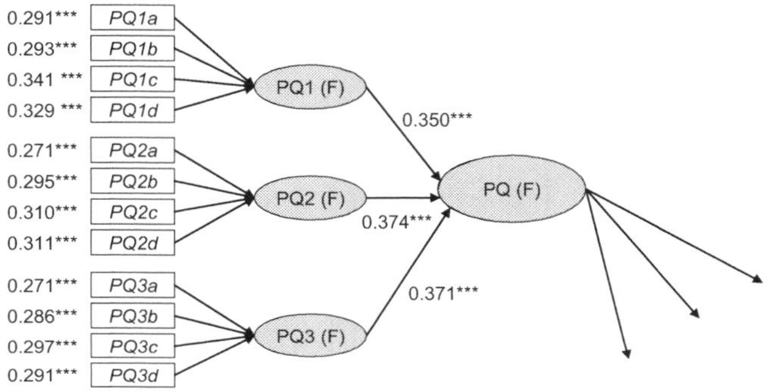

Legend: path weights: ^{ns} - not significant, *** - p<0.001, ** - p<0.01, * - p<0.05

As illustrated in Figure 7-3, the EAM to-be architecture and the EAM roadmap are almost equally important to the realization of EAM benefits. The path weights for the EAM as-is architecture is 2.1pp lower that those for the EAM roadmap quality. This conclusion appears to be reasonable because the goal of EAM is the transformation of the enterprise towards a target that must be clearly defined. The awareness of the as-is is thereby indeed a prerequisite that is required for the efficient execution of the transformation, but it does not guarantee the realization of the benefits that will result from achieving the actual target state.

Figure 7-3 Ranked Sub-dimensions of 'EAM Product Quality' by Path Weights

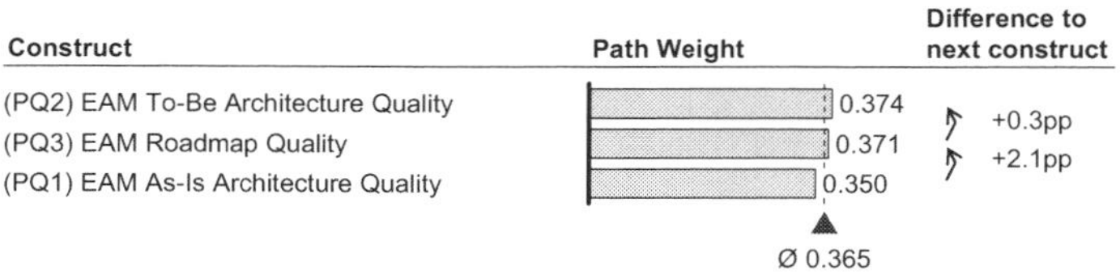

EAM Infrastructure Quality

The 'EAM infrastructure quality' dimension is comprised of the eight sub-dimensions '(IQ1) EAM mandate definition', '(IQ3) EAM governance formalization', '(IQ4) EAM framework availability', '(IQ5) EAM tool support availability', '(IQ6) EAM reference architectures availability', '(IQ7) EAM principle establishment', '(IQ8) EAM skills availability', and '(IQ9) EAM resources availability'. All of these sub-dimensions impact the overall 'EAM infrastructure quality' dimension significantly at p<0.001, as illustrated in Figure 7-4 for the respective model excerpts for the 'EAM infrastructure quality' dimension.

Figure 7-4 Model Excerpt for 'EAM Infrastructure Quality' Including Path Weights

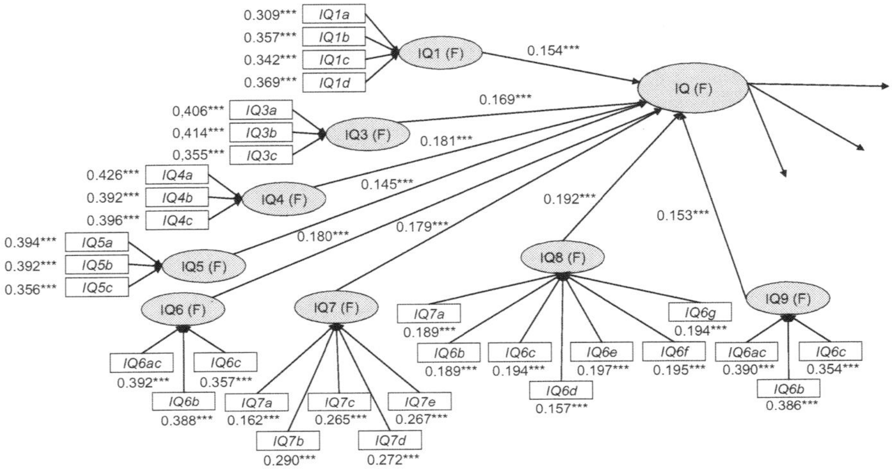

Legend: path weights: [ns] *- not significant,* *** *- p<0.001,* ** *- p<0.01,* * *- p<0.05*

Figure 7-5 illustrates the ranking of these eight dimensions according to their path weights. With a path weight that is 1.1pp higher than that of the next ranked sub-dimension, EAM skills are the most important sub-dimension of the EAM infrastructure in terms of their contribution to the realization of EAM benefits. With path weights that are only 0.1pp lower, the next three, almost equally important, sub-dimensions are the 'EAM framework availability', 'EAM reference architectures availability', and 'EAM principles establishment'. The people working in EAM are the most important component of the 'EAM infrastructure quality', followed by those infrastructure components that describe 'what to do' in EAM. This finding again confirms the importance of human capital, which has previously been discussed as contributing to the central role of EAM culture. The formal 'how to do' EAM constructs, namely 'EAM governance formalization' and 'EAM mandate', have path weights that are 1.0pp lower.

Finally, 'EAM resources availability' and 'EAM tool support availability' have the lowest path weights. The path weight for 'EAM resource availability' is 3.9pp less than the highest path weight, and the path weight for 'EAM tool support availability' is 4.7pp less than the highest path weight. Therefore, Expert 3, who stated that *"a fool with a tool is still a fool"*, appears to be right because tool support has the least influence on the realization of EAM benefits.[760]

Figure 7-5 Ranked Sub-dimensions of 'EAM Infrastructure Quality' by Path Weights

Construct	Path Weight	Difference to next construct
(IQ8) EAM Skill Availability	0.192	+1.1pp
(IQ4) EAM Framework Availability	0.181	+1.0pp
(IQ6) EAM Reference Architecture Availability	0.180	+0.1pp
(IQ7) EAM Principle Establishment	0.179	+1.0pp
(IQ3) EAM Governance Formalization	0.169	+1.5pp
(IQ1) EAM Mandate Definition	0.154	+0.1pp
(IQ9) EAM Resource Availability	0.153	+0.8pp
(IQ5) EAM Tool Support Availability	0.145	

Ø 0.169

EAM Service Delivery Quality

The third dimension, the 'EAM service delivery quality' dimension, includes the three sub-dimensions '(SQ1) EAM communication', '(SQ2) EAM management support', and '(SQ3) EAM project support'. As illustrated in the model excerpt in Figure 7-6, all of these sub-dimensions impact the overall 'EAM service delivery quality' dimension significantly at p<0.001.

Figure 7-6 Model Excerpt for 'EAM Service Delivery Quality' Including Path Weights

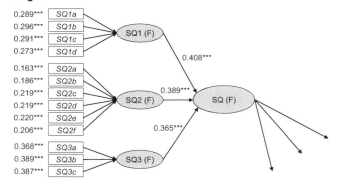

Legend: path weights: [ns] - not significant, *** - p<0.001, ** - p<0.01, * - p<0.05

'EAM communication' is the sub-dimension of the 'EAM service delivery' with the greatest impact on the realization of EAM benefits (see Figure 7-7). Next is 'EAM management

---

[760] See Section 4.2.1.

support', with a path weight that is 1.9pp lower. Interestingly, with a path weight that is 2.4pp lower, 'EAM project management' is the lowest ranked of these sub-dimensions. Although the full benefits of EAM are only achieved through the actual use of the planned architecture, the support for the transformation projects appears to be less relevant than the other two sub-dimensions. However, it could be argued that without value-oriented communications regarding the advantages of EAM and a fundamental commitment by the top management, an organization will not be able to implement the planned enterprise architecture; thus, 'EAM project support' is less important than the other two constructs. Furthermore, this finding again demonstrates the central role of EAM culture. Even if it has no direct impact on benefits, a strong EAM culture within an organization will encourage the use of EAM in the organization, i.e., within the transformation projects, which will make EAM project support less important than the EAM culture.

Figure 7-7 Ranked Sub-dimensions of 'EAM Service Delivery Quality' by Path Weights

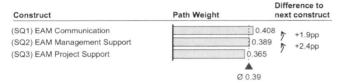

Construct	Path Weight	Difference to next construct
(SQ1) EAM Communication	0.408	+1.9pp
(SQ2) EAM Management Support	0.389	+2.4pp
(SQ3) EAM Project Support	0.365	

Ø 0.39

EAM Cultural Aspects

The fourth dimension, the 'EAM cultural aspects' dimension, includes the sub-dimensions '(CA1) EAM top-management commitment', '(CA2) EAM awareness', and '(CA3) EAM understanding'. As illustrated in Figure 7-8, in this dimension, all sub-dimensions and measurement items are significant at p<0.001.

Figure 7-8 Model Excerpt from 'EAM Cultural Aspects' Including Path Weights

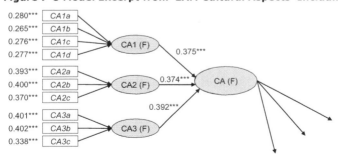

Legend: path weights: ^{ns} - not significant, *** - p<0.001, ** - p<0.01, * - p<0.05

Within this dimension, the most influential sub-dimension with respect to the realization of benefits from EAM is '(CA3) EAM understanding' (see Figure 7-9). With scoress that are 1.7pp and 1.8pp below that of the first sub-dimension, respectively, the remaining two sub-dimensions are relatively similar in terms of their impact. Hence, having a good understanding of EAM appears to be important because the latter may directly lead to the use of EAM. However, because the appropriate top-management commitment and the awareness of EAM have a significant influence on the use of EAM, these factors are also fairly close to the 'EAM understanding'.

Figure 7-9 Ranked Sub-dimensions of 'EAM Cultural Aspects' by Path Weights

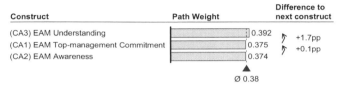

Construct	Path Weight	Difference to next construct
(CA3) EAM Understanding	0.392	+1.7pp
(CA1) EAM Top-management Commitment	0.375	+0.1pp
(CA2) EAM Awareness	0.374	

Ø 0.38

Legend: path weights plus difference to next ranked path in percent

Figure 7-10 Ranked Sub-dimensions 'EAM Organizational Benefits' by Path Weights

Construct	Path Weight	Difference to next construct
(OB1i) Reduce Cost	0.828	+4.0pp
(OB2c) Strategic Business-IT Alignment	0.788	+0.5pp
(OB1h) Increase Utilization	0.783	+0.1pp
(OB2d) Efficient Communication	0.782	+0.4pp
(OB1g) Control Complexity	0.778	+0.5pp
(OB1e) Consolidate Applications	0.773	+0.4pp
(OB3b) Respond to Market	0.769	+0.3pp
(OB1a) Integrate Applications	0.766	+1.7pp
(OB2b) Operational Business-IT Alignment	0.749	+0.3pp
(OB3c) Enable Innovation	0.746	+0.3pp
(OB2a) Global Optimization	0.743	+1.9pp
(OB3a) Identify Change	0.724	+0.1pp
(OB3d) Cooperate with Others	0.723	+0.2pp
(OB1j) Increase Revenue	0.721	+0.2pp
(OB1c) Standardize Applications.	0.719	+2.7pp
(OB1f) Consolidate Processes.	0.692	+1.4pp
(OB1b) Integrate Processes.	0.678	+2.5pp
(OB1d) Standardize Processes.	0.653	+0.4pp
(OB2e) Achieve Compliance	0.649	

Ø 0.74

EAM Benefits

Finally, we discuss the ranking of the perceived benefits of EAM. As discussed in Section 3.3, these benefits can be divided into those obtained at the organizational level and those obtained at the project level.

Figure 7-10 illustrates the ranking of the EAM benefits on the organizational level. The difference between the first and the last path weights is a remarkable 17.9pp. The top EAM benefit, cost reduction, has a path weight that is 4.0pp higher than that of the next benefit. Interestingly, the process-related benefits are at the bottom of the table, whereas the more IT-related benefits, e.g., the consolidation or integration of applications, are in the top ten. Furthermore, regulatory compliance is the lowest-ranked organizational benefit. Although regulatory compliance is considered as a key driver for EAM, our findings show that least benefits are realized from this factor. This discrepancy has also been identified in earlier research.[761]

At the project level, the greatest benefit of EAM is the ability to address complexity. This benefit may also be related to the above-discussed finding that EAM product quality is the only success dimension that directly yields EAM benefits (see Figure 7-11). EAM products create transparency for the as-is and to-be enterprise architecture, and such transparency facilitates the improved handling of organizational complexity.

Interestingly, the traditional benefits of program or project management, i.e., the ability to meet project budgets and project deadlines, are the lowest on this list. This finding is consistent with our discussion of the positioning of EAM in Section 2.1. We argued that EAM was the interface between the firm, its strategy and traditional program management, which partially implements the strategy. Because traditional program management only addresses budgets and deadlines, we argued that EAM is required to globally and fully implement a firm-level strategy. Consistent with this theory, this list demonstrates that EAM appears to deliver exactly the related benefits; the traditional program management benefits are ranked last, whereas the other project-related benefits that EAM should yield are at the top of the list. Interestingly, there is also a significant gap exactly at the demarcating line between obtaining the desired functionality (PB2b) and staying within the project budget (PB1a). The difference between these two constructs in terms of their contribution to the overall EAM benefits is 7.3pp.

---

[761] Lange, Mendling (2011)

Figure 7-11 Ranked Sub-dimensions of 'EAM Project Benefits' by Path Weights

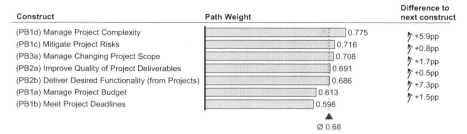

Construct	Path Weight	Difference to next construct
(PB1d) Manage Project Complexity	0.775	↗ +5.9pp
(PB1c) Mitigate Project Risks	0.716	↗ +0.8pp
(PB3a) Manage Changing Project Scope	0.708	↗ +1.7pp
(PB2a) Improve Quality of Project Deliverables	0.691	↗ +0.5pp
(PB2b) Deliver Desired Functionality (from Projects)	0.686	↗ +7.3pp
(PB1a) Manage Project Budget	0.613	↗ +1.5pp
(PB1b) Meet Project Deadlines	0.598	

Ø 0.68

7.3. Discussion of the Removed Constructs and Measurement Items

Having discussed the roles of the constructs that were included in this overall structural model and the details of each dimension in the previous sections, we now discuss the elements – i.e., the first-order constructs and measurement items – that have been removed aside from the above-discussed 'Satisfaction' construct. In total, one additional construct, namely the 'IQ2 Extent of centralization', and six measurement items have been removed. We now discuss the resulting implications in detail.

Removal of Constructs

Three statistical observations resulted in the removal of the construct '(IQ2) Extent of centralization.' First, during the assessment of the structural model, the average variance extracted (AVE) of this construct was below the threshold of 0.5. Second, the loading was not significant and showed no significant p-value.[762] Finally, the formative measurement items for this construct – 'IQ2a', i.e., the centrality of capital budgets, and 'IQ2c', i.e., the centrality of process improvement decisions, were problematic because of their low loadings and low weights.[763]

These three statistical observations indicate that the correlation between the construct 'IQ2' and the construct '(IQ) EAM infrastructure quality' is limited. Because the construct 'IQ2 Extent of centralization' indicates the degree of centralization of several decision-making areas, it can be argued based on the low loadings and weights that these areas have no direct, significant absolute or relative impact on the realization of EAM benefits. Whereas Radeke (2010) hypothesizes that centralization influences EAM outcomes and EAM use, our findings do not support this hypothesis.[764] Hence, due to the statistical

---

[762] See Section 6.5.

[763] See Section 6.3.

[764] Note that Radeke (2010) did not provide any empirical evidence for this hypothesis.

instability of this construct and its limited theoretical contribution to the realization of EAM benefits, we removed this construct completely. Based on these findings, it seems that the centrality of decision-making may not be an EAM success factor because both centralized and decentralized setup of EAM can be used depending on the organizational culture. An organization that has a decentralized decision-making culture might be better suited to a decentralized EAM, for example, and the other way around.

Removal of Measurement Items

When validating the measurement items, we identified six problematic measurement items. These items included one measurement item from the reflectively defined 'EAM Use' construct, the measurement item 'Use4', and the five formative measurement items 'PQ1e' 'PQ2e', 'PQ3e', 'IQ3d', and 'IQ3e'.

Although removing the measurement item 'Use4' from the reflective construct 'Use' has no direct impact on the definition of the construct due to the nature of reflective measurement items, removing a measurement item from a formatively defined construct needs to be handled with more care.[765] As discussed in Section 6.3, the reflective construct 'Use' is statistically problematic in two respects. First, the construct exhibited low reliability, and second, the measurement item 'Use4' exhibited problematic convergent validity. Therefore, we removed the item 'Use4' from the construct, improving reliability at the construct level. Because the remaining three items still sufficiently measure the 'Use' construct, removing the measurement item 'Use4' did not change the meaning or the definition of the construct. Hence, the interpretation of this construct has not changed due to the removal of this item.

The formative indicators are different in this respect. 'PQ1e' 'PQ2e', and 'PQ3e' within the dimension of EAM products represent the attribute 'available elsewhere' for the as-is architecture, the to-be architecture, and the roadmap, respectively. Based on the statistical analysis, it appears that the redundant availability of EAM information does not have an impact on the realization of EAM benefits.[766] This finding is supported by the fact that this characteristic of EAM product quality was not identified during the literature review for our a priori model or during the expert interviews for the revised a priori model. We identified this characteristic during the construct definition process because this is a commonly measured item in the context of the original DMSM. Therefore, we

---

[765] While reflective measurement items are unidimensional, i.e., the items measure all the same characteristic, formatively defined measurement items are multidimensional and each formative measurement item measures a distinct characteristic of the construct. See Section 5.2.1 for a detailed discussion of the difference between formative and reflective constructs.

[766] See Section 6.3.

argue that this characteristic appears to be relevant to traditional information systems because it is included in other measurement instruments for the DMSM but that it is not a distinct element of product quality in the domain of EAM. Because the information provided by EAM in some organizations is also generated in the context of other initiatives, e.g., parts of the business architecture can be documented during business process management initiatives, the uniqueness of the information provided appears not to be crucial to 'EAM product quality'. Instead, EAM needs to provide an overview of the relevant information that might be otherwise distributed across the organization but that might not be available as a holistic, integrated whole. Consequently, we argue that these items can be removed without compromising the definition of the formative constructs.

Similarly, the other two problematic indicators, 'IQ3d' and 'IQ3e' which represent the ignorance and the waiving of EAM principles, respectively, do not appear to have an impact on 'EAM governance formalization' according to the statistical analysis.[767] Although formal EAM governance determines how strictly the EAM implementation process proceeds, it can be argued that waiving or ignoring the EAM principles will not necessarily mean that the to-be architecture is not achieved in the future. Indeed, the EAM principles can also be fulfilled at a later stage, and their temporary non-compliance or waiving has no significant impact on the long-term benefits of EAM. Therefore, we believe that the removal of these items does not compromise the definition of the 'IQ3' construct; thus, we remove these items as well. However, the role of waivers and informal agreements in the realization of benefits should be researched in more detail.

7.4. Implications

In this section, we discuss the implications for research[768] as well as practice from this doctoral thesis.[769]

7.4.1.   Implications for Research

In summary, this research has shown that the DMSM is generally applicable to the domain of EAM and that both an EAM culture and EAM use play a central role in the realization of benefits from EAM. These findings have implications for both EAM research and IS success research.

First, the findings from this research suggest that the central role of an EAM culture and EAM use should be reflected in EAM research. These findings have implications both for behavioural science research and for design science research on EAM. In behavioural

---

[767] See Section 6.3.

[768] See Section 7.4.1.

[769] See Section 7.4.2.

science research on EAM, the existing empirical models, to the best of our knowledge, do not include cultural aspects. However, the findings from the present thesis suggest that EAM culture plays a central role in EAM. Including EAM culture in these models, either as a mediator or an independent variable depending on the model, could improve their explanatory power. For example, Boh et al.'s (2007) empirical research model on the use of and conformance to EAM principles does not include cultural aspects, as is discussed in their published work.[770] Including cultural aspects in their model could better explain the use of and conformance to EAM principles. The findings from this research support this particular example because the EAM principles influence EAM culture as part of our dimension 'EAM infrastructure quality'. In turn, EAM culture has an impact on EAM use, which is a central aspect of Boh et al.'s (2007) model. Similarly, the empirical work of Schmidt et al. (2011) and Foorthuis et al. (2010), discussed above, could benefit from an extension by these cultural aspects. Schmidt et al.'s (2011) model, which measures the IT benefits of EAM, could include the cultural aspects as a mediator to explain the realization of IT benefits and Foorthuis et al. (2010)'s model, which measures the EAM benefits resulting from project conformance to EAM, could use the cultural aspects as an additional contextural factor that explains the conformance to EAM. Furthermore, our findings regarding the central role of EAM culture also have implications for design science research on EAM. This research stream focuses on the design aspects of EAM, considering what EAM processes, EAM products, and EAM governance should ideally look like. Having indicated the importance of both EAM culture and EAM use, the findings from this doctoral thesis suggest that these aspects should also be incorporated into such research to increase the acceptance of the designed artifacts, which improves their effectiveness and efficiency. For example, Buckl et al. (2008) suggest a pattern-based approach to EAM.[771] An extension of this approach by cultural aspects that describes which patterns work in what culture best could improve the effectiveness and efficiency of EAM.

Second, the implications for IS success research are at least threefold. First, the application of the DMSM to the domain of EAM has shown that the model is applicable not only to traditional information systems in a narrower, more technical sense but also to socio-organizational disciplines such as EAM. This conclusion supports the findings from earlier research in which the DMSM has been applied to disciplines such as business process modeling or knowledge management.[772] It provides further evidence of such broader applicability of the DMSM. Consequently, these findings encourage the

---

[770] Boh et al. (2007)

[771] Buckl et al. (2008). See also Section 2.3 for a more detailed introduction.

[772] Kulkarni et al. (2006); Sedera et al. (2004d); Wu, Wang (2006)

application of the DMSM to other domains that may even be boundary disciplines of IS research such as organizational research. Such an application to other domains would create further insights that substantiate the applicability of the DMSM to other domains, and hence, the further generalizability of the model. Second, this research has identified the central role of EAM culture in the realization of benefits. Therefore, these findings suggest that cultural aspects have an influence that is not yet reflected in the original DMSM. Although other existing IS success models do not include cultural aspects either as having a direct influence or as a mediator, some scholars have suggested that these factors should be included in IS success research in particular.[773] Correspondingly, the findings from this research show the importance of cultural aspects in the domain of EAM. Therefore, it is reasonable to assume that these aspects also play an important role in other domains. Nevertheless, it is important to note that further evidence of the impact of these cultural aspects has yet to be accumulated in other domains. Because the DMSM was developed for more technical domains, these findings may only be relevant to the application of the DMSM to more socio-organizational domains. Third, the findings from this research suggest the viability of the use construct as an enabler of benefits. Previous research has presented only sporadic evidence of the impact of use on benefits.[774] However, following our discussion on the different possible perspectives on benefits and use,[775] it is important to differentiate what perspectives have been taken to research benefits and use when comparing the results. In this research, the DMSM has been implemented to measure *organizational benefits* and *use of a subgroup of people within an organization*: the EAM stakeholders. Given this context, use has exhibited a significant impact on benefits. Consequently, these findings suggest that use is an applicable mediator for benefits when use is a critical enabler for these benefits and when the resulting benefits can clearly be distinguished from use. In the context of EAM, this is as follows. Although the use of EAM by a subgroup of an organization, the EAM stakeholders, provides direct benefits for this subgroup, the majority of the resulting benefits accrue to the organization as a whole. Hence, the congruence of the benefits and use is limited. However, EAM benefits on the organizational level are only realized through EAM use as our research shows. Consequently, the use construct is required as an enabler. To generalize these findings, IS research must distinguish more clearly between the different perspectives on use. This will make it possible to distinguish different use constructs and compare only constructs that are genuinely equal. In

---

[773] E.g., Claver et al. (2001); Seddon (1997); Wainwrighta, Waring (2004)

[774] Petter et al. (2008)

[775] See Section 1.4.

addition, further evidence must be collected to generalize the applicability of the use construct when measuring organizational benefits.

7.4.2.   Implications for Practice

In addition to the academic relevance of this doctoral thesis and its implications for research, this thesis has implications for EAM practitioners and experts in at least three areas.

First, the findings from this research provide practitioners and experts with important insight into the factors that facilitate EAM benefits. These findings can inform organizations about how to approach EAM so as to improve the realization of EAM benefits. This research has highlighted a number of important factors that must be considered to ensure effective and efficient EAM. For example, organizations should be aware of the important role that cultural aspects play in a successful EAM. Rather than implementing EAM by focusing on related techniques and tools, organizations should focus on the human capital associated with EAM and build a broad understanding and awareness of EAM across the organization, persuading people of the importance of EAM. The findings of this thesis yield two actionable recommendations for improving the benefits of EAM. (1) Do not focus your EAM on techniques and model intensively your organization in an ivory tower; go into your transformation projects and be a role model for conducting good EAM to shape your EAM culture proactively. (2) Focus your EAM on people rather than on processes and formalizations; an EAM culture begins in people's minds and is not created by enforced guidelines and rules. This approach will ultimately yield the required use of EAM in organizations' transformation activities and the expected benefits. To develop an appropriate EAM culture, organizations should develop the appropriate setup for their EAM infrastructure and EAM service delivery that suits their overall organizational culture.

Second, the developed measurement instrument for EAM success factors and EAM benefits allows EAM practitioners to measure the degree of firm-level EAM benefit realization in their organization. This ability not only ensures a transparent view of the current state of the realization of EAM benefits but also allows the perceived EAM benefits to be tracked over time. For example, organizations can use the measurement instrument once a year to evaluate whether the measures that have been implemented to improve the realization of EAM benefits had the desired effect and to calculate the corresponding impact size.

Third, the measurement instrument not only enables the measurement of EAM benefits but also enables the identification of potential improvements. This benchmarking capacity can be used in two ways. First, organizations can use the measurement instrument within their organization to explore how EAM benefits are generated across different departments or different projects. Using this approach, organizations can both compare the different entities to each other and compare how different stakeholders perceive the realized EAM benefits. Based on this type of assessment, an organization can derive the measures required to improve the realization of EAM benefits in particular departments or projects. Second, the measurement instrument can serve as a benchmarking tool across organizations. Evaluating the realization of EAM benefits across different organizations not only allows the identification of combinations of EAM success factors that best provide the EAM benefits but also provides the opportunity to identify the distinct measures that have been applied by one organization that could help another organization to improve their situation. Such cross-organizational benchmarking makes it possible to identify best-practices that will yield EAM benefits and to share this knowledge across organizations.

7.5. Synopsis

In this chapter, we have discussed the findings generated by our statistical model regarding the realization of benefits from EAM. First, we discussed the role of the five dimensions that have a significant impact on the realization of EAM benefits. Then, we discussed each dimension in detail and have considered what sub-dimensions impact the particular dimensions and to what degree. Finally, we discussed the implications of removing the problematic constructs and measurement items during the statistical analyses for the measurement model and the structural model.

In summary, we can conclude based on this discussion of the dimensions of EAM success that EAM benefits are generated in two ways. First, the information transparency and communication capabilities associated with EAM products can generate the EAM benefits. However, the impact of these is relatively small compared to the influence of the second source of benefits. This second source, EAM use, has the greatest impact; the impact is approximately twice as great as the impact of EAM products. However, this dimension requires a deeper understanding of EAM and, hence, the establishment of an EAM culture in the long term. Thus, the three discussed EAM success factors – EAM products, EAM infrastructure, and EAM service delivery – are fundamental to shaping this central EAM culture.

8. Conclusion

Nothing is permanent
but change
Heraclitus

In this final chapter, we synthesize the material presented in this thesis and discuss the outcomes, contributions, and limitations of this research. The objective of this chapter is therefore to provide a summary of the findings and contributions that have been presented thus far. First, we summarize the results in Section 8.1. Then, we discuss the contributions of this doctoral thesis in Section 8.2 and its limitations in Section 8.3. Finally, in Section 8.4, we provide suggestions for future research.

8.1. Recapitulation

The need for an approach that could be used to evaluate the benefits of EAM motivated this research. Therefore, we answered two research questions:

- What are the dimensions and measures that affect the benefits of Enterprise Architecture Management?

- How can the benefits of Enterprise Architecture Management for an organization be explained and predicted?

To answer these research questions, we conducted a study based on a multi-method research design. This design included an exploratory phase and a confirmatory phase. In the exploratory phase, we developed a theoretical a priori model based on a review of the literature on EAM success factors and benefits. We refined and revised the a priori model by conducting semi-structured interviews with EAM experts. This revised a priori model provides a comprehensive conceptualization of the generation of EAM benefits based on six dimensions of success: EAM product quality, EAM infrastructure quality, EAM service delivery quality, EAM use and EAM satisfaction. We developed these dimensions not only based on the results of the literature review and expert interviews but also based on the DMSM, which suggests that similar dimensions are at work in the domain of information systems.

In the second, confirmatory phase, we operationalized this revised a priori model using a survey instrument and then used this survey instrument to test the model statistically. This data analysis showed strong support for four of the five identified dimensions.

Because the dimension of EAM satisfaction in our model did not exhibit any explanatory power, we removed this dimension. The model provided strong additional support for most of the hypotheses related to the relationships between the remaining four dimensions. In particular, the model demonstrates the important central role of EAM culture; the essential but not sufficient role of EAM product quality, EAM infrastructure quality, and EAM service delivery quality; and, finally, the essential role of EAM use in generating benefits from EAM. Figure 8-1 recapitulates this model of the realization of EAM benefits.

Figure 8-1 Recapitulation of the Resulting EAM Benefit Realization Model

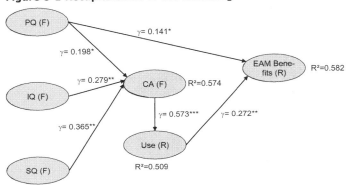

In developing this model, we have employed a rigorous positivist approach intended to incorporate as much empirical evidence as possible to validate the model. During the first phase of this research, we therefore explored 868 journal articles on EAM, conducted eleven semi-structured interviews with EAM experts, and (in preparing the survey) discussed the phases of our research with more than 50 different experts, consultants, colleagues, and students. We continuously and comprehensively incorporated the feedback gathered in this way. The global administration of the survey allowed us to capture responses from more than 300 participants.[776]

Overall, this doctoral thesis contributes to the existing body of knowledge on this subject by compiling EAM success factors from the literature and from practical observation and by using this collection of factors to develop and validate a model of the realization of EAM benefits. We developed this theoretical model by expanding on existing knowledge, i.e., the DMSM, and established theories regarding the generation of benefits from information systems. The empirical validation of this model indicated that the suggested

---

[776] From these over 300 responses, unfortunately, only 133 were complete and usable for the overall model. The 300 respondents, however, all answered parts of the survey.

model is appropriate and helps to explain the role of the different dimensions of EAM success in explaining the realization of EAM benefits.

8.2. Contributions

This doctoral thesis contributes to the existing body of knowledge in multiple ways. The central contribution of this doctoral thesis is the construction and empirical validation of the EAM Benefit Realization Model of the factors that influence the realization of EAM benefits. However, in the following, we discuss the details of the different detailed contributions. First, we elaborate on the different contributions of each chapter of the thesis; then, we discuss the appropriateness of our contributions based on Weber's (2012) framework for the evaluation of IS theories.[777]

Contributions of this Doctoral Thesis

First, we presented an overview of the existing approaches to EAM assessment in Chapter 2 of this thesis. This review of the literature on EAM assessment approaches contributes to the existing body of knowledge on the subject by organizing the existing knowledge and providing an overview of the existing gaps in the literature. Furthermore, we pointed out some potential directions for future research. This information may guide researchers seeking to fill the identified gaps.

2We then discussed the existing knowledge on EAM success factors and benefits in a structured literature review in Chapter 3 of this thesis. This literature review generated a deeper knowledge of theory regarding the EAM success factors and benefits and their relationships. Furthermore, we showed how existing theories of IS success – namely the DMSM – can be integrated with the findings from our literature review and adjusted to the domain of EAM.

Then, we conducted semi-structured interviews, presented in Chapter 4, that supplemented the findings from the literature by providing a practical perspective. This is one of the few studies in the domain of EAM that thereby presents empirical, practical insight into the 'real-world' realization of EAM benefits based on semi-structured interviews. Furthermore, the semi-structured interviews contributed to our initial validation of the a priori model of the realization of EAM benefits.

One of the central contributions of this doctoral thesis was presented in Chapter 5. In this chapter, we presented the operationalization of our model for the realization of EAM benefits into a set of measurement items that have been implemented as a web-based survey. These measurement items were used to capture the respondents' perceptions

---

[777] Weber (2012)

about the realization of EAM benefits and the necessary EAM success factors. The scale development procedure ensured a high level of construct and content validity and ensured the reliability of the measurement items. This procedure also made this thesis one of the few studies in IS that thoroughly develops measurement items for a mixed formative and reflective set of measurement items. The described procedure for validating these measurement items thereby leveraged different guidelines and recommendations from the various sources that are suggested for use in developing these mixed measurement items. Although this thesis reused some of the existing measurement items, it also developed new ones that contribute to the IS inventory of measurement items. These items can be reused in subsequent studies.

Fifth, we have validated our revised a priori model based on the data collected using the Web-based survey (as seen in Chapter 6). First, this data analysis was conducted using an SEM approach by MacKenzie et al. (2011) to empirically evaluate the mixed formative and reflective models.[778] This is one of the few empirical studies in the domain of EAM and one of the first studies in IS that have used this rigorous process of validating formative constructs. This thesis has shown the effectiveness of this and should encourage other IS researchers to validate their formative constructs in a similar manner.

Finally, in Chapter 7, we discussed the central contribution of this thesis: the validated EAM benefit realization model. As this chapter indicates, the empirically validated model communicates a viable theory that can explain the realization of EAM benefits. We have thus shown that the existing DMSM can be applied (with some limitations) to the domain of EAM. Second, the model demonstrates the relevance of the different dimensions of EAM success to the realization of EAM benefits. Third, it provides some empirical evidence of the benefits of EAM.

Evaluation of the Contributions of this Thesis

Some researchers argue that research, in addition to making these kinds of contributions to the existing body of knowledge, must also develop high-quality theory that can *"enhance practitioners' capabilities to operate effectively and efficiently in the domain covered by their theory."*[779] Weber (2012) therefore suggests that a framework for evaluating the quality of research should have four goals. First, the framework should evaluate the likely usefulness of a theory in predicting or explaining real-world phenomena. Second, it should pinpoint areas in which it may be challenging to empirically evaluate the theory. Third, it should indicate opportunities to improve or

---

[778] MacKenzie et al. (2011)

[779] Weber (2012)

refine the theory and, lastly, it should facilitate the development of new high-quality theory.[780] In this spirit, we evaluate the outcomes of this thesis in the Table 8-1.

Table 8-1 An Evaluation of the Outcomes of This Doctoral Thesis based on Weber's (2012) Framework for High-quality Theory Building

Criterion	Evaluation
Part	
Constructs	We have precisely defined the constructs of our model. For each construct, we have either reused existing definitions or developed and validated new definitions. All constructs have been defined based on a comprehensive literature review (see Section 3.3) and have been revised using the practical perspective generated from our expert interviews (see Section 4.2).
Associations	We have discussed the details of all associations between the constructs based on our literature review (see Section 3.3), and we have refined some of these associations based on our expert interviews (see Section 4.2).
States	The developed model does not explicitly differentiate between different degrees of realization of EAM benefits. In general, the model covers all levels of realization of EAM benefits as the model is defined at the moment. However, to gain a deeper understanding of the different phases of realization of EAM benefits, researchers could extend the model by considering these maturity levels in future research (see Section 8.4).
Events	We also did not differentiate between the different events that occur in the process of generating EAM benefits. In general, as indicated in the previous chapters, the model covers all of the different events through which EAM benefits are realized. However, again, differentiating between the various events that occur in the process of realizing EAM benefits might be helpful in future research (see Section 8.3).
Whole	
Importance	As we discussed in presenting the details of the motivation for this research in the introduction (see Section 1.1), we believe that our model of the realization of EAM benefits is of fundamental importance to both research and practice.
Novelty	As outlined in the introductory chapter (see Section 1.1), we believe, to the best of our knowledge, that this study of the realization of EAM benefits is the first in this research area.
Parsimony	Although the overall model includes many constructs and propositions, we aimed to keep the model as parsimonious as possible. We have defined the structural model hierarchically to increase parsimony. Furthermore, in evaluating the inner structural model, we have made trade-offs between parsimony and construct completeness. In particular, we removed the 'EAM Satisfaction' construct because it did not increase the explanatory power of the model and decreased its parsimony.
Level	We have framed the model as a mid-range theory, making it generally applicable to EAM. However, further generalizability might be possible in future research (see Section 8.4).
Falsifiability	We worked to articulate our model as precisely as possible to allow for rigorous empirical testing. We presented formulated all propositions as falsifiable hypotheses in Section 6.4.

Source: Adapted from Weber (2012)

---

[780] Weber (2012)

In summary, we believe that our EAM Benefit Realization Model fulfills Weber's (2012) criteria for high-quality theoretical contributions. Nevertheless, as we have indicated in the discussion above, some considerations should be further explored in future research. We elaborate on this potential in the last section of this chapter, in which we discuss potential future research directions.

8.3. Limitations

As with any other research, the research presented in this doctoral thesis has some limitations. Several of these limitations have already been discussed in the previous chapters. Table 8-2 summarizes the main limitations of this doctoral thesis and the different phases of this research.

Table 8-2 Limitations of this Doctoral Thesis

Phase of research	Limitation	Discussion
Research design	Determinism of positivist assumptions	In this thesis, we have adopted a positivist perspective. Although the positivistic research techniques encourage deterministic explanations of phenomena, research shows that it is wrong to suspect that this assumption is true in the case with information systems and human behavior.[781] The use of EAM in organizations is inevitably embedded in social contexts, influenced, for example, by time, politics, and, as noted in this thesis, culture. Therefore, we recognize that the generation of EAM benefits may be influenced by the organizational and political problems within an organization. These considerations, while relevant, are not part of this research; however, we also argue that these socio-organizational dimensions should be regarded not as enablers of EAM benefits but rather as inhibitors.
	Limited scope of EAM benefit realization	The research in this doctoral thesis focuses on a limited scope for EAM net benefits. As discussed in Section 1.5, various perspectives can be used to analyze the realization of EAM benefits. Clearly, this limited scope restricts the generalizability of the findings. The many additional perspectives on the realization of EAM benefits should be addressed in future research.
	Limited to a distinct set of research methods	This thesis could have employed a broad range of different research methods, such as experiments or case study research. However, we sought to employ a set of research methods that is suited to theory building in an exploratory investigation of EAM benefits and EAM success factors. Thus, we employed semi-structured interviews and literature reviews. We also focused on methods that were suited to theory testing, i.e., survey research. Although this set of research methods best supported our research objectives, we acknowledge that different research methods, e.g., case study research, would help to extend and enrich this research.

---

[781] Markus, Robey (1988); Orlikowski, Baroudi (1990)

Phase of research	Limitation	Discussion
Literature review	Limitation of the literature review to a predetermined scope	Although EAM is a comprehensive instrument that is related to various other IS topics, we focused our literature review by excluding literature from neighboring disciplines such as business-IT alignment or software architecture development. The literature review is thereby limited in its scope. However, we believe that our informed selection procedure allowed us to select the most important and relevant publications and to ensure a comprehensive view of the benefits and success factors associated with EAM benefits. Furthermore, we supplemented the literature review with semi-structured expert interviews, and we included a second evaluation period in the research design to confirm that no major factors were missing.
	Selection of the DMSM as an existing theory	In developing of the suggested model for the realization of EAM benefits, we have employed the DMSM. This model, we have argued, is well suited for the context of EAM benefits because the original theory regarding IS has overlaps significantly with EAM and because the original dimensions can be reinterpreted in the context of EAM.[782] Although our ex ante selection of an existing theory limits the interpretation of the results, we have delimited these limitations by exploring and evaluating different model alternatives during the model testing phase.[783]
	Subjectivity in proposition building	The process of identifying strategies for generating EAM benefits is partially dependent on the subjectivity of the researcher. However, we aimed to reduce this subjectivity by transparently discussing the decisions made and thereby demonstrating the validity and reliability of these judgments.
Model refine-ment	Validity and reliability of semi-structured interviews	Semi-structured interviews are typically prone to a lack of (internal and external) validity and reliability. These hazards also affect this research. However, by rigorously designing and conducting the semi-structured interviews based on guidelines and recommendations from previous research, we aspired to conduct high-quality interviews. Furthermore, we supplemented the interviews with complementary research methods, i.e., a literature review and survey research, to overcome these limitations.
	Limited number of semi-structured interviews	When conducting the semi-structured interviews, we were limited to eleven interviews due to time and resource constraints. Although a broader set of interview partners might have yielded additional insights, we have made every effort to conduct as many interviews as possible and to identify instances of theoretical saturation. After we had conducted the eleven interviews, no new EAM benefits or success factors were identified.
Model operatio-nalization	Limitation of the selected hypothesis	Although we have explored all possible relationships between the constructs in light of the research objectives of this doctoral thesis, other interesting hypotheses might have been chosen that could have yielded other interesting

---

[782] See Section 3.1.

[783] See Section 6.4 and 6.4.2.

Phase of research	Limitation	Discussion
		insights. However, given the scope of this thesis, we believe that all of the relevant hypotheses have been explored and that only potential hypotheses that are irrelevant to the research objectives have been neglected.
	Limitations of survey research	Although survey research has a number of inherent limitations (see Section 5.1), we aimed to mitigate these limitations by carefully planning and designing the survey research and by complementing our use of this research method with the use of semi-structured interviews.
	Limitations of instrument development	The instrument development process conducted in this doctoral thesis has at least three limitations. First, some measurement items used in this research were reused from previous research without extensive further validation. Second, we assessed the content validity of the newly developed measurement items a priori by validating them with eight students only. Third, although many individuals helped to develop the measurement items, bias may remain a factor. Nevertheless, the evaluation of the measurement items used during the scale development process suggests that the measurement items demonstrate an appropriate level of reliability and validity.
	Limitation of perceptual measures	The measurement instrument has been implemented using perceptual measures. The legitimacy of perceptual measures as a proxy for objective measures is still a matter for question in IS because it is possible that interviewees exaggerate their views and because the difficulty of evaluating organizational performance makes it difficult to accurately assess even perceived benefits.[784] However, because research proves that there is a strong correlation between perceived firm-level performance and the results obtained using traditional objective measures,[785] we acknowledge the associated bias and consider the consequences in discussing the findings.
	Potential presence of common method variance	The measurement items employed in this doctoral thesis captured the respondents' self-reported, perceived beliefs about the independent and dependent variables. Using the same methods for both types of variables may inflate the perceived correlations. This is a commonly known issue with these types of measures.[786] Potential future research might address this problem by using different methods for the dependent and independent variables. In the meantime, for this research, this potential limitation must be considered when we interpret the results.
	Limitations of the survey sample	The sample from the survey research also has some limitations. The preferred random sampling strategy for survey research could not be used because of the limited information available about the overall population. This limitation may have restricted the generalizability and robustness of the results. However, by transparently

---

[784] Tallon et al. (2000)

[785] Venkatraman, Ramanujam (1987)

[786] Meade et al. (2007)

Phase of research	Limitation	Discussion
		discussing the resulting statistics and comparing them with those presented in earlier research, we tried to validate the representativeness of the sample as extensively as possible.
Data analysis	Limitations of the selected data analysis strategy	In the data analysis, a PLS approach was selected because of its appropriateness when formative, complex constructs are used. However, covariance-based SEM techniques could also be used and might have yielded different results. For instance, using a PLS approach instead of a covariance-based SEM approach can inflate the indicator loadings and weights.[787] This potential inflation needs to be considered when we interpret the results.
	Limitations related to the construct validation	To validate the measurement model and the structural model in this doctoral thesis, we have employed the approach suggested by MacKenzie et al. (2011).[788] However, due to the time and resource constraints associated with this doctoral thesis, we did not conduct a full analysis. The last two steps (namely, a cross-validation of the scale and the development of norms for the scale) have not been conducted. These steps would provide further evidence of the validity and reliability of the measurement items and would facilitate a better understanding of the latter. We acknowledge the resulting limitations. Future empirical studies should take into account these limitations and employ these two steps.
	Limited number of model variants explored	The validation of the structural model included an exploration of the different model variants. This exploration employed only six models. Although we have selected these models based on the different hypothesized relationships between the main constructs, it would also have been possible to include additional variants. To do so might have further improved the explanatory power of the selected model. However, we believe that the logical combination of changes that we employed allowed us to generate a comprehensive set of models and to identify the relevant improvement effects.

8.4. Future Research

The model developed in this thesis is, to the best of our knowledge, one of the first studies of the realization of EAM benefits. This research therefore has the potential to encourage a variety of related research projects that can further develop the implications of this research. To stimulate future research in this area, we suggest some potential future research directions that may be worth investigating in this last section. This list is by no means exhaustive but should nevertheless be helpful. Future research might fall into one of the four following categories: (1) additional model testing, (2) the extension

---

[787] Diamantopoulos (2011)

[788] MacKenzie et al. (2011)

of the model, (3) research in related areas, and (4) the application of the model to different domains, including its further generalization.

First, the proposed model should be tested further to establish additional evidence in support of the underlying theory. This model testing could repeat the procedures used in the present thesis or could extend or vary the scope of the model. Because the data collected using our Web-based survey did not allow for the cross-validation of the measurement instrument or make it possible to norm the scale, future research should pursue these objectives. Furthermore, testing the model with different stakeholders, across different industries, or between different countries would generate additional evidence of the validity of the proposed model and could yield important findings regarding the potential differences between the suggested areas. Given the large number of contextual factors impacting EAM, the theoretical model developed in this doctoral thesis could be a sound basis for future empirical studies that might identify these factors and demonstrate their impact on the realization of EAM benefits.

Second, this thesis related the EAM success factors to the EAM benefits using a variance model. This variance model identifies the factors that create variance in the EAM benefits. To this end, the model does not consider in particular the aspects timing and change-causing event sequences. An extension of the model that takes into account these two aspects would provide deeper insight into the influence of EAM maturity and other time-dependent contextual success factors. Because EAM maturity is discussed in EAM research as an important aspect of EAM, extending the model in this way should provide deeper insight and motivate researchers to explore the details of the timing-related aspects of EAM benefits. In addition, the measurement instrument suggested in this research relies on beliefs about EAM benefits as perceived by the EAM stakeholder. Such perceptual measures are affected by the subjectivity of the respondent. Therefore, future research can extend the work of this thesis by using more objective and tangible measures of EAM benefits. Although measuring EAM benefits using these measures requires extensive efforts in data-gathering, such efforts would increase objectivity and might make it possible to establish a monetary business case for EAM.

Third, in discussing the different EAM success factors and benefits, the model has addressed many aspects of EAM that require deeper understanding and further research. These boundary areas can not only generate deeper insight into EAM but also be used to refine the model presented in this research. Such boundary areas might include the relationships between the different EAM benefits, which remain unexplored on an empirical level. The EAM benefits discussed in this doctoral thesis are of various types. Some are more tangible, whereas others are less tangible. Some are more monetary; others are less monetary. Although this thesis provides insight into the relative contribution of each of these benefits to EAM success overall, we did not explore how the different EAM benefits relate to each other. Such research would provide a deeper understanding of the EAM benefits and their dependencies. Another boundary area is the role of culture in EAM. Although this research has shown that cultural aspects play a crucial role in the realization of EAM benefits, the characteristics of this EAM culture remain unexplored. For instance, one interesting area to investigate might be the relationship between EAM culture, the overall culture of an organization, and what type of EAM culture is desirable. Research on EAM culture can provide a deeper understanding of what type of culture is required in a particular context to improve the realization of EAM benefits. To empirically validate the suggested model, we have collected an extensive data set that can be analyzed in many of these directions. Thus, the collected data can serve as a foundation for further exploration of neighboring research areas.

Lastly, this research has shown that the DMSM can be applied to the domain of EAM, just as previous research has applied the DMSM to other domains. In addition, the findings demonstrate the central role of cultural aspects in this domain of EAM. Because our model of the realization of EAM benefits adapts the DMSM to a domain with a socio-organizational focus rather than a technical focus, the increased importance of cultural aspects becomes evident. In contrast, the original domain of the DMSM, traditional IS, is more technically oriented. Therefore, further evidence of the role of cultural aspects in this original domain of the DMSM must be gathered before these findings can be generalized. In addition to generalizing the findings to the original DMSM, the present research model could also serve as a reference point for the application of the model to other domains with a socio-organizational focus in which the realization of benefits is not directly measurable and tangible. Such areas might include traditional strategic planning, change management, or research and development. Based on the insights generated by applying the model to these domains, the further generalization of the model within socio-organizational disciplines might become possible.

In summary, the research described in this doctoral thesis constitutes a first step in the research on the benefits of EAM. More research in this area is clearly required, and we believe that the opportunities for future research on the realization of EAM benefits are manifold. We hope that this doctoral thesis stimulates additional research in this area, thereby improving the domain of EAM in terms of both research and practice.

A. Appendix – Introduction

A.1. Key EAM Stakeholders, their Areas and Organizational Levels

Table A-1 Key EAM Stakeholders, their Aspect Areas and Organizational Levels.

	Business	Information	Information systems	Technical infrastructure
Enterprise	▪ CEO ▪ CFO ▪ COO ▪ Board of Directors	▪ CIO	▪ CIO	▪ CTO
Domain	▪ Head of BD/BU ▪ Business change manager	▪ DIO, ▪ IT manager,	▪ DIO, ▪ IT change manager	▪ Platform manager ▪ Platform subject matter expert
Project	▪ Business project manager ▪ Business analyst	▪ Information analyst	▪ Software development project manager, Software designer / architect	▪ Infrastructure project manager ▪ Infrastructure engineer
Operational	▪ Operational business ▪ Business process administrator ▪ End-user	▪ Database administrator, ▪ End-user	▪ Application management, ▪ Application administrator, ▪ End User	▪ Data center management ▪ Infrastructure administrator

Source: Adapted from van der Raadt et al. (2010)

B. Appendix - Research Background

B.1. Identified Research by Research Methods

Table B-1 Identified Research by Research Methods

Research	Research method			
	Conceptual	Qualitative empiric	Quantitative empiric	Literature Review
EAM scenario analysis				
de Boer et al. (2005)	✓			
Buschle et al. (2010); Ekstedt et al. (2009a); Ekstedt et al. (2009b); Franke et al. (2009b); Franke et al. (2009a); Gammelgård et al. (2007); Gustafsson et al. (2009); Holschke et al. (2010); Höök et al. (2009); Johnson et al. (2007a); Johnson et al. (2006), (2007b); Lagerström (2010); Lagerström et al. (2009a); Lagerström et al. (2009b); Lagerström et al. (2007); Närman et al. (2009a); Raderius et al. (2009); Ullberg et al. (2010); Ullberg et al. (2008a), (2008b), Lagerström et al. (2010); Närman et al. (2007); Närman et al. (2009b)	✓	✓		
Aliee et al. (2010); Davoudi et al. (2009a), (2009b), (2009c); Davoudi et al. (2009d); Davoudi et al. (2009e); Davoudi et al. (2011)		✓		
Iacob et al. (2005)	✓			
Buckl et al. (2009a); Buckl et al. (2009b)	✓			
(2010)	✓			
Yu et al. (2006)		✓		
Javanbakht et al. (2009)		✓		
EAM process evaluation				
Hirvonen et al. (2003)	✓			
Ylimäki et al. (2007)		✓		
Lim et al. (2009)	✓			
Buckl et al. (2008)	✓			
Overall EAM benefit assessment				
Ross et al. (2005)		✓		
Boucharas et al. (2010); van Steenbergen et al. (2008)				✓
Foorthuis et al. (2010)			✓	
Kluge et al. (2006)		✓		
Niemi et al. (2009)	✓			
van der Raadt et al. (2010); van der Raadt et al. (2005); van der Raadt et al. (2007); van der Raadt et al. (2009)		✓	✓	
Lux et al. (2010)		✓		

Table B-2 Identified Research by Addressed Element

Research	Goals	EAM products				EAM processes			EAM governance			Benefit
		Principles	Model	Architecture	System	Decision-making	Conformance	EAM delivery	Bodies	Roles	Responsibilities	
EAM scenario analysis												
de Boer et al. (2005)					✓							
Buschle et al. (2010); Ekstedt et al. (2009a); Ekstedt et al. (2009b); Franke et al. (2009b); Franke et al. (2009a); Gammelgård et al. (2007); Gustafsson et al. (2009); Holschke et al. (2010); Höök et al. (2009); Johnson et al. (2007a); Johnson et al. (2006), (2007b); Lagerström (2010); Lagerström et al. (2009a); Lagerström et al. (2009b); Lagerström et al. (2007); Närman et al. (2009a); Raderius et al. (2009); Ullberg et al. (2010); Ullberg et al. (2008a), (2008b), Lagerström et al. (2010); Närman et al. (2007); Närman et al. (2009b)		✓	✓									
Aliee et al. (2010); Davoudi et al. (2009a), (2009b), (2009c); Davoudi et al. (2009d); Davoudi et al. (2009e); Davoudi et al. (2011)		✓	✓	✓								
Iacob et al. (2005)		✓										
Buckl et al. (2009a); Buckl et al. (2009b)		✓										
(2010)		✓										
Yu et al. (2006)		✓										
Javanbakht et al. (2009)		✓										
EAM process evaluation												
Hirvonen et al. (2003)						✓		✓				
Ylimäki et al. (2007)												
Lim et al. (2009)						✓		✓				
Buckl et al. (2008)						✓		✓				
Overall EAM benefit assessment												
Ross et al. (2005)												✓✓
Boucharas et al. (2010); van Steenbergen et al. (2008)												✓✓

Research	Goals	EAM products				EAM processes			EAM governance			Benefit
		Principles	Model	Architecture	System	Decision-making	Conformance	EAM delivery	Bodies	Roles	Responsibilities	
Foorthuis et al. (2010)		✓	✓	✓	✓	✓		✓		✓	✓	
		✓	✓	✓	✓	✓		✓		✓	✓	✓✓
Kluge et al. (2006)			✓		✓	✓		✓		✓	✓	
			✓		✓	✓		✓		✓	✓	✓✓
Niemi et al. (2009)		✓	✓	✓	✓	✓		✓		✓	✓	
		✓	✓	✓	✓	✓		✓		✓	✓	✓✓
van der Raadt et al. (2010); van der Raadt et al. (2005); van der Raadt et al. (2007); van der Raadt et al. (2009)		✓	✓	✓	✓	✓		✓		✓	✓	
		✓	✓	✓	✓	✓		✓		✓	✓	✓✓
Lux et al. (2010)		✓	✓	✓	✓	✓		✓		✓	✓	
		✓	✓	✓	✓	✓		✓		✓	✓	✓✓

C. Appendix - Model Refinement

C.1. Questionnaire Semi-structured Interviews

Note: All remarks for the interviewer are marked enclosed in '[' and ']' in the following

[Introductory remarks

Important: Please do not introduce EAM benefit realization model upfront. The objective of the first three sections is to have an open discussion about EAM benefits and success factors that is not influenced by the researcher's model.

Please open interview with sincere appreciation for the participation

Next, introduce yourself as the interviewer and give some background about yourself

Briefly introduce background of this study talking about

- *EAM benefit realization as an open research question*
- *Relevance in practice (can also be used as a hook to start a discussion how interviewee perceives the topic)*
- *Developed model for the realization of benefits from EAM*
- *Next steps in the research: Empirical validation of the model and development of measurement instrument that allows benchmarking in practice*

Please remark: We will treat all information confidential and anonymous. The data is used for our research about Enterprise Architecture only.]

Section Demographics

Before we start with EAM-related questions, we want to discuss some demographic and personal factors that might influence your EA approach.

D.1 What industry does your company belong to?

Automotive&Assembly, Electronics & Semiconductors, Aerospace & Defence, Information Technology, Consumer, Engery, Basic Materials, Chemicals, Banking, Insurance, Healthcare, Private Equity, Public Services, Telecom & Media, Travel, Transport & Logistics

D.2 How many total employees work in your company?

D.3 How many total employees work in your IT department?

D.4 What is your IT budget (EUR m)? Can you break it down in CTB (Change-the-business) and RTB (Run-the-business) (EUR m)?

D.5 In how many countries are you present? (1, 1-5, >5)

D.6 On how many continents are you present? (1, 2, >2)

Section Personal

P.1 What is your current role?

P.2 How many years do you have experience in Enterprise Architecture Management?

Section EA Introduction questions

First, we want to discuss briefly your understanding of EA and how your company approaches EA currently.

I.1 When was Enterprise Architecture in your company introduced?

I.2 Do you have a dedicated organizational unit for Enterprise Architecture?

I.3 How many employees are involved in Enterprise Architecture at your company?

I.4 How do you define Enterprise Architecture?

Section 1. EAM benefits

One of our main objectives is to understand what benefits EAM yields in organizations. The following section discusses your experience about what benefits your organization realizes with EAM.

B.1 What benefits do you realize with EAM?

B.2 How do these benefits differ on an organizational and project-level?

Section 2. EAM success factors

In the following we want to discuss, the success factors that enable the just discussed EAM benefits.

S.1 Based on your experience, what are the success factors for EAM?

S.2 How do these success factors link to the benefits of EAM?

Section 3. Discussion of the EAM benefit realization model

Based on a comprehensive literature review, we have developed a model for the realization of benefits from EAM. Building on the benefits and success factors we have discussed so far, I would like to introduce the model now and then discuss with you the different elements. [Explain elements of the model based on slides prepared for the interviews. [789]]

---

[789] The model is illustrated in and Figure C-2.

[Go through the following two questions for all constructs in the model to discuss the construct and the related proposition with the interviewee. Apply the laddering technique to gain deeper insights in the reasoning of the interviewee.]

C.1 How did you experience [insert different model constructs] as a success factor for EAM?

C.2 How does [insert different model constructs] lead to EAM benefits?

- EA as-is architecture quality
- EA to-be architecture quality
- EA roadmap quality
- EA mandate setup
- EA formality setup
- EA decision-making setup
- EA frameworks & tools
- EA principles definition
- EA skill quality
- EA communication quality
- EA management support quality
- EA project support quality
- EA stakeholder awareness
- EA leadership involvement
- Common EA understanding establishment
- Use
- Satisfaction

[After finishing all constructs as interviewee for final remarks.

If no further remarks, express your sincere appreciation and thank the interviewee for participation.

Also, use the opportunity to ask whether further discussions would be possible and give an outlook of the next steps of this research (empirical validation by Web-based survey).

State again that interviewee will receive the results of this research.]

C.2. Supplementary Slides for Interviews

Figure C-1 Screenshot of Slide Introducing High-level View on Model

Based on literature review and expert discussion
EA benefit realization model has been defined

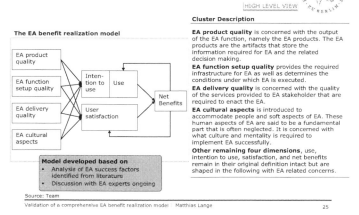

HIGH LEVEL VIEW

Cluster Description

EA product quality is concerned with the output of the EA function, namely the EA products. The EA products are the artifacts that store the information required for EA and the related decision making.

EA function setup quality provides the required infrastructure for EA as well as determines the conditions under which EA is executed.

EA delivery quality is concerned with the quality of the services provided to EA stakeholder that are required to enact the EA.

EA cultural aspects is introduced to accommodate people and soft aspects of EA. These human aspects of EA are said to be a fundamental part that is often neglected. It is concerned with what culture and mentality is required to implement EA successfully.

Other remaining four dimensions, use, intention to use, satisfaction, and net benefits remain in their original definition intact but are shaped in the following with EA related concerns.

Source: Team

Validation of a comprehensive EA benefit realization model | Matthias Lange   25

Figure C-2 Screenshot of Slide Detailing Model

For each of the constructs definitions and
hypotheses are detailed in the following

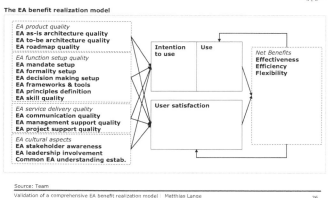

Source: Team

Validation of a comprehensive EA benefit realization model | Matthias Lange   26

D. Appendix – Model Operationalization

D.1. Construct Definition

Table D-1 Overview of Conceptual Construct Definitions

(Sub-) Construct Name	Con-struct Order	Definition	Inter-nal Refe-rence
EAM Product Quality			
(PQ1) As-Is Architecture	1st	An EAM stakeholder's perceived extent to which all desirable information about the as-is architecture is provided to satisfy the organization's needs.	see below
(PQ1a) Timeliness	2nd	An EAM stakeholder's perceived extent to which all desirable information about the as-is architecture is provided timely.	(P1a)
(PQ1b) Completeness	2nd	An EAM stakeholder's perceived extent to which all desirable information about the as-is architecture is provided completely.	(P1b)
(PQ1c) Level of Detail	2nd	An EAM stakeholder's perceived extent to which all desirable information about the as-is architecture is provided in the right level of detail.	(P1c)
(PQ2) To-Be Architecture	1st	An EAM stakeholder's perceived extent to which all desirable information about the to-be architecture is provided to satisfy the organization's needs.	see below
(PQ2a) Timeliness	2nd	An EAM stakeholder's perceived extent to which all desirable information about the to-be architecture is provided timely.	(P2a)
(PQ2b) Completeness	2nd	An EAM stakeholder's perceived extent to which all desirable information about the to-be architecture is provided completely.	(P2b)
(PQ2c) Level of Detail	2nd	An EAM stakeholder's perceived extent to which all desirable information about the to-be architecture is provided in the right level of detail.	(P2c)
(PQ3) Roadmap	1st	An EAM stakeholder's perceived extent to which all desirable information about the roadmap is provided to satisfy the organization's needs.	see below
(PQ3a) Timeliness	2nd	An EAM stakeholder's perceived extent to which all desirable information about the roadmap is provided timely.	(I1p)
(PQ3b) Completeness	2nd	An EAM stakeholder's perceived extent to which all desirable information about the roadmap is provided completely.	(P3b)
(PQ3c) Level of Detail	2nd	An EAM stakeholder's perceived extent to which all desirable information about the roadmap is provided in the right level of detail.	(I1p)
(PQ3d) Feasability	2nd	An EAM stakeholder's perceived extent to which all projects on the roadmap are feasible.	(P3a)
(PQ3e) Consideration of dependencies	2nd	An EAM stakeholder's perceived extent to which all dependencies between projects on the roadmap have been considered.	(P3c)
EAM Infrastructure Quality			
(IQ1) EAM mandate	1st	An EAM stakeholder's perceived extent to which the appointed scope of the EA function has been	see below

240

(Sub-) Construct Name	Con-struct Order	Definition	Inter-nal Refe-rence
		defined.	
(IQ1a) Organizational Scope	2nd	An EAM stakeholder's perceived extent to which the appointed organizational scope of the EA function has been defined.	(F1a)
(IQ1b) Covered business-IT aspects	2nd	An EAM stakeholder's perceived extent to which the scope of covered business-IT aspects of the EA function, i.e., EA layers, has been defined.	(I2f)
(IQ1c) Organizational business-IT focus	2nd	An EAM stakeholder's perceived extent to which the EA function is positioned as an organizational function rather than IT function.	(I2f)
(IQ1d) Alignment with other functions	2nd	An EAM stakeholder's perceived extent to which the EA function is aligned with other organizational functions (e.g., strategy or project management).	(F1c)
(IQ2) Extent of centralization	1st	An EAM stakeholder's perceived extent to which a central decision-making has been defined.	see below
(IQ2a) Capital budgets	2nd	An EAM stakeholder's perceived extent to which a central decision-making for capital budgets has been defined.	(F2a)
(IQ2b) Operational process optimization and implementation	2nd	An EAM stakeholder's perceived extent to which a central decision-making for operational process optimization and implementation has been defined.	(F2b)
(IQ2c) Application development projects prioritization and approval	2nd	An EAM stakeholder's perceived extent to which a central decision-making for application development projects prioritization and approval has been defined.	(F2c)
(IQ2d) IT development and implementation	2nd	An EAM stakeholder's perceived extent to which a central decision-making for IT development and implementation has been defined.	(F2d)
(IQ2e) Infrastructure planning and management	2nd	An EAM stakeholder's perceived extent to which a central decision-making for infrastructure planning and management has been defined.	(F2e)
(IQ2f) Compliance management	2nd	An EAM stakeholder's perceived extent to which a central decision-making for compliance management has been defined.	(I3f)
(IQ2e) EA definition and implementation	2nd	An EAM stakeholder's perceived extent to which a central decision-making for EA definition and implementation has been defined.	(I3f)
(IQ3) EA governance formalization	1st	An EAM stakeholder's perceived extent to which the EA governance mechanisms are formalized.	see below
(IQ3a) Formally defined approval process	2nd	An EAM stakeholder's perceived extent to which the EA approval processes are formally defined.	(F3a)

(Sub-) Construct Name	Construct Order	Definition	Internal Reference
(IQ3b) EA principle compliance	2nd	An EAM stakeholder's perceived extent to which the projects formally need to comply with EA principles.	(F3b)
(IQ3c) Occurrence of informal agreements	2nd	An EAM stakeholder's perceived extent to which the informal agreements are reached to annul EA principles.	(I4f)
(IQ3d) Penalties for EA principle violations	2nd	An EAM stakeholder's perceived extent to which penalties enforce the adherence to EA principles.	(F3d)
(IQ3e) Frequent waivers	2nd	An EAM stakeholder's perceived extent to which the waivers prevent adherence to EA principles.	(I4f)
(IQ4) EAM framework	1st	An EAM stakeholder's perceived extent to which EAM frameworks support EAM activities.	see below
(IQ4a) Standardized FW in place	2nd	An EAM stakeholder's perceived extent to which EAM frameworks have been established to support EAM activities.	(C2f)
(IQ4b) Use industry standards	2nd	An EAM stakeholder's perceived extent to which EAM frameworks use industry standards.	(C2f)
(IQ4c) Accepted among stakeholders	2nd	An EAM stakeholder's perceived extent to which used EAM frameworks are accepted among EAM stakeholders.	(C2f)
(IQ5) EAM tool support	1st	An EAM stakeholder's perceived extent to which EAM tools support EAM activities.	see below
(IQ5a) Established tool support	2nd	An EAM stakeholder's perceived extent to which EAM tool support have been established to support EAM activities.	(C2f)
(IQ5b) Central repository provided	2nd	An EAM stakeholder's perceived extent to which a central repository has been established to support EAM activities.	(C2f)
(IQ5c) Accepted among stakeholders	2nd	An EAM stakeholder's perceived extent to which the used EAM tool support is accepted among EAM stakeholders.	(C2f)
(IQ6) EA reference architectures	1st	An EAM stakeholder's perceived extent to which EAM reference architectures support EAM activities.	see below
(IQ6a) Established reference architecture	2nd	An EAM stakeholder's perceived extent to which EAM reference architectures have been established to support EAM activities.	(A7f)
(IQ6b) Guide to-be design	2nd	An EAM stakeholder's perceived extent to which EAM reference architectures guide the design of the to-be architecture.	(A7f)
(IQ6c) Used without major adjustments	2nd	An EAM stakeholder's perceived extent to which EAM reference architectures are used without major adjustments.	(A7f)
(IQ7) EA principles	1st	An EAM stakeholder's perceived extent to which EA principles have been established.	see below

(Sub-) Construct Name	Construct Order	Definition	Internal Reference
(IQ7a) Business architecture	2nd	An EAM stakeholder's perceived extent to which EA principles have been established for the business architecture.	(I5f)
(IQ7b) Application architecture	2nd	An EAM stakeholder's perceived extent to which EA principles have been established for the application architecture.	(I5f)
(IQ7c) Technology architecture	2nd	An EAM stakeholder's perceived extent to which EA principles have been established for the technology architecture.	(I5f)
(IQ7d) Integration architecture	2nd	An EAM stakeholder's perceived extent to which EA principles have been established for the integration architecture.	(I5f)
(IQ7e) Data architecture	2nd	An EAM stakeholder's perceived extent to which EA principles have been established for the data architecture.	(I5f)
(IQ8) EA skills	1st	An EAM stakeholder's perceived extent to which all desirable EA skills are available to the EA function.	see below
(IQ8a) Defined EA roles	2nd	An EAM stakeholder's perceived extent to which all desirable EA roles are clearly defined.	(F6a)
(IQ8b) Ongoing training	2nd	An EAM stakeholder's perceived extent to which all EA staff receives ongoing training.	(F6b)
(IQ8c) Good communication skills	2nd	An EAM stakeholder's perceived extent to which all EA staff has good communication skills.	(F6c)
(IQ8d) Extensive networking in organization	2nd	An EAM stakeholder's perceived extent to which all EA staff has a good network in the organization.	(F6d)
(IQ8e) High EA expert knowledge	2nd	An EAM stakeholder's perceived extent to which all EA staff has a high degree of EA expert knowledge.	(F6c)
(IQ8f) Role differentiation from other functions	2nd	An EAM stakeholder's perceived extent to which all desirable EA roles are clearly differentiated from other function's roles.	(F6e)
(IQ8g) Job rotation	2nd	An EAM stakeholder's perceived extent to which all desirable EA staff rotates through different jobs to receive needed skills in practice.	(I6f)
(IQ9) EA resources	1st	An EAM stakeholder's perceived extent to which all desirable EA resources are available to the EA function.	see below
(IQ9a) Financial resources	2nd	An EAM stakeholder's perceived extent to which sufficient financial resources are available to the EA function.	(A6f)
(IQ9b) People resources	2nd	An EAM stakeholder's perceived extent to which sufficient people resources are available to the EA function.	(A6f)
(IQ9c) Time resources	2nd	An EAM stakeholder's perceived extent to which sufficient time is given for EAM tasks.	(A6f)
EAM Service Delivery Quality			
(SQ1) EA communication	1st	An EAM stakeholder's perceived extent to which the communication of the EA function fulfills the varying EAM stakeholders' needs.	see below

(Sub-) Construct Name	Construct Order	Definition	Internal Reference
(SQ1a) Stakeholder-specific communications	2nd	An EAM stakeholder's perceived extent to which the EA function communicates according to EAM stakeholders' needs.	(D1a)
(SQ1b) Communication of the Benefits of EA	2nd	An EAM stakeholder's perceived extent to which the EA function communicates the value of EAM to EAM stakeholders.	(D1b)
(SQ1c) Proactive communication	2nd	An EAM stakeholder's perceived extent to which the EA function communicates proactively with EAM stakeholders.	(D1c)
(SQ1d) Simple and understandable communication	2nd	An EAM stakeholder's perceived extent to which the EA function communicates simple and understandable with EAM stakeholders.	(I7s)
(SQ2) EAM Management Support	1st	An EAM stakeholder's perceived extent to which the EA function provides desired services to the management.	see below
(SQ2a) Projects checked for conformance	2nd	An EAM stakeholder's perceived extent to which projects are regularly checked for EA principle compliance.	(D2a)
(SQ2b) Top management involved in decision-making	2nd	An EAM stakeholder's perceived extent to which top-management is involved in EA decision-making.	(D2b)
(SQ2c) Regular EA principle review	2nd	An EAM stakeholder's perceived extent to which EA principles are regularly reviewed.	(I9s)
(SQ2d) Management briefing	2nd	An EAM stakeholder's perceived extent to which top-management is briefed regarding EA review results.	(D2d)
(SQ2e) Top management is actively involved in EA planning	2nd	An EAM stakeholder's perceived extent to which top-management is involved in EA planning.	(I8s)
(SQ2f) Top management involved in execution	2nd	An EAM stakeholder's perceived extent to which top-management is involved in executing EA decisions.	(I8s)
(SQ3) EA project support	1st	An EAM stakeholder's perceived extent to which the EA function provides desired services to the projects.	see below
(SQ3a) Active involvement	2nd	An EAM stakeholder's perceived extent to which the EA staff is consult implementation projects.	(D3a)
(SQ3b) Active project role	2nd	An EAM stakeholder's perceived extent to which the EA staff has an active role in implementation projects.	(D3b)
(SQ3c) Integrating role across projects	2nd	An EAM stakeholder's perceived extent to which the EA staff has an integrating role across implementation projects.	(A10s)

(Sub-) Construct Name	Construct Order	Definition	Internal Reference
EAM Cultural Aspects			
(CA1) Top-management commitment	1st	An EAM stakeholder's perceived extent to which top management is engaged in EA.	see below
(CA1a) Resource commitment	2nd	An EAM stakeholder's perceived extent to which top management allocates sufficient time for EA.	(C1a)
(CA1b) Assigned importance	2nd	An EAM stakeholder's perceived extent to which top management allocate adequate resources for EA.	(C1b)
(CA1c) Time commitment	2nd	An EAM stakeholder's perceived extent to which EA is of high importance to top managers.	(C1c)
(CA1d) Communication of importance	2nd	An EAM stakeholder's perceived extent to which top management communicates the importance of EA.	(C1d)
(CA2) EA awareness	1st	An EAM stakeholder's perceived extent to which the organization is aware of EAM.	see below
(CA2a) Stakeholders' awareness	2nd	An EAM stakeholder's perceived extent to which EA stakeholder are aware of the EA function.	(C2a)
(CA2b) Stakeholders understanding of importance	2nd	An EAM stakeholder's perceived extent to which EA stakeholders understand the importance of EA.	(C2b)
(CA2c) Stakeholder education	2nd	An EAM stakeholder's perceived extent to which EA stakeholders not working in the EA function are trained on EA topics.	(C2c)
(CA3) EA understanding	1st	An EAM stakeholder's perceived extent to which a common EA understanding has been established among all EAM stakeholders.	see below
(CA3a) Shared vision	2nd	An EAM stakeholder's perceived extent to which business and IT employees have a common EA understanding.	(C3a)
(CA3b) Shared understanding	2nd	An EAM stakeholder's perceived extent to which business and IT employees have a common long-term EA vision.	(C3b)
(CA3c) Alignment of common goals	2nd	An EAM stakeholder's perceived extent to which current business objectives are in line with the organization's overall EA approach.	(C3c)
Use / Satisfaction			
(Use) Use	1st	An EAM stakeholder's perceived extent to which a person intends to continue to engage in Enterprise Architecture.	(Use)
(Sat) Satisfaction	1st	An EAM stakeholder's perceived extent to which a person feels satisfied about his or her overall experience with the use of Enterprise Architecture.	(Sat)
EAM Benefits			
(OB1) Organizational Efficiency	1st	An EAM stakeholder's perceived extent to which the EA practice yields organizational effectiveness improvements.	see below
(OB1a) Integrate Application/Pro	2nd	An EAM stakeholder's perceived extent to which the EA practice improves the integration of applications and processes.	(B1a)

(Sub-) Construct Name	Construct Order	Definition	Internal Reference
cesses			
(OB1b) Standardize Applications/Processes	2nd	An EAM stakeholder's perceived extent to which the EA practice improves the standardization of applications and processes.	(B1b)
(OB1c) Consolidate Application/Processes	2nd	An EAM stakeholder's perceived extent to which the EA practice improves the consolidation of applications and processes.	(B1c)
(OB1d) Control Complexity	2nd	An EAM stakeholder's perceived extent to which the EA practice improves the controllability of organizational complexity.	(B1d)
(OB1e) Increase Utilization	2nd	An EAM stakeholder's perceived extent to which the EA practice yields improved utilization.	(B1e)
(OB1f) Reduce Cost	2nd	An EAM stakeholder's perceived extent to which the EA practice yields reduced cost.	(B1f)
(OB1g) Increase revenue	2nd	An EAM stakeholder's perceived extent to which the EA practice yields increased revenues.	(A1b)
(OB2) Organizational Effectiveness	1st	An EAM stakeholder's perceived extent to which the EA practice yields organizational effectiveness improvements.	see below
(OB2a) Global optimization	2nd	An EAM stakeholder's perceived extent to which the EA practice yields a global (instead of local) optimization.	(B2a)
(OB2b) Operational business-IT Alignment	2nd	An EAM stakeholder's perceived extent to which the EA practice yields operational business-IT alignment.	(A2b)
(OB2c) Efficient communication	2nd	An EAM stakeholder's perceived extent to which the EA practice improves communication.	(B2c)
(OB2d) Strategic business-IT Alignment	2nd	An EAM stakeholder's perceived extent to which the EA practice yields strategic business-IT alignment.	(A2b)
(OB3) Organizational Flexibility	1st	An EAM stakeholder's perceived extent to which the EA practice yields organizational flexibility improvements.	see below
(OB3a) Identify change	2nd	An EAM stakeholder's perceived extent to which the EA practice improves the identification of required change.	(B3a)
(OB3b) Respond to market	2nd	An EAM stakeholder's perceived extent to which the EA practice yields improved respondence to market changes.	(B3b)
(OB3c) Enable innovation	2nd	An EAM stakeholder's perceived extent to which the EA practice enables innovation.	(B3c)
(OB3d) Cooperate with others	2nd	An EAM stakeholder's perceived extent to which the EA practice enables to co-operate with others more effectively and efficiently.	(B3d)
(PB1) Project Efficiency	1st	An EAM stakeholder's perceived extent to which the EA practice yields project-related effectiveness improvements.	

(Sub-) Construct Name	Construct Order	Definition	Internal Reference
(PB1a) Manage Project Budget	2nd	An EAM stakeholder's perceived extent to which the EA practice allows meeting project budgets.	(B1g)
(PB1b) Meet Project Deadlines	2nd	An EAM stakeholder's perceived extent to which the EA practice allows meeting project deadlines.	(B1h)
(PB1c) Mitigate Project Risks	2nd	An EAM stakeholder's perceived extent to which the EA practice allows mitigating project risks.	(B1i)
(PB1d) Manage Project Complexity	2nd	An EAM stakeholder's perceived extent to which the EA practice allows managing project complexity.	(B1j)
(PB2) Project Effectiveness	1st	An EAM stakeholder's perceived extent to which the EA practice yields project-related effectiveness improvements.	see below
(PB2a) Improve quality of project deliverables	2nd	An EAM stakeholder's perceived extent to which the EA practice improves the quality of project deliverables.	(A3b)
(PB2b) Deliver desired functionality (from projects)	2nd	An EAM stakeholder's perceived extent to which the EA practice allows delivering desired functionality better.	(A4b)
(PB3) Project Flexibility	1st	An EAM stakeholder's perceived extent to which the EA practice yields project-related flexibility improvements.	see below
(PB3a) Manage changing project scope	2nd	An EAM stakeholder's perceived extent to which the EA practice allows managing changing project scopes more effectively and efficiently.	(A5b)

D.2. Assessment of Construct Dimensionality

Questions to Determine the Multidimensionality of the Construct[790]

- (Q1a) How distinctive are the essential characteristics from each other? (Answers: D = distinctive, ND = non distinctive)

- (Q1b) Would eliminating any of the characteristics restrict the domain of the construct in a significant or important way? (Answers: R = restriction, NR = no restriction)

---

[790] MacKenzie et al. (2011)

Questions to Determine how Multidimensional Constructs Relate to their Sub-constructs[791]

- (Q2a) Are the sub-dimensions manifestations of the construct or are they defining characteristics? (Answers: M = manifestation, D = defining)

- (Q2b) Does the construct exist separately of its sub-dimensions or is the construct a function of its sub-dimensions? (answers: E = exist separately, F = function of sub-dimension)

- (Q2c) Would a change in the construct result necessarily in a change of all sub-dimensions or could a change result in a change of only one sub-dimension? (Answers: A = all sub-dimensions change, O = one sub-dimension changes)

Source: Adopted from MacKenzie et al. (2011)

Table D-2 Dimensionality Assessment of the Constructs of the Revised A Priori Model

(Sub-)Construct Name	Q 1a	Q 1b	Q 2a	Q 2b	Q 2c	Result
EAM Product Quality						
(PQ1) As-Is Architecture	D	R	D	F	O	Multidimensional formative construct
(PQ1a) Timeliness	D	NR				Onedimensional characteristic of formative construct
(PQ1b) Completeness	D	NR				Onedimensional characteristic of formative construct
(PQ1c) Level of Detail	D	NR				Onedimensional characteristic of formative construct
(PQ2) To-Be Architecture	D	R	D	F	O	Multidimensional formative construct
(PQ2a) Timeliness	D	NR				Onedimensional characteristic of formative construct
(PQ2b) Completeness	D	NR				Onedimensional characteristic of formative construct
(PQ2c) Level of Detail	D	NR				Onedimensional characteristic of formative construct
(PQ3) Roadmap	D	R	D	F	O	Multidimensional formative construct
(PQ3a) Timeliness	D	NR				Onedimensional characteristic of formative construct
(PQ3b) Completeness	D	NR				Onedimensional characteristic of formative construct
(PQ3c) Level of Detail	D	NR				Onedimensional characteristic of formative construct
(PQ3d) Feasability	D	NR				Onedimensional characteristic of formative construct

---

[791] MacKenzie et al. (2011)

(Sub-)Construct Name	Q 1a	Q 1b	Q 2a	Q 2b	Q 2c	Result
(PQ3e) Consideration of dependencies	D	NR				Onedimensional characteristic of formative construct
EAM Infrastructure Quality						
(IQ1) EA mandate	D	R	D	F	O	Multidimensional formative construct
(IQ1a) Organizational Scope	D	NR				Onedimensional characteristic of formative construct
(IQ1b) Covered business-IT aspects	D	NR				Onedimensional characteristic of formative construct
(IQ1c) Organizational business-IT focus	D	NR				Onedimensional characteristic of formative construct
(IQ1d) Alignment with other functions	D	NR				Onedimensional characteristic of formative construct
(IQ2) Extent of centralization	D	R	D	F	O	Multidimensional formative construct
(IQ2a) Capital budgets	D	NR				Onedimensional characteristic of formative construct
(IQ2b) Operational process optimization and implementation	D	NR				Onedimensional characteristic of formative construct
(IQ2c) Application development projects prioritization and approval	D	NR				Onedimensional characteristic of formative construct
(IQ2d) IT development and implementation	D	NR				Onedimensional characteristic of formative construct
(IQ2e) Infrastructure planning and management	D	NR				Onedimensional characteristic of formative construct
(IQ2f) Compliance management	D	NR				Onedimensional characteristic of formative construct
(IQ2e) EA definition and implementation	D	NR				Onedimensional characteristic of formative construct
(IQ3) EA governance formalization	D	R	D	F	O	Multidimensional formative construct
(IQ3a) Formally defined approval process	D	NR				Onedimensional characteristic of formative construct
(IQ3b) EA principle compliance	D	NR				Onedimensional characteristic of formative construct
(IQ3c) Occurrence of informal agreements	D	NR				Onedimensional characteristic of formative construct
(IQ3d) Penalties for EA principle violations	D	NR				Onedimensional characteristic of formative construct
(IQ3e) Frequent waivers	D	NR				Onedimensional characteristic of formative construct
(IQ4) EAM framework	D	R	D	F	O	Multidimensional formative construct
(IQ4a) Standardized FW in place	D	NR				Onedimensional characteristic of formative construct
(IQ4b) Use industry standards	D	NR				Onedimensional characteristic of formative construct
(IQ4c) Accepted among stakeholders	D	NR				Onedimensional characteristic of formative construct
(IQ5) EAM tool support	D	R	D	F	O	Multidimensional formative construct

(Sub-)Construct Name	Q 1a	Q 1b	Q 2a	Q 2b	Q 2c	Result
(IQ5a) Established tool support	D	NR				Onedimensional characteristic of formative construct
(IQ5b) Central repository provided	D	NR				Onedimensional characteristic of formative construct
(IQ5c) Accepted among stakeholders	D	NR				Onedimensional characteristic of formative construct
(IQ6) EA reference architectures	D	R	D	F	O	Multidimensional formative construct
(IQ6a) Established reference architecture	D	NR				Onedimensional characteristic of formative construct
(IQ6b) Guide to-be design	D	NR				Onedimensional characteristic of formative construct
(IQ6c) Used without major adjustments	D	NR				Onedimensional characteristic of formative construct
(IQ7) EA principles	D	R	D	F	O	Multidimensional formative construct
(IQ7a) Business architecture	D	NR				Onedimensional characteristic of formative construct
(IQ7b) Application architecture	D	NR				Onedimensional characteristic of formative construct
(IQ7c) Technology architecture	D	NR				Onedimensional characteristic of formative construct
(IQ7d) Integration architecture	D	NR				Onedimensional characteristic of formative construct
(IQ7e) Data architecture	D	NR				Onedimensional characteristic of formative construct
(IQ8) EA skills	D	R	D	F	O	Multidimensional formative construct
(IQ8a) Defined EA roles	D	NR				Onedimensional characteristic of formative construct
(IQ8b) Ongoing training	D	NR				Onedimensional characteristic of formative construct
(IQ8c) Good communication skills	D	NR				Onedimensional characteristic of formative construct
(IQ8d) Extensive networking in organization	D	NR				Onedimensional characteristic of formative construct
(IQ8e) High EA expert knowledge	D	NR				Onedimensional characteristic of formative construct
(IQ8f) Role differentiation from other functions	D	NR				Onedimensional characteristic of formative construct
(IQ8g) Job rotation	D	NR				Onedimensional characteristic of formative construct
(IQ9) EA resources	D	R	D	F	O	Multidimensional formative construct
(IQ9a) Financial resources	D	NR				Onedimensional characteristic of formative construct
(IQ9b) People resources	D	NR				Onedimensional characteristic of formative construct
(IQ9c) Time resources	D	NR				Onedimensional characteristic of formative construct

EAM Service Delivery Quality

(Sub-)Construct Name	Q 1a	Q 1b	Q 2a	Q 2b	Q 2c	Result
(SQ1) EA communication	D	R	D	F	O	Multidimensional formative construct
(SQ1a) Stakeholder-specific communications	D	NR				Onedimensional characteristic of formative construct
(SQ1b) Communication of the Benefits of EAM	D	NR				Onedimensional characteristic of formative construct
(SQ1c) Proactive communication	D	NR				Onedimensional characteristic of formative construct
(SQ1d) Simple and understandable communication	D	NR				Onedimensional characteristic of formative construct
(SQ2) EA Management Support	D	R	D	F	O	Multidimensional formative construct
(SQ2a) Projects checked for conformance	D	NR				Onedimensional characteristic of formative construct
(SQ2b) Top management involved in decision-making	D	NR				Onedimensional characteristic of formative construct
(SQ2c) Regular EA principle review	D	NR				Onedimensional characteristic of formative construct
(SQ2d) Management briefing	D	NR				Onedimensional characteristic of formative construct
(SQ2e) Top management is actively involved in EA planning	D	NR				Onedimensional characteristic of formative construct
(SQ2f) Top management involved in execution	D	NR				Onedimensional characteristic of formative construct
(SQ3) EA project support	D	R	D	F	O	Multidimensional formative construct
(SQ3a) Active involvement	D	NR				Onedimensional characteristic of formative construct
(SQ3b) Active project role	D	NR				Onedimensional characteristic of formative construct
(SQ3c) Integrating role across projects	D	NR				Onedimensional characteristic of formative construct
EAM Cultural Aspects						
(CA1) Top-management commitment	D	R	D	F	O	Multidimensional formative construct
(CA1a) Resource commitment	D	NR				Onedimensional characteristic of formative construct
(CA1b) Assigned importance	D	NR				Onedimensional characteristic of formative construct
(CA1c) Time commitment	D	NR				Onedimensional characteristic of formative construct
(CA1d) Communication of importance	D	NR				Onedimensional characteristic of formative construct
(CA2) EA awareness	D	R	D	F	O	Multidimensional formative construct
(CA2a) Stakeholders' awareness	D	NR				Onedimensional characteristic of formative construct
(CA2b) Stakeholders understanding of importance	D	NR				Onedimensional characteristic of formative construct

(Sub-)Construct Name	Q 1a	Q 1b	Q 2a	Q 2b	Q 2c	Result
(CA2c) Stakeholder education	D	NR				Onedimensional characteristic of formative construct
(CA3) EA understanding	D	R	D	F	O	Multidimensional formative construct
(CA3a) Shared vision	D	NR				Onedimensional characteristic of formative construct
(CA3b) Shared understanding	D	NR				Onedimensional characteristic of formative construct
(CA3c) Alignment of common goals	D	NR				Onedimensional characteristic of formative construct
Use / Satisfaction						
(Use) Use	D	R	M	E	A	Multidimensional reflective construct
(Sat) Satisfaction	D	R	M	E	A	Multidimensional reflective construct
EAM Benefits						
(OB1) Organizational Efficiency	D	R	M	E	A	Multidimensional reflective construct
(OB1a) Integrate Application/Processes	D	NR				Onedimensional manifestation of reflective construct
(OB1b) Standardize Applications/Processes	D	NR				Onedimensional manifestation of reflective construct
(OB1c) Consolidate Application/Processes	D	NR				Onedimensional manifestation of reflective construct
(OB1d) Control Complexity	D	NR				Onedimensional manifestation of reflective construct
(OB1e) Increase Utilization	D	NR				Onedimensional manifestation of reflective construct
(OB1f) Reduce Cost	D	NR				Onedimensional manifestation of reflective construct
(OB1g) Increase revenue	D	NR				Onedimensional manifestation of reflective construct
(OB2) Organizational Effectiveness	D	R	M	E	A	Multidimensional reflective construct
(OB2a) Global optimization	D	NR				Onedimensional manifestation of reflective construct
(OB2b) Operational business-IT Alignment	D	NR				Onedimensional manifestation of reflective construct
(OB2c) Efficient communication	D	NR				Onedimensional manifestation of reflective construct
(OB2d) Strategic business-IT Alignment	D	NR				Onedimensional manifestation of reflective construct

(Sub-)Construct Name	Q 1a	Q 1b	Q 2a	Q 2b	Q 2c	Result
(OB3) Organizational Flexibility	D	R	M	E	A	Multidimensional reflective construct
(OB3a) Identify change	D	NR				Onedimensional manifestation of reflective construct
(OB3b) Respond to market	D	NR				Onedimensional manifestation of reflective construct
(OB3c) Enable innovation	D	NR				Onedimensional manifestation of reflective construct
(OB3d) Cooperate with others	D	NR				Onedimensional manifestation of reflective construct
(PB1) Project Efficiency	D	R	M	E	A	Multidimensional reflective construct
(PB1a) Manage Project Budget	D	NR				Onedimensional manifestation of reflective construct
(PB1b) Meet Project Deadlines	D	NR				Onedimensional manifestation of reflective construct
(PB1c) Mitigate Project Risks	D	NR				Onedimensional manifestation of reflective construct
(PB1d) Manage Project Complexity	D	NR				Onedimensional manifestation of reflective construct
(PB2) Project Effectiveness	D	R	M	E	A	Multidimensional reflective construct
(PB2a) Improve quality of project deliverables	D	NR				Onedimensional manifestation of reflective construct
(PB2b) Deliver desired functionality (from projects)	D	NR				Onedimensional manifestation of reflective construct
(PB3) Project Flexibility	D	R	M	E	A	Multidimensional reflective construct
(PB3a) Manage changing project scope	D	NR				Onedimensional manifestation of reflective construct

D.3. Adopted Construct Definitions

Table D-3 Overview of Adopted Construct Definitions

Con-struct	Adopted construct definition	Original construct definition	Adopted from
(PQ1) as-is archi-tecture quality	An EAM stakeholder's perceived extent to which all desirable information about the as-is architecture is provided to satisfy the organization's needs.	Information-Quality is concerned with the quality of (the IS) outputs: namely, the quality of the information the system produces in reports and on-screen.	E.g., Gable et al. (2008)
(PQ2) to-be archi-tecture quality	An EAM stakeholder's perceived extent to which all desirable information about the to-be architecture is provided to satisfy the organization's needs.	Information-Quality is concerned with the quality of (the IS) outputs: namely, the quality of the information the system produces in reports and on-screen.	E.g., Gable et al. (2008)
(PQ3) road-map quality	An EAM stakeholder's perceived extent to which all desirable information about the roadmap is provided to satisfy the organization's needs.	Information-Quality is concerned with the quality of (the IS) outputs: namely, the quality of the information the system produces in reports and on-screen.	E.g., Gable et al. (2008)
(IQ2) Deci-sion-making centra-lization	An EAM stakeholder's perceived extent to which a central decision-making has been defined.	What is the extent of centralization for the following IT services in your company? (Five-point scale bounded by 'centralized in corporate IT group' and 'decentralized in lines of business.')	E.g., Boh et al. (2007)
(IQ7) EA princi-ples estab-lish-ment	An EAM stakeholder's perceived extent to which EA principles have been established.	Please rate the extent to which your company has defined formal architecture guidelines and internal standards.	E.g., Boh et al. (2007)
(Use) Use	An EAM stakeholder's perceived extent to which a person intends to continue to engage in Enterprise Architecture.	The extent to which a person intends to continue to use a particular artifact.	E.g., Bhattacher jee (2001); Spreng et al. (1996); Recker (2007)
(Sat) Satis-faction	An EAM stakeholder's perceived extent to which a person feels satisfied about his or her overall experience with the use of Enterprise Architecture.	The extent to which a person feels satisfied about his or her overall experience with the use of an artifact.	E.g., Bhattacher jee (2001); Spreng et al. (1996), (1996) ; Recker (2007)

Con-struct	Adopted construct definition	Original construct definition	Adopted from
(OB) Organi-zational Bene-fits	An EAM stakeholder's perceived extent to which the EA practice yields organizational benefits.	EA turns out to be a good instrument for organizational benefits.	E.g., Foorthuis et al. (2010)
(PB) Project-related Bene-fits	An EAM stakeholder's perceived extent to which the EA practice yields project-related benefits.	EA turns out to be a good instrument for project benefits.	E.g., Foorthuis et al. (2010)

D.4. Adoptions to Measurement Items for Benefit Construct

Table D-4 Overview of Adoptions to Measurement Items for Benefits Constructs

Original definition	Related construct	Adopted
EA turns out to be a good instrument to...		
B1. ... accomplish enterprise-wide goals	(OB2a) Global optimization	Adopted
B2. ...achieve an optimal fit between IT and the business processes it supports.	(OB2b) Operational business-IT Alignment	Adopted
B3. ...provide insight into the complexity of the organization.		Removed due overlap w/ (OB1d)
B4. ...control the complexity of the organization	(OB1d) Control Complexity	Adopted
B5. ...integrate, standardize and/or deduplicate related processes and systems.	(OB1a) Integrate Application	Split
	(OB1b) Standardize Applications	Split
	(OB1c) Consolidate Application	Split
	(OB1a) Integrate Processes	Split
	(OB1b) Standardize Processes	Split
	(OB1c) Consolidate Processes	Split
B6. Control costs	(OB1f) Reduce Cost	Adopted
B7. Respond to changes in the outside world in an agile fashion	(OB3b) Respond to market	Adopted
B8. ...co-operate with other organizations effectively and efficiently.	(OB3d) Cooperate with others	Adopted
B9. ...depict a clear image of the desired future situation.		Removed as in (IQ2) included
B10. EA turns out to be a good frame of reference to enable different stakeholders to communicate with each other effectively.	(OB2c) Efficient communication	Adopted

Original definition	Related construct	Adopted
B11. EA, in general, turns out to be a good instrument.		Removed as general measure
B12. ...exceed their budgets less often than projects that do not have to conform to EA.	(PB1a) Manage Project Budget	Adopted
B13. ...exceed their deadlines less often than projects that do not have to conform to EA.	(PB1b) Meet Project Deadlines	Adopted
B14. ...be better equipped to deal with risks than projects that do not have to conform to EA.	(PB1c) Mitigate Project Risks	Adopted
B15. ...deliver the desired quality more often than projects that do not have to conform to EA.	(PB2a) Improve quality of project deliverables	Adopted
B16. ...deliver the desired functionality more often than projects that do not have to conform to EA.	(PB2b) Deliver desired functionality (from projects)	Adopted
B17. ...be better equipped to deal with complexity (of the project and/or its immediate environment) than projects that do not have to conform to EA.	(PB1d) Manage Project Complexity	Adopted
B18. ...get initialized faster than projects that do not have to conform to EA.		Removed as overlapping with B13
	(OB1g) Increase revenue	Introduced
	(OB1e) Increase Utilization	Introduced
	(OB2d) Strategic business-IT Alignment	Introduced
	(OB3a) Identify change	Introduced
	(OB3c) Enable innovation	Introduced
	(PB3a) Manage changing project scope	Introduced

D.5. Overview of Results from ANOVA Test for Construct Validity

Table D-5 Overview of Results from ANOVA Test for Construct Validity (Group 1)

	Valid N	*EAM Infrastructure Quality* PQ1	PQ2	PQ3	*EAM Infrastructure Quality* IQ1	IQ2	IQ3	IQ4	IQ5	IQ6	IQ7	F	Highest Construct
PQ1a	4	**4,0**	1,8	1,5	1,3	2,0	1,5	1,5	1,3	1,3	1,3	10,5	PQ1
PQ1b	4	**4,5**	1,5	1,5	2,0	1,5	1,5	1,5	1,0	1,3	1,5	15,3	PQ1
PQ1c	4	**3,5**	2,0	1,8	1,5	1,3	2,0	1,5	1,5	1,5	1,3	9,5	PQ1
PQ1d	4	**4,3**	1,5	1,5	1,5	1,5	1,3	1,5	1,3	1,5	1,8	11,4	PQ1
PQ1e	4	**4,5**	2,0	1,5	1,3	1,8	1,0	1,5	2,0	1,3	1,5	18,8	PQ1
PQ1f	4	**3,8**	1,5	1,5	1,8	1,5	1,5	1,8	1,3	1,3	1,8	11,2	PQ1
PQ1g	4	**4,8**	1,5	1,8	1,3	1,0	2,0	1,3	1,0	1,5	1,5	28,8	PQ1
PQ1h	4	**4,5**	1,3	1,0	1,5	1,3	1,8	1,8	1,3	1,8	1,3	20,6	PQ1
PQ2a	4	1,8	**4,3**	1,8	1,8	1,5	1,5	1,8	1,5	1,5	1,3	12,3	PQ2
PQ2b	4	1,3	**4,8**	1,5	2,0	1,3	1,8	1,3	1,5	1,0	1,8	26,6	PQ2
PQ2c	4	1,5	**3,5**	1,5	1,3	1,8	1,8	1,5	1,5	1,5	1,8	9,0	PQ2
PQ2d	4	1,8	**3,8**	1,3	1,8	1,8	1,0	1,3	2,0	1,3	1,8	17,2	PQ2
PQ2e	4	1,8	**4,5**	1,8	1,5	1,8	1,0	1,0	1,5	1,5	1,5	20,8	PQ2
PQ2f	4	1,3	**3,5**	1,8	1,5	2,0	1,5	1,0	1,5	1,8	1,5	9,3	PQ2
PQ2g	4	1,3	**3,5**	1,5	1,5	1,5	1,0	1,5	1,3	1,8	1,0	10,9	PQ2
PQ2h	4	1,8	**4,0**	1,5	2,0	1,5	1,5	1,3	1,5	1,8	1,0	14,1	PQ2
PQ3a	4	1,3	1,8	**3,8**	1,5	1,8	1,8	1,5	1,3	1,8	1,8	12,3	PQ3
PQ3b	4	1,5	1,3	**4,8**	1,3	1,5	1,5	2,0	1,5	1,3	1,0	24,2	PQ3
PQ3c	4	1,3	1,5	**4,8**	1,8	1,0	1,3	1,5	1,5	1,5	1,3	21,5	PQ3
PQ3d	4	1,5	1,5	**4,0**	1,3	1,3	1,5	1,5	1,3	1,3	1,5	10,6	PQ3
PQ3e	4	1,5	2,0	**3,8**	1,5	1,5	1,5	1,5	1,8	1,5	1,8	9,6	PQ3
PQ3f	4	1,5	1,5	**3,8**	1,5	1,5	1,0	1,5	1,8	1,3	1,8	11,9	PQ3
PQ3g	4	2,0	1,8	**3,0**	1,5	1,3	1,3	1,5	1,3	1,5	1,5	8,4	PQ3
PQ3h	4	1,5	1,8	**3,8**	1,3	1,3	1,5	1,8	1,8	1,3	1,3	9,5	PQ3
IQ1a	4	1,3	1,5	2,0	**4,3**	1,5	1,5	1,3	1,5	1,0	1,8	14,6	IQ1
IQ1b	4	1,8	1,5	2,0	**3,5**	1,5	1,5	1,5	1,3	1,0	1,3	9,1	IQ1
IQ1c	4	1,8	1,0	1,5	**3,5**	1,5	1,5	1,0	1,8	1,3	1,8	12,0	IQ1
IQ2a	4	1,3	1,5	1,3	1,5	**3,5**	1,5	1,0	1,5	1,5	1,5	9,0	IQ2
IQ2b	4	1,0	1,5	1,8	1,3	**4,0**	1,8	2,0	2,0	1,8	1,3	18,1	IQ2
IQ2c	4	1,5	1,3	1,8	1,8	**4,5**	1,5	1,8	1,8	1,5	1,5	13,8	IQ2
IQ2d	4	1,3	1,3	1,5	1,8	**3,8**	1,8	1,8	1,5	1,5	1,8	9,5	IQ2
IQ2e	4	1,8	1,8	1,5	1,5	**4,0**	1,5	1,5	1,8	1,3	2,0	12,8	IQ2
IQ2f	4	1,5	1,5	1,3	1,5	**4,5**	1,5	1,3	1,5	1,8	1,3	13,1	IQ2
IQ2g	4	2,0	1,8	1,5	1,5	**3,3**	1,3	1,5	1,5	2,0	1,5	10,3	IQ2
IQ2h	4	1,3	1,3	1,5	1,5	**4,3**	1,0	1,5	1,5	1,5	1,8	15,9	IQ2
IQ2i	4	1,5	1,8	1,8	1,8	**3,8**	2,0	1,3	1,5	1,3	1,3	13,8	IQ2
IQ3a	4	1,5	1,5	1,3	1,5	1,3	**3,8**	1,8	1,8	1,5	1,0	9,8	IQ3

		EAM Infrastructure Quality			EAM Infrastructure Quality								
	Valid N	PQ1	PQ2	PQ3	IQ1	IQ2	IQ3	IQ4	IQ5	IQ6	IQ7	F	Highest Construct
IQ3b	4	1,8	1,0	1,5	1,3	2,0	**4,0**	1,0	1,3	1,5	1,5	12,5	IQ3
IQ3c	4	1,5	1,8	1,8	1,3	2,0	**4,0**	1,3	1,5	1,8	1,5	13,2	IQ3
IQ3d	4	1,3	1,8	1,5	1,5	1,3	**5,0**	1,3	1,5	1,5	1,3	24,1	IQ3
IQ3e	4	1,5	1,5	1,3	1,3	1,8	**3,5**	1,8	1,5	1,5	1,5	7,2	IQ3
IQ4a	4	1,0	1,0	1,0	1,0	1,8	1,5	**3,8**	1,3	1,5	2,0	16,2	IQ4
IQ4b	4	1,0	1,0	1,0	1,3	1,5	2,0	**4,0**	1,8	1,5	1,8	19,0	IQ4
IQ4c	4	1,0	1,0	1,0	1,5	1,3	1,8	**3,8**	1,5	1,8	1,8	12,8	IQ4
IQ4d	4	1,0	1,0	1,0	1,5	1,5	1,5	**3,3**	1,3	1,5	1,3	10,2	IQ4
IQ4e	4	1,0	1,0	1,0	1,5	1,5	1,8	**4,0**	1,5	1,3	1,8	12,3	IQ4
IQ5a	4	1,0	1,0	1,0	1,3	1,5	1,8	1,5	**4,3**	1,3	1,3	22,3	IQ5
IQ5b	4	1,0	1,0	1,0	1,8	1,5	1,5	1,5	**4,0**	1,5	1,8	15,2	IQ5
IQ5c	4	1,0	1,0	1,0	1,3	1,8	1,5	2,0	**4,0**	1,8	2,0	38,1	IQ5
IQ6a	4	1,0	1,0	1,0	1,3	1,5	1,8	2,0	1,3	**4,0**	1,3	14,5	IQ6
IQ6b	4	1,0	1,0	1,0	1,0	1,0	1,3	1,5	1,8	**3,5**	1,8	19,5	IQ6
IQ6c	4	1,0	1,0	1,0	1,8	1,5	1,5	1,3	1,3	**4,0**	1,5	15,3	IQ6
IQ7a	4	1,0	1,0	1,0	1,3	1,8	1,5	2,0	2,0	1,0	**3,3**	24,4	IQ7
IQ7b	4	1,0	1,0	1,0	1,3	1,5	1,3	1,3	1,5	1,5	**4,5**	23,3	IQ7
IQ7c	4	1,0	1,0	1,0	1,8	1,5	1,8	1,5	1,8	1,8	**3,8**	13,1	IQ7
IQ7d	4	1,0	1,0	1,0	1,5	1,8	1,5	1,8	1,5	1,5	**4,3**	15,9	IQ7
IQ7e	4	1,0	1,0	1,0	1,3	1,3	1,3	1,5	1,5	1,3	**3,3**	10,8	IQ7

Table D-6 Overview of Results from ANOVA Test for Construct Validity (Group 2)

		EAM Infrastructure Quality		EAM Service Delivery Quality			EAM Cultural Aspects			EAM Benefits			
Item	N	IQ8	IQ9	SQ1	SQ2	SQ3	CA1	CA2	CA3	OB	PB	F	Highest Construct
IQ8a	4	**4,0**	1,5	1,3	1,8	1,8	1,3	1,5	2,0	1,5	1,3	13,1	IQ8
IQ8b	4	**4,0**	1,8	1,5	1,3	1,5	1,8	1,5	2,0	1,0	1,8	11,7	IQ8
IQ8c	4	**4,5**	1,8	1,8	1,3	1,5	1,3	1,3	1,8	1,8	1,5	14,5	IQ8
IQ8d	4	**3,8**	2,0	1,8	1,3	1,0	1,3	1,5	1,8	1,3	1,5	11,8	IQ8
IQ8e	4	**4,5**	1,5	1,8	1,5	1,8	1,5	1,5	1,5	1,3	1,3	16,2	IQ8
IQ8f	4	**3,8**	1,5	1,5	1,5	1,8	1,5	1,3	1,3	1,5	1,5	8,4	IQ8
IQ8g	4	**4,3**	1,8	1,5	1,5	2,0	1,5	1,8	1,0	1,3	1,3	15,2	IQ8
IQ9a	4	1,5	**4,3**	1,3	1,5	2,0	1,8	2,0	1,0	1,5	1,8	17,2	IQ9
IQ9b	4	1,5	**4,3**	1,5	2,0	1,3	1,3	1,5	1,5	1,5	1,5	12,6	IQ9
IQ9c	4	1,5	**4,3**	1,5	1,8	1,5	1,5	1,3	1,8	1,8	1,3	15,1	IQ9
SQ1a	4	1,0	1,3	**4,0**	1,0	1,3	1,8	1,5	1,3	2,0	1,8	24,7	SQ1
SQ1b	4	1,5	2,0	**4,0**	1,0	1,5	1,5	1,5	1,8	1,8	1,5	11,0	SQ1
SQ1c	4	1,8	1,8	**4,0**	1,3	1,5	1,5	1,5	1,0	1,3	1,0	18,7	SQ1
SQ1d	4	1,3	2,0	**4,5**	1,3	2,0	1,8	1,3	1,8	2,0	2,0	34,1	SQ1
SQ2a	4	1,0	1,5	1,5	**3,8**	1,3	1,5	1,5	1,3	1,8	1,5	11,7	SQ2
SQ2b	4	1,3	1,5	1,5	**4,5**	1,5	1,5	1,5	1,8	1,0	1,3	14,2	SQ2

258

Item	N	EAM Infrastructure Quality		EAM Service Delivery Quality			EAM Cultural Aspects			EAM Benefits			Highest Construct
		IQ8	IQ9	SQ1	SQ2	SQ3	CA1	CA2	CA3	OB	PB	F	
SQ2c	4	1,5	1,5	1,3	**3,8**	1,5	1,5	1,5	1,8	1,5	1,3	8,4	SQ2
SQ2d	4	1,3	1,5	2,0	**3,8**	1,5	2,0	1,0	1,5	1,5	1,5	12,0	SQ2
SQ2e	4	1,5	2,0	1,3	**4,3**	1,5	1,8	1,5	1,5	1,5	1,8	13,1	SQ2
SQ2f	4	1,3	1,5	1,8	**4,5**	1,8	1,8	1,8	1,8	1,3	1,5	18,2	SQ2
SQ3a	4	1,3	1,3	1,8	1,5	**4,0**	1,8	1,5	2,0	1,5	1,0	14,5	SQ3
SQ3b	4	1,0	1,8	1,5	1,5	**4,0**	1,3	1,3	1,5	1,3	1,8	12,7	SQ3
SQ3c	4	1,3	1,5	1,3	2,0	**5,0**	1,8	1,5	1,3	2,0	1,3	34,0	SQ3
CA1a	4	1,8	1,0	1,5	1,5	1,3	**3,8**	1,0	2,0	1,5	1,5	16,0	CA1
CA1b	4	1,5	1,3	1,3	1,5	1,8	**4,0**	1,8	1,5	1,3	1,8	11,7	CA1
CA1c	4	2,0	1,8	1,3	1,8	1,0	**3,8**	1,8	1,3	2,0	1,5	14,2	CA1
CA1d	4	1,8	1,8	1,5	1,8	1,8	**4,0**	2,0	1,5	1,5	1,5	12,9	CA1
CA2a	4	1,3	1,5	1,5	1,8	1,3	1,8	**4,0**	1,8	1,3	1,8	12,2	CA2
CA2b	4	1,5	1,8	1,5	2,0	1,3	1,8	**4,0**	1,0	1,5	1,3	14,5	CA2
CA2c	4	1,5	1,8	1,3	1,3	1,8	1,3	**3,5**	1,5	1,3	1,5	9,3	CA2
CA3a	4	1,8	1,0	1,3	1,5	1,8	1,8	1,8	**4,3**	1,8	1,8	14,9	CA3
CA3b	4	2,0	1,8	1,3	1,8	1,8	1,5	1,5	**3,5**	1,8	1,8	11,8	CA3
CA3c	4	1,3	1,0	1,3	1,5	1,3	1,5	2,0	**3,8**	1,8	1,5	14,6	CA3
OB1a	4	1,5	1,5	1,3	1,3	1,8	1,8	1,3	1,8	**4,0**	1,3	12,0	OB
OB1b	4	1,3	1,5	1,5	1,5	1,8	1,3	1,3	1,8	**3,5**	1,3	9,3	OB
OB1c	4	1,3	1,5	1,5	1,5	1,5	2,0	1,5	1,5	**4,3**	1,8	12,7	OB
OB1d	4	1,8	1,3	1,3	1,3	1,8	1,0	1,8	1,5	**3,8**	1,0	11,8	OB
OB1e	4	1,3	1,8	1,8	1,3	2,0	1,3	1,8	1,8	**4,3**	1,5	19,2	OB
OB1f	4	1,8	1,5	1,3	1,5	1,5	1,3	1,3	1,8	**4,3**	1,3	12,4	OB
OB1g	4	1,3	1,8	1,3	1,5	2,0	1,5	1,8	1,0	**4,0**	2,0	24,1	OB
OB2a	4	1,8	1,5	1,8	1,3	1,8	1,8	1,8	1,5	**3,3**	1,3	9,0	OB
OB2b	4	1,8	1,0	1,3	2,0	1,3	1,5	1,5	1,3	**4,0**	1,5	14,3	OB
OB2c	4	1,3	1,3	1,5	1,5	1,5	1,8	1,8	1,5	**4,5**	1,8	16,8	OB
OB2d	4	1,3	1,0	1,0	1,3	1,5	1,3	1,0	1,5	**4,3**	1,5	21,0	OB
OB2e	4	1,5	1,5	1,5	1,8	1,5	1,5	1,3	1,5	**3,5**	1,5	8,2	OB
OB3a	4	1,5	1,0	1,8	1,5	1,8	1,8	1,0	1,3	**4,0**	1,8	11,9	OB
OB3b	4	1,3	2,0	1,3	1,8	1,5	1,5	1,8	1,5	**4,8**	1,5	22,0	OB
OB3c	4	1,5	1,5	2,0	1,8	1,5	1,5	1,3	1,3	**4,5**	1,0	20,8	OB
OB3d	4	1,3	1,5	1,3	1,8	1,5	1,5	1,3	1,0	**3,5**	1,5	7,8	OB
PB1a	4	1,8	1,5	1,5	1,5	1,5	1,3	1,8	2,0	1,5	**4,3**	13,1	PB
PB1b	4	1,3	1,8	1,5	1,3	1,3	1,5	1,8	1,5	1,3	**4,3**	12,4	PB
PB1c	4	1,8	1,8	1,3	1,5	1,5	2,0	1,3	1,5	1,8	**3,5**	11,1	PB
PB1d	4	1,5	1,3	1,3	1,3	1,8	2,0	1,8	1,0	1,8	**4,0**	15,7	PB
PB2a	4	1,8	1,8	1,5	1,5	1,3	1,5	1,8	1,5	1,8	**3,5**	9,5	PB
PB2b	4	1,8	2,0	1,8	1,0	1,0	1,5	1,5	1,8	1,5	**3,5**	14,3	PB
PB3a	4	1,8	1,5	1,5	1,8	1,8	1,5	1,3	1,3	1,8	**3,8**	9,5	PB

D.6. Screenshot of Access Website to Survey

Figure D-1 Screenshot of Access Website to Survey with Referral

Figure D-2 Screenshot of Access Website to Survey without Referral

D.7. Used Survey Instrument

Dear Participant,

Thank you for your interest in our survey.

This research project seeks to develop an understanding of how Enterprise Architecture (EA) creates business benefits. Therefore, the following survey investigates different aspects of your organization's EA approach and resulting benefits.

The survey takes about 30 minutes and is intended to be answered by stakeholders that are involved in Enterprise Architecture on all levels in organizations.

As a participant of this study, we offer you to receive the final report with the results of this study providing you the insight which elements of an EA approach have highest impact on business benefits. In addition, we would like to offer you a benchmark of your answers compared to your industry. To receive the results and to participate in this free benchmarking, please indicate your interest below.

Your participation in this survey is voluntary, and you may decline to answer any question at any time. We guarantee you that your identity will be kept completely confidential. Data gathered in this survey will be used solely for aggregate statistics, and not to specifically identify you or your organization to any third parties.

When answering the questions, please be as accurate as you can. If you don't have the information, please provide your best estimate.

Furthermore, if you encounter any difficulties in completing this survey, or have any concerns or questions, feel free to contact us via email (matthias.lange@wiwi.hu-berlin.de)

Please indicate now which results you would like to receive:

☐ General results in form of a study report   ☐ Individual comparison of my answers to industry

Please provide us your email address to which we can send the results (as selected above):

Thank you very much; your support in this study is highly appreciated. Please press the next button to start the survey.

Matthias Lange
Humboldt-University Berlin
Institute of Information Systems
Spandauer Straße 1, 10178 Berlin, Germany
matthias.lange@wiwi.hu-berlin.de

Prof. Dr. Jan Mendling
Vienna University of Economics
Institute for Information Business
Augasse 2-6, A-1090 Vienna, Austria
jan.mendling@wu.ac.at

2. Organization's Demographics

In the following section, we would like to ask you some questions about **your organization's** demographics.

Please answer all questions in the following survey from the broadest perspective you can. Before doing so, please specify from which organizational perspective you are answering all following question in this survey (please choose one)?

○ All business units of your organization

○ A subset of the firm (e.g., a single business unit, geography, etc.)

What is the type of your organization (please choose one)?

○ Publicly traded   ○ Non-profit

○ Privately held   ○ Government

What industry does your organization belong to (select most applicable)?

○ Aerospace & Defence   ○ Consumer Goods   ○ Private Equity

○ Automotive & Assembly   ○ Electronics & Semiconductors ○ Public Services

○ Basic Materials   ○ Energy   ○ Retail & Wholesale

○ Banking   ○ Healthcare   ○ Telecom & Media

○ Chemicals   ○ Information Technology   ○ Travel, Transport & Logistics

○ Consultancy   ○ Insurance

Other (please specify)

_____

Where is the headquarters of your organization located?

_____

In how many countries is your organization present?

_____

How many employees worked in your organization in 2010?

_____

How many employees worked in your EA function in 2010?

_____

What was your organization's total 2010 revenue? (Non-Profits, Educational organizations, and Government please report total budget)

_____

What was your organization's total 2010 IT spending as a percentage of revenues? Please include operating and capital spending excluding depreciation. (Non-Profits, Educational organizations, and Government please report IT spending as a % of total budget)

_____

How many years does your organization engage in EA?

What describes your business strategy best (please choose one)?

◯ Cost leadership   ◯ Niche leadership

◯ Quality leadership   ◯ Don't know

◯ Innovation leadership

Demographic Comments - If you have any questions related to your answers above, please enter your comments and ideas here:

3. Personal Demographics

In the following section, we would like to ask you some questions about **your personal** demographics.

What is your primary job function?

[   ]

How is your current role positioned between an operational (e.g. business analyst), managerial (e.g. line manager) or executive (e.g. CxO) role (Please rate on a scale from 1 being operational to 4 being managerial to 7 being executive)?

○ 1
(Operational)
○ 2
○ 3
○ 4
(Managerial)
○ 5
○ 6
○ 7
(Executive)

What percentage of your time do you spend on specific projects (as opposed to line functions)?

[   ]

How would you rate the following statements (Please rate them on a scale from 1 being IT-oriented to 7 being business-oriented)?

	1 (IT-oriented)	2	3	4 (Both)	5	6	7 (Business-oriented)
My current role is organizationally positioned mostly...	○	○	○	○	○	○	○
With regards to Enterprise Architecture, I consider myself as having expertise that is mostly...	○	○	○	○	○	○	○

How many years of experience do you have with Enterprise Architecture in total (from your current position as well as former positions)?

[   ]

Personal demographic Comments - If you have any questions related to your answers above, please enter your comments and ideas here:

[   ]

264

In the following section, we would like to ask you some questions about **your organization's** EA products.

Definition of terms we use in this section of the survey:
*The **As-Is architecture** is the description and documentation of the current architectural landscape covering all information from business goals, to business processes, to IT applications, to infrastructure.*
*The **To-be architecture** is the description and documentation of the desired architectural landscape covering all information from business goals, to business processes, to IT applications, to infrastructure.*
*The **Roadmap** schedules the transformation steps (i.e. the implementation projects) that evolve the as-is architecture to a to-be architecture.*

How would you rate the following statements (Please rate on a scale from 1 being strongly disagree to 7 being strongly agree)?

Information provided by the EA function about the AS-IS architecture is...

	Don't know	1 (strongly disagree)	2	3	4 (neutral)	5	6	7 (strongly agree)
...detailed	O	O	O	O	O	O	O	O
...easy to understand	O	O	O	O	O	O	O	O
...complete	O	O	O	O	O	O	O	O
...always timely	O	O	O	O	O	O	O	O
...unavailable elsewhere	O	O	O	O	O	O	O	O

Information provided by the EA function about the TO-BE architecture is...

	Don't know	1 (strongly disagree)	2	3	4 (neutral)	5	6	7 (strongly agree)
...detailed	O	O	O	O	O	O	O	O
...easy to understand	O	O	O	O	O	O	O	O
...complete	O	O	O	O	O	O	O	O
...always timely	O	O	O	O	O	O	O	O
...unavailable elsewhere	O	O	O	O	O	O	O	O

Information provided by the EA function about the ROADMAP is...

	Don't know	1 (strongly disagree)	2	3	4 (neutral)	5	6	7 (strongly agree)
...detailed	O	O	O	O	O	O	O	O
...easy to understand	O	O	O	O	O	O	O	O
...complete	O	O	O	O	O	O	O	O
...always timely	O	O	O	O	O	O	O	O
...unavailable elsewhere	O	O	O	O	O	O	O	O

EA Product Comments - If you have any questions related to your answers above, please enter your comments and ideas here:

In the following section, we would like to ask you some questions about **your organization's** EA function setup.

Definition of terms we use in this section of the survey:
EA activities *are all tasks and activities executed for the purpose of EA.*
EA approach *is the overall "way" an organization conducts EA; for example consisting of the tasks and roles, created end products as well as the processes executed to generate these products.*
The **EA framework** *defines how to organize the structure and views associated with an Enterprise Architecture (e.g. TOGAF, Zachman).*
EA function *is the organizational unit responsible for EA.*
EA principles *are the standards and rules that guide the definition and implementation of the architecture.*
EA procedures *are the processes and activities that are executed for the purpose of EA.*
EA reference architectures *are industry standards and best-practice architectures (such as eTOM, ITIL, etc.) that are used as a guideline.*

How would you rate the following statements regarding your EA function's mandate (Please rate on a scale from 1 being strongly disagree to 7 being strongly agree)?

	Don't know	1 (strongly disagree)	2	3	4 (neutral)	5	6	7 (strongly agree)
Organizational entities and subsidiaries covered by our EA function have been clearly specified.	○	○	○	○	○	○	○	○
Our EA function takes care of both business as well as IT aspects.	○	○	○	○	○	○	○	○
Our EA function has an organizational/ business focus rather than an IT focus.	○	○	○	○	○	○	○	○
Our EA function is well aligned with other boundary functions (such as project portfolio management, strategic planning)	○	○	○	○	○	○	○	○

How would you rate the extent of centralization for the respective decision making in your company (Please rate on a scale from 1 being "decentralized along business lines" to 7 being "centralized")?

	Don't know	1 (decentralized in lines of business)	2	3	4	5	6	7 (centralized in corporate IT group)
Capital budget	O	O	O	O	O	O	O	O
Enterprise Architecture definition and implementation	O	O	O	O	O	O	O	O
Operational process optimization and implementation	O	O	O	O	O	O	O	O
Application development projects prioritization and approval	O	O	O	O	O	O	O	O
IT development and implementation	O	O	O	O	O	O	O	O
Infrastructure planning and management	O	O	O	O	O	O	O	O
Compliance Management	O	O	O	O	O	O	O	O

How would you rate the following statements regarding the extent of your organization's EA formally introduced governance mechanisms (Please rate on a scale from 1 being strongly disagree to 7 being strongly agree)?

	Don't know	1 (strongly disagree)	2	3	4 (neutral)	5	6	7 (strongly agree)
We have well-defined approval processes to ensure project conformance to EA principles.	O	O	O	O	O	O	O	O
Internal directives require compliance with EA principles for all projects.	O	O	O	O	O	O	O	O
There are penalties for violating EA principles.	O	O	O	O	O	O	O	O
EA principles are ignored and informal agreements are reached to handle some situations.	O	O	O	O	O	O	O	O
Waivers of EA principles are often granted.	O	O	O	O	O	O	O	O

How would you rate the following statements regarding your organization's EA framework (Please rate on a scale from 1 being strongly disagree to 7 being strongly agree)?

	Don't know	1 (strongly disagree)	2	3	4 (neutral)	5	6	7 (strongly agree)
We have a standardized EA framework in place.	○	○	○	○	○	○	○	○
We employ elements of industry standards (e.g. TOGAF) to complement our own EA framework.	○	○	○	○	○	○	○	○
Our EA framework is accepted by all EA stakeholders.	○	○	○	○	○	○	○	○

How would you rate the following statements regarding your EA tool support (Please rate on a scale from 1 being strongly disagree to 7 being strongly agree)?

	Don't know	1 (strongly disagree)	2	3	4 (neutral)	5	6	7 (strongly agree)
We have established software tool support for our EA activities.	○	○	○	○	○	○	○	○
We have software tools that provide access to a central repository.	○	○	○	○	○	○	○	○
Our software tools for EA are accepted among all relevant stakeholders.	○	○	○	○	○	○	○	○

How would you rate the following statements regarding established EA reference architectures in your organization (Please rate on a scale from 1 being strongly disagree to 7 being strongly agree)?

	Don't know	1 (strongly disagree)	2	3	4 (neutral)	5	6	7 (strongly agree)
We have established EA reference architectures.	○	○	○	○	○	○	○	○
EA reference architectures are used to guide the definition of our to-be architecture.	○	○	○	○	○	○	○	○
We use EA reference architectures without major adjustments.	○	○	○	○	○	○	○	○

How would you rate the following statements regarding your EA principles (Please rate on a scale from 1 being strongly disagree to 7 being strongly agree)? We have effective EA principles in place for our ...

	Don't know	1 (strongly disagree)	2	3	4 (neutral)	5	6	7 (strongly agree)
Business architecture	O	O	O	O	O	O	O	O
Application architecture	O	O	O	O	O	O	O	O
Technology architecture	O	O	O	O	O	O	O	O
Integration architecture	O	O	O	O	O	O	O	O
Data architecture	O	O	O	O	O	O	O	O

How would you rate the following statements regarding your EA skills (Please rate on a scale from 1 being strongly disagree to 7 being strongly agree)?

	Don't know	1 (strongly disagree)	2	3	4 (neutral)	5	6	7 (strongly agree)
We have job descriptions for EA roles.	O	O	O	O	O	O	O	O
EA roles are clearly distinguished from other roles outside the EA function (such as IT portfolio managers).	O	O	O	O	O	O	O	O
EA staff receives ongoing training.	O	O	O	O	O	O	O	O
EA staff participate in a job rotation.	O	O	O	O	O	O	O	O
EA staff have a high level of communication skills.	O	O	O	O	O	O	O	O
EA staff have a high level of EA expert knowledge.	O	O	O	O	O	O	O	O
EA staff are well networked in the organization.	O	O	O	O	O	O	O	O

How would you rate the following statements regarding your EA resources (Please rate on a scale from 1 being strongly disagree to 7 being strongly agree)?

	Don't know	1 (strongly disagree)	2	3	4	5	6	7 (strongly agree)
Our EA function receives sufficient funding.	O	O	O	O	O	O	O	O
Our EA function has adequate staffing to support its needs.	O	O	O	O	O	O	O	O
Our EA function has sufficient time to complete its tasks.	O	O	O	O	O	O	O	O

EA Function Setup Comments - If you have any questions related to your answers above, please enter your comments and ideas here:

In the following section, we would like to ask you some questions about **your organization's** EA service delivery.

Definition of terms we use in this section of the survey:
EA function is the organizational unit responsible for EA.
EA principles are the standards and rules that guide the definition and implementation of the architecture.

How would you rate the following statements regarding your organization's EA communication (Please rate on a scale from 1 being strongly disagree to 7 being strongly agree)?

The EA function communicates...

	Don't know	1 (strongly disagree)	2	3	4 (neutral)	5	6	7 (strongly agree)
... with all stakeholder groups according to their needs.	◯	◯	◯	◯	◯	◯	◯	◯
... proactively with all stakeholder groups.	◯	◯	◯	◯	◯	◯	◯	◯
... with all stakeholders always as simple and understandable as possible.	◯	◯	◯	◯	◯	◯	◯	◯
... successfully the value of EA to all EA stakeholders.	◯	◯	◯	◯	◯	◯	◯	◯

How would you rate the following statements regarding your organization's EA reviews and EA management support in practice (Please rate on a scale from 1 being strongly disagree to 7 being strongly agree)?

	Don't know	1 (strongly disagree)	2	3	4 (neutral)	5	6	7 (strongly agree)
We regularly review our EA principles.	◯	◯	◯	◯	◯	◯	◯	◯
Projects are regularly checked for conformance with EA principles.	◯	◯	◯	◯	◯	◯	◯	◯
Top-management is briefed regarding review results.	◯	◯	◯	◯	◯	◯	◯	◯
Top-management is involved in EA decision making.	◯	◯	◯	◯	◯	◯	◯	◯
Top-management is actively involved in EA planning.	◯	◯	◯	◯	◯	◯	◯	◯
Top-management is involved in executing EA decisions.	◯	◯	◯	◯	◯	◯	◯	◯

How would you rate the following statements regarding your organization's EA project support (Please rate on a scale from 1 being strongly disagree to 7 being strongly agree)?

	Don't know	1 (strongly disagree)	2	3	4 (neutral)	5	6	7 (strongly agree)
Enterprise Architects consult implementation projects regarding architectural considerations.	○	○	○	○	○	○	○	○
Enterprise Architects play an active role in implementation projects working actively on project teams.	○	○	○	○	○	○	○	○
Enterprise Architects take an integrating role across projects.	○	○	○	○	○	○	○	○

EA Service Comments - If you have any questions related to your answers above, please enter your comments and ideas here:

In the following section, we would like to ask you some questions about **your organization's** EA culture.

Definition of terms we use in this section of the survey:
EA approach *is the overall "way" an organization conducts EA; for example consisting of the tasks and roles, created end products as well as the processes executed to generate these products.*
EA function *is the organizational unit responsible for EA.*

How would you rate the following statements regarding your organization's EA leadership commitment (Please rate on a scale from 1 being strongly disagree to 7 being strongly agree)?

	Don't know	1 (strongly disagree)	2	3	4 (neutral)	5	6	7 (strongly agree)
Top-level managers allocate sufficient time for EA.	○	○	○	○	○	○	○	○
Top-level managers allocate adequate resources for EA.	○	○	○	○	○	○	○	○
EA is of high importance to top-level managers.	○	○	○	○	○	○	○	○
Top-level managers communicate the importance of EA to the organization.	○	○	○	○	○	○	○	○

How would you rate the following statements regarding your organization's EA stakeholder awareness (Please rate on a scale from 1 being strongly disagree to 7 being strongly agree)?

	Don't know	1 (strongly disagree)	2	3	4 (neutral)	5	6	7 (strongly agree)
EA stakeholders are aware of the EA function.	○	○	○	○	○	○	○	○
EA stakeholders understand the importance of EA.	○	○	○	○	○	○	○	○
EA stakeholders who not work in the EA function but are involved in EA are frequently trained to better understand EA.	○	○	○	○	○	○	○	○

How would you rate the following statements regarding your organization's **EA understanding (Please rate on a scale from 1 being strongly disagree to 7 being strongly agree)?**

	Don't know	1 (strongly disagree)	2	3	4 (neutral)	5	6	7 (strongly agree)
Business and IT employees have a shared understanding of EA.	○	○	○	○	○	○	○	○
Business and IT employees have a shared vision for EA.	○	○	○	○	○	○	○	○
Our current business objectives are in line with our EA approach.	○	○	○	○	○	○	○	○

EA Culture Comments - If you have any questions related to your answers above, please enter your comments and ideas here:

In the following section, we would like to ask you some questions about **your organization's** intention to use EA and **your organization's** user satisfaction with EA.

Definition of terms we use in this section of the survey:
EA approach is the overall "way" how an organization conducts EA; consisting for example of the tasks and roles, created end products as well as the processes executed to generate these products.

How would you rate the following statements regarding your organization's EA use (Please rate on a scale from 1 being strongly disagree to 7 being strongly agree)?

	Don't know	1 (strongly disagree)	2	3	4 (neutral)	5	6	7 (strongly agree)
If we remain with our EA approach, EA stakeholder's intention would be to continue to engage in EA.	○	○	○	○	○	○	○	○
In the future, I expect that EA stakeholder will continue to engage in EA.	○	○	○	○	○	○	○	○
EA stakeholders prefer to continue to use our approach to EA over other approaches to EA.	○	○	○	○	○	○	○	○
Regulatory requirements mandate the use of Enterprise Architecture in our organization.	○	○	○	○	○	○	○	○

How would you rate the following statements regarding your organization's EA satisfaction (Please rate on a scale from 1 being strongly disagree to 7 being strongly agree)?
EA stakeholders feel...

	Don't know	1 (strongly disagree)	2	3	4 (neutral)	5	6	7 (strongly agree)
...contented about their overall experience with our approach to EA.	○	○	○	○	○	○	○	○
...satisfied about their overall experience with our approach to EA.	○	○	○	○	○	○	○	○
...delighted about their overall experience with our approach to EA.	○	○	○	○	○	○	○	○

Use and User Satisfaction Comments - If you have any questions related to your answers above, please enter your comments and ideas here:

In the following section, we would like to ask you some questions about the benefits **your organization's** EA approach generates.

Definition of terms we use in this section of the survey:
EA approach *is the overall "way" how an organization conducts EA; consisting for example of the tasks and roles, created end products as well as the processes executed to generate these products.*

How would you rate the following statements regarding the EA benefits your organization achieves on an organizational level (Please rate on a scale from 1 being strongly disagree to 7 being strongly agree)?
Our EA approach turns out to be a good instrument to...

	Don't know	1 (strongly disagree)	2	3	4 (neutral)	5	6	7 (strongly agree)
...integrate applications.	○	○	○	○	○	○	○	○
...integrate processes.	○	○	○	○	○	○	○	○
...standardize applications.	○	○	○	○	○	○	○	○
...standardize processes.	○	○	○	○	○	○	○	○
...consolidate applications.	○	○	○	○	○	○	○	○
...consolidate processes.	○	○	○	○	○	○	○	○
...control the complexity of the organization.	○	○	○	○	○	○	○	○
...increase the utilization of resources.	○	○	○	○	○	○	○	○
...reduce costs.	○	○	○	○	○	○	○	○
...increase revenue.	○	○	○	○	○	○	○	○
...accomplish enterprise-wide goals, instead of (possibly conflicting) local optimizations.	○	○	○	○	○	○	○	○
...achieve an optimal fit between IT and the business processes it supports.	○	○	○	○	○	○	○	○
...achieve an optimal fit between IT strategy and business strategy.	○	○	○	○	○	○	○	○
...effectively communicate among different stakeholders.	○	○	○	○	○	○	○	○
...achieve compliance to regulatory requirements.	○	○	○	○	○	○	○	○
...identify and trigger required changes in the organization.	○	○	○	○	○	○	○	○
...enable the organization to respond to changes in the outside world in an agile fashion.	○	○	○	○	○	○	○	○

	Don't know	1 (strongly disagree)	2	3	4 (neutral)	5	6	7 (strongly agree)
...enable innovation.	○	○	○	○	○	○	○	○
...co-operate with other organizations effectively and efficiently.	○	○	○	○	○	○	○	○

How would you rate the following statements regarding the EA benefits your organization achieves within projects (Please rate on a scale from 1 being strongly disagree to 7 being strongly agree)?

Our projects leveraging EA turn out to ...

	Don't know	1 (strongly disagree)	2	3	4 (neutral)	5	6	7 (strongly agree)
...meet their budget more often than projects that do not leverage EA.	○	○	○	○	○	○	○	○
...meet their deadlines more often than projects that do not leverage EA.	○	○	○	○	○	○	○	○
...mitigate risks better than projects that do not leverage EA.	○	○	○	○	○	○	○	○
...be better equipped to deal with complexity than projects that do not leverage EA.	○	○	○	○	○	○	○	○
...deliver the desired quality more often than projects that do not leverage EA.	○	○	○	○	○	○	○	○
...deliver the desired functionality more often than projects that do not leverage EA.	○	○	○	○	○	○	○	○
...be able to adjust their scope to changing requirements more easily than projects that do not leverage EA.	○	○	○	○	○	○	○	○

EA Benefits Comments - If you have any questions related to your answers above, please enter your comments and ideas here:

10. Ending

Thank you for participating in our survey.

If you have indicated your interest earlier, we will provide you the results and benchmarking as soon as possible.

In addition to this survey, we also would like to offer you a cross-department benchmarking within your organization. This analysis would interview various stakeholders in your organization and provide you insights in how different stakeholders perceive your EA function. For further details please contact us directly (matthias.lange@wiwi.hu-berlin.de) or indicate your interest below.

☐ Please contact me to discuss further details on the cross-department benchmark.

Finally, we would like to ask you whether you know anyone who would be interested in completing this survey as well (Please enter the names as well as the email addresses)?

Thanks again for participating in our survey.

Final Comments - If you have any questions related to your answers above, please enter your comments and ideas here:

D.8. Survey Invitations

D.8.1.   Personalized Invitation E-mails

Subject: Invitation to research survey about "Value of Enterprise Architecture Management"

Body:

Dear XXX,

have you ever asked yourself, what elements of Enterprise Architecture Management have which contribution to your organization's success?

Today, we would like to invite you to our research study "Benefits of Enterprise Architecture Management" which is conducted by the Humboldt-University Berlin and Vienna University of Economics. This study investigates whether Enterprise Architecture contributes to an organization's success and how claimed benefits can be realized.

As a participant of this study, we offer you to receive the final report with the results of this study providing you insights in the elements of an EA approach that have high impact on business benefits. In addition, we would like to offer you a benchmark of your answers compared to your industry.

You can access our survey now under http://ea-research.net/?c=[Referral]

Your participation in this survey is voluntary, and you may decline to answer any question at any time. We guarantee you that your identity will be kept completely confidential. Data gathered in this survey will be used solely for aggregate statistics, and not to specifically identify you or your organization to any third parties.

Furthermore, if you encounter any difficulties in completing this survey, or have any concerns or questions, feel free to contact us via e-mail (matthias.lange@wiwi.hu-berlin.de).

Thank you very much; your support in this study is highly appreciated.

Best regards,

Matthias Lange and Prof. Dr. Jan Mendling

D.8.2.   Personalized Survey Invitation for Referrals

Subject: Personal Invitation to Study on "Benefits of Enterprise Architecture Management"

Body:

Dear Mr./Mrs. XXX,

I'm writing you today as your colleague XXX indicated that you might be interested in our research on the benefits of Enterprise Architecture Management.

We would like to invite you to our research study "Benefits of Enterprise Architecture Management" which is conducted by the Humboldt-University Berlin and WU Vienna. This study investigates whether Enterprise Architecture contributes to an organization's success and how claimed benefits can be realized.

As a participant of this study, we offer you to receive the final report with the results of this study providing you insights in the elements of an EA approach that have high impact on business benefits. In addition, we would like to offer you a benchmark of your answers compared to your industry.

You can access our survey now under http://ea-research.net/?c=REI914

Your participation in this survey is voluntary, and you may decline to answer any question at any time. We guarantee you that your identity will be kept completely confidential. Data gathered in this survey will be used solely for aggregate statistics, and not to specifically identify you or your organization to any third parties.

Furthermore, if you encounter any difficulties in completing this survey, or have any concerns or questions, feel free to contact us via e-mail (matthias.lange@wiwi.hu-berlin.de).

Thank you very much; your support in this study is highly appreciated.

Best regards,

Matthias Lange and Prof. Dr. Jan Mendling

D.8.3.   Offered Personalized EAM Benchmark

Figure D-3 Screenshot of Offered Personalized EAM Benchmark

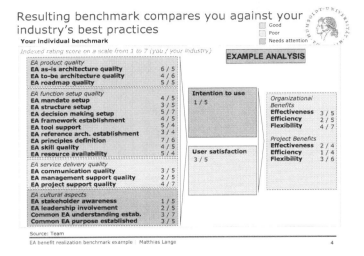

Source: Team

EA benefit realization benchmark example | Matthias Lange   4

D.8.4.   Personalized Follow-up E-mail for Participation

Dear Mr./Mrs. XXX,

a couple of days ago, I have sent you the invitation to my survey about the realization of organizational benefits from Enterprise Architecture.

I want to thank you for taking the time to participate in my study. If you have not yet had the time to complete my survey, I would appreciate if you do so today. I know that you are busy but your response will determine the success of my study.

You find my survey under http://ea-research.net/?c=[Referral]

If you have any questions, don't hesitate to reach out to me under matthias.lange@wiwi.hu-berlin.de or +49 (171) 2839040.

Thank you very much for participating in my study. I highly appreciate your support.

All the best,

Matthias

D.8.5. Personalized Follow-up E-mail for Completion

Subject: Follow-up on your participation in our study on „Benefits of Enterprise Architecture Management"

Body:

Dear Mr./Mrs. XXX,

I want to thank you for taking the time to participate in our study „Benefits of Enterprise Architecture Management".

Unfortunately, it seems as if you have not yet had the time to complete my survey and I would appreciate if you do so today. I know that you are busy but your response will determine the success of my study.

You can just go back to my survey under http://ea-research.net/?c=[Referral] and continue from where you have stopped*.

If you have any questions, don't hesitate to reach out to me under matthias.lange@wiwi.hu-berlin.de or +49 (171) 2839040 (CET Time)

Thank you very much for participating in my study. I highly appreciate your support.

All the best,
Matthias

* Enabled cookies are required for this. If you have not enabled cookies you have to start again unfortunately.

E. Appendix – Data Analysis

E.1. Descriptive Statistics

Table E-1 Overview of Participants Demographics

Aspect	Values	Frequency	Percentage
Organizational demographics			
Type of organization	Publicly traded	51	38.35%
	Privately held	49	36.84%
	Government	23	17.29%
	Non-Profit	10	7.52%
Industry	Information and communication	34	25.56%
	Financial and insurance activities	32	24.06%
	Public administration (including defense)	16	12.03%
	Manufacturing and construction	14	10.53%
	Other	21	15.79%
	Unspecified	16	12.03%
Location of Headquarters	Europe	69	51.88%
	North America	32	24.06%
	Australasia	21	15.79%
	South America	4	3.01%
	Africa	2	1.50%
	N/A	5	3.76%
Employees	<1,000	29	21.80%
	1,001-5,000	30	22.56%
	5,001-25,000	33	24.81%
	26,001-50,000	12	9.02%
	>50,000	23	17.29%
	N/A	6	4.51%
Revenue (in mil. Euro)	1-100	21	15.79%
	101-1,000	23	17.29%
	1,001-5,000	19	14.29%
	5,001-25,000	21	15.79%
	>25,000	14	10.53%
	N/A	35	26.32%
Personal demographics			
Job function	Architect	90	67.67%
	Chief Architect	13	9.77%
	Head of EAM	20	15.04%
	CxO	5	3.75%
	VP	2	1.50%
	N/A	3	2.26%
Managerial Positioning	1	5	3.76%
	2	8	6.02%
	3	33	24.81%
	4	30	22.56%
	5	34	25.56%
	6	13	9.77%
	7	10	7.52%
Time on Projects	<=10%	14	10.53%
	>10 to 25%	18	13.53%
	>25% to 50%	44	33.08%
	>50%	55	41.35%

Aspect	Values		Frequency	Percentage
	N/A		2	1.50%
Pers. EAM	<=1		14	10.53%
Experience	1-5		50	37.59%
	5-10		40	30.08%
	>10		26	19.55%
	N/A		3	2.26%

Table E-2 Descriptive Statistics of Measurement Items

Measurement item	N	Mean	Min	Max	Median	Std. Deviation	Kurtosis	Skewness
PQ1a	133	4,113	0	7	4	1,617	-0,404	-0,338
PQ1b	133	4,308	0	7	4	1,657	-0,462	-0,240
PQ1c	133	3,398	0	7	3	1,825	-0,803	0,340
PQ1d	133	3,301	0	7	3	1,595	-0,268	0,188
PQ1e	129	4,069	0	7	4	1,934	-0,523	-0,448
PQ2a	133	3,872	0	7	4	1,885	-0,912	-0,144
PQ2b	133	4,271	0	7	5	1,915	-0,712	-0,427
PQ2c	133	3,579	0	7	4	1,884	-0,807	0,027
PQ2d	133	3,571	0	7	4	1,839	-0,741	-0,015
PQ2e	127	4,215	0	7	5	2,231	-0,916	-0,539
PQ3a	133	3,609	0	7	4	1,870	-0,853	-0,177
PQ3b	133	4,165	0	7	5	1,908	-0,696	-0,433
PQ3c	133	3,489	0	7	4	1,869	-0,903	0,060
PQ3d	133	3,617	0	7	4	1,812	-0,637	-0,071
PQ3e	127	3,985	0	7	4	2,142	-0,856	-0,412
IQ1a	133	4,316	0	7	5	1,986	-0,908	-0,365
IQ1b	133	4,639	1	7	5	1,768	-0,894	-0,396
IQ1c	133	3,752	1	7	4	1,868	-0,940	0,170
IQ1d	133	4,263	0	7	4	1,792	-0,744	-0,267
IQ2a	129	4,366	0	7	5	2,324	-1,163	-0,481
IQ2b	131	4,432	0	7	6	2,475	-1,528	-0,403
IQ2c	131	3,720	0	7	3,5	2,054	-1,124	0,095
IQ2d	131	4,129	0	7	5	2,266	-1,417	-0,218
IQ2e	131	4,402	0	7	5	2,376	-1,423	-0,406
IQ2f	131	4,515	0	7	6	2,549	-1,520	-0,452
IQ2g	129	3,863	0	7	5	2,468	-1,483	-0,226
IQ3a	133	4,105	0	7	4	1,912	-1,077	-0,192
IQ3b	133	4,045	0	7	4	2,026	-1,032	-0,251
IQ3c	131	2,333	0	7	2	1,831	-0,153	0,911
IQ3d	133	4,075	0	7	4	1,654	-0,482	-0,376
IQ3e	129	3,695	0	7	4	1,893	-0,530	-0,539
IQ4a	133	4,338	0	7	5	1,981	-1,026	-0,315
IQ4b	133	4,632	1	7	5	1,848	-0,940	-0,358
IQ4c	133	4,128	0	7	4	1,998	-0,840	-0,306

Measurement item	N	Mean	Min	Max	Median	Std. Deviation	Kurtosis	Skewness
IQ5a	131	4,402	0	7	5	2,030	-0,927	-0,356
IQ5b	131	4,439	0	7	5	2,127	-1,083	-0,413
IQ5c	131	3,636	0	7	4	1,891	-0,763	-0,053
IQ6a	129	4,366	0	7	5	1,910	-0,874	-0,410
IQ6b	129	4,305	0	7	5	1,965	-0,889	-0,343
IQ6c	129	3,519	0	7	4	1,807	-0,711	-0,039
IQ7a	127	3,854	0	7	4	1,985	-1,066	-0,018
IQ7b	129	4,817	0	7	5	1,749	-0,112	-0,731
IQ7c	129	5,053	0	7	5	1,600	0,107	-0,741
IQ7d	127	4,723	0	7	5	1,800	-0,368	-0,605
IQ7e	129	4,145	0	7	4	1,877	-0,892	-0,157
IQ8a	133	4,789	0	7	5	2,056	-0,731	-0,646
IQ8b	133	4,729	0	7	5	2,129	-0,982	-0,610
IQ8c	133	3,970	0	7	4	2,037	-1,128	-0,177
IQ8d	129	2,771	0	7	2	1,900	-0,613	0,622
IQ8e	131	4,659	0	7	5	1,790	-0,307	-0,690
IQ8f	131	4,462	0	7	5	1,809	-0,722	-0,472
IQ8g	133	4,602	0	7	5	1,754	-0,366	-0,595
IQ9a	133	3,459	0	7	3	1,893	-0,835	0,140
IQ9b	131	3,235	0	7	3	1,840	-0,664	0,356
IQ9c	127	3,154	0	7	3	1,745	-0,382	0,471
SQ1a	131	4,364	0	7	5	1,631	-0,158	-0,658
SQ1b	129	4,046	0	7	4	1,635	-0,579	-0,203
SQ1c	129	4,130	0	7	4	1,693	-0,475	-0,322
SQ1d	131	3,591	0	7	4	1,676	-0,686	0,057
SQ2a	133	3,812	0	7	4	1,814	-0,843	-0,094
SQ2b	131	4,030	0	7	4	1,981	-1,048	-0,186
SQ2c	131	3,621	0	7	3	1,932	-1,172	0,126
SQ2d	133	4,000	0	7	4	2,049	-1,162	-0,242
SQ2e	133	3,699	0	7	4	2,000	-1,106	-0,027
SQ2f	133	3,654	0	7	4	1,996	-1,109	-0,068
SQ3a	133	4,722	0	7	5	1,798	0,054	-0,781
SQ3b	131	4,485	0	7	5	1,793	-0,325	-0,492
SQ3c	123	4,656	0	7	5	1,934	-0,635	-0,557
CA1a	133	3,188	0	7	3	1,750	-0,715	0,293
CA1b	133	3,135	0	7	3	1,691	-0,697	0,252
CA1c	133	3,421	0	7	3	1,793	-1,069	0,019
CA1d	131	3,098	0	7	3	1,751	-0,601	0,376
CA2a	133	4,158	0	7	5	1,833	-0,340	-0,626
CA2b	133	3,767	0	7	4	1,714	-0,556	-0,400
CA2c	133	2,699	0	7	2	1,710	-0,745	0,295
CA3a	133	3,293	0	7	3	1,641	-0,897	-0,044
CA3b	133	2,992	0	7	3	1,699	-0,703	0,322

Measurement item	N	Mean	Min	Max	Median	Std. Deviation	Kurtosis	Skewness
CA3c	129	3,855	0	7	4	1,966	-0,864	-0,300
USE1	129	4,229	0	7	5	1,892	-0,253	-0,696
USE2	133	4,722	0	7	5	1,768	0,655	-1,012
USE3	129	3,977	0	7	4	2,062	-0,367	-0,696
USE4	91	3,080	0	7	3	2,202	-1,307	0,164
SAT1	133	3,970	0	7	4	1,813	0,098	-0,806
SAT2	133	3,805	0	7	4	1,764	-0,156	-0,689
SAT3	133	3,083	0	7	3	1,775	-0,803	-0,119
OB1a	131	4,902	0	7	5	1,675	0,621	-0,989
OB1b	99	4,379	0	7	4	1,677	-0,438	-0,372
OB1c	133	4,820	0	7	5	1,842	-0,105	-0,757
OB1d	99	4,397	0	7	5	1,739	-0,260	-0,530
OB1e	133	4,857	0	7	5	1,720	0,525	-0,873
OB1f	99	4,267	0	7	4	1,741	-0,208	-0,450
OB1g	133	4,564	0	7	5	1,872	-0,387	-0,611
OB1h	131	4,235	0	7	4	1,803	-0,330	-0,414
OB1i	133	4,481	0	7	5	1,726	-0,118	-0,560
OB1j	133	3,722	0	7	4	1,777	-0,337	-0,343
OB2a	133	4,617	0	7	5	1,808	-0,119	-0,746
OB2b	131	4,553	0	7	5	1,691	0,278	-0,732
OB2c	127	4,615	0	7	5	1,745	0,240	-0,752
OB2d	129	4,321	0	7	5	1,665	-0,017	-0,482
OB2e	131	4,129	0	7	4	1,855	-0,243	-0,541
OB3a	133	4,008	0	7	4	1,848	-0,712	-0,340
OB3b	133	4,045	0	7	4	1,890	-0,677	-0,325
OB3c	133	4,128	0	7	4	1,844	-0,595	-0,426
OB3d	131	4,455	0	7	5	1,687	0,407	-0,812
PB1a	133	3,737	0	7	4	1,907	-0,172	-0,768
PB1b	133	3,662	0	7	4	1,914	-0,402	-0,643
PB1c	133	4,331	0	7	5	2,022	0,259	-1,071
PB1d	131	4,644	0	7	5	1,970	0,653	-1,171
PB2a	133	4,203	0	7	5	2,025	0,014	-0,876
PB2b	133	4,180	0	7	4	2,029	-0,176	-0,813
PB3a	131	4,159	0	7	4	2,071	-0,290	-0,756

E.2. Detailed Analysis Results from Measurement Item Testing

Table E-3 Measurement Item Loadings and Cross-loadings

	PQ1	PQ2	PQ3	IQ1	IQ2	IQ3	IQ4	IQ5	IQ6	IQ7	IQ8	IQ9	SQ1	SQ2	SQ3	CA2	CA3	Benefit	Use	CA1	Sat
PQ1a	**0,77**	0,60	-0,56	0,06	-0,04	-0,10	0,21	-0,03	-0,06	0,07	0,08	-0,15	0,00	0,01	0,09	0,08	-0,05	0,09	-0,09	-0,05	0,15
PQ1b	**0,76**	-0,28	0,19	0,11	0,01	-0,12	-0,05	0,03	0,02	-0,11	0,20	-0,15	0,08	0,05	-0,05	0,14	-0,12	-0,17	0,30	0,02	-0,26
PQ1c	**0,86**	-0,32	0,16	-0,07	0,00	-0,08	0,02	-0,05	0,11	0,05	0,00	0,00	0,01	-0,03	-0,13	-0,11	0,28	0,08	-0,14	-0,02	0,04
PQ1d	**0,83**	0,00	0,16	-0,09	0,04	0,25	-0,17	0,05	-0,10	-0,01	-0,10	0,03	0,01	-0,01	0,09	-0,08	-0,11	-0,02	-0,04	0,04	0,05
PQ1e	**0,05**	0,56	0,32	0,04	-0,14	0,33	0,06	0,02	0,29	-0,29	-0,11	0,12	0,27	-0,31	0,10	0,01	-0,50	0,04	-0,11	0,13	0,20
PQ2a	0,00	**0,81**	-0,11	-0,02	0,04	0,01	0,26	-0,03	-0,10	0,02	-0,44	0,10	-0,07	0,14	-0,01	-0,13	0,32	-0,12	0,00	-0,17	0,15
PQ2b	0,05	**0,87**	-0,12	0,06	-0,01	-0,13	0,02	-0,07	-0,06	0,06	0,36	-0,19	-0,05	0,03	0,10	0,01	-0,02	-0,13	0,21	0,07	-0,12
PQ2c	0,24	**0,87**	0,08	-0,08	0,00	-0,08	-0,13	0,00	0,03	0,04	0,12	-0,04	-0,08	0,06	-0,16	-0,15	0,21	0,06	-0,03	-0,07	0,03
PQ2d	0,05	**0,88**	0,10	-0,03	0,00	0,11	-0,30	0,15	0,09	-0,04	-0,01	0,06	0,23	-0,09	0,03	0,10	-0,17	0,16	-0,13	0,08	-0,06
PQ2e	-0,78	0,38	0,09	0,15	-0,23	0,20	0,41	-0,13	0,07	-0,18	-0,15	0,17	0,01	-0,29	0,09	0,37	-0,70	0,04	-0,11	0,15	0,04
PQ3a	0,03	0,25	**0,86**	0,07	0,03	-0,03	0,27	-0,04	-0,16	0,08	-0,29	0,12	-0,03	-0,01	-0,11	-0,03	0,25	-0,06	0,12	-0,19	0,08
PQ3b	0,10	-0,05	**0,88**	0,14	-0,05	-0,11	-0,06	-0,08	-0,07	-0,02	0,28	-0,20	0,01	0,09	0,08	-0,19	-0,06	-0,03	0,12	0,14	0,01
PQ3c	0,17	-0,27	**0,91**	-0,02	0,05	-0,06	-0,15	0,08	0,14	0,03	0,16	-0,08	-0,21	0,05	-0,06	0,06	0,13	0,03	-0,17	-0,03	-0,03
PQ3d	0,09	-0,09	**0,87**	-0,17	0,05	0,06	-0,26	0,07	0,06	0,04	-0,04	0,06	0,21	0,02	0,01	0,07	-0,14	0,07	-0,06	0,07	-0,11
PQ3e	-0,88	0,39	0,39	-0,02	-0,18	0,30	0,47	-0,08	0,05	-0,27	-0,27	0,26	0,07	-0,35	0,19	0,19	-0,40	-0,04	-0,02	0,03	0,12
IQ1a	-0,03	-0,18	-0,18	**0,67**	-0,07	-0,02	-0,16	0,05	-0,15	0,14	0,12	0,07	-0,11	0,16	0,14	0,54	-0,32	-0,04	-0,15	0,04	-0,11
IQ1b	0,20	0,05	-0,25	**0,73**	-0,15	-0,11	0,33	-0,11	-0,07	0,11	-0,01	-0,17	0,17	-0,05	-0,22	-0,01	0,06	0,13	0,04	-0,09	-0,18
IQ1c	0,03	-0,32	0,34	**0,71**	0,02	0,04	-0,02	0,21	0,16	-0,34	-0,04	-0,17	0,02	0,17	-0,16	-0,42	0,19	0,05	0,01	-0,08	0,20
IQ1d	-0,19	0,17	0,08	**0,77**	0,18	0,08	-0,15	-0,13	0,05	0,09	-0,06	0,25	-0,09	-0,24	0,24	-0,08	0,05	-0,14	0,09	0,12	0,08
IQ2a	-0,12	-0,35	0,35	-0,02	**0,39**	-0,01	-0,21	-0,21	0,18	0,13	0,10	-0,14	-0,03	0,02	0,10	0,14	0,51	-0,06	-0,45	-0,02	-0,08
IQ2b	-0,17	0,31	-0,10	-0,21	**0,61**	0,08	0,14	-0,19	0,08	0,09	0,00	-0,09	-0,06	-0,24	0,04	-0,08	-0,16	-0,20	0,73	0,15	-0,26
IQ2c	-0,02	0,05	-0,17	-0,18	**0,48**	0,03	0,30	0,05	0,16	0,14	-0,18	0,21	0,17	0,21	-0,39	-0,19	0,00	0,03	0,42	-0,24	-0,16
IQ2d	0,17	-0,01	-0,20	0,17	**0,73**	0,21	-0,11	0,08	-0,16	-0,12	0,27	-0,20	0,04	-0,13	-0,03	-0,29	-0,03	0,08	0,07	0,02	0,19
IQ2e	0,14	-0,10	0,18	0,18	**0,66**	0,02	-0,04	0,21	-0,17	0,00	-0,26	0,17	0,11	-0,09	0,02	-0,12	-0,03	0,14	-0,38	0,01	0,30
IQ2f	-0,11	-0,08	0,11	0,19	**0,69**	-0,30	-0,01	-0,05	0,09	-0,18	-0,02	0,18	-0,19	0,11	0,20	0,27	-0,04	0,06	-0,31	0,03	-0,06
IQ2g	0,03	0,10	-0,09	-0,15	**0,55**	-0,03	-0,06	0,02	-0,04	0,07	0,06	-0,16	-0,01	0,21	-0,01	0,35	-0,07	-0,11	-0,10	-0,02	-0,05
IQ3a	0,13	-0,15	-0,11	0,17	-0,02	**0,87**	-0,02	-0,09	0,01	0,11	-0,03	0,02	-0,09	-0,06	0,20	0,03	-0,15	0,00	-0,08	0,26	0,07
IQ3b	0,14	0,03	-0,12	-0,05	0,07	**0,90**	-0,02	-0,06	-0,04	0,00	0,14	0,05	-0,12	0,01	0,11	-0,02	0,12	0,02	0,06	-0,03	-0,12
IQ3c	-0,24	-0,01	0,27	-0,02	-0,03	**0,75**	0,00	0,22	0,09	-0,20	0,02	0,00	0,05	0,10	-0,41	-0,03	0,06	0,04	-0,11	-0,23	0,13
IQ3d	-0,32	0,04	0,04	-0,21	-0,15	**0,02**	0,13	0,28	0,13	0,04	-0,59	-0,20	0,57	0,02	0,18	-0,29	-0,27	-0,05	0,08	-0,10	0,19
IQ3e	-0,23	0,46	-0,01	-0,38	-0,09	**0,23**	0,15	-0,15	-0,15	0,21	-0,47	-0,24	0,62	-0,10	0,16	0,08	-0,09	-0,19	0,38	-0,12	-0,22
IQ4a	0,06	0,10	-0,04	0,02	0,08	0,05	**0,87**	0,07	0,00	0,09	-0,19	0,05	-0,36	0,16	0,08	0,07	-0,17	0,05	-0,12	0,06	0,16
IQ4b	0,08	0,10	0,02	-0,04	-0,02	-0,03	**0,80**	-0,12	0,07	-0,12	-0,02	-0,13	0,41	-0,20	0,05	-0,15	-0,06	-0,03	0,28	0,04	-0,27
IQ4c	-0,14	0,08	-0,09	-0,04	0,10	0,08	**0,82**	0,04	-0,07	0,02	0,22	0,08	-0,02	0,02	-0,13	0,08	0,24	-0,02	-0,15	-0,10	0,09
IQ5a	0,03	0,06	-0,14	0,02	0,01	0,02	0,07	**0,91**	-0,03	0,04	-0,11	-0,02	-0,04	0,01	0,06	0,03	-0,20	0,01	0,04	0,02	0,06
IQ5b	0,02	0,08	-0,09	0,03	-0,08	0,02	-0,10	**0,91**	-0,05	0,06	-0,13	-0,06	0,05	0,01	0,05	-0,32	-0,04	0,05	-0,01	0,13	0,10
IQ5c	-0,06	-0,15	0,25	-0,04	0,10	-0,04	0,03	**0,83**	0,09	-0,11	0,26	0,08	-0,01	-0,03	-0,12	0,32	0,26	-0,06	-0,04	-0,16	-0,17

	PQ1	PQ2	PQ3	IQ1	IQ2	IQ3	IQ4	IQ5	IQ6	IQ7	IQ8	IQ9	SQ1	SQ2	SQ3	CA2	CA3	Benefit	Use	CA1	Sat
IQ6a	0,23	-0,18	0,00	0,06	-0,10	-0,18	0,11	-0,09	**0,90**	0,09	0,04	0,03	-0,03	0,12	-0,09	-0,13	0,07	0,07	-0,03	0,01	-0,02
IQ6b	0,10	0,10	-0,14	0,03	0,04	0,07	-0,05	0,03	**0,90**	0,05	-0,13	0,02	0,03	0,08	0,08	-0,06	-0,13	-0,01	0,06	0,07	0,10
IQ6c	-0,14	0,09	0,16	-0,09	0,06	0,12	-0,06	0,06	**0,82**	-0,14	0,11	-0,05	-0,01	-0,21	0,00	0,21	0,07	-0,06	-0,04	-0,09	-0,09
IQ7a	0,01	0,30	-0,28	0,22	-0,21	-0,06	0,31	0,02	-0,03	0,49	-0,26	-0,05	0,35	0,41	-0,37	-0,36	0,17	0,00	0,26	-0,33	-0,03
IQ7b	-0,10	0,02	-0,16	-0,06	-0,06	-0,05	-0,07	-0,04	0,10	**0,87**	0,09	-0,07	0,20	0,11	-0,18	0,01	0,13	0,02	-0,02	-0,23	-0,06
IQ7c	0,17	0,07	-0,21	0,08	0,05	0,05	0,03	-0,05	-0,30	**0,82**	0,13	-0,07	0,13	-0,17	0,07	0,32	0,13	-0,02	-0,20	0,34	0,08
IQ7d	-0,04	-0,06	0,30	-0,11	0,05	-0,10	0,02	-0,02	0,06	**0,80**	0,16	0,13	-0,05	-0,36	0,14	0,02	-0,11	0,04	0,13	0,12	-0,08
IQ7e	-0,03	-0,22	0,26	-0,05	0,10	0,14	0,16	0,11	0,16	**0,78**	-0,24	0,04	-0,31	0,17	0,21	-0,14	0,29	-0,04	-0,07	-0,02	0,09
IQ8a	0,07	-0,26	0,24	0,07	-0,04	-0,13	0,14	0,01	0,03	-0,07	**0,75**	0,20	-0,21	-0,13	0,14	0,24	-0,36	0,15	-0,25	0,21	-0,04
IQ8b	-0,12	0,16	-0,16	0,02	0,03	0,13	0,14	0,02	-0,11	-0,02	**0,78**	0,09	-0,20	-0,23	0,19	0,38	-0,48	0,13	-0,27	0,23	0,26
IQ8c	-0,24	-0,35	0,36	0,01	-0,09	0,11	0,02	0,04	0,04	0,01	**0,80**	0,26	0,11	-0,12	-0,23	-0,02	-0,25	0,31	-0,01	0,10	-0,12
IQ8d	-0,07	-0,01	-0,06	-0,04	0,01	0,21	-0,23	0,09	0,22	-0,04	**0,62**	-0,05	-0,17	0,19	-0,24	-0,32	0,46	-0,25	-0,01	-0,07	0,28
IQ8e	-0,07	0,33	-0,07	0,00	-0,01	-0,16	-0,03	-0,06	-0,04	-0,05	**0,79**	-0,12	0,25	0,16	0,07	-0,23	0,14	-0,13	0,27	-0,11	-0,20
IQ8f	0,27	-0,07	-0,02	0,00	0,03	-0,09	-0,11	-0,10	0,10	-0,11	**0,79**	-0,17	0,20	0,08	-0,06	-0,09	0,36	-0,16	0,17	-0,23	-0,09
IQ8g	0,15	0,19	-0,30	-0,06	0,07	-0,02	0,01	-0,03	-0,19	0,28	**0,78**	-0,22	-0,03	0,07	0,09	-0,01	0,20	-0,09	0,08	-0,14	-0,03
IQ9a	-0,12	-0,15	0,10	0,08	-0,02	0,05	-0,04	0,00	0,03	0,05	0,13	**0,92**	0,19	-0,14	-0,14	0,02	-0,04	0,05	-0,02	0,10	-0,05
IQ9b	-0,03	-0,25	-0,24	-0,12	0,01	0,05	0,03	-0,07	-0,14	0,05	0,00	**0,91**	-0,01	-0,05	0,10	-0,05	0,04	-0,06	0,17	-0,05	0,06
IQ9c	0,16	-0,10	0,15	0,02	0,01	-0,09	0,01	0,08	0,12	-0,07	-0,14	**0,84**	-0,20	0,20	0,04	0,03	0,00	0,02	-0,16	-0,06	-0,02
SQ1a	-0,04	-0,14	0,00	0,02	-0,09	-0,08	-0,04	-0,05	0,06	0,10	-0,09	-0,01	**0,88**	0,09	0,10	-0,09	-0,18	-0,02	-0,01	0,11	0,04
SQ1b	0,13	0,00	0,00	0,13	-0,05	-0,06	0,05	-0,08	-0,05	0,09	0,08	0,03	**0,90**	0,03	-0,03	0,07	0,05	-0,04	-0,03	-0,16	-0,07
SQ1c	-0,06	0,15	-0,16	-0,06	-0,03	0,01	-0,08	0,12	-0,01	-0,06	0,01	0,01	**0,88**	-0,13	0,13	-0,20	-0,10	0,16	-0,02	0,07	0,07
SQ1d	-0,04	0,20	0,07	-0,10	0,18	0,13	0,20	0,02	-0,01	-0,14	0,00	-0,03	**0,85**	0,15	-0,20	0,13	0,25	-0,11	0,07	-0,01	-0,05
SQ2a	0,10	-0,17	-0,19	-0,06	-0,01	-0,17	0,08	0,08	-0,15	0,17	0,07	-0,09	0,30	**0,66**	0,03	0,03	-0,07	-0,19	0,04	-0,03	0,03
SQ2b	0,12	0,16	-0,41	-0,07	-0,01	0,33	0,12	-0,02	-0,21	0,10	0,08	0,09	0,06	**0,72**	0,49	-0,02	-0,06	-0,01	-0,07	0,09	0,08
SQ2c	0,05	0,03	-0,09	0,03	-0,03	0,12	0,12	0,00	-0,10	-0,02	0,06	0,09	-0,19	**0,82**	-0,08	-0,01	0,09	-0,20	-0,08	0,20	0,01
SQ2d	-0,09	-0,15	0,20	0,21	0,05	-0,09	-0,07	-0,06	0,18	-0,10	0,08	-0,08	-0,08	**0,88**	-0,16	0,02	0,12	-0,05	0,06	0,04	-0,07
SQ2e	-0,01	-0,04	0,07	-0,01	0,01	-0,03	-0,14	0,01	0,13	-0,11	-0,11	0,10	0,08	**0,89**	-0,13	-0,11	0,02	0,20	0,08	-0,09	-0,13
SQ2f	0,13	0,16	-0,03	-0,11	0,10	-0,13	-0,03	-0,06	0,07	0,02	-0,14	0,12	-0,09	**0,85**	-0,07	0,09	-0,13	0,19	-0,04	-0,19	0,11
SQ3a	-0,04	-0,01	-0,08	-0,07	-0,02	-0,02	-0,03	-0,03	0,07	0,03	0,03	0,00	0,00	-0,03	**0,87**	0,15	-0,21	-0,08	-0,04	0,07	0,15
SQ3b	-0,04	0,13	0,10	0,00	-0,02	0,01	0,11	-0,06	0,01	0,02	0,04	-0,01	-0,09	-0,01	**0,91**	-0,09	0,13	-0,04	0,15	-0,13	-0,06
SQ3c	-0,09	-0,13	0,10	0,07	-0,07	-0,10	-0,10	0,08	0,08	-0,05	0,04	0,01	0,00	0,04	**0,90**	-0,06	0,08	0,12	-0,12	0,06	-0,09
CA2a	-0,26	0,09	-0,02	0,07	0,09	0,06	-0,04	-0,09	0,06	-0,11	0,17	-0,04	0,11	-0,02	-0,05	**0,87**	0,00	-0,05	0,11	-0,08	-0,13
CA2b	0,14	0,02	-0,07	0,00	-0,06	-0,13	0,03	0,02	0,05	0,05	-0,26	0,02	0,18	-0,13	0,19	**0,85**	0,02	0,04	0,05	0,20	-0,09
CA2c	0,07	-0,12	0,10	-0,02	0,00	0,08	0,08	0,08	-0,11	0,06	0,09	0,03	-0,30	0,15	-0,14	**0,80**	-0,02	0,01	-0,17	-0,12	0,24
CA3a	0,07	-0,02	-0,03	-0,02	0,00	-0,01	0,14	-0,04	0,00	-0,04	0,03	-0,02	-0,02	0,01	-0,13	0,00	**0,92**	-0,12	-0,04	-0,04	-0,06
CA3b	0,06	-0,13	0,04	0,07	0,04	0,05	-0,12	0,03	0,08	0,06	0,11	0,04	0,04	-0,07	-0,12	0,06	**0,92**	0,10	-0,16	-0,05	0,08
CA3c	-0,03	0,18	-0,01	0,15	-0,04	-0,04	-0,03	-0,01	0,03	-0,02	-0,17	0,00	-0,03	0,07	0,30	0,00	**0,77**	0,02	0,23	0,10	-0,03
OB1a	0,09	-0,46	0,26	0,15	-0,04	-0,14	0,02	0,04	0,28	0,21	0,10	0,00	-0,25	0,08	0,30	0,00	0,11	**0,77**	-0,18	-0,03	0,08
OB1b	0,09	-0,42	0,35	-0,17	-0,01	-0,06	-0,10	0,08	0,08	0,03	-0,18	-0,08	-0,13	0,38	-0,16	-0,13	0,45	**0,68**	0,19	-0,49	-0,42
OB1c	0,07	-0,56	0,37	0,07	-0,05	-0,10	-0,03	-0,17	-0,08	0,45	0,23	-0,01	-0,31	0,23	0,17	0,23	0,16	**0,72**	0,19	-0,26	-0,10
OB1d	-0,01	-0,48	0,37	-0,28	-0,07	0,11	0,00	-0,06	0,13	0,23	0,07	-0,01	-0,18	0,59	-0,06	-0,12	0,33	**0,65**	0,45	-0,50	-0,38
OB1e	-0,03	-0,27	0,03	-0,06	-0,01	-0,25	-0,12	-0,13	0,07	0,34	0,43	-0,22	0,01	0,21	-0,06	0,12	0,17	**0,77**	0,07	-0,16	-0,22
OB1f	-0,16	-0,13	0,22	-0,29	-0,05	-0,11	-0,04	-0,21	0,32	0,14	0,07	0,12	0,05	0,49	-0,23	-0,14	0,35	**0,69**	0,52	-0,45	-0,45

	PQ1	PQ2	PQ3	IQ1	IQ2	IQ3	IQ4	IQ5	IQ6	IQ7	IQ8	IQ9	SQ1	SQ2	SQ3	CA2	CA3	Benefit	Use	CA1	Sat
OB1g	0,27	-0,21	-0,16	0,17	-0,15	-0,16	-0,14	-0,12	-0,02	0,10	0,29	0,01	0,07	0,19	-0,17	0,02	0,05	**0,78**	0,21	-0,12	-0,25
OB1h	0,25	0,12	-0,27	0,12	0,03	0,10	-0,07	-0,14	-0,12	0,00	0,04	-0,13	-0,06	-0,02	-0,13	0,06	0,01	**0,78**	0,25	0,09	-0,14
OB1i	0,18	0,11	-0,30	0,03	0,07	0,12	-0,02	-0,16	-0,10	0,01	0,04	-0,02	0,13	-0,22	0,11	0,28	-0,10	**0,83**	0,08	0,10	-0,14
OB1j	-0,04	0,09	-0,03	0,00	0,07	0,15	0,16	-0,25	0,05	0,01	-0,40	0,12	0,34	-0,36	-0,33	0,03	0,31	**0,72**	0,27	-0,12	0,07
OB2a	-0,16	0,01	-0,01	0,26	0,01	-0,19	-0,13	-0,01	0,09	0,22	0,21	0,15	-0,20	-0,27	-0,12	0,07	-0,29	**0,74**	-0,11	0,38	0,29
OB2b	0,26	-0,25	-0,18	0,25	-0,09	-0,29	-0,34	-0,03	0,00	0,18	0,44	-0,03	-0,07	0,08	-0,10	-0,14	0,02	**0,75**	0,02	0,22	-0,06
OB2c	0,03	0,14	-0,32	0,21	-0,01	-0,26	-0,30	0,07	-0,15	0,14	0,36	0,10	0,00	0,05	-0,14	-0,05	-0,17	**0,79**	-0,05	0,16	-0,04
OB2d	0,29	-0,03	-0,45	0,27	-0,12	-0,18	-0,20	0,04	-0,05	-0,02	0,28	0,01	0,27	0,00	-0,17	-0,06	-0,16	**0,78**	0,16	0,19	-0,08
OB2e	0,46	0,26	-0,74	0,00	-0,03	0,32	-0,25	0,07	0,08	-0,18	-0,01	-0,27	0,19	0,05	0,10	-0,22	-0,02	**0,65**	0,11	-0,07	0,13
OB3a	0,35	0,20	-0,44	0,19	-0,01	-0,15	-0,12	0,02	0,01	-0,21	-0,02	-0,01	0,19	0,21	-0,29	-0,02	-0,18	**0,72**	0,24	-0,03	-0,21
OB3b	0,17	0,12	0,01	0,19	-0,12	-0,06	0,01	-0,05	0,19	-0,16	-0,11	-0,06	0,07	-0,17	-0,13	0,00	-0,19	**0,77**	0,10	0,29	-0,18
OB3c	0,33	0,07	-0,12	0,16	0,06	-0,05	-0,06	0,08	-0,10	-0,19	0,06	-0,19	-0,21	0,11	-0,08	0,10	-0,13	**0,75**	0,21	0,03	-0,16
OB3d	-0,05	-0,11	-0,15	0,16	-0,08	0,06	0,02	0,00	0,06	0,03	0,12	-0,15	-0,24	-0,01	-0,29	-0,05	-0,20	**0,72**	-0,13	0,19	0,00
PB1a	-0,13	0,36	0,04	-0,09	0,12	0,28	0,27	0,21	-0,17	-0,34	-0,34	0,08	-0,19	-0,25	0,16	0,19	-0,20	**0,61**	-0,61	0,20	0,58
PB1b	-0,31	0,30	0,25	-0,27	0,09	0,29	0,33	0,26	-0,18	-0,31	-0,46	0,11	-0,19	-0,04	0,20	0,03	-0,03	**0,60**	-0,45	-0,11	0,38
PB1c	-0,55	0,18	0,44	-0,31	0,06	0,32	0,38	0,11	-0,07	-0,14	-0,36	0,13	0,10	-0,30	0,14	0,04	-0,05	**0,72**	-0,23	-0,11	0,21
PB1d	-0,37	0,16	0,32	-0,12	0,02	0,11	0,27	0,13	-0,02	-0,24	-0,20	0,03	-0,02	-0,25	0,39	0,08	-0,13	**0,78**	-0,36	0,11	0,11
PB2a	-0,40	0,40	0,27	-0,33	0,16	0,10	0,20	0,08	-0,05	-0,18	-0,23	0,02	0,03	-0,28	0,27	-0,10	0,00	**0,69**	-0,40	0,06	0,37
PB2b	-0,33	0,38	0,25	-0,26	0,11	0,11	0,11	0,19	-0,03	-0,16	-0,41	0,11	-0,07	-0,23	0,28	-0,22	0,09	**0,69**	-0,50	0,07	0,52
PB3a	-0,36	0,16	0,39	-0,28	0,08	0,15	0,22	0,16	-0,12	-0,09	-0,32	0,09	-0,14	-0,22	0,42	-0,07	-0,10	**0,71**	-0,24	0,03	0,31
USE1	0,06	0,13	-0,15	0,12	0,04	-0,04	-0,11	-0,04	-0,01	-0,03	0,09	-0,02	-0,11	0,07	0,07	0,16	-0,08	-0,13	**0,89**	0,12	-0,05
USE2	-0,04	-0,01	0,01	-0,03	0,02	-0,13	0,08	-0,13	-0,09	0,00	0,10	-0,06	-0,07	0,02	0,19	0,11	0,01	0,00	**0,88**	0,01	-0,26
USE3	-0,35	-0,13	0,34	-0,07	0,01	-0,04	-0,02	0,01	0,17	0,00	0,02	0,15	0,03	-0,15	-0,13	-0,08	-0,11	0,15	**0,79**	0,16	0,31
USE4	0,05	-0,01	-0,25	-0,04	-0,11	0,32	0,07	0,24	-0,08	0,03	-0,32	-0,09	0,23	0,06	-0,21	-0,30	0,26	-0,01	**0,58**	-0,41	0,05
CA1a	0,05	-0,07	0,07	0,09	-0,07	-0,13	0,02	0,00	-0,01	-0,01	0,05	0,06	-0,08	0,05	0,03	-0,02	-0,08	-0,03	-0,13	**0,93**	0,08
CA1b	0,06	0,12	-0,24	-0,02	-0,02	0,13	-0,08	0,01	-0,09	0,02	-0,19	0,30	0,16	-0,16	0,04	0,05	-0,04	0,09	0,01	**0,87**	-0,08
CA1c	-0,05	0,05	0,06	-0,08	0,03	0,03	0,05	0,01	0,06	-0,10	0,05	-0,22	-0,04	0,00	0,08	-0,06	0,06	-0,03	0,11	**0,92**	-0,02
CA1d	-0,06	-0,10	0,10	0,00	0,06	-0,01	0,01	-0,02	0,03	0,09	0,08	-0,13	-0,04	0,10	-0,15	0,03	0,06	-0,03	0,02	**0,90**	0,02
SAT1	-0,10	-0,13	0,18	0,12	0,06	0,08	0,03	0,02	-0,02	-0,03	0,07	-0,05	0,00	-0,05	0,01	0,06	-0,02	0,01	-0,04	-0,04	**0,95**
SAT2	-0,07	0,00	0,02	0,01	0,00	-0,03	0,00	-0,01	0,00	0,07	0,03	0,02	-0,01	-0,04	0,04	0,07	-0,08	-0,01	-0,03	-0,03	**0,98**
SAT3	0,18	0,14	-0,20	-0,01	-0,06	-0,05	-0,03	-0,01	0,02	-0,05	-0,11	0,02	0,01	0,10	-0,05	-0,14	0,10	0,01	0,07	-0,03	**0,91**

Table E-4 Construct Correlations and Square Roots of AVEs on Diagonal

	PQ1	PQ2	PQ3	IQ1	IQ2	IQ3	IQ4	IQ5	IQ6	IQ7	IQ8	IQ9	SQ1	SQ2	SQ3	CA1	CA2	CA3	Use	Sat	Benefit
PQ1	**0,72**	0,71	0,68	0,38	0,11	0,54	0,49	0,35	0,54	0,57	0,56	0,53	0,56	0,54	0,47	0,45	0,45	0,46	0,37	0,38	0,42
PQ2	0,71	**0,79**	0,83	0,45	0,09	0,53	0,36	0,30	0,46	0,54	0,56	0,43	0,56	0,53	0,45	0,40	0,46	0,44	0,31	0,34	0,43
PQ3	0,68	0,83	**0,81**	0,52	0,05	0,52	0,33	0,28	0,37	0,56	0,56	0,42	0,58	0,55	0,45	0,41	0,49	0,47	0,42	0,43	0,49
IQ1	0,38	0,45	0,52	**0,72**	0,16	0,45	0,41	0,32	0,41	0,52	0,48	0,32	0,48	0,48	0,45	0,31	0,34	0,41	0,36	0,27	0,44
IQ2	0,11	0,09	0,05	0,16	**0,60**	0,09	0,05	0,03	0,08	0,15	0,03	0,14	0,19	0,14	0,19	-0,05	-0,05	-0,07	0,00	-0,01	0,10
IQ3	0,54	0,53	0,52	0,45	0,09	**0,66**	0,46	0,25	0,47	0,54	0,53	0,53	0,61	0,61	0,50	0,46	0,46	0,46	0,30	0,32	0,46
IQ4	0,49	0,36	0,33	0,41	0,05	0,46	**0,83**	0,49	0,64	0,50	0,48	0,32	0,52	0,51	0,50	0,41	0,44	0,39	0,41	0,39	0,44
IQ5	0,35	0,30	0,28	0,32	0,03	0,25	0,49	**0,88**	0,47	0,41	0,50	0,30	0,39	0,34	0,30	0,29	0,36	0,36	0,46	0,36	0,31
IQ6	0,54	0,46	0,37	0,41	0,08	0,47	0,64	0,47	**0,87**	0,58	0,53	0,39	0,46	0,51	0,46	0,41	0,46	0,38	0,43	0,39	0,41
IQ7	0,57	0,54	0,56	0,52	0,15	0,54	0,50	0,41	0,58	**0,77**	0,56	0,36	0,54	0,55	0,51	0,41	0,44	0,42	0,44	0,36	0,56
IQ8	0,56	0,56	0,56	0,48	0,03	0,53	0,48	0,50	0,53	0,56	**0,76**	0,58	0,63	0,56	0,53	0,46	0,56	0,49	0,37	0,47	0,45
IQ9	0,53	0,43	0,42	0,32	0,14	0,53	0,32	0,30	0,39	0,36	0,58	**0,89**	0,58	0,55	0,50	0,53	0,43	0,45	0,30	0,37	0,27
SQ1	0,56	0,56	0,58	0,48	0,19	0,53	0,52	0,39	0,46	0,54	0,63	0,58	**0,88**	0,71	0,61	0,52	0,61	0,55	0,49	0,57	0,52
SQ2	0,54	0,53	0,55	0,48	0,14	0,61	0,51	0,34	0,51	0,55	0,56	0,55	0,71	**0,81**	0,51	0,64	0,59	0,56	0,53	0,53	0,54
SQ3	0,47	0,45	0,45	0,45	0,19	0,50	0,50	0,30	0,46	0,51	0,53	0,50	0,61	0,51	**0,89**	0,35	0,50	0,43	0,40	0,33	0,51
CA1	0,45	0,40	0,41	0,31	-0,05	0,46	0,41	0,29	0,41	0,41	0,46	0,53	0,52	0,64	0,35	**0,91**	0,59	0,68	0,57	0,45	0,52
CA2	0,45	0,46	0,49	0,34	-0,05	0,46	0,44	0,36	0,46	0,44	0,56	0,43	0,61	0,59	0,50	0,59	**0,84**	0,68	0,65	0,66	0,61
CA3	0,46	0,44	0,47	0,41	-0,07	0,46	0,39	0,36	0,38	0,42	0,49	0,45	0,55	0,56	0,43	0,68	0,68	**0,87**	0,56	0,52	0,64
Use	0,37	0,31	0,42	0,36	0,00	0,30	0,41	0,46	0,43	0,44	0,37	0,30	0,49	0,53	0,40	0,57	0,65	0,56	**0,79**	0,71	0,62
Sat	0,38	0,34	0,43	0,27	-0,01	0,32	0,39	0,36	0,39	0,36	0,47	0,36	0,57	0,53	0,33	0,45	0,66	0,52	0,71	**0,95**	0,54
Benefit	0,42	0,43	0,49	0,44	0,10	0,46	0,44	0,31	0,41	0,56	0,45	0,27	0,52	0,54	0,51	0,52	0,61	0,64	0,62	0,54	**0,73**

E.3. Detailed Results from Validation of Structure Model

Table E-5 Overview of Path Standard Errors for Each Model Variant

Path	Model 1	Model 2	Model 3	Model 4	Model 5	Model 6
PQ->Ben	0,092	0,092	0,087	0,087	0,087	0,087
IQ->Ben	0,155	0,155	0,149	0,149	0,15	0,15
SQ->Ben	0,133	0,133	0,125	0,125	0,126	0,126
CA->Ben	0,147	0,147	0,121	0,121	0,12	0,12
Use->Ben			0,089	0,089	0,095	0,095
Sat->Ben			0,097	0,097		
PQ->Use			0,083	0,083	0,082	0,082
IQ->Use			0,112	0,112	0,118	0,118
SQ->Use			0,101	0,101	0,12	0,12
CA->Use			0,114	0,114	0,121	0,121
Use->Use			0	0		
Sat->Use			0,085	0,085		
PQ->Sat				0,088		
IQ->Sat				0,127		
SQ->Sat				0,145		
CA->Sat				0,127		
PQ->CA		0,094		0,094	0,094	
IQ->CA		0,112		0,111	0,111	
SQ->CA		0,13		0,129	0,129	

F. References

The Standard for Program Management: An American National Standard ANSI/PMI 08-002-2008. 2. Aufl. (2008), The Stationery Office/Tso. Newton Square, Pennsylvania.

Aagesen, G. et al. (2011): The Entanglement of Enterprise Architecture and IT-Governance: The Cases of Norway and the Netherlands. In: Proceedings of the 44th Hawaii International Conference on Systems Sciences. Kauai, HI: IEEE Computer Society, 1–10.

Ahlemann, Frederik; Stettiner, Eric; Messerschmidt, Marcus; Legner, Christine (2012): Strategic Enterprise Architecture Management: Challenges, Best Practices, and Future Developments, Springer. Berlin, New York.

Aier, S. et al. (2011a): Construction and Evaluation of a Meta-Model for Enterprise Architecture Design Principles. In: Proceedings of the 10th International Conference on Wirtschaftsinformatik WI 2011. Zürich, Switzerland: Association for Information Systems, 637–644.

Aier, S. et al. (2011b): Understanding Enterprise Architecture Management Design – An Empirical Analysis. In: Proceedings of the 10th International Conference on Wirtschaftsinformatik WI 2011. Zürich, Switzerland: Association for Information Systems, 645–654.

Aier, S.; Schelp, J. (2009): A Reassessment of Enterprise Architecture Implementation. In: Proceedings of the 4th Workshop on Trends in Enterprise Architecture Research (TEAR 2009). Berlin: Springer Verlag, 35–47.

Aier, Stephan; Riege, Christian; Winter, Robert; Artikels, Art (2008): Classification of Enterprise Architecture Scenarios – An Exploratory Analysis. International Journal of Enterprise Modelling and Information Systems Architectures, 3 (1), 14–23.

Akella, Janaki; Buckow, Helge; Lange, Matthias (2012): Reconfiguring Enterprise Architecture to Drive Business Value in the Bank. In: McKinsey & Company (Eds.): IT in digital banking. Düsseldorf.

Alaranta, M. (2006): Combining Theory-testing and Theory-building Analyses of Case Study Data. In: Proceedings of the 14th European Conference on Information Systems. Göteborg, Sweden: Association for Information Systems, 695–706.

Aliee, Fereidoon Shams; Davoudi, Mahsa Razavi; Badie, Kambiz (2010): An Approach towards Enterprise Architecture Quality Attribute Assessment based on Fuzzy AHP. Journal of Information Technology Management, 2 (4), 79–98.

Almutairi, H.; Subramanian, G. H. (2005): An Empirical Application of the DeLone and McLean Model in the Kuwaiti Private Sector. Journal of Computer Information Systems, 45 (3), 113–122.

Anastasi, A.; Urbina, S. (1996): Psychological Testing. 7th Edition, Prentice Hall. Upper Saddle River, New Yersey.

Andersin, A.; Hämäläinen, N. (2007): Enterprise Architecture Process of a Telekommunication Company - A Case Study on Initialization. In: Proceedings of HAAMAHA 2007 Conference - Managing Enterprise of the Future. Poznan, Poland: IEA Press .

Anderson, J. C.; Gerbing D. (1988): Structural Equation Modeling in Practice: A Review and Recommended Two-Step Approach. Psychological Bulletin, 103 (3), 411–423.

Anderson, J. C.; Gerbing, D.W (1991): Predicting the Performance of Measures in a Confirmatory Factor Analysis with a Pretest Assessment of Their Substantive Validates. Journal of Applied Psychology, 76 (5), 732–740.

Andrews, Dorine; Nonnecke, Blair; Preece, Jennifer (2003): Electronic Survey Methodology: A Case Study in Reaching Hard-to-Involve Internet Users. International Journal on Human-Computer Interaction, 16 (2), 185–210.

Armour, Frank J.; Kaisler, Stephan H.; Liu, Simon Y. (1999): A Big-Picture Look at Enterprise Architectures. IEEE Professional, 1 (1), 35–42.

Armstrong, J. S. (1982): The Value of Formal Planning for Strategic Decisions: Review of Empirical Research. Strategic Management Journal, 3 (3), 197–211.

Asfaw, Tamrat; Bada, Abiodun; Allario, Frank (2009): Enablers and Challenges in Using Enterprise Architecture to Drive Transformation: Perspectives from Private Organizations and Federal Government Agencies. The Journal of Enterprise Architecture, 5 (3), 9–17.

Attewell, P.; Rule, J. B. (1991): Survey and Other Methodologies Applied to IT Impact Research: Experiences From a Comparative Study of Business Computing. In: Kraemer, K. L. (Eds.): The Information Systems Research Challenge: Survey Research. Boston, Massachusetts: Harvard Business School Press, 299–315.

Avison, David E.; Pries-Heje, Jan (Hg.) (2005): Research in Information Systems: A Handbook for Research Supervisors and their Students. Amsterdam, Boston, London: Elsevier.

Avital, M.; Te'eni D. (2009): From Generative Fit to Generative Capacity: Exploring an Emerging Dimension of Information Systems Design and Task Performance. Information Systems Journal, 19 (4), 345–367.

Avital, Michel; Boland, R. J.; Lyytinen, Kalle (2009): Introduction to Designing Information and Organizations with a Positive Lens. Information and Organization, 19 (3), 153–161.

Aziz, Sohel; Obitz, Thomas (2007): Infosys - EA Survey 2007.

Bachmann, D.; Elfrink, J. (1996): Tracking the Progress of Email versus Snail-mail. Marketing Research, 8 (2), 31–35.

Bagnoli, A. (2009): Beyond the Standard Interview: The Use of Graphic Elicitation and Arts-based Methods. Qualitative Research, 9 (5), 547–570.

Bagozzi, Richard P. (1979): The Role of Measurement in Theory Construction and Hypothesis Testing: Toward a Holistic Model. In: Conceptual and Theoretical Developments in Marketing. Chicago, IL: American Marketing Association.

Bagozzi, Richard P. (1980): Causal Modeling in Marketing, Wiley & Sons. New York, NY.

Bagozzi, Richard P.; Phillips, Lynn W. (1982): Representing and Testing Organizational Theories: A Holistic Construal. Administrative Science Quarterly, 27 (3), 459–489.

Baker, Michael J. (2000): Writing a Literature Review. Marketing Review, 1 (2), 219.

Ballantine, J.; Bonner, M.; Levy, M.; Martin, A.; Munro, I.; Powell, P. L. (1996): The 3-D Model of Information Systems Success: the Search for the Dependent Variable Continues. Information Resources Management Journal, 9 (4), 5–15.

Bandara, W. et al. (2006): Business Processing Modeling Success: An Empirically Tested Measurement Model. In: Proceedings of the 27th International Conference on Information Systems 2006. Milwakee, USA: Association for Information Systems, 895–913.

Barclay, D.; Higgins, C.; Thompson, Ronald L. (1995): The Partial Least Squares (PLS) Approach to Causal Modeling: Personal Computer Adoption and Use as an Illustration. Technology Studies, 2 (2), 285–309.

Barki, H. (2008): Thar's Gold in Them Thar Constructs. ACM SIGMIS Database, 39 (3), 9–20.

Barki, H.; Hartwick, J. (1989): Rethink the Concept of User Involvement. MIS Quarterly, 13 (1), 53–63.

Barnes, S. J. (2005): Assessing the Value of IS Journals. Communication of ACM, 48 (1), 110–112.

Bartis, E.; Mitev, N. (2008): A Multiple Narrative Approach to Information Systems Failure: A Successful System that Failed. European Journal of Information Systems, 17 (2), 112–124.

Bass, Len; Clements, Paul C.; Kazman, Rick (2002): Software Architecture in Practice, Addison-Wesley. Boston.

Baxter, R. (2009): Reflective and Formative Metrics of Relationship Value: A Commentary Essay. Journal of Business Research, 62 (12), 1370–1377.

Bean (2010): Re-thinking Enterprise Architecture using Systems and Complexity Approaches. Journal of Enterprise Architecture, 6 (4), 7–13.

Becker, Jörg; Niehaves, Björn (2007): Epistemological Perspectives on IS Research: A Framework for Analysing and Systematizing Epistemological Assumptions. Information Systems Research (17), 197–214.

Bem, D. J. (1995): Writing a Review Article for Psychological Bulletin. Psychological Bulletin, 118 (2), 172-172.

Benbasat, Izak; Goldstein, D. K.; Mead, M. (1987): The Case Study Strategy in Studies of Information Systems. MIS Quarterly, 11 (3), 369–388.

Bentley, Colin (2010): PRINCE2: A Practical Handbook. 3. Aufl., Elsevier. Amsterdam.

Bergmann, G. (1957): Philosophy of Science, The University of Wisconsin Press. Madison, WI.

Bhattacherjee, Anol (2001): Understanding Information Systems Continuance: An Expectation-Confirmation Model. MIS Quarterly, 25 (3), 351–370.

Bhattacherjee, Anol (2012): Social Science Reseaerch. 2nd, University of South Florida. Tempa, Florida, USA.

Blalock, H.M (1969): Theory Construction, Prentice Hall. Englewood Cliffs, NJ.

Boh, W.; Fonga, I.; Yellin, Daniel (2007): Using Enterprise Architecture Standards in Managing Information Technology. Journal of Management Information Systems, 23 (3), 163–207.

Bohm, D. (1957): Causality and Chance Modern Physics, Routledge Kegan Paul. London.

Bollen, Kenneth A. (1989): Structural Equations with Latent Variables, Wiley & Sons. New York, NY.

Bollen, Kenneth A. (2007): Interpretational Confounding is Due to Misspecification, Not to Type of Indicator: Comment on Howell, Breivik, and Wilcox. Psychological Bulletin, 12 (2), 219–228.

Bollen, Kenneth A. (2011): Evaluating Effect, Composite, and Causal Indicators in Structural Equation Models. MIS Quarterly, 35 (2), 359–372.

Bollen, Kenneth A.; Lennox, R. (1991): Conventional Wisdom on Measurement: A Structural Equation Perspective. Psychological Bulletin, 110 (2), 305–314.

Boucharas, V. et al. (2010): The Contribution of Enterprise Architecture to the Achievement of Organizational Goals: A Review of the Evidence. In: Proceedings of the 5th Trends in Enterprise Architecture Research Conference. Berlin: Springer Verlag, 1–15.

Boudreau, Marie-Claude; Gefen, David; Straub, Detmar W. (2001): Validation in Information Systems Research: A State-of-the-Art Assessment. MIS Quarterly, 25 (1), 1.

Bradley, Randy V.; Pridmore, Jeannie; Byrd, Terry (2006): Information Systems Success in the Context of Different Corporate Cultural Types: An Empirical Investigation. Journal of Management Information Systems, 23 (2), 267–294.

Bricknall, R. et al. (2006): Enterprise Architecture: Critical Factors Affecting Modelling and Management. In: Proceedings of the 14th European Conference on Information Systems. Goteborg, Sweden: Association for Information Systems .

Buchanan, R. D.; Boddy, D.; McCalman, J. (1988): Getting in, Getting on, Getting out, and Getting back. In: Bryman, Alan (Eds.): Doing Research in Organizations. London: Routledge Kegan Paul, 53–67.

Bucher, Tobias; Fischer, Ronny; Kurpjuweit, Stephan; Winter, Robert (2007): Analysis and Application Scenarios of Enterprise Architecture: An Exploratory Study. Journal of Enterprise Architecture, 3 (3), 33–43.

Buckl, S. et al. (2008): Enterprise Architecture Management Patterns - Exemplifying the Approach. In: Proceedings of the 12th International IEEE Enterprise Distributed Object Computing Conference. München, Germany: IEEE, 393–402.

Buckl, S. et al. (2009a): A Pattern-based Approach to Quantitative Enterprise Architecture Analysis. In: Proceedings of the 15th Americas Conference on Information Systems (AMCIS). San Francisco, USA: Association for Information Systems, 316–327.

Buckl, S. et al. (2009b): Towards a Language for Enterprise Architecture Documentation and Analysis – Extending the Meta Object Facility. In: Proceedings of the The 4th International Workshop on Vocabularies, Ontologies and Rules for The Enterprise (VORTE 2009).

Buckl, S.; Matthes, F. (2010): Towards a Method Framework for Enterprise Architecture Management–A Literature Analysis from a Viable System Perspective. In: Proceedings of the 5th International Workshop on Business/IT Alignment and Interoperability (BUSITAL 2010). Hammamet, 46–60.

Buckl, Sabine; Schweda, Christian M.; Matthes, Florian (2010): A situated approach to enterprise architecture management. In: Proceedings of the 2010 IEEE International Conference on Systems, Man, and Cybernetics (SMC). Istanbul, Turkey, 587–592.

Burkell, Jacquelyn (2003): The Dilemma of Survey Nonresponse. Library & Information Science Research, 25 (3), 239–263.

Burns, Peter; Neutens, Michael; Newman, Daniel; Power, Tim (2009): Building Value through Enterprise Architecture: A Global Study, Booz&Company. New York, NY.

Burt, R. S. (1976): Interpretational Confounding of Unobserved Variables in Structural Equation Models. Sociological Methods & Research, 5 (1), 3–52.

Buschle, M. et al. (2010): A Tool for Enterprise Architecture Analysis Using the PRM Formalism. In: Proceeding of the 22nd International Conference on Advanced Information Systems Engineering. Hammamet, Tunisia, 108–121.

Byrd, T. A.; Thrasher, E. H.; Lang, T.; Davidson, N. W. (2006): A Process-oriented Perspective of IS Success: Examining the Impact of IS on Operational Cost. Omega, 34 (5), 448–460.

Cameron, K. S.; Whetten, D. A. (1983): Some Conclusions About Organizational Effectiveness. In: Organizational Effectiveness: A Comparison of Multiple Models. New York, NY: Academy Press, 261-177.

Campbell, Donald T.; Fiske, Donald W. (1959): Convergent and Discriminant Validation by the Multitrait-multimethod Matrix. Psychological Bulletin, 56 (2), 81–105.

Carroll, John S.; Hatakenaka, Sachi (2001): Driving Organizational Change in the Midst of Crisis. MIT Sloan Management Review, 42 (3), 70–79.

Cenfetelli, Ronald T.; Bassellier, Geneviève (2009): Interpretation of Formative Measurement in Information Systems Research. MIS Quarterly, 33 (4), 689–707.

Cha-Jan Chang, Jerry; King, W. R. (2005): Measuing the Performance of Information Success: A Functional Scorecard. Journal of Management Information Systems, 22 (1).

Chan, Yolahfde E. (2000): IT Value: The Great Divide Between Qualitative and Quantitative and Individual and Organizational Measures. Journal of Management Information Systems, 16 (4), 225–261.

Chan, Yolande E.; Reich, Blaize Horner (2007): IT alignment: What Have We Learned? Journal of Information Technology Management, 22 (4), 297–315.

Chaplin, W. F.; John, O. P.; Goldberg, L. R. (1988): Conceptions of States and Traits: Dimensional Attributes with Ideals as Prototypes. Journal of Personality and Social Psychology, 54 (4), 541–557.

Chau, Patrick Y. K.; Kuan, Kevin K. Y.; Liang, Ting-Peng (2007): Research on IT Value: What We Have Done in Asia and Europe. European Journal of Information Systems, 16 (3), 196–201.

Chen, WenShin; Hirschheim, Rudy (2004): A Paradigmatic and Methodological Examination of Information Systems Research from 1991 to 2001. Information Systems Journal (14), 197–235.

Cheung, C. M. K.; Lee, M. K. O. (2005): The Assymetric Effect of Website Attribute Performance on Satisfaction: An Empirical Study. In: Proceedings of the 38th Hawaii International Conference on System Sciences. Big Island, Hawaii: IEEE, 175–187.

Chin, W. W. (2001): PLS-Graph User's Guide, Version 3.0. University of Houston.

Chin, Wynne W. (1998): The Partial Least Squares Approach to Structural Equation Modeling. In: Marcoulides, G.A (Eds.): Modern Methods for Business Research. London, 295–336.

Chin, Wynne W.; Dibbern, J. (2009): A Permutation Based Procedure for Multi-Group PLS Analysis: Results of Tests of Differences on Simulated Data and a Cross of Information System Services between Germany and the USA. In: Vinzi, W. E.; Chin, Wynne W.; Henseler, J. Ringle; Wang, H. (Eds.): Handbook of Partial Least Squares: Concepts, Methods and Applications. Berlin: Springer Verlag, 171–193.

Chin, Wynne W.; Marcolin, Barbara L.; Newsted, Peter R. (2003): A Partial Least Squares Latent Variable Modeling Approach for Measuring Interaction Effects: Results from a Monte Carlo Simulation Study and an Electronic-Mail Emotion/Adoption Study. Information Systems Research, 14 (2), 189–217.

Chin, Wynne W.; Newsted, Peter R. (1999): Structural Equation Modeling Analysis with Small Samples Using Partial Least Squares. In: Hoyle, R. (Eds.): Statistical Strategies for Small Sample Research. Thousand Oaks, Calif: Sage Publications, 1307–1341.

Chua, Wai Fong (1986): Radical Developments in Accounting Thought. The Accounting Review, 61 (4), 601–632.

Churchill, G. A. (1979): A Paradigm for Developing Better Measures of Marketing Constructs. Journal of Marketing Research, 16 (1), 64–73.

Clark, L. A.; Watson, D. (1995): Constructing Validity: Basic Issues in Objective Scale Development. Psychological Assessment, 7 (3), 309–319.

Claver, Enrique; Llopis, Juan; González, M. Reyes; Gascó, José L. (2001): The Performance of Information Systems through Organizational Culture. Information Technology & People, 14 (3), 247–260.

Clay, P. F. et al. (2005): Factors Affecting the Loyal Use of Knowledge Management Systems. In: Proceedings of the 38th Hawaii International Conference on System Sciences. Big Island, Hawaii: IEEE, 251–253.

Cleland, David I.; King, W. R. (1974): Developing A Planning Culture for More Effective Strategic Planning. Long Range Planning, 7 (3), 70–74.

Clemons, E. K.; Reddi, S. P.; Row, M. C. (1993): The Impact of Information on the Organization of Economic Activity: The 'Move to the Middle' hypothesis. Journal of Management Information Systems, 10 (2), 9–35.

Clemons, E. K.; Row, M. C. (1993): Limits to Interfirm Coordination through Information Technology: Results of a Field Study in Consumer Packaged Goods Distribution. Journal of Management Information Systems, 10 (1), 73–95.

Cobanoglu, Cihan; Cobanoglu, Nesrin (2003): The Effect of Incentives in Web Surveys: Application and Ethical Considerations. International Journal of Market Research, 45 (4), 475–488.

Cobanoglu, Cihan; Warde, Bill; Moreo, Patrick J. (2001): A Comparison of Mail, Fax and Web-based Survey Methods. International Journal of Market Research, 43 (4), 441–452.

Cohen, J. (1988): Statistical Power Analysis for the Behavioral Sciences, Lawrence Erlbaum Associates, Publishers. Hillsdale, NJ.

Cohen, J. (1992): Statistical Power Analysis for the Behavioral Sciences. Psychological Bulletin, 112 (1), 155–159.

Cole, S. T. (2005): Comparing Mail and Web-Based Survey Distribution Methods: Results of Surveys to Leisure Travel Retailers. Journal of Travel Research, 43 (4), 422–430.

Cook, C.; Heath, F.; Thompson, R. L. (2000): A Meta-Analysis of Response Rates in Web- or Internet-Based Surveys. Educational and Psychological Measurement, 60 (6), 821–836.

Corbin, Juliet M.; Strauss, Anselm L. (2008): Basics of Qualitative Research: Techniques and Procedures for Developing Grounded Theory. 3. Aufl., Sage Publications. Los Angeles, Calif.

Couper, M. P.; Traugott, M. W. Lamias M. J. (2001): Web Survey Design and Administration. Public Opinion Quarterly, 65 (2), 230–253.

Covey, Stephen R. (2004): The 7 Habits of Highly Effective People: Restoring the Character Ethic. [Rev. ed.]., Free Press. New York.

Cronbach, L. J.; Meehl, O. E. (1955): Construct Validity in Psychological Tests. Psychological Bulletin, 52 (4), 281–302.

Cronk M. C.; Fritzgerald, E. P. (1997): A Conceptual Framework for Furthering Understanding of 'IT Business Value' and its Dimensions. In: Proceedings of the 3rd Asia Conference on Information Systems. Brisbane, Australia, 405–415.

Crowstone, K.; Myers, Michael D. (2004): Information Technology and Transformation of Industries: Three Research Perspectives. Journal of Strategic Information Systems, 13 (1), 5–28.

D'Agostino, Ralph; Belanger, Albert; D'Agostino, Ralph B., JR. (1990): A Suggestion for Using Power and Informative Tests of Normality. The American Statistican, 44 (4), 316–321.

Danziger, J. N.; Kraemer, K. L. (1991): Survey Research and Multiple Operationism: The URBIS Project Methodology. In: Kraemer, K. L. (Eds.): The Information Systems Research Challenge. Survey Research Methods. Boston, Massachusetts: Harvard Business School Press, 351–371.

Darling, Rory (2008): A Survey of Enterprise Architecture Model Transformation Efficiency. Journal of Enterprise Architecture, 4 (2), 35–64.

Davis, C. J.; Hufnagel, E. M. (2007): Through the Eyes of Experts: A Sociocognitive Perspective on the Automation of Fingerprinting Work. MIS Quarterly, 31 (4), 681–703.

Davis, Fred D. (1989): Perceived Usefulness, Perceived Ease of Use, and User Acceptance of Information Technology. MIS Quarterly, 13 (3), 319–340.

Davoudi, Mahsa Razavi; Aliee, Fereidoon Shams (2009a): A New AHP-based Approach towards Enterprise Architecture Quality Attribute Analysis. In: Proceedings of the Third International Conference on Research Challenges in Information Science (RCIS 2009), 333–342.

Davoudi, Mahsa Razavi; Aliee, Fereidoon Shams (2009b): An Approach towards Enterprise Interoperability. Lecture Notes in Business Information Processing, 38 (1), 52–65.

Davoudi, Mahsa Razavi; Aliee, Fereidoon Shams (2009c): Characterization of Enterprise Architecture Quality Attributes. In: Proceedings of the IEEE EDOC AQuSerM Workshop, 131–137.

Davoudi, Mahsa Razavi; Aliee, Fereidoon Shams; Mohsenzadeh, Mehran (2009d): A New Approach towards Enterprise Architecture Analysis. Lecture Notes in Business Information Processing, 38 (1), 44–51.

Davoudi, Mahsa Razavi; Aliee, Fereidoon Shams; Sarabadani, Amir Esmaeil (2009e): A Fuzzy AHP Based Approach Towards Enterprise Architecture Evaluation. In: Proceedings of the 2009 European Conference on information Management and Evaluation (ECIME 2009), 408–421.

Davoudi, Mahsa Razavi; Shams Aliee, Fereidoon; Badie, Kambiz (2011): An AHP-based Approach toward Enterprise Architecture Analysis based on Enterprise Architecture Quality Attributes. Knowledge and Information Systems, 28 (2), 449–472.

de Boer, F. S. et al. (2005): Enterprise Architecture Analysis with XML. In: Proceedings of the 38th Hawaii International Conference on System Sciences. Big Island, Hawaii: IEEE, 222–234.

DeLone, William H.; McLean, Ephraim R. (1992): Information Systems Success: The Quest for the Dependent Variable. Information Systems Research, 3 (1), 60–95.

DeLone, William H.; McLean, Ephraim R. (2003): The DeLone and McLean Model of Information Systems Success: A Ten-Year Update. Journal of Management Information Systems, 19 (4), 9–30.

Department Of Defence Architecture Framework Group: DoD Architecture Framework Version 1.0. Online available at https://acc.dau.mil/CommunityBrowser.aspx?id=22209, last accessed on 06.03.2012.

Dess, Gregory G.; Davis, Peter S. (1984): Porter's (1980) Generic Strategies as Determinants of Strategic Group Membership and Organizational Performance. The Academy of Management Journal, 27 (3), 467–488.

Deutskens, Elisabeth; Ruyter, Ko de; Wetzel, Martin; Oosterveld, Paul (2004): Response Rate and Response Quality of Internet-Based Surveys: An Experimental Study. Marketiong Letters, 15 (1), 21–36.

DeVellis, Robert F. (1991): Scale Development: Theory and Application, Sage Publications. Newbury Park, CA.

Diamantopoulos, Adamantios (2010): Reflective and Formative Metrics of Relationship Value: Response to Baxter's Commentary Essay. Journal of Business Research, 63 (1), 91–93.

Diamantopoulos, Adamantios (2011): Incorporating Formative Measures into Covariance-based Structural Equation Models. MIS Quarterly, 35 (2), 335–358.

Diamantopoulos, Adamantios; Siguaw, J. A. (2006): Formative Versus Reflective Indicators in Organizational Measure Development: A Comparison and Empirical Illustration. British Journal of Management, 17 (4), 263–282.

Diamantopoulos, Adamantios; Winklhofer, Heidi M. (2001): Index Construction with Formative Indicators: An Alternative to Scale Development. Journal of Marketing Research, 38 (2), 269–277.

Dietz, J.L.G (2008): Architecture: Building Strategy into Design, Academic Service. Den Haag.

Dillman, D. A. (2000): Mail and Web-based Survey: The Tailored Design Method, Wiley & Sons. New York, NY.

Dillman, D. A.; Reips, U.-D; Matzat U. (2010): Advice in Surveying the General Public Over the Internet. International Journal of Internet Science, 5 (1), 1–4.

Dillman, D. A.; Tortora, Robert D.; Bowker, Dennis (1999): Principles for Constructing Web Surveys. In: SESRC Technical Report. Pullman, Washington, 98-50.

Doll, William J.; Xia, Weidong; Torkzadeh, Gholamreza (1994): A Confirmatory Factor Analysis of the End-User Computing Satisfaction Instrument. MIS Quarterly, 18 (4), 453–461.

Dooley, Larry M.; Lindner, James R. (2003): The Handling of Nonresponse Error. Human Resource Development Quarterly, 14 (1), 99–110.

Dubé, Line; Paré, Guy (2003): Rigor in Information Systems Positivist Case Research: Current Practices, Trends, and Recommendations. MIS Quarterly, 27 (4), 597–635.

Edwards, Jeffrey R. (2001): Multidimensional Constructs in Organizational Behavior Research: An Integrative Analytical Framework. Organizational Research Methods (4), 144–192.

Edwards, Jeffrey R.; Bagozzi, Richard P. (2000): On the Nature and Direction of Relationships between Constructs and Measures. Psychological Methods, 5 (2), 155–174.

Eisenhardt, Kathleen M. (1989): Building Theories from Case Study Research. Academy of Management Journal, 14 (4), 532–550.

Ekstedt, M. et al. (2009a): A Tool for Enterprise Architecture Analysis of Maintainability. In: Proceedings of the 13th European Conference on Software Maintenance and Reengineering: IEEE, 327–328.

Ekstedt, Mathias; Sommestad, Teodor (2009b): Enterprise Architecture Models for Cyber Security Analysis. In: Proceedings of the 2009 Power Systems Conference and Exposition: IEEE, 1–6.

Ellison, R. J.; Moore, A. P. (2003): Trustworthy Refinement Through Intrusion-Aware Design (TRIAD). Carnegie Mellon University, SEI. Pittsburgh.

Espinosa, J. A. et al. (2011): The Organizational Impact of Enterprise Architecture: A Research Framework. In: Proceedings of the 44th Hawaii International Conference on Systems Sciences. Kauai, HI: IEEE Computer Society .

Evermann, Joerg; Tate. Mary (2011): Fitting Covariance Models for Theory Generation. Journal of the AIS, 12 (9), 632–661.

Falkenberg, Eckhard D. (1998): A Framework of Information System Concepts: The FRISCO Report (Web edition), University of Leiden, Department of Computer Science. Leiden.

Fan, Weiguo; Yan, Zheng (2010): Factors Affecting Response Rates of the Web Survey: A Systematic Review. Computers in Human Behavior, 26 (2), 132–139.

Fishbein, Martin; Ajzen, Icek (1975): Belief, Attitude, Intention and Behavior: An Introduction to Theory and Research, Addison-Wesley. Reading, Mass. [u.a.].

Flynn, B. B.; Sakakibara, Sadao; Schroeder, Roger G.; Bates, Kimberly A.; Flynn, E.James (1990): Empirical Research Methods in Operations Management. Journal of Operations Management, 9 (2), 250–284.

Fontana, A.; Frey, J. H. (2000): The Interview: from Structured Questions to Negotiated Text. In: Denzin, Norman K.; Lincoln, Yvonna S. (Eds.): Handbook of Qualitative Research. 2. Aufl. Thousand Oaks, Calif: Sage Publications, 645–672.

Foorthuis, R. et al. (2010): On Cource, But Not There Yet: Enterprise Architecture Conformance and Benefits in Systems Development. In: Proceedings of the 31st International Conference on Information Systems (ICIS2010). St. Louis, Missouri, USA: Association for Information Systems, 110.

Fornell, Claes; Larcker, David F. (1981): Structural Equation Models with Unobservable Variables and Measurement Error: Algebra and Statistics. Journal of Marketing Research, 18 (3).

Fowler, Floyd J. (2009): Survey Research Methods. 4. Aufl., Sage Publications. Los Angeles (i.e. Thousand Oaks, Calif.).

Franke, U. et al. (2009a): Enterprise Architecture Analysis Using Fault Trees and MODAF. In: Proceedings of the CAiSE Forum 2009, 61–66.

Franke, U. et al. (2009b): Enterprise Architecture Dependency Analysis Using Fault Trees and Bayesian Networks. In: Proceedings of the 2009 Spring Simulation Multiconference: Society for Computer Simulation International, 209–216.

Fricker, R. D.; Schonlau, M. (2002): Advantages and Disadvantages of Internet Research Surveys: Evidence from the Literature. Field Methods, 14 (4), 347–367.

Froehle, Craig M.; Roth, Aleda V. (2004): New Measurement Scales for Evaluating Perceptions of the Technology-mediated Customer Service Experience. Journal of Operations Management, 22 (1), 1–21.

Gable, G. G. et al. (2003): Enterprise Systems Success: A Measurement Model. In: Proceedings of the 24th International Conference on Information Systems. Seattle, Washington, USA: Association for Information Systems, 576–591.

Gable, Guy G. (1994): Integrating Case Study and Survey Reserach Methods: An Example in Information Systems. European Journal of Information Systems, 3 (2), 112–126.

Gable, Guy G. (1996): A Multidimensional Model of Client Success When Engaging External Consultants. Management Science, 42 (8), 1175–1198.

Gable, Guy G.; Sedera, Darshana; Chan, Taizan (2008): Re-conceptualizing Information System Success: The IS-Impact Measurement Model. Journal of the Asociation for Information Systems, 9 (7), 377–408.

Gallagher, C. A. (1974): Perception of the Value of a Management Information System. Academy of Management Journal, 17 (1), 46–55.

Galliers, R.D; Markus, M.L; Newell, S. (2006): Exploring Information Systems Research Approaches, Routledge Kegan Paul. New York, New York, USA.

Gammelgård, Magnus; Ekstedt, Mathias; Närman, Per (2007): Architecture Scenario Analysis – Estimating the Credibility of the Results. In: Proceedings of the 11th IEEE International Enterprise Distributed Object Computing Conference (EDOC 2007) .

Garland, R. (1990): A Comaprison of Three Forms of the Semantic Differential. Marketing Bulletin, 1 (1), 19–24.

Garrity, E. J.; Glassberg, B.; Kim, Y. J.; Sanders, G. L.; Shin, S. K. (2005): An Experimental Investigation of Webbased Information Systems Success in the Context of Electronic Commerce. Decision Support Systems, 39 (3), 485–503.

Gefen, David; Rigdon, Edward E.; Straub, Detmar W. (2011): An Update and Extension to SEM Guidelines for Administrative and Social Science Research. MIS Quarterly, 35 (2), iii–xiv.

Gefen, David; Straub, Detmar W.; Boudreau, Marie-Claude (2000): Structural Equation Modeling and Regression, Guidelines for Research Practice. Communications of the AIS, 4 (7).

Geldermann, M. (2002): Task Difficulty, Task Variability and Satisfaction with Management Support Systems. Information & Management, 39 (7), 593–604.

Glaser, Barney G.; Strauss, Anselm L. (1969): The Discovery of Grounded Theory: Strategies for Qualitative Research. The British Journal of Sociology, 20 (2), 227–228.

Glaser, Barney G.; Strauss, Anselm L. (2008): The Discovery of Grounded Theory: Strategies for Qualitative Research. Third paperback printing., Aldine Transaction. New Brunswick.

Glock, C.Y (1967): Survey Research in the Social Sciences, Russell Sage Foundation. New York, NY.

Goodhue, D. L. et al. (2012): Marcoulides & Saunders/Editor's Comments: PLS Modeling. Online available at http://www.misq.org/skin/frontend/default/misq/BLOG/11961.pdf, last accessed on 06.03.2012, last accessed on 06.03.2012.

Goodhue, Dale L.; Lewis, William; Thompson, Ronald L. (2006): PLS, Small Sample Size, and Statistical Power in MIS Research. In: Proceedings of the 39th Hawaii International Conference on System Sciences, 202–212.

Goodhue, Dale L.; Thompson, Ronald L. (1995): Task-Technology Fit and Individual Performance. MIS Quarterly, 19 (2), 213–236.

Google Analytics (2012). Google.

Gordon, George G.; DiTomaso, Nancy (2007): Predicting Corporate Performance From Organizational Culture. Journal of Management Studies, 29 (6), 783–798.

Gravetter, Frederick J.; Wallnau, Larry B. (2011): Essentials of Statistics for the Behavioral Sciences. 7. Aufl., Wadsworth. Belmont, CA.

Greefhorst, Danny; Proper, Erik (2011): Architecture Principles: The Cornerstones of Enterprise Architecture, Springer Verlag. Berlin.

Greer, S. (1969): The Logic of Social Inquiry, Aldine Publishing. Chicago, IL.

Gregor, Shirley (2006): The Nature of Theory in Information Systems. MIS Quarterly, 30 (3), 611–642.

Grover, V.; Jeong, Seung R.; Segras, A. H. (1996): Information Systems Effectiveness: The Construct Space and Patterns of Application. Information & Management, 31 (4), 177–191.

Guadagnoli, Edward; Velicer, Wayne F. (1988): Relation to Sample Size to the Stability of Component Patterns. Psychological Bulletin, 103 (2), 265–275.

Gustafsson, Pia; Nordström, Lars (2009): Enterprise Architecture: A Framework Supporting Organizational Performance Analysis. In: Proceedings of the 20th International Conference on Electricity Distribution, 867–871.

Hair, J. F.; Black, W. C.; Babin, B. J.; Anderson, R. E. (2010): Multivariate Data Analysis, Prentice Hall. Englewood Cliffs, NJ.

Hair, Joseph F. (1995): Multivariate Data Analysis with Readings. 4. Aufl., Prentice Hall. Englewood Cliffs, N.J.

Halley, Marc R.; Drive, Colshire; Bashioum, Chris (2005): Enterprise Transformation to a Service Oriented Architecture: Successful Patterns in the Transformation to SOA. In: Proceedings of the IEEE International Conference on Web Services (ICWS'05): IEEE, 781–782.

Handfield, R. B.; Melnyk, S. A. (1998): The Scientific Theory-Building Process: A Primer Using the Case of TQM. Journal of Operations Management, 16 (4), 321–339.

Hardgrave, B. C.; Johnson, R. A. (2003): Towards an Information Systems Development Acceptance Model: The Case of Object-Oriented Systems Development. IEEE Transactions on Engineering Management, 20 (1), 322–336.

Hart, C. (1999): Doing a Literature Review. Releasing the Social Science Imagination, Sage Publications. London.

Haynes, S. N.; Richard, D. C. S.; Kubany, E. S. (1995): Content Validity in Psychological Assessment: A Functional Approach to Concepts and Methods. Psychological Assessment, 7 (3), 238–247.

Heiskanen, A.; Newman, M. (1997): Bridging the Gap between Information Systems Research and Practice: the Reflective Practitioner as a Researcher. In: Proceedings of the 18th International Conference on Information Systems. Atlanta, Georgia, USA: Association for Information Systems .

Henderson, J. C.; Venkatraman, N. (1993): Strategic Alignment: Leveraging Information Technology for Transforming Organizations. IBM Systems Journal, 38 (2).

Henseler, Jörg; Ringle, Christian M.; Sinkovics, R. R. (2009): The Use of Partial Least Squares Path Modeling in International Marketing. Advances in International Marketing (AIM), 20, 277–319.

Hermanns, Harry (2004): Interviewing as an Activity. In: Flick, Uwe; Kardorff, Ernst von; Steinke, Ines (Eds.): A Companion to Qualitative Research. London [u.a.]: Sage Publications, 209–213.

Hesse-Biber, Sharlene Nagy; Leavy, Patricia (2005): The Practice of Qualitative Research, Sage Publications. Thousand Oaks, Calif.

Hevner, Alan R.; March, Salvatore T.; Park, Jinsoo; Ram, Sudha (2004): Design Science in Information Systems Research. MIS Quarterly, 28 (1), 75–105.

Hill, Charles W. L.; Jones, Gareth R. (2008): Strategic Management: An Integrated Approach. 8. Aufl., Houghton Mifflin. Boston.

Hinkin, T. R. (1995): A Review of Scale Development Practices in the Study of Organizations. Journal of Management, 21 (5), 967–988.

Hinkin, T. R.; Tracey, J. B. (1999): An Analysis of Variance Approach to Content Validation. Organizational Research Methods, 2 (2), 175–186.

Hirschheim, Rudy (1992): Information Systems Epistemology: An Historical Perspective. In: R. Galliers (Eds.): Information Systems Research: Issues, Methods and Practical Guidelines. Oxford: Blackwell Scientific Publications, 28–60.

Hirvonen, A. et al. (2003): Evaluation of Enterprise IT Architecture Solutions–How can an ICT Consultant Tell What is Best for You? In: Proceedings of the 10th European Conference on Information Technology Evaluation. Madrid, Spain, 327–338.

Hjort-Madsen, K.; Pries-Heje, J. (2009): Enterprise Architecture in Government: Fad or Future? In: Proceedings of the 42nd Hawaii International Conference on System Sciences. Manoa, Hawaii: IEEE.

Hoerl, Roger Wesley; Snee, Ronald D. (2012): Statistical Thinking: Improving Business Performance. Second Edition, John Wiley & Sons, Inc. Hoboken, New Jersey.

Holmström, Jan; Ketokivi, Mikko; Hameri, Ari-Pekka (2009): Bridging Practice and Theory: A Design Science Approach. Decision Sciences, 40 (1), 65–87.

Holschke, Oliver; Närman, Per; Flores, Waldo Rocha; Ericsson, Evelina; Schönherr, Marten (2010): Using Enterprise Architecture Models and Bayesian Belief Networks for Failure Impact Analysis. The Journal of Enterprise Architecture, 6 (2), 7–18.

Hoogervorst, Jan (2004): Enterprise Architecture: Enabling Integration, Agility and Change. International Journal of Cooperative Information Systems, 13 (3), 213–233.

Hoogervorst, Jan (2009): Enterprise Governance and Enterprise Engineering, Springer Verlag. Berlin, Heidelberg, New York.

Höök, David; Gustafsson, Pia; Nordström, Lars; Johnson, Pontus (2009): An enterprise architecture based method enabling quantified analysis of IT support system's impact on maintenance management. PICMET '09 - 2009 Portland International Conference on Management of Engineering & Technology, 3176–3189.

Horan, Thomas A. (2000): Digital Places: Building our City of Bits, ULI-the Urban Land Institute. Washington, D.C.

Howell, R. D.; Breivik, E.; Wilcox, J. B. (2007): Reconsidering Formative Measurement. Psychological Methods, 12 (2), 205–218.

Hu, P. J.-H. (2003): Evaluating Telemedicine Systems Success: A Revised Model. In: Proceedings of the 36th Hawaii International Conference on System Sciences. Big Island, Hawaii: IEEE, 184–206.

Huber, George P.; Power, Danial J. (1985): Retrospective Reports of Strategic-level Managers: Guidelines for Increasing their Accuracy. Strategic Management Journal, 6 (2), 171–180.

Hunter, M. G. (1997): The use of RepGrids to Gather Interview Data about Information Systems Analysts. Information Systems Journal, 7 (67–81).

Iacob, M.-e.; Jonkers, H. (2005): Quantitative Analysis of Enterprise Architectures. In: Proceedings of the First International Conference on Interoperability of Enterprise Software and Applications. Geneva, Switzerland, 239–252.

IDS Scheer (2005): Enterprise Architectures and ARIS Process Platform. Saarbrücken.

IEEE (2000): IEEE 1471:2000: Recommended Practice for Architectural Description, Institute of Electrical and Electronics Engineers.

Iivari, Juhani (2005): An Empirical Test of the DeLone-McLean Model of Information System Success. ACM SIGMIS Database, 36 (2).

Iivari, Juhani; Hirschheim, Rudy; Klein, Heinz K. (2004): Towards a Distinctive Body of Knowledge for Information Systems Experts: Coding ISD Process Knowledge in Two IS Journals. Information Systems Journal, 14 (4), 313–342.

Inji Wijegunaratne; Peter Evans-Greenwood; George Fernandez (2011): EA Heavy and EA Light: Two Examples of Successful Enterprise Architecture. Journal of Enterprise Architecture, 7 (2), 50–64.

ISO/IEC (2001): Software Engineering - Product Quality.

Isomäki, H.; Liimatainen, K. (2008): Challenges of Government Enterprise Architecture Work – Stakeholders' Views. In: Electronic Government 7th International Conference EGOV 2008. Turin, Italy: Springer Verlag, 364–374.

Ives Blake; Olson, Margrethe H. (1984): User Involvement and MIS Success: A Review of Research. Management Science, 30 (5), 586–603.

Jarvis, C. B.; MacKenzie, S. B.; Podsakoff, P. M. (2003a): Critical Review of Construct Indicators and Measurement Model Misspecification in Marketing and Consumer Research. Journal of Consumer Research, 30 (2), 199–218.

Jarvis, Cheryl Burke; MacKenzie, Scott B.; Podsakoff, Philip M. (2003b): A Critical Review of Construct Indicators and Measurement Model Misspecification in Marketing and Consumer Research. Journal of Consumer Research, 30 (2), 199–218.

Javanbakht, M. et al. (2009): A New Method for Enterprise Architecture Assessment and Decision-Making about Improvement or Redesign. In: Proceedings of the 2009 Fourth International Multi-Conference on Computing in the Global Information Technology, 69–76.

Jick, T. D. (1983): Mixing Qualitative and Quantitative Methods: Triangulation in Action. In: van Maanen, J. (Eds.): Qualitative Methodology. Beverly Hills, CA: Sage Publications, 135–148.

Johnson, P. et al. (2006): Extended Influence Diagrams for Enterprise Architecture Analysis. In: Proceedings of the 10th IEEE International Enterprise Distributed Object Computing Conference (EDOC'06), 3–12.

Johnson, P. et al. (2007a): A Tool for Enterprise Architecture Analysis. In: Proceedings of the 11th IEEE International Enterprise Distributed Object Computing Conference (EDOC 2007), 142–152.

Johnson, Pontus; Ekstedt, Mathias; Silva, Enrique; Plazaola, Leonel (2004): Using Enterprise Architecture for CIO Decision-Making. Proceedings of the 2nd Annual Conference on Systems Engineering Research (DoD).

Johnson, Pontus; Lagerström, Robert; Närman, Per; Simonsson, Mårten (2007b): Enterprise architecture analysis with extended influence diagrams. Information Systems Frontiers, 9 (2-3), 163–180.

Jonkers, Henk; Lankhorst, Marc M.; ter Doest, Hugo W. L.; Arbab, Farhad; Bosma, Hans; Wieringa, Roel J. (2006): Enterprise architecture: Management Tool and Blueprint for the Organisation. Information Systems Frontiers, 8 (2), 63–66.

Kaisler, S. H. et al. (2005): Enterprise Architecting: Critical Problems. In: Proceedings of the 38th Hawaii International Conference on System Sciences. Big Island, Hawaii: IEEE.

Kamogawa, T.; Okada, H. (2005): A Framework for Enterprise Architecture Effectiveness. In: Proceedings of ICSSSM '05. 2005 International Conference on Services Systems and Services Management, 2005, 740–745.

Kaplan, Andreas M. (1964): The Conduct of Inquiry, Chandler. San Francisco, CA.

Kaplan, B.; Duchon, D. (1988): Combining Qualitative and Quantitative Methods in Information Systems Research: A Case Study. MIS Quarterly, 12 (4), 571–586.

Kaplan, R. S.; Norton, D. P. (2004): Strategy Maps: Converting Intangibale Assests into Tangible Outcomes, Harvard Business School Press. Boston, Massachusetts.

Kaplowitz, M. D.; Hadlock, T. D.; Levine, R. (2004): A Comparison of Web and Mail Survey Response Rates. Public Opinion Quarterly, 68 (1), 94–101.

Kappelman, Leon Allan; McGinnis, Tom; Pettite, Alex; Salmans, Brian; Sidorova, Anna (2010): Enterprise Architecture: Charting the Territory for Academic Research. In: Kappelman, Leon Allan (Eds.): The SIM guide to enterprise architecture. Boca Raton. Fla: CRC Press, 96–110.

Keen, P. G. W. (1980): MIS Research: Reference Disciplines and a Cumulative Tradition. In: Proceedings of the First International Conference on Information Systems, 9–18.

Kehoe, C. M.; Pitkow, J. E. (1996): Surveying the Territory: GVU's Five Www User Surveys. The World Wide Web Journal, 1 (3), 77–84.

Kelly, G. A. (1955): The Psychology of Personal Constructs, Norton.

Kerlinger, F. N. (1986): Foundations of Behavioral Research, Holt, Rhinehart, & Winston. New York, NY.

Khalifa, M.; Verner, J. M. (2000): Drivers for Software Development Model Usage. IEEE Transactions on Engineering Management, 47 (3), 360–369.

Kiesler, S.; Sproull, L. S. (1986): Response Effects in the Electronic Survey. Public Opinion Quarterly, 50 (3), 402–413.

Kim, Young-Gul; Everest, Gordon C. (1994): Building an IS Architecture : Collective Wisdom from the Field. Information & Management, 26 (1), 1–11.

King, W. R.; He, J. (2005): External Validity in IS Survey Research. Communications of the AIS, 16 (45), 880–894.

Klein, Heinz K.; Myers, Michael D. (1999): A Set of Principles for Conducting and Evaluating Interpretive Field Studies in Information Systems. MIS Quarterly, 23 (1), 67.

Kluge, C. et al. (2006): How to Realise Corporate Value from Enterprise Architecture. In: Proceedings of the 14th European Conference on Information Systems. Göteborg, Sweden: Association for Information Systems, 1572–1581.

Kock, Ned (2011): WarpPLS 2.0, ScriptWarp Systems. Laredo, Texas.

Kotter, John P. (1995): Leading Change: Why Transformation Efforts Fail. Harvard Business Review (March-April), 59–67.

Kozlowski, S. W. J.; Klein, K. J. (2000): A Multilevel Approach to Theory and Research in Organizations: Contextual, Temporal, and Emergent Processes. In: Klein, K. J.; Kozlowski, S. W. J. (Eds.): Multilevel Theory, Research, and Methods in Organizations: Foundations, Extensions, and New Direction. San Francisco, CA: Jossey-Bass, 3–90.

Krejjcie, R. T. (1970): Determining Sample Size for Research Activities. Educational and Psychological Measurement, 30 (3), 607–610.

Kuechler, Bill; Vaishnavi, Vijay (2008): On Theory Development in Design Science Research: Anatomy of a Research Project. European Journal of Information Systems, 17 (5), 489–504.

Kulkarni, U. R.; Ravindran, S.; Freeze, R. (2006): A Knowledge Management Success Model: Theoretical Development and Empirical Validation. Journal of MIS, 23 (3), 309–347.

Lagerström, R. (2010): Enterprise Systems Modifiability Analysis: An Enterprise Architecture Modeling Approach for Decision Making.

Lagerström, Robert; Franke, Ulrik; Johnson, Pontus; Ullberg, Johan (2009a): A method for Creating Enterprise Architecture Metamodels - Applied to Systems Modifiability Analysis. International Journal of Computer Science and Applications, 6 (5), 89–120.

Lagerström, Robert; Johnson, Pontus; Höök, David (2009b): An Enterprise Architecture Management Pattern for Software Change Project Cost Analysis. In: Proceedings of the Patterns in Enterprise Architecture Management (PEAM2009) Workshop, 1–11.

Lagerström, Robert; Johnson, Pontus; Höök, David (2010): Architecture Analysis of Enterprise Systems Modifiability – Models, Analysis, and Validation. Journal of Systems and Software, 83 (8), 1387–1403.

Lagerström, Robert; Johnson, Pontus; Närman, Per (2007): Extended Influence Diagram Generation for Interoperability Analysis. Enterprise Interoperability II (5), 599–602.

Lange, M. et al. (2012): A Comprehensive EA Benefit Realization Model – An Exploratory Study. In: Proceedings of the 45th Hawaii International Conference on Systems Sciences, 4230–4239.

Lange, M.; Mendling, J. (In Review): Enterprise Architecture Benefit Assessment – A Literature Review and Research Directions.

Lange, Matthias; Mendling, Jan (2011): An Experts' Perspective on Enterprise Architecture Goals, Framework Adoption and Benefit Assessment. In: Proceedings of the 6th Trends in Enterprise Architecture Research Workshop (EDOCW'11), 304–313.

Lankhorst, M. M. et al. (2009): Enterprise Architecture at Work: Modelling, Communication and Analysis. Dietz, Jan; Proper, Erik; Tribolet, José (Hg.). Berlin, Heidelberg, Springer Verlag.

Lassila, K.S; Brancheau, J.C (1999): Adoption and Utilization of Commercial Software Packages: Exploring Utilization Equilibria, Transitions, Triggers, and Tracks. Journal of Management Information Systems, 16 (2), 63–90.

Latham, A. (2003): Research, Performance and Doing Human Geography: Some Reflections on the Diary-photograph, Diary-interview Method. Environment and Planning A, 35 (11), 1993–2017.

Law, K. S.; Wong, C. S.; Mobley, W. H. (1998): Toward a Taxonomy of Multidimensional Constructs. Academy of Management Review, 23 (4), 741–755.

Lawshe, C. H. (1975): A Quantitative Approach to Content validity. Personnel Psychology, 28 (4), 563–575.

Lazar, J.; Preece, J. (1999): Designing and Implementing Web-based Surveys. Journal of Computer Information Systems, 39 (4), 63–67.

Lee, A. S. (2001): Editorial. MIS Quarterly, 25 (1), pp. iii–vii.

Lee, A. S.; Baskerville, Richard (2003): Generalizing Generalizability in Information Systems Research. Information Systems Research, 14 (3), 221–243.

Lee, Allen S. (1989): A Scientific Methodology for MIS Case Studies. MIS Quarterly, 13 (1), 32–50.

Lee, Siew Kim Jean; Yu, Kelvin (2004): Corporate Culture and Organizational Performance. Journal of Managerial Psychology, 19 (4), 340–359.

Leedy, Paul D.; Ormrod, Jeanne Ellis (2009): Practical Research: Planning and Design. 9. Aufl., N.J.; Pearson Education. Upper Saddle River.

Leidner, D. E.; Elam, J. J. (1994): Executive Information Systems: Their Impact On Executive Decision-Making. Journal of Management Information Systems, 10 (3), 139–156.

Lewis, Bruce R.; Templeton, Gary F.; Byrd, Terry A. (2005): A Methodology for Construct Development in MIS Research. European Journal of Information Systems, 14 (4), 388–400.

Lickert, R. (1932): A Technique for Measurement of Attributes. Archives of Psychology, 140 (1), 5–53.

Lim, N. et al. (2009): A Comparative Analysis of Enterprise Architecture Frameworks Based on EA Quality Attributes. In: Proceedings of the 10th ACIS International Conference on Software Engineering, Artificial Intelligences, Networking and Parallel/Distributed Computing, 283–288.

Lincoln, Y. S.; Guba, E. G. (1985): Naturalistic Inquiry, Sage Publications. Beverly Hills, CA.

Lindström, Åsa; Johnson, Pontus; Johansson, Erik; Ekstedt, Mathias; Simonsson, Mårten (2006): A Survey on CIO Concerns - Do Enterprise Architecture Frameworks Support Them? Information Systems Frontiers, 8 (2), 81–90.

Loke, S. D.; Gilbert, B. O. (1995): Method of Psychological Assessment, Self Disclosure, and Experiential Differences: A Study of Computer, Questionnaire and Interview Assessment Formats. Journal of Social Behaviour and Personality, 10 (3), 255–263.

Lux, J. et al. (2010): Understanding the Performance Impact of Enterprise Architecture Management Understanding the Performance Impact of Enterprise Architecture Management. In: Proceedings of the 16th Americas Conference on Information Systems (AMCIS).

Lyons, J. (1977): Semantics, University Press. Cambridge.

MacKenzie, Scott B. (2003): The Dangers of Poor Construct Conceptualization. Journal of the Academy of Marketing Science, 31 (3), 323–326.

MacKenzie, Scott B.; House, R. (1978): Paradigm Development in the Social Sciences: A Proposed Research Strategy. The Academy of Management Review, 3 (1), 7–23.

MacKenzie, Scott B.; Podsakoff, Philip M.; Jarvis, Cheryl Burke (2005): The Problem of Measurement Model Misspecification in Behavioral and Organizational Research and Some Recommended Solutions. Journal of Applied Psychology, 90 (4), 710–730.

MacKenzie, Scott B.; Podsakoff, Philip M.; Podsakoff, Nathan P. (2011): Construct Measurement and Validation Procedures in MIS and Behavioral Research, Integrating New and Existing Techniques. MIS Quarterly, 35 (2), 293–334.

Magalhaes, Rodrigo; Zacarias, Marielba; Tribolet, José (2007): Making Sense of Enterprise Architectures as Tools of Organizational Self-Awareness. Journal of Enterprise Architecture, 3 (4).

Mao, E.; Ambrose, P. (2004): A Theoretical and Empirical Validation of IS Success Models in a Temporal and Quasi Volitional Technology Usage Context. In: Proceedings of the 10th Americas Conference on Information Systems. New York City, NY, USA: Association for Information Systems, 476-475.

Marcoulides, George A.; Chin, Wynne W.; Saunders, Carol (2009): A Critical Look at Partial Least Squares Modeling. MIS Quarterly, 33 (1), 171–175.

Marcoulides, George A.; Saunders, Carol (2006): PLS: A Silver Bullet? MIS Quarterly, 30 (2).

Markus, M.L; Robey, Daniel (1988): Information Technology and Organizational Change: Causal Structure in Theory and Research. Management Science, 34 (5), 583–598.

Mason, R. O. (1978): Measuring Information Output: A Communcation System Approach. Information & Management, 1 (5), 219–234.

Mathieson, Kieran; Peacock, Eileen (2001): Extending the Technology Acceptance Model: The Influence of Perceived User Resources. The DATA BASE for Advances in IS, 32 (3), 86–112.

Matthee, M. C.; Tobin, P. K. J.; van der Merwe, P. (2007): The Status Quo of Enterprise Architecture Implementation in South African Financial Services Companies. South African Journal of Business Management, 38 (1).

McCoy, S. et al. (2001): Using Electronic Surveys to Collect Data: Experiences from the Field. In: Proceedings of the 7th Americas Conference on Information Systems, 290–300.

McKinsey (2009): Willkommen in der Volatilen Welt. Düsseldorf.

Meade, A. W. et al. (2007): Assessing Common Methods Bias in Organizational Research. In: Proceedings of the 22nd Annual Meeting of the Society for Industrial and Organizational Psychology, 1–10.

Meskendahl, Sascha; Jonas, Daniel; Kock, Alexander; Gemünden, Hans Georg (2011): The Art of Project Portfolio Management, TU Berlin. Berlin.

Michael, S. (2005): The promise of appreciative inquiry as an interview tool for field research. Development in Practice, 15 (2), 222–230.

Miles, Matthew B.; Huberman, A. M. (1994): Qualitative data analysis: An expanded sourcebook. 2. Aufl., Sage Publications. Thousand Oaks.

Miller, Larry E.; Smith, Keith L. (1983): Handling Nonresponse Issues. Journal of extension, 21 (5), 45–50.

Mlhotra, M. K.; Grover, V. (1998): An Assessment of Survey Research in POM: From Construct to Theory. Journal of Operations Management, 16 (4), 407–425.

Moore, G. C.; Benbasat, I. (1991): Development of an Instrument to Measure the Perceptions of Adopting an Information Technology Innovation. Information Systems, 1991 (2), 192–222.

Morganwalp, Jillian M.; Sage, Andrew P. (2004): Enterprise Architecture Measures of Effectiveness. International Journal of Technology, Policy and Management, 4 (1), 81–94.

Morkevicius, Aurelijus; Gudas, Saulius; Silingas, Darius (Hg.) (2010): Model-driven Quantitative Performance Analysis of UPDM-based Enterprise Architecture.

Mulholland, Andy; Thomas, Chris S.; Kurchina, Paul; Woods, Dan (2006): Mashup Corporations: The End of Business as Usual. 1. Aufl., Evolved Technologist Press. New York.

Myers, Michael D. (1997): Qualitative Research in Information Systems. MIS Quarterly, 21 (2), 241–242.

Myers, Michael D. (1999): Investigating Information Systems with Ethnographic Research. Communications of the AIS, 23 (2), 1–20.

Myers, Michael D. (2009): Qualitative Research in Business & Management, Sage Publications. Los Angeles, London.

Myers, Michael D.; Newman, Michael (2007): The Qualitative Interview in IS Research: Examining the Craft. Information and Organization, 17 (1), 2–26.

Napier, N. P.; Keil M.; Tan F. B. (2009): IT Project Managers' Construction of Successful Project Management Practice: A Repertory Grid Investigation. Information Systems Journal, 19 (3), 255–282.

Närman, P. et al. (2009a): Enterprise Architecture Analysis for Data Accuracy Assessments. In: Proceedings of the 13th International IEEE Enterprise Distributed Object Computing Conference, 24–33.

Närman, P. et al. (2009b): Using Enterprise Architecture Models for System Quality Analysis. In: Proceedings of the 13th International IEEE Enterprise Distributed Object Computing Conference, 14–23.

Närman, Per; Johnson, Pontus; Nordström, Lars (2007): Enterprise Architecture: A Framework Supporting System Quality Analysis. In: Proceedings of the 11th IEEE International Enterprise Distributed Object Computing Conference (EDOC 2007), 130–142.

Nederhof, A. J. (1985): Methods of Coping with Social Desirability Bias. European Journal of Social Psychology, 15 (3), 263–280.

Nelson, R. R.; Todd, P. A.; Wixom, B. H. (2005): Antecedents of Information and System Quality: An Empirical Examination Within the Context of Data Warehousing. Journal of Management Information Systems, 21 (4), 199–235.

Newman, Michael; Robey, Daniel (1992): A Social Process Model of User-Analyst Relationships. MIS Quarterly, 16 (2), 249–266.

Newsted, P. et al. (1998): Survey Instruments in IS Database. Online available at http://home.aisnet.org/displaycommon.cfm?an=1&subarticlenbr=675, last accessed on 08.03.2012, last accessed on 06.03.2012.

Niemi, E.; Pekkola, S. (2009): Adapting the DeLone and McLean Model for the Enterprise Architecture Benefit Realization Process. In: Proceedings of the 42nd Hawaii International Conference on System Sciences. Manoa, Hawaii: IEEE, 1–10.

Niemi, E.; Soliman, K. S. (2006): Enterprise Architecture Benefits: Perceptions from Literature and Practice. In: Proceedings of the 7th International Business Information Management Association (IBIMA) Conference Internet & Information Systems in the Digital Age: Challenges & Solutions.

Norman, K. L.; Friedman, Z.; Norman, K.; Stevenson, R. (2001): Navigational Issues in the Design of Online Self-administered Questionnaires. Behaviour&Information Technology, 20 (1), 37–45.

Northcutt, Norwell; McCoy, Danny (2004): Interactive Qualitative Analysis: A Systems Method for Qualitative Research, Sage Publications. Thousand Oaks (Calif.).

Nunnally, J. C.; Bernstein, I. H. (1994): Psychometric Theory, McGraw-Hill. New York, NY.

OGC (2012): ITIL, last updated on26.2.2012.

Ogden, C. K.; Richards, I. A. (1923): The Meaning of Meaning: A Study of the Influence of Language Upon Thought and of the Science of Symbolism, Harcourt & Brace. New York.

Op 't Land, Martin; Arnold, B.; Engels, A. (2000): Fps: Another Way of Looking at Components and Architecture in the Financial World. In: Proceedings of the Second National Architecture Conference (LAC2000) .

Op 't Land, Martin; Proper, Erik; Waage, Maarten; Cloo, Jeroen; Steghuis, Claudia (2009): Enterprise Architecture: Creating Value by Informed Governance, Springer Verlag. Berlin, Heidelberg.

OpenGroup, 2012: ArchiMate 2.0.

Oppenheim, A. N. (1992): Questionnaire Design, Interviewing and Attitude Measurement, Pinter Publisher. New York, NY.

Orlikowski, Wanda J. (2001): Technology and Institutions: What Can Research on Information Technology and Research on Organizations Learn From Each Other? MIS Quarterly, 25 (2), 145–165.

Orlikowski, Wanda J.; Baroudi, J. J. (1991): Studying Information Technology in Organizations: Research Approaches and Assumptions. Information Systems Research, 2 (1), 1–28.

Orlikowski, Wanda; Baroudi, Jack J. (1990): Studying Information Technology in Organizations: Research Approaches and Assumptions. New York, NY, Stern School of Business, New York University.

Palvia, Prashant; Mao, En; Midha, Vishal (2004): Research Methodologies in MIS: An Update. Communications of the AIS, 14 (4), 526–542.

Paolo, A. M.; Bonamino, G. A.; Gibson, C.; Patridge, T.; Kallail, K. (2000): Response Rate Comparisons of E-mail and Mail-distributed Student Evaluations. Teaching and Learning in Medicine, 12 (2), 81–84.

Paré, G. et al. (2005): Evaluating PACS Success: A Multidimensional Model. In: Proceedings of the 38th Hawaii International Conference on System Sciences. Big Island, Hawaii: IEEE .

Pearl, Dennis K.; Fairley, David (1985): Testing for the Potential for Nonresponse Bias in Sample Surveys. Public Opinion Quarterly, 43 (553-560).

Perkins, G. H. (2004): Will Libraries' Web-based Survey Methods Replace Existing Non-electronic Survey Methods? Information Technology & Libraries, 23 (3), 122–126.

Peterson, Ryan (2000): Constructing Effective Questionaires, Sage Publications. Thousand Oaks, CA.

Peterson, Ryan (2004): Crafting Information Technology Governance. Information Systems Management, 32 (6), 7–22.

Petter, Stacie; DeLone, William H.; McLean, Ephraim R. (2008): Measuring Information Systems Success: Models, Dimensions, Measures, and Interrelationships. European Journal of Information Systems, 17 (3), 236–263.

Petter, Stacie; McLean, Ephraim R. (2009): A Meta-analytic Assessment of the DeLone and McLean IS Success Model: An Examination of IS Success at the Individual level. Information & Management, 46 (3), 159–166.

Petter, Stacie; Straub, Detmar W.; Rai, Arun (2007): Specifying Formative Constructs in Information Systems Research. MIS Quarterly, 31 (4), 623–656.

Phillips, B. S. (1976): Social Research: Strategy and Tactics, Macmillan. New York, NY.

Pinsonneault, Alain; Kraemer, Kenneth L. (1993): Survey Research Methodology in Management Information Systems: An Assessment. Journal of Management Information Systems, 10 (2), 75–105.

Podsakoff, P. M.; MacKenzie, Scott B.; Lee, J. Y.; Podsakoff, Nathan P. (2003): Common Method Biases in Behavioural Research: A Critical Review of the Literature and Recommended Remedies. Journal of Applied Psychology, 85 (5), 879–903.

Polites, Greta L.; Roberts, Nicholas; Thatcher, Jason (2011): Conceptualizing models using multidimensional constructs: a review and guidelines for their use. European Journal of Information Systems (1), 1–27.

Polkinghorne, D. E. (2005): Language and Meaning: Data Collection in Qualitative Research. Journal of Counseling Psychology, 52 (2), 137–145.

Popper, K.R (1961): The Logic of Scientific Discovery, Science Editions. New York, NY.

Porter, M. E. (1980): Competitive Startegy, Free Press. New York, NY.

Preece. J.; Rogers, Y.; Sharp, S. (2002): Interaction design: Beyond human-computer interaction, Wiley & Sons. New York, NY.

Project Management Institute: A guide to the Project Management Body of Knowledge (PMBOK® Guide). 4. Aufl. (2008), Project Management Institute. Newtown Square, Pa.

Proper, Erik; Greefhorst, Danny (2011): Principles in an Enterprise Architecture Context. Journal of Enterprise Architecture (1), 8–16.

Pulkkinen, Mirja (2006): Systemic Management of Architectural Decisions in Enterprise Architecture Planning. Four Dimensions and Three Abstraction Levels. In: Proceedings of the 39th Hawaii International Conference on System Sciences.

Qian, Z.; Bock, G.-W. (2005): An Empirical Study on Measuring the Success of Knowledge Repository Systems. In: Proceedings of the 38th Hawaii International Conference on System Sciences. Big Island, Hawaii: IEEE.

Quinn, R. E.; Rohrbaugh, J. (1983): A Spatial Model Of Effectiveness Criteria: Towards A Competing Values Approach To Organizational Analysis. Management Science, 29 (3), 363–377.

Radeke (2011): Toward Understanding Enterprise Architecture Management's Role in Strategic Change: Antecedents, Processes, Outcomes. In: Proceedings of the 10th International Conference on Wirtschaftsinformatik WI 2011. Zürich, Switzerland: Association for Information Systems.

Radeke, F. (2010): Awaiting Explanation in the Field of Enterprise Architecture Management. In: Proceedings of the 16th Americas Conference on Information Systems (AMCIS): Association for Information Systems.

Raderius, Jakob; Närman, Per; Ekstedt, Mathias (2009): Assessing System Availability Using an Enterprise Architecture Analysis Approach. Lecture Notes in Computer Science, 2009 (5472), 351–362.

Rai, Arun; Lang, Sandra; Welker, Robert B. (2002): Assessing the validity of IS success models: An empirical test and theoretical analysis. Information Systems Research, 13 (1), 50–69.

Ravald, Annika; Grönroos, Christian (1996): The Value Concept and Relationship Marketing. European Journal of Marketing, 30 (2), 19–30.

Recker, J. (2008): Understanding Process Modelling Grammar Continuance. PhD Thesis. Supervised by Michael Rosemann, Marlon Dumas und Peter Green. Brisbane, Australia. Queensland University of Technology.

Reynolds, T. J.; Gutman J. (1988): Laddering Theory, Method, Analysis and Interpretation. Journal of Advertising Research, 28 (1), 11–21.

Richardson, Gary L.; Jackson, Brad M.; Dickson, Gary W. (1990): A Principles-Based Enterprise Architecture: Lessons from Texaco and Star Enterprise. MIS Quarterly, 14 (4), 385–403.

Riege, Christian; Aier, Stephan (2009): A Contingency Approach to Enterprise Architecture Method Engineering. Journal of Enterprise Architecture, 5 (1), 36–48.

Ringle, C. M. et al. (2005): SmartPLS 2.0 (beta).

Roberts, R. E.; Lewinsohn, P. M.; Seeley, J. R. (1993): A Brief Measure of Loneliness: Suitable for Use with Adolescents. Psychological Reports, 72 (3), 1379–1391.

Robson, Colin (2011): Real World Research: A Resource for Users of Social Research Methods in Applied Settings. 3. Aufl., Wiley & Sons. Chichester, West Sussex.

Rodrigues, Luis Silva; Amaral, Luis (2010): Issues in Enterprise Architecture Value. The Journal of Enterprise Architecture, 6 (4).

Rogers, F. T. (1976): Interviews by Telephone and in Person: Quality of Response and Field performance. The Public Opinion Quaterly, 40 (1), 51–65.

Ross, J. W.; Weill, P. (2005): Understanding the Benefits of Enterprise Architecture.

Ross, Jeanne W. (2003): Creating a Strategic IT Architecture Competency: Learning in Stages. MIS Quarterly Executive, 2 (1).

Ross, Jeanne W.; Beath, C.; Goodhue, Dale L. (1996): Develop Long-term Competitiveness Through IT Assets. Sloan Management Review, 28 (1), 31–45.

Ross, Jeanne W.; Weill, Peter; Robertson, David C. (2009): Enterprise Architecture as Strategy: Creating a Foundation for Business Execution, Harvard Business School Press. Boston, Mass.

Rubin, Herbert J.; Rubin, Irene (2005): Qualitative Interviewing: The Art of Hearing Data. 2. Aufl., Sage Publications. Thousand Oaks, Calif.

Salant, P.; Dillman, D. A. (1994): How to Conduct Your Own Survey, John Wiley & Sons. New York, NY.

Salmans, Brian; Kappelman, Leon Allan (2010): The State of EA: Progress, Not Perfection. In: Kappelman, Leon Allan (Eds.): The SIM guide to enterprise architecture. Boca Raton. Fla: CRC Press, 165–187.

Sánchez-Fernández, Juan; Muñoz-Leiva, Francisco; Montoro-Ríos, Francisco Javier (2012): Improving Retention Rate and Response Quality in Web-based Surveys. Computers in Human Behavior, 28, 507–514.

Sarstedt, Marko; Henseler, Jörg; Ringle, Christian M. (2011): Multigroup Analysis in Partial Least Squares (PLS) Path Modeling: Alternative Methods and Empirical Results. Advances in International Marketing (AIM), 22 (3), 195–218.

Sartori, G.: Guidelines for Concept Analysis. In: Sartori, G. (Eds.): Social Science Concepts: A Systematic Analysis. Beverly Hills, CA: Sage Publications, 15–85.

Sawyer, S.; Wigand, R. T.; Crowstone, K. (2005): Redefining Access: Uses and Roles of Information and Communication Technologies in the U.S. Residential Real Estate Industrie from 1995 to 2005. Journal of Information Technology Management, 20 (4), 213–223.

Schaefer, D. R.; Dillman, D. A. (1998): Development of Standard E-mail Methodology: Results of an Experiment. Public Opinion Quarterly, 62 (3), 378–397.

Schaupp, L. C.; Fan, Weiguo; Belanger, F. (2006): Determining Success for Different Website Goals. In: Proceedings of the 39th Hawaii International Conference on System Sciences.

Scheer, A.-W (1999): ARIS - Business Process Frameworks, Springer Verlag. Berlin et al.

Schekkerman, Jaap (2006): How to Survive in the Jungle of Enterprise Architecture Frameworks: Creating or Choosing an Enterprise Architecture Framework, Trafford. Victoria, B.C.

Schmidt, Christian; Buxmann, Peter (2011): Outcomes and Success Factors of Enterprise IT Architecture Management: Empirical Insight from the International Financial Services Industry. European Journal of Information Systems, 20 (2), 168–185.

Schönherr, Marten (2009): Towards a Common Terminology in the Discipline of Enterprise Architecture. Lecture Notes in Computer Science, 5472, 400–413.

Schriesheim, C. A.; Powers, K. J.; Scandura, T. A.; Gardiner, C. C. Lankau M. J. (1993): Improving Construct Measurment in Management Research: Contents and a Quantitative Approach for Assessing the Theoretical Adequacy of Paper-and-Pencil Survey-Type Instruments. Journal of Management, 19 (2), 385–417.

Schultze, Ulrike; Avital, Michel (2011): Designing interviews to generate rich data for information systems research. Information and Organization, 21, 1–16.

Schwab, D. P. (1980): Construct Validity in Organizational Behavior. In: Staw, B. M.; Cummings, L. L. (Eds.): Research in Organizational Behavior (Vol. 2). Greenwich, CT: JAI Press, 3–43.

Schwarz, Norbert (1995): What Respondents Learn from Questionaires: The Survey Interview and the Logic of Conversation. International Statistics Review, 63 (2), 153–168.

Schwarz, Norbert; Strack, Fritz; Mai, Hans-Peter (1991): Assimilation and Contrast Effects in Part-Whole Question Sequences: A conversational logic analysis. Public Opinion Quarterly, 55 (1), 3–23.

Scornavacca, E. Jr.; Becker, J. L.; Barnes, S. J. (2004): Developing Automated e-Survey and Control Tools: An Application in Industrial Management. Industrial Management & Data Systems, 104 (3), 189–200.

Seddon, Peter B. (1997): A Respecification and Extension of the DeLone and McLean Model of IS success. Information Systems Research, 8 (3), 240–253.

Seddon, Peter B.; Staples, S.; Patnayakuni, R.; Bowtell, M. (1999): Dimensions of Information System Success. Communications of the AIS, 2 (3), 1–61.

Sedera, D. (2006): An empirical investigation of the salient characteristics of IS-Success models. In: Proceedings of the 12th Americas Conference on Information Systems.

Sedera, D. et al. (2004a): Knowledge Management as an Antecedent of Enterprise System Success. In: Proceedings of the 10th Americas Conference on Information Systems. New York City, NY, USA: Association for Information Systems.

Sedera, D. et al. (2006): Identifying and Evaluating the Importance of Multiple Stakeholder Perspective in Measuring ES-Success. In: Proceedings of the 16th European Conference on Information Systems.

Sedera, D.; Gable, G. (2004b): A Factor and Structural Equation Analysis of the Enterprise Systems Success Measurement Model. In: Proceedings of the 25th International Conference on Information Systems, 449–465.

Sedera, D.; Gable, G. G. (2004c): A Factor and Structural Equation Analysis of the Enterprise Systems Success Measurement Model. In: Proceedings of the 37th Hawaii International Conference on System Sciences.

Sedera, Darshana; Tan, Felix Ter Chian (2005): User Satisfaction: An Overarching Measure of Enterprise System Success. Proceedings of the PACIS 2005.

Sedera, W. et al. (2004d): Measuring Process Modelling Success. In: Proceedings of the 10th European Conference on Information Systems. Turku, Finland: Association for Information Systems .

Segars, A. H. (1997): Assessing the Unidimensionality of Measurement: A Paradigm and Illustration Within the Context of Information Systems Research. Omega, 25 (1), 107–121.

Seppänen, Ville; Heikkilä, Jukka; Liimatainen, Katja (2009): Key Issues in EA-Implementation: Case Study of Two Finnish Government Agencies. In: Proceedings of the 2009 IEEE Conference on Commerce and Enterprise Computing.

Sessions, R.: A Comparison of the Top Four Enterprise-Architecture Methodologies. Online available at http://msdn.microsoft.com/en-us/library/bb466232.aspx, last accessed on 06.03.2012.

Shanks, Graeme (2002): Guidelines for Conducting Positivist Case Study Research in Information Systems. Australasian Journal of Information Systems, 10 (1), 76–85.

Shannon, C. E.; Weaver, W. (1949): The Mathematical Theory of Communication, University of Illinois Press. Urbana, USA.

Shaw, D. (1995a): Bibliographic Database Searching by Graduate Students in Language and Literature: Search Strategies, System Interfaces, and Relevance Judgments. Library & Information Science Research, 17 (4), 327–345.

Shaw, J. (1995b): A Schema Approach to the Formal Literature Review in Engineering Theses. System Sciences (HICSS), 2010 43rd Hawaii International Conference on, 23 (3), 325–335.

Shaw, N. C.; DeLone, William H.; Niedermann, F. (2002): Sources of Dissatisfaction in End-user Support: an Empirical Study. ACM SIGMIS Database, 33 (2), 41–56.

Sheehan, K. B.; McMillan, S. J. (1999): Response Variation in E-mail Surveys: An Exploration. Journal of Advertising Research, 39 (4), 45–54.

Shin, B. (2003): An Exploratory Investigation of System Success Factors in Data Warehousing. Journal of the AIS, 4 (2), 141–170.

Sidorova, Anna; Kappelman, Leon Allan (2011): Better Business-IT Alignment Through Enterprise Architecture. Journal of Enterprise Architecture, 7 (1), 39–47.

Silver, M. S.; Markus, M.L; Beath, Cynthia M. (1995): The Information Technology Interaction Model: A Foundation for the MBA Core Course. MIS Quarterly, 19 (3), 361–390.

Sivio, Stephan A.; Saunders, Carol; Chang, Qing; Jiang, James J. (2006): How Low Should You Go? Low Response Rates and the Validity of Inference in IS Questionnaire Research. Journal of the AIS, 6 (6), 351–414.

Smith, C. B. (1997): Casting the net: Surveying an Internet Population. Journal of Computer Mediated Communication, 3 (1).

Smolander, Kari; Rossi, Matti; Purao, Sandeep (2008): Software Architectures: Blueprint, Literature, Language or Decision? European Journal of Information Systems, 17 (6), 575–588.

Spector, P. E. (1992): Summated Rating Scale Construction: An Introduction, Sage Publications. Newbury Park, CA.

Spreng, Richard A.; MacKenzie, Scott B.; Olshavsky, Richard W. (1996): A Reexamination of the Determinants of Consumer Satisfaction. The Journal of Marketing, 60 (3), 15–32.

Stanton, J. M. (1998): An Empirical Assessment of Data Collection using the Internet. Personnel Psychology, 51, 709–726.

Steinfield, Charles William; Fulk, Janet (1990): The Theory Imperative. In: Fulk, Janet; Steinfield, Charles William (Eds.): Organizations and Communication Technology. Newbury Park, Calif: Sage Publications.

Stelzer, D. (2009): Enterprise Architecture Principles: Literature Review and Research Directions. In: Proceedings of the 4th Workshop on Trends in Enterprise Architecture Research. Berlin: Springer Verlag, 21–36.

Stevens, James (2009): Applied multivariate statistics for the social sciences. 5. Aufl., Routledge. New York.

Stinchcombe, A.L (1968): Constructing Social Theories, Harcourt & Brace. Brace World, New York.

Stratman, J. K.; Roth, A. V. (2002): Enterprise Resource Planing (ERP) Competence Constructs: Two-Stage Multi-Item Scale Development and Validation. Decision Sciences, 33 (4), 601–628.

Straub, Detmar W. (1989): Validating Instruments in MIS Research. MIS Quarterly, 1989 (13), 147–169.

Straub, Detmar W.; Boudreau, Marie-Claude; Gefen, David (2004): Validation Guidelines for IS Positivist Research. Communications of the AIS, 13 (24), 380–427.

Struck, V. et al. (2010): Enterprise Architecture Management from a Knowledge Management Perspective - Results from an Empirical Study. In: Proceedings of the 5th Mediterranean Conference on Information Systems. TelAviv, paper 84.

Sue, Valerie M.; Ritter, Lois A. (2007): Conducting Online Surveys, Sage Publications. Los Angeles.

Tallon, Paul P.; Kraemer, Kenneth L.; Gurbaxani, Viijay (2000): Executives' Perceptions of the Business Value of Information Technology: A Process-Oriented Approach. Journal of Management Information Systems, 16 (4).

Tamm, Toomas; Seddon, Peter B.; Shanks, Graeme; Reynolds, Peter (2011): How Does Enterprise Architecture Add Value to Organisations? Communications of the Association for Information Systems, 28 (1).

Tan F. B.; Hunter, M. G. (2002): The Repertory Grid Technique: A Method for the Study of Cognition in Information Systems. MIS Quarterly, 26 (1), 39–57.

Tanigawa, Utako (2004): Decision Processes in Enterprise Architecture: Descriptive Study. In: Proceedings of the 10th American Conference on Information Systems.

Tanur, J.M (1982): Advances in Methods for Large-scale Surveys and Experiments. In: Mcadams, R.; Smelser, N. J.; TreimanD.J. (Eds.): Behavioral and Social Science Research: A National Resource, Part II. Washington, D.C: National Academy Press, 1–71.

Tapscott, Don (1996): The Digital Economy: Promise and Peril in the Age of Networked Intelligence, McGraw-Hill. New York.

Taylor, H. (2000): Does Internet Research Work? Comparing Electronic Survey Results with Telephone Survey. International Journal of Market Research, 42 (1), 51–63.

Tenenhaus, Michel; Vinzi, Vincenzo Esposito; Chatelin, Yves-Marie; Lauro, Carlo (2005): PLS Path Modeling. Computational Statistics & Data Analysis, 48 (1), 159–205.

Teo, T. S.; Wong, P. K. (1998): An Empirical Study of the Performance Impact of Computerization in the Retail Industry. Omega: International Journal of Management Science, 16 (5), 611–621.

The Open Group (2005): The Open Group Architecture Framework, Version 8 Enterprise Edition. Reading, U.K.

Thode, Henry C. (2002): Testing for Normality, Marcel Dekker. New York.

Thong, J. Y. L.; Yap, C. (1995): Information Systems Effectiveness: A User Satisfaction Approach. Information Processing and Management, 32 (5), 601–610.

tmforum: eTOm Business Process Framework. tmforum. Online available at 26.02.2012.

Trochim, W. M.: The Research Methods Knowledge Base. 2nd Edition. Online available at http://www.socialresearchmethods.net/kb/, last accessed on 05.03.2012, last accessed on 06.03.2012.

Ullberg, Johan; Franke, Ulrik; Buschle, Markus; Johnson, Pontus (2010): A Tool for Interoperability Analysis of Enterprise Architecture Models using Pi-OCL. In: Popplewell, Keith; Harding, Jenny; Poler, Raul; Chalmeta, Ricardo (Eds.): Enterprise Interoperability IV - Making the Internet of the Future for the Future of Enterprise. Berlin et al: Springer Verlag, 81–90.

Ullberg, Johan; Lagerström, Robert; Johnson, Pontus (2008a): A Framework for Service Interoperability Analysis using Enterprise Architecture Models. In: Proceedings of the 2008 IEEE International Conference on Services Computing: IEEE, 99–107.

Ullberg, Johan; Lagerström, Robert; Johnson, Pontus (2008b): Enterprise Architecture: A Service Interoperability Analysis Framework. In: Mertins, Kai; Ruggaber, Rainer; Popplewell, Keith; Xu, Xiaofei (Eds.): Enterprise Interoperability III New Challenges and Industrial Approaches: Springer Verlag, 611–623.

2008: International Standard Industrial Classification of All Economic Activities, Rev.4.

Urbach, Nils; Ahlemann, Frederik (2010): Structural Equation Modeling in Information Systems Research Using Partial Least Squares. Journal of Information Technology Theory and Application, 11 (2), 5–40.

Urbach, Nils; Smolnick, Stefan; Riempp, Gerold (2008): A Methodological Examination of Empirical Research on Information Systems Success: 2003 to 2007. In: Proceedings of the 14th Americas Conference on Information Systems (AMCIS).

van de Ven, A. H. (1989): Nothing is Quite so Practical as a Good Theory. Academy of Management Review, 14 (4), 486–489.

van der Raadt, Bas; Bonnet, Marc; Bruijne, Mark de; van Den Berg, Jan; van Vliet, Hans (2004): Effectiveness of Enterprise Architecture. International Journal of Technology, 4 (1), 81–94.

van der Raadt, Bas; Bonnet, Marc; Schouten, Sander; van Vliet, Hans (2010): The Relation between EA Effectiveness and Stakeholder Satisfaction. Journal of Systems and Software, 83 (10), 1954–1969.

van der Raadt, Bas; Hoorn, Johan F.; van Vliet, Hans (2005): Alignment and maturity are silibings in architecture assessment. In: Proceedings of the 17th International Conference on Advanced Information Systems Engineering, 357–371.

van der Raadt, Bas; Slot, Raymond; van Vliet, Hans (2007): Experience Report: Assessing a Global Financial Services Company on its Enterprise Architecture Effectiveness Using NAOMI. Proceedings of the 40th Annual Hawaii International Conference on System Sciences (HICSS'07), 218–228.

van der Raadt, Bas; van Vliet, Hans (2008): Designing the Enterprise Architecture Function. Lecture Notes in Computer Science, 2008 (5281), 103–118.

van der Raadt, Bas; van Vliet, Hans; Proper, Erik; Harmsen, Frank; Dietz, Jan L. G. (2009): Assessing the Efficiency of the Enterprise Architecture Function. Advances in Enterprise Engineering II: First NAF Academy Working Conference on Practice-Driven Research on Enterprise Transformation, PRET 2009, Held at CAiSE 2009.

van Steenbergen, Marlies; Brinkkemper, Sjaak (2008): Modeling the Contribution of Enterprise Architecture Practice to the Achievement of Business Goals. In: Proceedings of the 17th International Conference on Information Systems Development (ISD 2008), 1–12.

Veludo-de-Oliveira, Tânia Modesto; Ikeda, Ana Akemi; Campomar, Marcos Cortez (2006): Laddering in the Practice of Marketing Research: Barriers and Solutions. Qualitative Market Research: An International Journal, 9 (3), 297–306.

Venkatesh, Viswanath; Brown, Susan A.; Bala, Hillol (Forthcoming): Bridging the Qualitative–Quantitative Divide: Guidelines for Conducting Mixed Methods Research in Information Systems. MIS Quarterly.

Venkatesh, Viswanath; Morris, Michael G.; Davis, Gordon B.; Davis, Fred D. (2009): User Acceptance of Information Technology: Towards a Unified View. Management Information Systems, 27 (3), 425–478.

Venkatraman, N. (1989): The Concept of Fit in Strategy Research: Towards Verbal and Statistical Correspondence. Academy of Management Review, 14 (3), 423–444.

Venkatraman, N.; Ramanujam, V. (1987): Measurement of Business Economic Performance: An examination of Method Convergence. Journal of Management Information Systems, 13 (1), 109–122.

314

Wade, Michael R.; Parent, Michael (2001): Relationships Between Job Skills and Performance: A Study of Webmasters. Journal of Management Information Systems, 18 (3), 71–96.

Wainwrighta, David; Waring, Teresa (2004): Three Domains for Implementing Integrated Information Systems: Redressing the Balance between Technology, Strategic and Organisational Analysis. International Journal of Information Management, 24, 329–346.

Walsham, Geoff (2006): Doing Interpretive Research. European Journal of Information Systems, 15 (3), 320–330.

Webb, E.; Campbell, D. T.; Shwartz, R.; Sechrest, L. (1966): Unobtrusive Measures: Nonreactive Research in the Social Sciences,, Rand McNally. Chicago, Illinois.

Weber, Ron (2004): Editor's Comment: The Rhetoric of Positivism Versus Interpretivism: A Personal View. MIS Quarterly, 28 (1), iii–xii.

Weber, Ron (2012): Evaluating and Developing Theories in the Information Systems Discipline. Journal of the AIS, 13 (1), 1–30.

Webster, Jane; Watson, Richard T. (2002): Guest Editorial: Analyzing the Past to Prepare for the Future: Writing a literature Review. MIS Quarterly, 26 (2).

Weick, Karl E. (1989): Theory Construction as Disciplined Imagination. Academy of Management Review, 14 (4), 516–531.

Weill, Peter; Ross, Jeanne W. (2009): IT Governance: How Top Performers Manage IT Decision Rights for Superior Results, Harvard Business School Press. Boston, Mass.

Wetzels, Martin; Odekerken-Schröder, Gaby (2009): Using PLS Path Modelling for Assessing Hierarchical Construct Models: Guidelines and Empirical Illustration. MIS Quarterly, 33 (1), 177–195.

Whetten, D. A. (1989): What Constitutes a Theoretical Contribution? Academy of Management Review, 14 (4), 490–495.

Wilcox, J. B.; Howell, R. D.; Breivik, E. (2008): Questions About Formative Measurement. Journal of Business Research, 61 (12), 1219–1228.

Wilkin, C.; Castleman, T. (2003): Development of an Instrument to Evaluate the Quality of Delivered Information Systems. In: Proceedings of the 36th Hawaii International Conference on System Sciences. Big Island, Hawaii: IEEE.

Wilkinson (2006): Designing an 'Adaptive' Enterprise Architecture. BT Technology Journal, 24 (4).

Wilson, Jeffery A.; Mazzuchi, Thomas; Sarkani, Shahram (2011): Evaluating the Effectiveness of Reference Models in Federating Enterprise Architectures. Journal of Enterprise Architecture, 7 (2), 40–49.

Winter, Robert (2008): Design Science Research in Europe. European Journal of Information Systems, 17 (5), 470–475.

Winter, Robert; Fischer, Ronny (2007): Essential Layers, Artifacts, and Dependencies of Enterprise Architecture. Journal of Enterprise Architecture, 2007 (May), 1–12.

Witmer, D. F.; Colman, R. W.; Katzman, S. L. (1999): From Paper-and-pencil to Screen-and-keyboard. In: Jones, S. (Eds.): Doing Internet Research: Critical Issues and Methods for Examining the Net. Thousand Oaks, CA: Sage Publications, 145–162.

Wixom, B. H.; Todd, P. A. (2005): A Theoretical Integration of User Satisfaction and Technology Acceptance. Information Systems Research, 16 (1), 85–102.

Wold, H. (1966): Estimation of Principal Components and Related Models by Iterative Least Squares. New York, NY.

Wong, C. S.; Law, K. S.; Huang, G. H. (2008): On the Importance of Conducting Construct-Level Analysis for Multidimensional Constructs in Theory Development and Testing. Journal of Management, 34 (4), 744–764.

Wright, Kevin B. (2005): Researching Internet-Based Populations: Advantages and Disadvantages of Online Survey Research, Online Questionnaire Authoring Software Packages, and Web Survey Services. Journal of Computer-Mediated Communication, 10 (3).

Wright, Ryan T.; Campbell; Damon E.; Thatcher, Jason Bennett; Roberts, Nicholas (2012): Operationalizing Multidimensional Constructs in Structural Equation Modeling: Recommendations for IS Research. Communications of the AIS, 30 (23).

Wu, J.-H; Wang, Y.-M (2006): Measuring KMS Success: A Respecification of the DeLone and McLean's Model. Information & Management, 43 (6), 728–739.

Wyatt, Jeremy C. (2000): When to Use Web-based Surveys. Journal of the American Medical Informatics Association, 7 (4), 426–429.

Yao, Grace; Wu, Chia-huei; Yang, Cheng-ta (2007): Examining the Content Validity of the WHOQOL-BREF from Respondents' Perspective by Quantitative Methods. Social Indicators Research, 85 (3), 483–498.

Yin, R. K. (2003): Case Study Reserach: Design and Methods, Sage Publications. Thousand Oaks, California.

Yin, Robert K. (2011): Qualitative Research from Start to Finish, Guilford Press. New York.

Ylimäki, Tanja; Niemi, Eetu; Hämäläinen, Niina (2007): Enterprise Architecture Compliance: The Viewpoint of Evaluation. In: Proceedings of the European Conference on Information Management and Evaluation.

Yoon, Y.; Guimaraes, T. (1995): Assessing Expert Systems Impact on Users' Jobs. Journal of Management Information Systems, 12 (1), 225–249.

Yu, Eric; Strohmaier, Markus; Deng, Xiaoxue (2006): Exploring Intentional Modeling and Analysis for Enterprise Architecture. Proceedings of the 10th IEEE International Enterprise Distributed Object Computing Conference (EDOC'06) (paper 32).

Yun, G. W.; Trumbo, C. W. (2000): Comparative Response to a Survey Executed by Post, E-mail, & Web Form. Journal of Computer Mediated Communication, 6 (1).

Zachman, J. A. (1987): A Framework for Information Systems Architecture. IBM Systems Journal, 26 (3), 454–470.

Zachman, J. A. (2003): The Zachman Framework For Enterprise Architecture: Primer for Enterprise Engineering and Manufacturing, Zachman International.

Zeithaml, V. A. (1988): Consumer Perception of Price, Quality and Value: A Means-end Model and Synthesis of Evidence. Journal of Marketing Research, 52 (July), 2–22.

Zink, Gregory (2009): How to Restart an Enterprise Architecture Program After Initial Failure. Journal of Enterprise Architecture, 5 (2), 31–41.

Zuh, K.; Kraemer, K. L. (2005): Post-adoption Variations in Usage and Value of E-business by Organizations: Cross-country Evidence from the Retail Industry. Information Systems Research, 16 (1), 61–84.

G. Statement of Original Authorship

Ich bezeuge durch meine Unterschrift, dass meine Angaben über die bei der Abfassung meiner Dissertation benutzten Hilfsmittel, über die mir zuteil gewordene Hilfe sowie über frühere Begutachtungen meiner Dissertation in jeder Hinsicht der Wahrheit entsprechen.

Translation: I testify with my signature that all information about the preparation of this dissertation with respect to used resources, about received assistance, and about earlier appraisals of this dissertation in all respects reflect the truth.

Düsseldorf, April 19, 2012.

(Matthias Lange)

Made in the USA
Charleston, SC
13 July 2013